RENAULT 16 1965–70 AUTOBOOK

Workshop Manual for the Renault 16
1965–70 and the 16TS 1968–70

by

Kenneth Ball
G I Mech E
and the
Autopress team of Technical Writers

AUTOPRESS LTD
BENNETT ROAD BRIGHTON BN2 5JG ENGLAND

ISBN 0 85147 122 6

Books by the same author:

1100 MK 1 1962–67 AUTOBOOK
1100 MK 2, 1300, AMERICA 1968–69 AUTOBOOK
1800 AUTOBOOK
AUSTIN A30, A35, A40 AUTOBOOK
AUSTIN HEALEY 100/6, 3000 1956–68 AUTOBOOK
AUSTIN MAXI 1969 AUTOBOOK
BMC AUTOBOOK THREE
BMC AUTOBOOK FOUR
FIAT 500 1957–69 AUTOBOOK
FIAT 600, 600D 1955–69 AUTOBOOK
FIAT 850 1964–69 AUTOBOOK
FORD ANGLIA PREFECT 100E AUTOBOOK
FORD CAPRI 1968–69 AUTOBOOK
FORD CONSUL, ZEPHYR, ZODIAC 1, 2 1950–62 AUTOBOOK
FORD ESCORT 1967–69 AUTOBOOK
FORD ZEPHYR, ZODIAC MK 3 1962–66 AUTOBOOK
FORD ZEPHYR V4, V6 ZODIAC 1966–69 AUTOBOOK
HILLMAN MINX 1 to 5 1956–65 AUTOBOOK
HILLMAN MINX 1965–67 AUTOBOOK
HILLMAN SUPER MINX 1, 2, 3 1961–65 AUTOBOOK
JAGUAR XK120, 140, 150 MK 7, 8, 9 1948–61 AUTOBOOK
JAGUAR 2.4, 3.4, 3.8 MK 1, 2 1955–67 AUTOBOOK
MG TA–TF 1936–55 AUTOBOOK
MGA, MGB 1955–69 AUTOBOOK
MINI 1959–70 AUTOBOOK
MINI COOPER 1961–70 AUTOBOOK
MORRIS MINOR 1952–69 AUTOBOOK
RENAULT R8, R10, 1100 1962–69 AUTOBOOK
ROVER 60–110 1953–64 AUTOBOOK
ROVER 2000 1963–69 AUTOBOOK
ROVER 3 LITRE 1958–67 AUTOBOOK
SPRITE, MIDGET AUTOBOOK
SUNBEAM RAPIER ALPINE 1959–65 AUTOBOOK
TRIUMPH TR2, TR3, TR3A 1952–62 AUTOBOOK
TRIUMPH TR4, TR4A 1961–67 AUTOBOOK
VAUXHALL VELOX CRESTA 1957–69 AUTOBOOK
VAUXHALL VICTOR 1, 2, FB 1957–64 AUTOBOOK
VAUXHALL VICTOR 101 1964–67 AUTOBOOK
VAUXHALL VICTOR FD 1600, 2000 1967–69 AUTOBOOK
VAUXHALL VIVA HA 1964–66 AUTOBOOK
VAUXHALL VIVA HB 1966–69 AUTOBOOK
VOLKSWAGEN BEETLE 1964–67 AUTOBOOK

The AUTOBOOK series of Workshop Manuals covers the majority of British and Continental motor cars. For a full list see the back of this manual.

CONTENTS

First Edition November 1970

Printed in England by
G. Beard & Son
Brighton

ACKNOWLEDGEMENT

My thanks are due to Renault Limited for their unstinted co-operation and also for supplying data and illustrations.

I am also grateful to a considerable number of owners who have discussed their cars at length and many of whose suggestions have been included in this manual.

Ditchling

Kenneth Ball G I Mech E
Associate Member Guild of Motoring Writers

INTRODUCTION

This do-it-yourself Workshop Manual has been specially written for the owner who wishes to maintain his car in first class condition and to carry out his own servicing and repairs. Considerable savings on garage charges can be made, and one can drive in safety and confidence knowing the work has been done properly.

Comprehensive step-by-step instructions and illustrations are given on all dismantling, overhauling and assembling operations. Certain assemblies require the use of expensive special tools, the purchase of which would be unjustified. In these cases information is included but the reader is recommended to hand the unit to the agent for attention.

Throughout the Manual hints and tips are included which will be found invaluable, and there is an easy to follow fault diagnosis at the end of each chapter.

Whilst every care has been taken to ensure correctness of information it is obviously not possible to guarantee complete freedom from errors or to accept liability arising from such errors or omissions.

Instructions may refer to the righthand or lefthand sides of the vehicle or the components. These are the same as the righthand or lefthand of an observer standing behind the car and looking forward.

CHAPTER 1

THE ENGINE

1 :1 Description

The engine used in the Renault R.1150 is shown in **FIG 1 :1.** The engine operates on the four stroke cycle of operations and has four cylinders which are layed out in the conventional in-line layout. The crankshaft has five main bearings giving the crankshaft very good rigidity. Power units bearing the type number 697-01 have a compression ratio of 8.6:1 and give 63 bhp at 5000 revs/min, those having type number 697-02 have a compression ratio of 7.6:1 and give a bhp of 60 at 5000 revs/min. A compression ratio of 7.25:1 exists on type number 697-03. The cylinders of the R.1150 power unit have a bore (diameter) of 2.992 inch (76 mm) and stroke (the distance the piston travels from Top Dead Centre to Bottom Dead Centre) of 3.189 inch (81 mm). The cubic capacity of the R.1150 power unit is 90 cu in (1480 cc).

The power unit fitted to the Renault R.1151 is illustrated in **FIG 1 :2** and like the unit fitted to the R.1150 model operates on the four stroke cycle, has four cylinders situated in-line and the crankshaft fitted has the same number of main journals. The bhp rating is 87.5 at 5750 rev/min, much higher than the R.1150 and this is mainly due to the superior cylinder head design and the larger capacity of 95.50 cu in (1565 cc), the greater capacity is due to an increased bore size of 3.032 inch (77 mm) and stroke of 3.307 inch (84 mm).

Both units are constructed in a similar manner. The Timing gears of both engines are driven by a chain and each uses the same distributor, sparking plugs and firing order although the spark advance curve is different for some distributors, the reason for the difference being explained in **Chapter 3.** Fuel is drawn to the carburetter by two similar fuel pumps, although the carburetters fitted are very different (see **Chapter 3**).

Lubrication of both engines is achieved by the action of an eccentric rotor pump driven by skew gearing off the camshaft. The pump draws oil from a sump and passes the oil to the various moving parts via a fullflow filter and pressure relief valve. The fullflow filter filters all the oil delivered to the bearings and has a relief valve fitted inside the filter body to allow the oil to bypass the filter if the filter becomes unduly clogged. The pressure relief valve relieves excessive oil pressure so preventing burst pipes and seals.

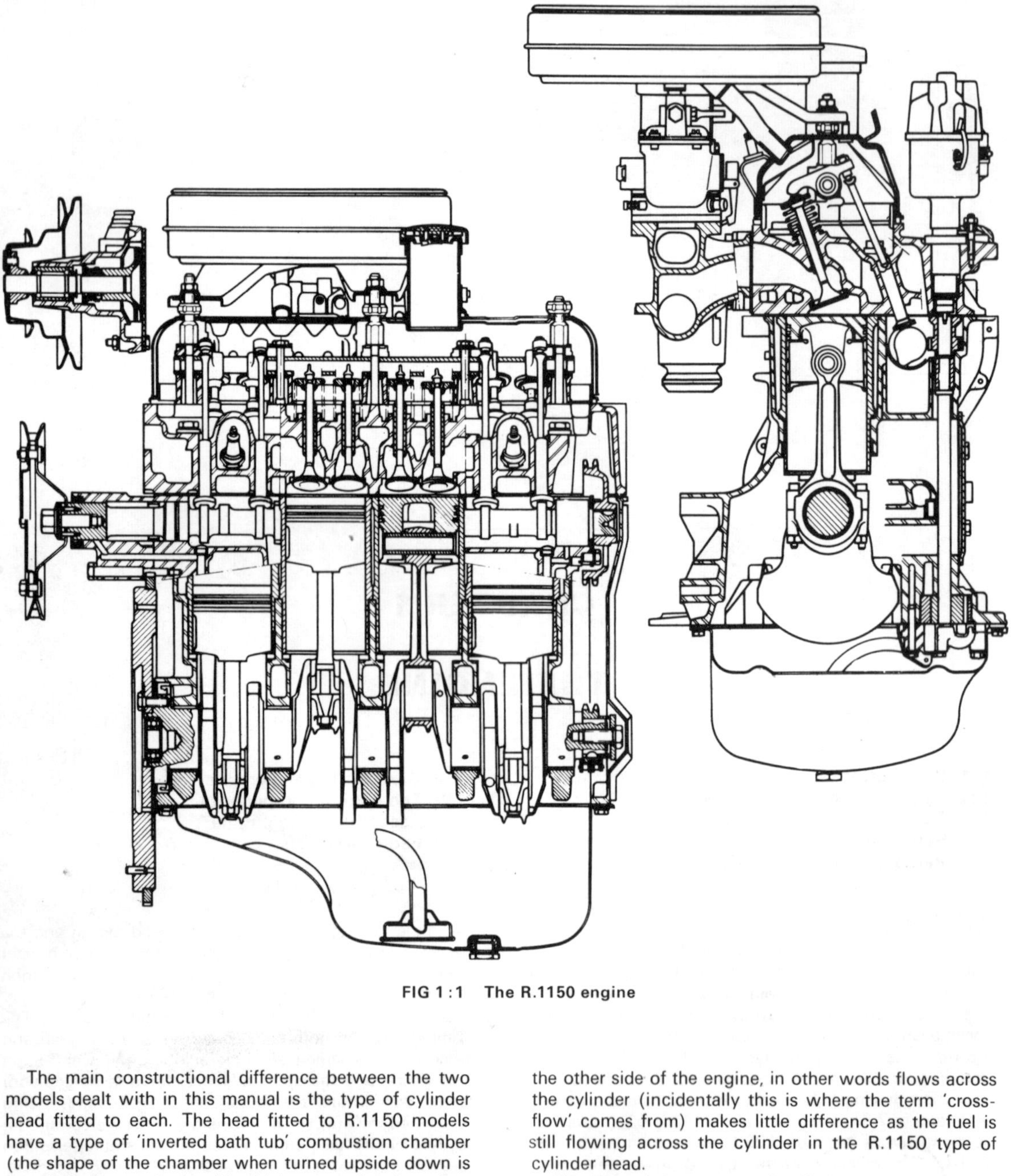

FIG 1 : 1 The R.1150 engine

The main constructional difference between the two models dealt with in this manual is the type of cylinder head fitted to each. The head fitted to R.1150 models have a type of 'inverted bath tub' combustion chamber (the shape of the chamber when turned upside down is not dissimilar to a bath tub) which means that the valves are placed next to one another and therefore the size of the valves have to be limited. On R.1151 models a 'hemispherical' type of combustion chamber (the shape is basically half a sphere, hence the term hemispherical) is used which allows the valves to be inclined so in turn allowing larger valves to be used. A larger valve will quite obviously allow a greater quantity of fuel into the cylinders and more fuel means more power. The fact that the fuel comes in one side of the engine and leaves the other side of the engine, in other words flows across the cylinder (incidentally this is where the term 'cross-flow' comes from) makes little difference as the fuel is still flowing across the cylinder in the R.1150 type of cylinder head.

The Renault has a type of cylinder construction that differs from most of its competitors, instead of a cast block being bored out and the bored holes becoming the cylinders the cylinders are in the form of wet liners. This is a sleeve which is placed in the cylinder block with appropriate seals to stop the cooling water leaking to the sump and combustion chambers. This form of construction has several advantages over the conventional method of cylinder construction, firstly the cooling water is in direct contact with the cylinder wall and secondly if the

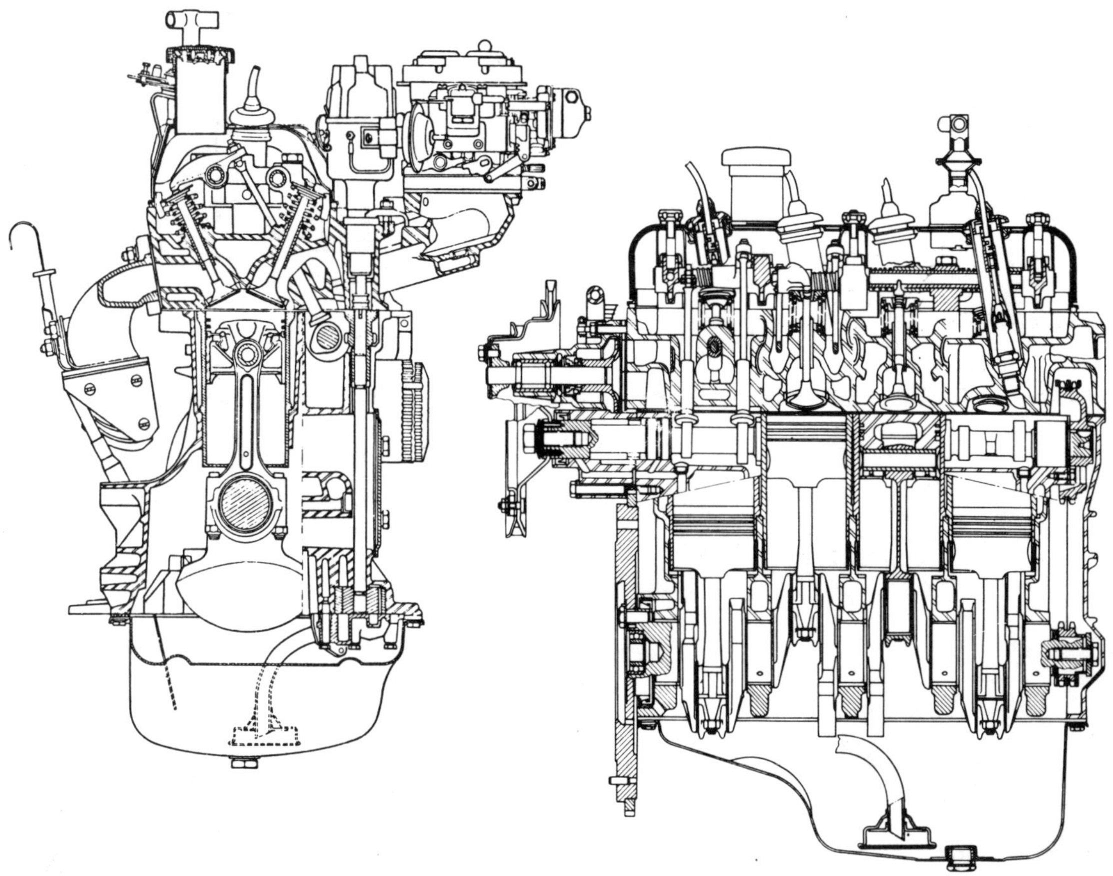

FIG 1:2 The R.1151 engine

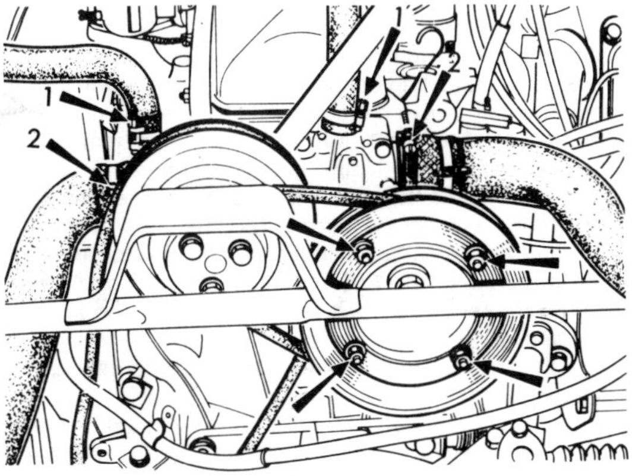

FIG 1:3 The water hose connections

Key to Fig 1:3 1 Heater hoses 2 Radiator hoses

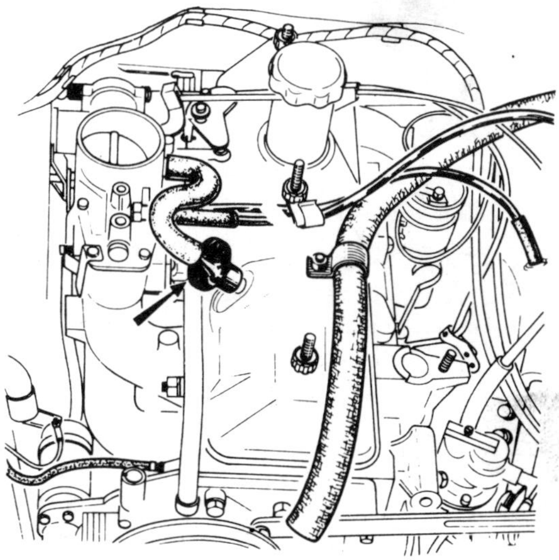

FIG 1:4 The emission capsule

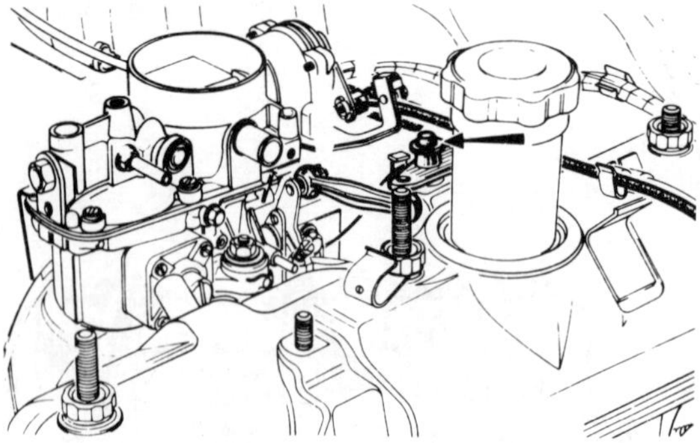

FIG 1:5 The accelerator idle lever

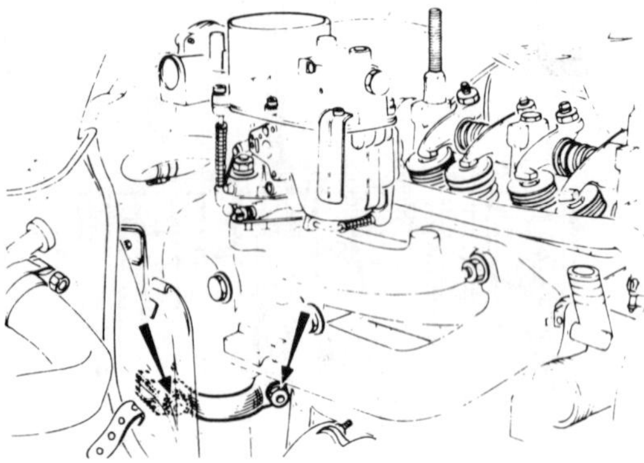

FIG 1:6 Exhaust clamp securing bolts

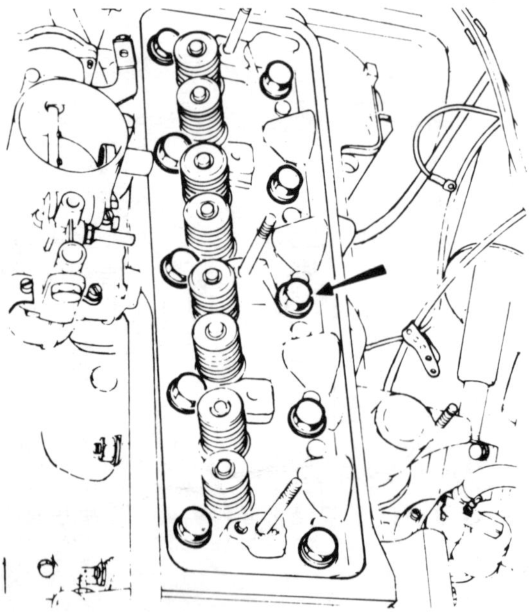

FIG 1:7 Centre head bolt

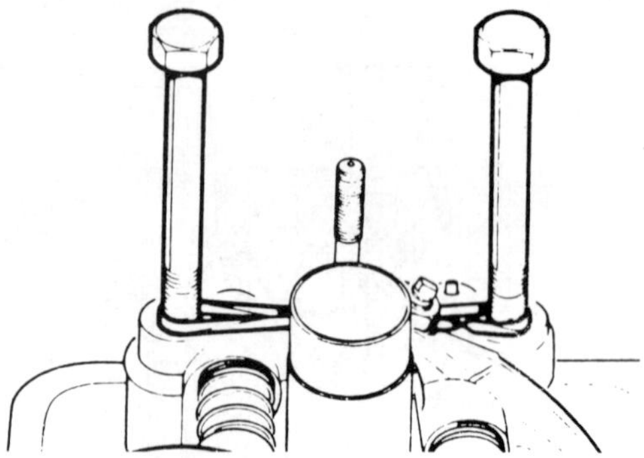

FIG 1:8 The two rocker shaft bolts

cylinder wall becomes too damaged (for the maximum rebore of a normal type of engine) to eliminate it, would mean a costly replacement of the complete block whereas on the Renault it would simply mean replacing the damaged liner. The main advantage however lies in the fact that the grade of cast iron that has good wearing qualities is not the same grade as that which had good casting properties, so with the normal layout a 'happy medium' has to be achieved whereas with a liner arrangement the grade that cast well is used to make the block and the grade that has the best wear properties is used in the manufacture of the liners. This advantage is not put to use on the R.1150 and R.1151 as the cylinder blocks are made of aluminium.

1:2 Removing the cylinder head

Removal:

Disconnect the battery and remove the spare wheel. Drain the cooling system as detailed in **Chapter 4** and take off the air filter. Disconnect the plug leads, the distributor input leads, the alternator leads and the vacuum pipe at the distributor. Undo the nuts and bolts securing the alternator and distributor and remove the distributor and alternator.

On R.1150 models, with regard to **FIG 1:3** disconnect the heater hoses 1 and radiator hoses 2 at the water pump and unscrew the nuts, arrowed in **FIG 1:3,** securing the outer flange on the camshaft pulley. Remove the outer flange and adjusting shims then take off the water pump and alternator drive belts. Pull out the emission capsule, arrowed in **FIG 1:4** and disconnect the temperature switch lead, the fuel pipe and the carburetter vacuum pipe. If the heater hose is secured to the rocker arm cover by a clip, remove the clip. Disconnect the accelerator link and choke cable. Remove the accelerator idle lever clip, arrowed in **FIG 1:5** and free it from the brackets on the rocker arm cover. Disconnect the input lead from the coil and remove the coil, the rocker cover securing nuts and the rocker cover. Undo the nuts, arrowed in **FIG 1:6,** securing the exhaust manifold clamp.

On R.1151 models carry out all the instructions layed out in the previous paragraph, except for the removal of the accelerator idle lever, and disconnect the vacuum pipe connecting the inlet manifold to the master-vac braking power unit, the throttle spring, the fuel pump pipes and finally remove the cable fitting on the rocker arm cover.

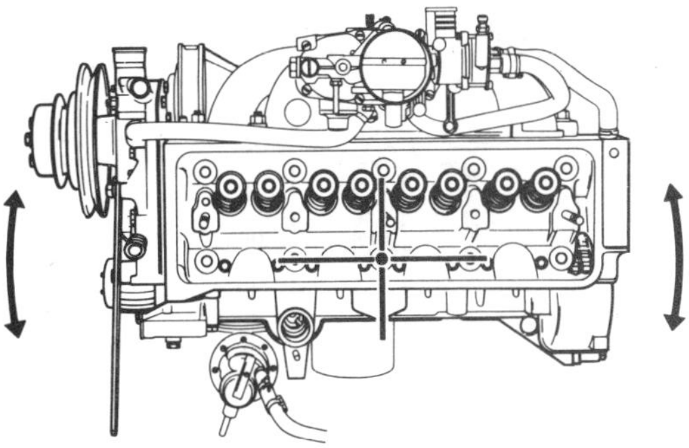

FIG 1:9 Removing the cylinder head

On R.1150 models unscrew the rocker arm adjusting screws and on R.1151 models remove the rocker arm assembly. Lift out the pushrods putting them aside in the order in which they are removed.

As the cylinder head gasket sticks to the cylinder head, cylinder block and liners it is very important that the head is not lifted as this would cause the liners to come unstuck at their bottom seatings and result in dirt entering and damage to the lower seals. Unscrew and remove the cylinder head bolts except for the centre bolt on the distributor side on R.1150 models (see **FIG 1:7**) and the centre and last two bolts on R.1151 models. Loosen the bolts left and on R.1151 models lift the two end bolts as far as they will go holding them with a piece of elastic in the manner shown in **FIG 1:8.** With regard to **FIG 1:9** free the cylinder head by tapping its end **horizontally using a plastic or hide mallet only.** Remove the centre bolt and gently lift the cylinder head. Remove the tappets putting them aside in the order in which they are removed and then lift the cylinder head away.

Cleaning the gasket face:

With regard to **FIG 1:9a** fit tool MOT.12 to retain the liner flanges. It is very important that the gasket faces on the cylinder block and head are not scraped off with a sharp tool as any distortion of the block or head face, however small, can cause leakage past the cylinder head gasket. Use only trichlorethylene to remove any part of the gasket that remains sticking to the cylinder head and on the cylinder block.

Place a straight edge over the liner and check by using feeler gauges that the gap between the liner and cylinder block face, i.e. the projection of the liner is between .005 and .0075 inch (.12 to .19 mm).

Remove the oil in securing holes A in **FIG 1:9a** using a syringe, otherwise when the bolt is tightened the oil being compressed will give an incorrect reading on the torque wrench, and clean hole B with a rag. Finally remove the liner retaining flanges.

Positioning the gasket and cylinder head:

To position the gasket and cylinder head on R.1150 models tool MOT.412, shown in **FIG 1:10** will have to be used. With reference to **FIG 1:11** screw the gasket locating dowel 1 into the front of the cylinder block on the camshaft side and fit the gauge 2 in the front hole of the cylinder block, with the two lugs T parallel with the longitudinal centre line of the engine. Fit the cylinder head gasket **and ensure that it is not removed. Should it be so (if the cylinder head were incorrectly positioned for example) a new gasket must be fitted.** Fit the tappet compartment rubber gasket making sure the ends do not overlap the cylinder head gasket. Place the tappets in the cylinder head, in their correct order, and tap them lightly so that they stick in their locations. Ensure that the distributor drive pinion is in its correct position that is to say that with number one piston

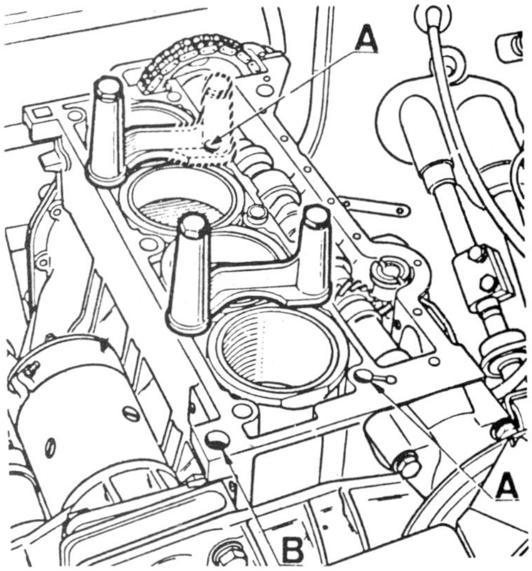

FIG 1:9a The liner retaining washers

Key to Fig 1:9a **A** Hole **B** Hole

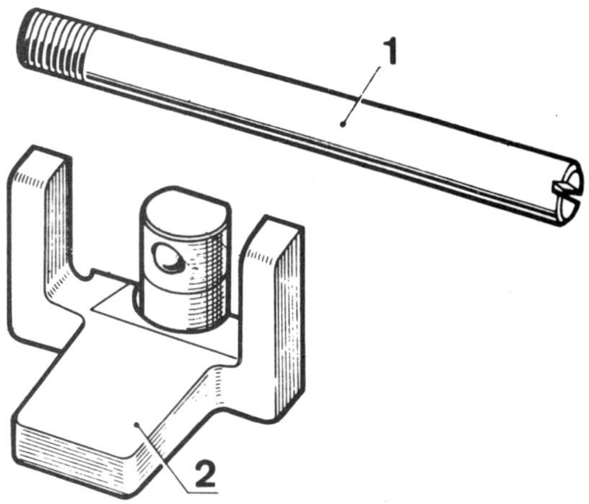

FIG 1:10 Tool MOT.412

Key to Fig 1:10 1 Locating dowel 2 Cylinder head positioning gauge

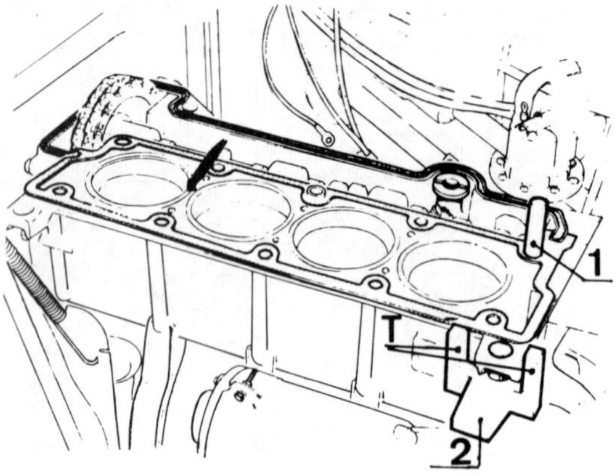

FIG 1:11 Fitting tool MOT.412

Key to Fig 1:11 T Lugs 1 Dowel 2 Gauge

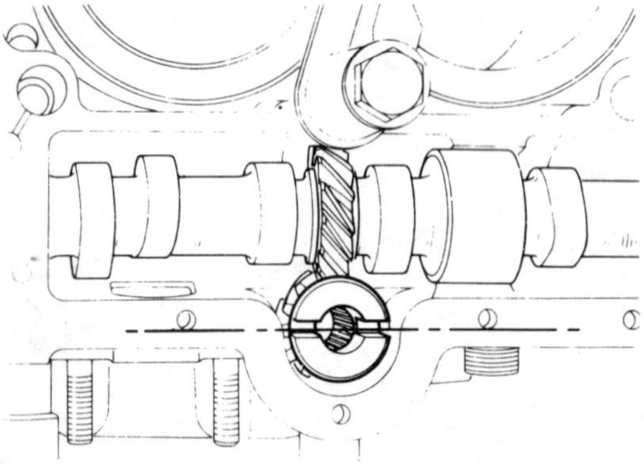

FIG 1:12 Pinion position (R.1150)

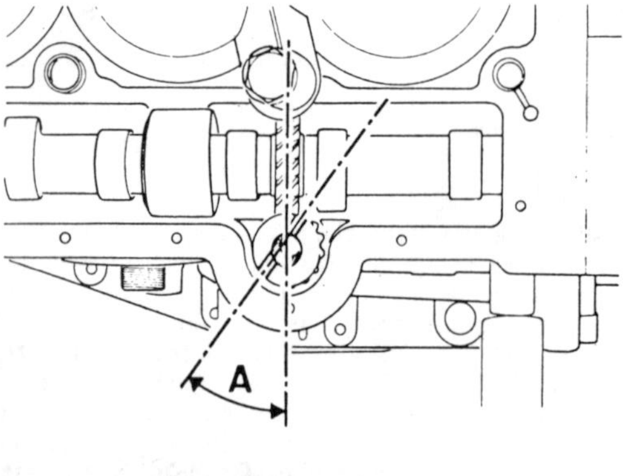

FIG 1:12a Pinion position (R.1151)

Key to Fig 1:12a A 53 deg. angle

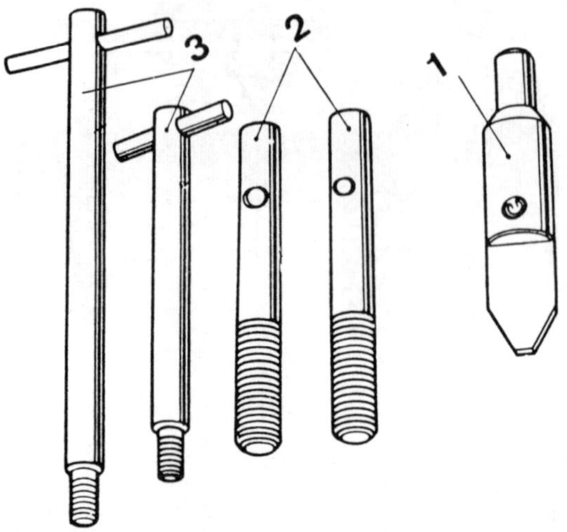

FIG 1:13 Tool MOT.446

Key to Fig 1:13 1 Gauge 2 Studs 3 Tools

at TDC and the cams on number four cylinder in balance the pinion slot on R.1150 models is parallel with the engine longitudinal centre line with the largest offset on the camshaft side (see **FIG 1:12**), and on R.1151 models with the largest offset on the camshaft side and angle A in **FIG 1:12a** formed by the slot in the pinion and the centre line which is square with the camshaft centre line equal to 53 deg. Position the cylinder head and place it on the cylinder block ensuring that its manifold face is placed against the two lugs T on the gauge and that the tappet compartment gasket is not moved. **From this point the cylinder head is not to be touched.** Remove the gasket locating dowel, lubricate the cylinder head bolt threads with engine oil and fit the bolts screwing them in slowly.

Positioning the gasket and head on R.1151 models requires the use of tool MOT.446 illustrated in **FIG 1:13.** With regard to **FIG 1:14** fit the gauge 1 in the cylinder block upper front securing hole and ensure that the cylinder head locating dowel, arrowed in **FIG 1:14** is in fact in position in the cylinder block. Fit the cylinder head gasket; **again ensure that it is not removed. Should it be so (if the cylinder head were incorrectly positioned for example) a new gasket must be fitted.** Screw the studs 2 in **FIG 1:14** into the position shown in the illustration until the balls make contact with the cylinder head gasket, this action will force the gasket against the cylinder block. Fit the tappet compartment rubber gasket, avoiding it overlapping the cylinder head at the ends. Place the tappets in the cylinder head in the correct order and tap them lightly so that they stick in their locations. Fit the rocker arm assembly in position taking care to correctly fit the two supports with holes in them and to ensure that they fit over their locating dowels correctly. Place the last two (shortest) bolts so that they project above the rocker arm supports by approximately $\frac{1}{4}$ inch (6 mm) and hold them in place with an elastic band in the manner illustrated in **FIG**

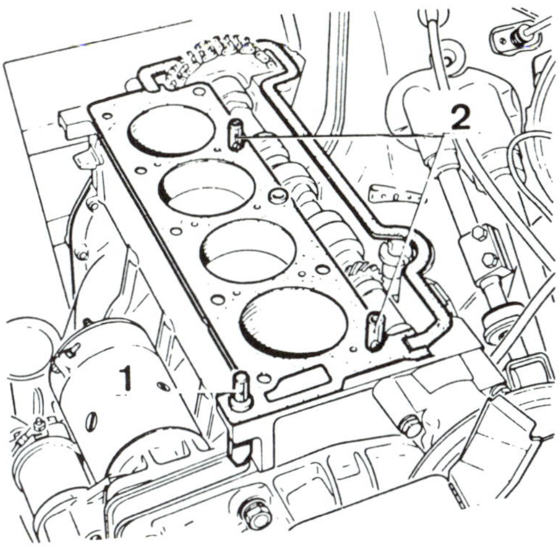

FIG 1:14 Fitting tool MOT.446

Key to Fig 1:14 1 Gauge 2 Studs

1:15. Refer to the previous paragraph and ensure that the distributor drive pinion is correctly in position. With the help of a friend (the weight of the cylinder head/manifold makes this necessary) position the head on the block. Using guide tool 3 in **FIG 1:16** remove the guide dowels. Lubricate the cylinder head bolt screw threads with engine oil then fit the bolts and screw them slowly in.

Refitting:

Tightening the cylinder head bolts must be carried out accurately and smoothly, if leakage past the gasket is to be avoided and it is for this reason that the manufacturer forbids a 'break-back' release type of torque wrench to be used and insists that the bolts are tightened initially in two separate movements.

1 Tighten the bolts to a torque of 30 lb ft (4 mkg) for R.1150 models in the order layed out in **FIG 1:17** and in the sequence layed down in **FIG 1:18** on R.1151 models.
2 Loosen the bolts by a quarter of a turn and then tighten them to a torque of 55 lb ft (8 mkg) in the same order.

If the bolts 'jerk' and will not tighten smoothly and positively screw them in and out a number of times. In the case of both models remove the positioning gauge.

Fit the pushrods, noting that on R.1151 models the exhaust pushrods are longer than those for the inlet rocker arms. On R.1150 models fit the rocker arm and tighten the securing nuts and bolts to 20 lb ft (2.75 mkg). torque. Lightly tap the rocker adjusting screws to make sure that the tappets are resting on their cams. The valve clearances will have to be set next. The clearance between the rocker arm and inlet valve is .008 inch (.20 mm) and between rocker arm and exhaust valve .010 inch (.25 mm) with the engine cold. Slacken the locknut and press down on the adjusting screw when checking in order that any oil trapped inside the pushrod

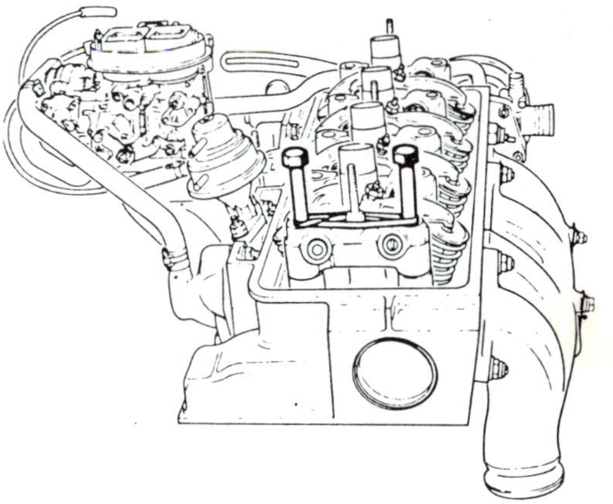

FIG 1:15 Securing the rocker shaft to the cylinder head

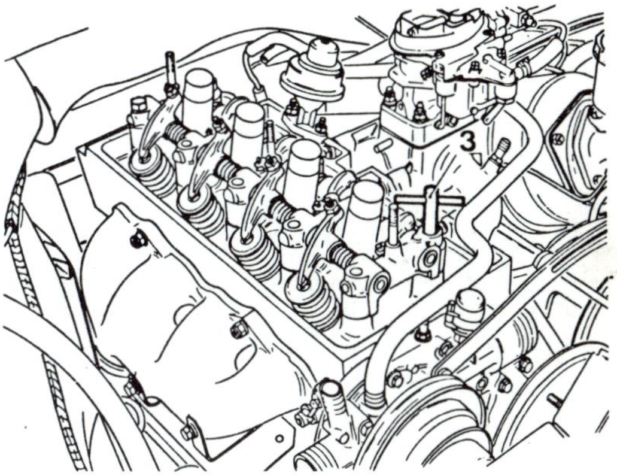

FIG 1:16 Positioning tools of tool MOT.446

Key to Fig 1:16 3 Tool

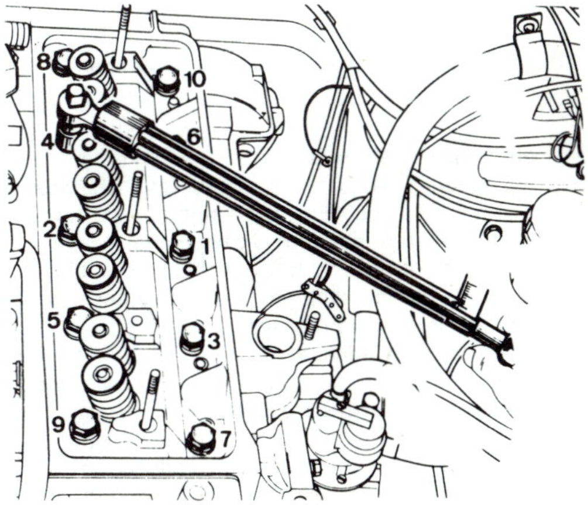

FIG 1:17 Cylinder head bolt tightening sequence (R.1150)

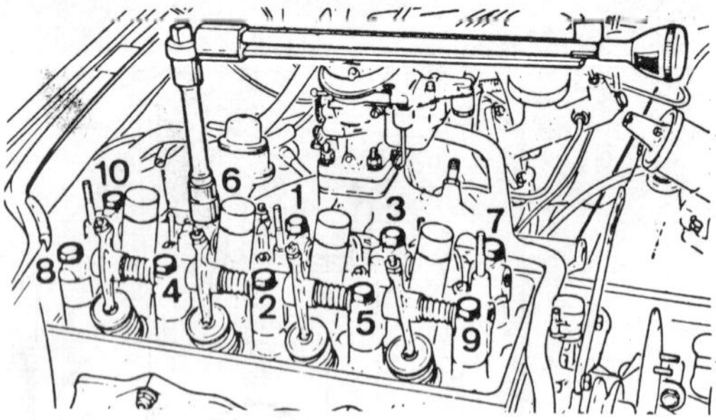

FIG 1 : 18 Cylinder head bolt tightening sequence (R.1151)

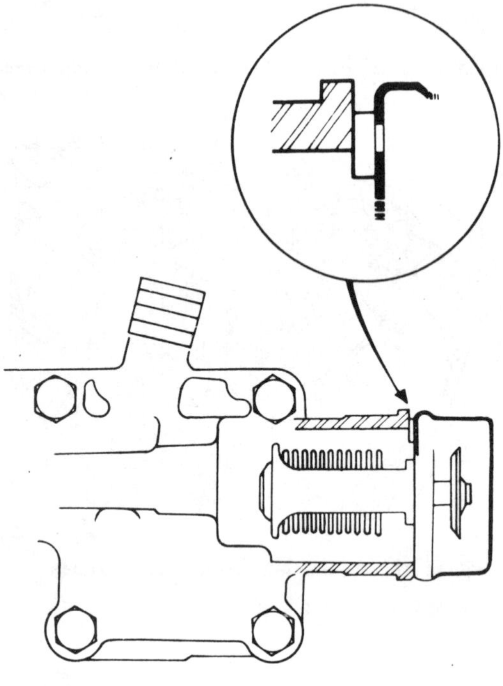

FIG 1 : 19 Thermostat leakage hole

cup can be dispersed, otherwise the oil will result in an incorrect reading. Adjust the screw until the correct clearance is obtained and then tighten the locknut. Recheck the clearance as it might have altered when the locknut was tightened. It is as well to note that it is impossible to obtain accurate valve clearances if the valve and or end of the rocker arm are worn.

The clearance of each valve must be set when the valve is on the back of its cam. This can be easily carried out by following the sequence layed out below:

Adjust No. 1 rocker with No. 8 valve fully open.
Adjust No. 2 rocker with No. 7 valve fully open.
Adjust No. 3 rocker with No. 6 valve fully open.
Adjust No. 4 rocker with No. 5 valve fully open.
Adjust No. 5 rocker with No. 4 valve fully open.

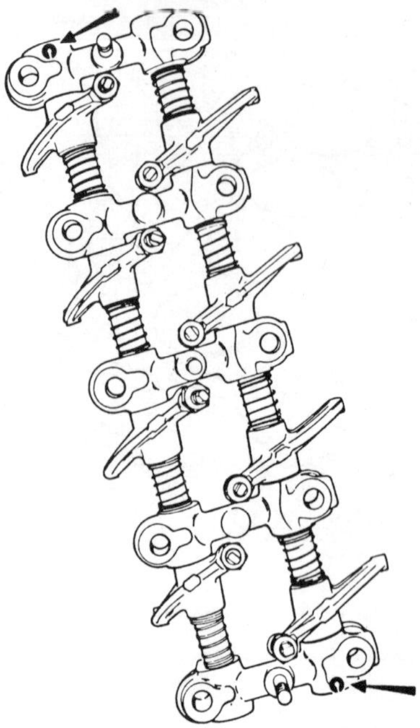

FIG 1 : 20 Rocker assembly (R.1151)

Adjust No. 6 rocker with No. 3 valve fully open.
Adjust No. 7 rocker with No. 2 valve fully open.
Adjust No. 8 rocker with No. 1 valve fully open.

Note that the numbers in each case add up to nine, remember this and it is easy to check without constant reference to the table. To rotate the camshaft to adjust the valve clearances, jack up one side of the vehicle, engage top gear and turn the jacked up road wheel in the forward drive direction. **The camshaft must never be turned by using the camshaft pulley bolt.**

Complete reassembling by securing the exhaust pipe clamp, refitting the rocker cover and on R.1150 models the ignition coil and accelerator idle lever. On R.1151 models connect up the throttle cable, throttle link and spring, temperature switch lead, braking power unit vacuum pipe and the fuel pump pipes whereas on R.1150 connect up the accelerator cable, accelerator link, choke cable and temperature switch lead. On both models connect the heater and radiator hoses and check that the thermostat leakage hole, shown in **FIG 1 : 19,** is upwards and in line with the slot in the pump body. Refit the distributor, connect up the leads and set it to a static timing of 0 deg. $\pm$ 2 deg. (see **Chapter 3**). Refit the alternator and connect up the leads. Fit the alternator belt and tension it until there is a deflection of $\frac{9}{64}$ to $\frac{13}{64}$ inch (3.6 to 5 mm) along its longest run. Fit the water pump drive belt adjusting shims, the belt and the outer pulley flange. Slowly tighten the outer flange securing bolts while turning the engine in order to avoid damage to the belt. The engine must be turned by again rotating the jacked up road wheel and never by turning the camshaft pulley securing bolt. Check the belt deflection which should be between $\frac{3}{32}$ and $\frac{5}{32}$ inch (2.5 to 4 mm). If the

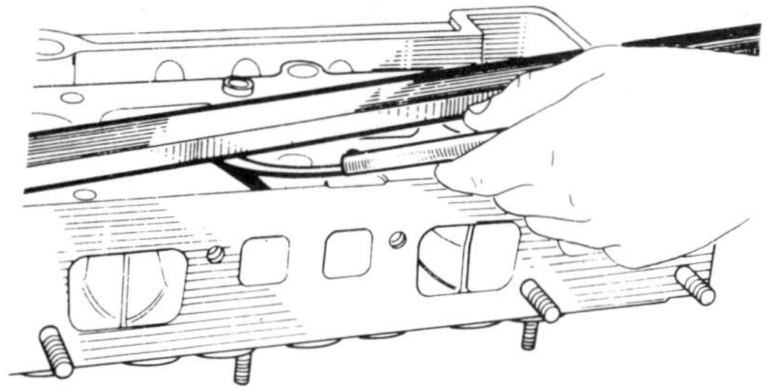

FIG 1 : 21 Checking for cylinder head distortion

deflection is incorrect add or remove shims between the two pulley flanges. Top up the cooling system and reconnect the battery.

Start the engine and allow it to warm up for 10 minutes then switch off and allow it to cool for 50 minutes. Disconnect the battery, remove the rocker cover, loosen the cylinder head bolts $\frac{1}{4}$ of a turn and then retighten them to a torque of 60 lb ft (8.75 mkg). Adjust the valve clearances, refit the rocker cover and connect up the battery.

Whenever the cylinder head gasket has been replaced, after 300 miles the cylinder head bolts must be retorqued in the manner described in the previous paragraph.

1 : 3 Overhauling the cylinder head

Dismantling:

Remove the spark plugs, water pump pulley, water pump and its backplate with the alternator tensioner, the alternator, bracket and the temperature switch. Using a suitable valve spring compressor, compress the valve springs and remove the collets, spring and seat washers. Take out the valves and put them aside in the order in which they were removed. On R.1150 models dismantle all the rocker arm assembly components, note that the plugs at the end of the shafts are force fitted and cannot be removed. On R.1151 models remove the roll pins arrowed in **FIG 1 : 20**, which retains the rocker arm shafts and separate and clean the various parts.

Examination:

Clean all the parts noting that it is very important not to scrape the cylinder head gasket face and that only trichlorethylene must be used to dissolve any part of the cylinder head gasket that remains sticking to the cylinder head.

Using a straight edge and feeler gauge in the manner illustrated in **FIG 1 : 21** check that the cylinder head distortion is no greater than .002 inch (.05 mm). If it is distorted beyond limits it may be refaced, provided that no more than .012 inch (.3 mm) is removed. If the cylinder head required more metal to be removed than the maximum .012 inch (.3 mm) allowed, it must be replaced.

On R.1150 models inspect the free length of each valve spring, that is the length of the spring when it is not under load, which should be $1\frac{29}{32}$ inch (48.4 mm) and replace any spring whose length is less. The inlet and exhaust valve springs are identical.

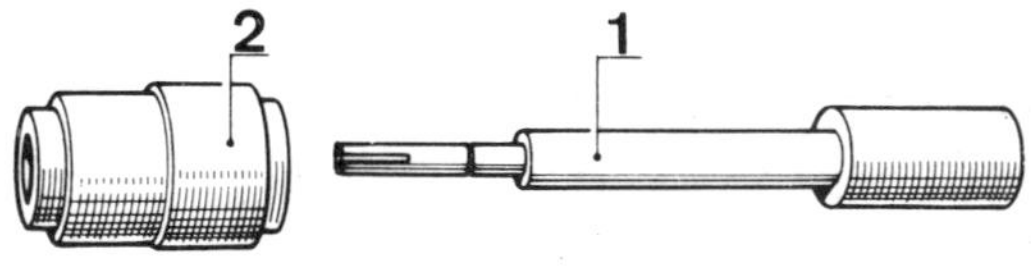

FIG 1 : 22 Tool MOT.356

Key to Fig 1 : 22 1 Mandrel 2 Guide stop

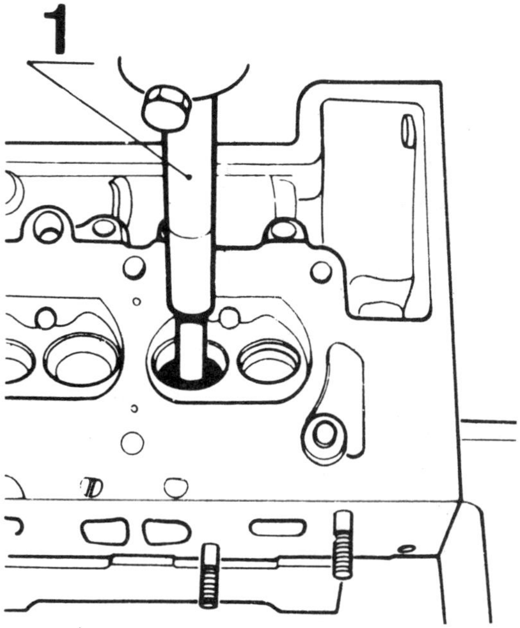

FIG 1 : 23 Pressing the old guide out

Key to Fig 1 : 23 1 Mandrel

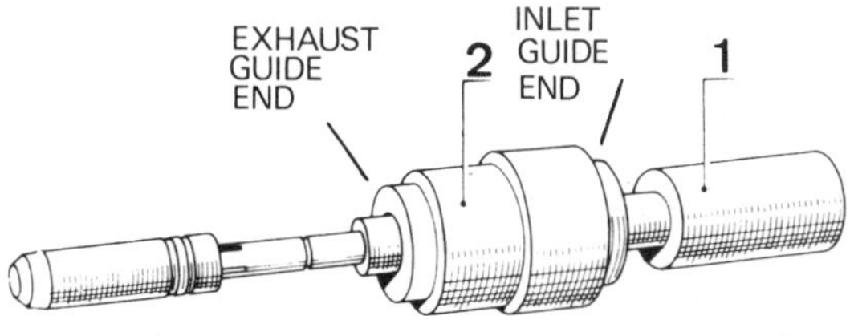

FIG 1 : 24 Placing the guide on tool MOT.356

Key to Fig 1 : 24 1 Mandrel 2 Guide stop

On R.1151 models like the R.1150 models the inlet and exhaust valve springs are identical. The free length of the valve outer springs should be $2\frac{5}{32}$ inch (54.3 mm) and that of the inner springs $1\frac{3}{4}$ inch (44.7 mm). Again replace any spring whose length is less.

Check the fit of each valve stem in its corresponding guide and if there is undue side movement of the valve the guide will have to be replaced.

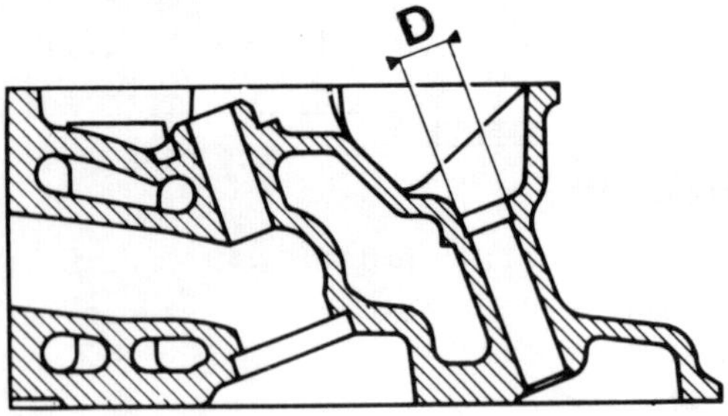

FIG 1 : 25 Diameter of the tappet counterbore

Key to Fig 1 : 25 D Diameter

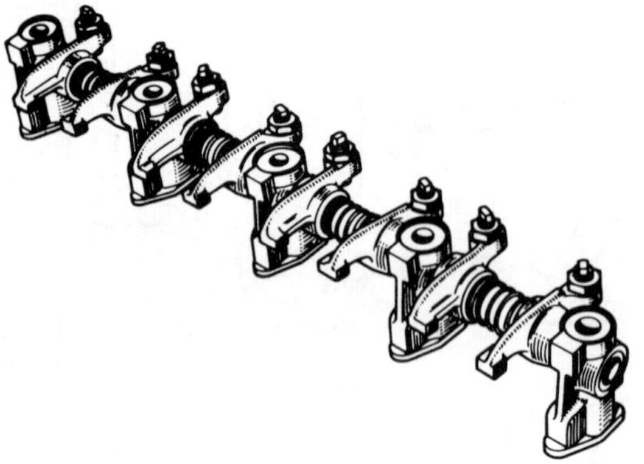

FIG 1 : 26 Rocker shaft assembly

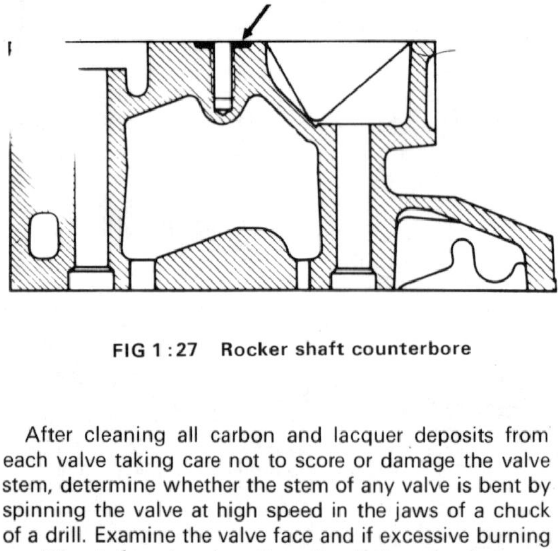

FIG 1 : 27 Rocker shaft counterbore

After cleaning all carbon and lacquer deposits from each valve taking care not to score or damage the valve stem, determine whether the stem of any valve is bent by spinning the valve at high speed in the jaws of a chuck of a drill. Examine the valve face and if excessive burning or pitting is found replace the valve. If the valve faces are not excessively damaged but are too pitted for the pitting to be removed by grinding in the valve with grinding paste have a garage recut the face at a 45 deg. angle asking them to ensure that the face width of the inlet valve does not exceed .063 inch (1.6 mm) and that of the exhaust valve is not greater than .079 inch (2 mm).

Examine the valve seats of the cylinder head for pitting

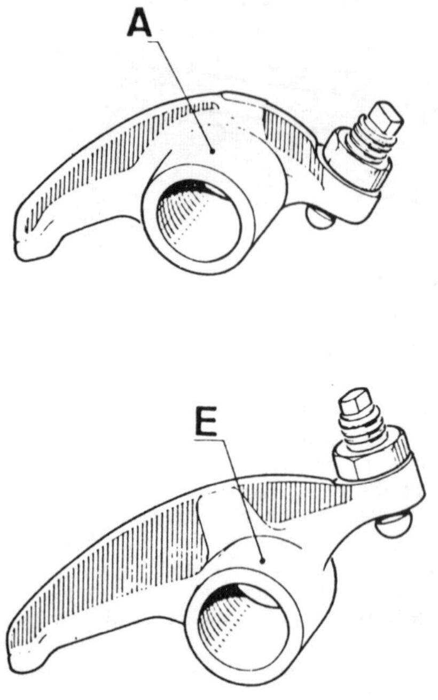

FIG 1 : 28 Inlet and exhaust rockers (R.1151)

Key to Fig 1 : 28 A Inlet rocker E Exhaust rocker

and scoring and if they are found to be excessive have a garage recut the seats at the 45 deg. angle specified.

Check that where the valve rocker arm comes into contact with the valve stem there is not a groove as this will result in incorrect setting of the valve rocker clearance. Any arm that has undue wear can have the contact face reground to eliminate this wear.

If new thread inserts are fitted to the sparking plug tappings take care to grind off the 2 or 3 threads which project into the combustion chamber.

Replacing a valve guide (R.1150 models only):

Tool MOT.356 shown in **FIG 1 : 22** will be required for this operation. Support the head so that it is tilted at about 30 deg. and using the mandrel 1 in **FIG 1 : 23** push out the guide. Measure the outside diameter of the guide to check whether it is an original one or whether it has already been replaced. An original guide measures .512 inch (13 mm) and is identified by one groove whereas the oversize guide measures .522 inch (13.25 mm) and is identified by two grooves. If the guide removed is an original one the guide locating bore will have to be reamed out to suit the oversize guide. If the guide pressed out is an oversize one a new head will have to be obtained.

Ream out the guide locating bore using the reamer in tool MOT.357 which corresponds to the diameter of the new guide. Fit the mandrel 1 into the guide stop 2 in the manner shown in **FIG 1 : 24** ensuring that the guide stop is fitted the correct way round depending whether the guide in question is an inlet or an exhaust guide. Place the guide on the end of the mandrel with the chamfer of the guide towards the outside. Lubricate the guide.

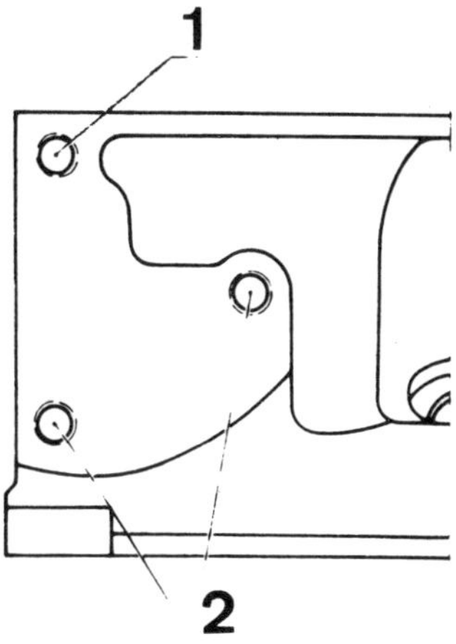

FIG 1 : 29 The alternator securing holes

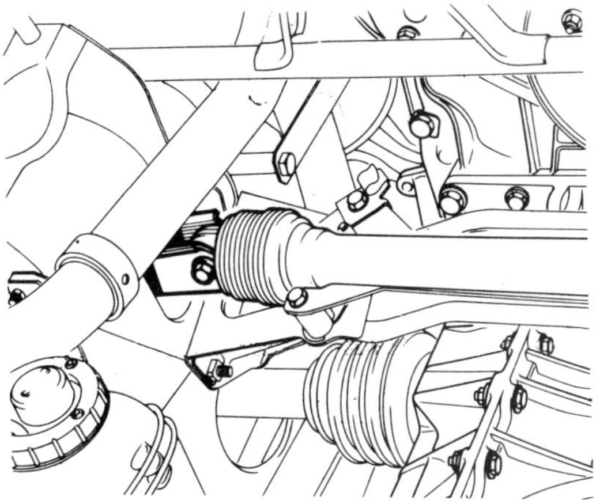

FIG 1 : 30 Steering link

Place the assembly on the cylinder head and press in the guide until the shoulder of the mandrel contacts the guide stop. Using the reamer in MOT.357 which has a diameter of .315 inch (8 mm) ream out the inside of the guide.

Replacing the tappets (R.1150 models only):

If the tappet blocks are a sloppy fit in the head, oversize tappets can be obtained which are .007 inch (.2 mm) larger in diameter than the standard sized tappets. Fitting oversize tappets necessitates reaming out the tappet locations in the cylinder head and for this task the reamer bearing tool kit number MOT.366 must be used. Check the diameter, D in **FIG 1 : 25**, is .512 inch (13 mm) after reaming is completed. If it is less than this it is to be opened up to .512 inch (13 mm).

Reassembling:

On R.1150 models fit the rocker arm assembly supports, the rocker arms and spring to the rocker arm shaft in the order shown in **FIG 1 : 26**. Ensure that the holes in the support are in line with those in the shaft and that the lubrication holes in the shaft face towards the pushrod side. It must be noted that when the counterbores, shown arrowed in **FIG 1 : 27**, were discontinued the rocker shaft supports were modified and the screwed length of the studs were also increased. The old type of support must not be fitted to a new cylinder head although the new type of support can be fitted to the earlier type of cylinder head. When fitting the new support the identification groove must be placed on the stud extension side. On R.1151 models it is as well to note that the intermediate bearings for the rocker shafts are identical except that the one at the timing gear end has a locating dowel, that the central bearing and extreme bearing at the timing gear end are the same except that the end bearing has a hole in it for the rocker arm shaft set pin and that the extreme bearing at the clutch end has a rocker arm lubrication oil hole in it. Note also that the machined face on the bearings should always be pointed towards the clutch end and that the inlet rocker arms are different from the exhaust rocker arms (see **FIG 1 : 28**).

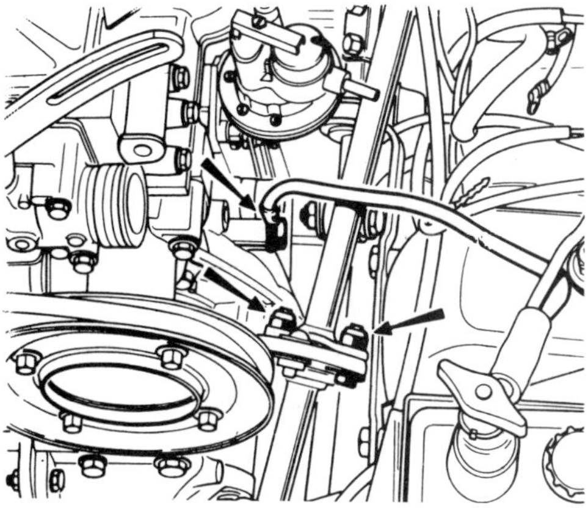

FIG 1 : 31 Flexible coupling securing bolts

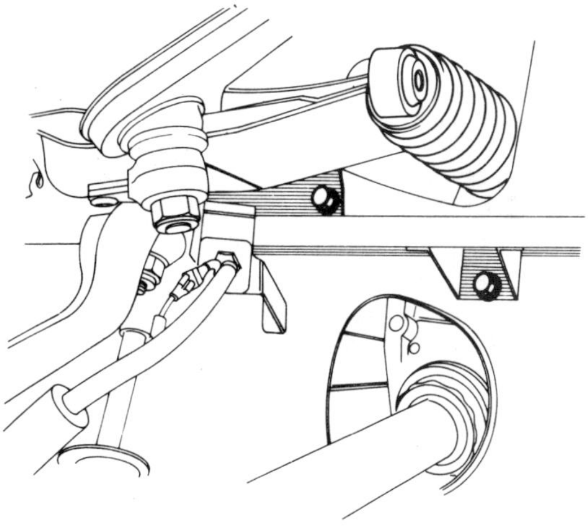

FIG 1 : 32 Steering crossmember securing bolts

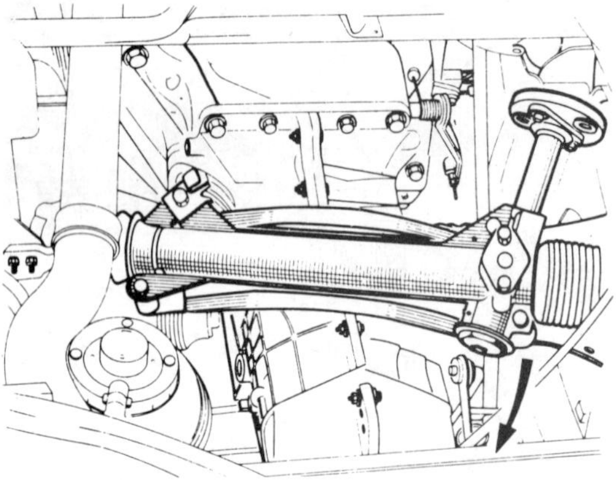

FIG 1:33 Removing the steering crossmember

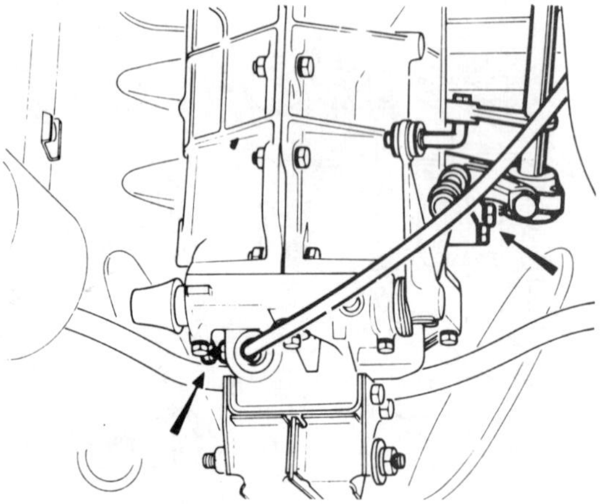

FIG 1:34 Gearshift level link

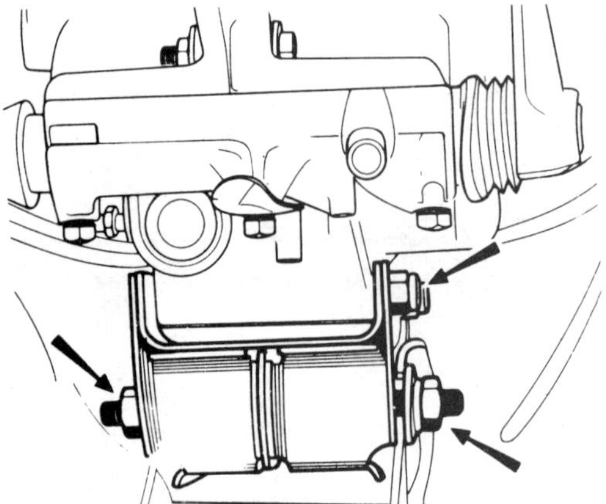

FIG 1:35 The mounting pad

FIG 1:36 Removing the roll-pins

Fit the valves in their correct order, place the valve spring seat washers, valve springs and valve collars in position and using a suitable valve spring compressor, compress the springs. Fit the collets noting that the inlet valve collets are different from the exhaust valve collets. Fit the water pump, alternator tensioner, water pump pulley and temperature switch.

Before fitting the alternator bracket, as the thickness of the bracket upper securing point has been increased, check the depth of the tapping in the securing holes 1 and 2 in **FIG 1:29.** If the upper hole 1 depth is $\frac{5}{8}$ inch (16 mm) and the depth of the lower holes 2 are $\frac{45}{64}$ inch (18 mm) it is a later type of cylinder head whereas if the depth of all the holes are $\frac{33}{64}$ inch (13 mm) it is an early type of head. The old type of bracket can be fitted to a new cylinder head and the later type of bracket to an early head provided a $\frac{5}{64}$ inch (2 mm) washer is placed behind the upper securing bolt head.

1:4 Removing the engine (R.1150)

Removal:

1. Disconnect the battery, remove the spare wheel and drain the cooling system and the transmission. Remove the bonnet retaining clip and lift the bonnet to its maximum extent.
2. Remove the fan and its casing, the air filter and the spare wheel carrier crossmember. Disconnect the leads from the alternator, the inlet pipe at the fuel pump, the fuel return pipe to the tank, the input lead at the ignition coil, the accelerator spring and accelerator link.
3. Remove the accelerator cable idle lever and disconnect the heater and radiator hoses and the water pump. Disconnect the lead from the temperature switch and leads from the starter and remove the exhaust pipe clamp and the upper bolt on the starter. Disconnect the oil pressure switch lead.

FIG 1 : 37 Transmission shaft rubber bellows

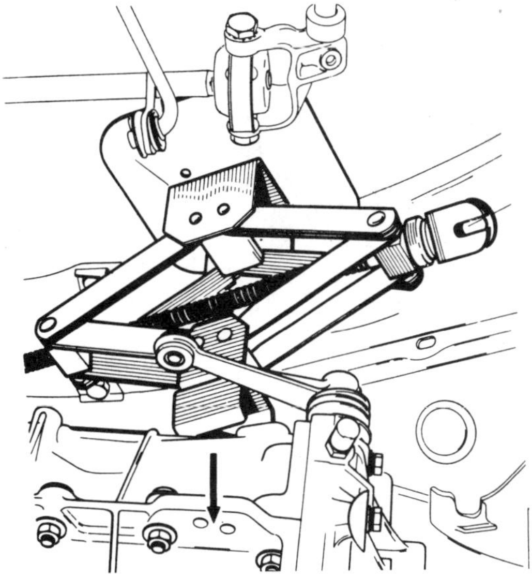

FIG 1 : 38 Freeing the transmission shaft

4 Turn the steering to the left and disconnect the righthand steering link from the adjustable end fitting (see **FIG 1 : 30**). Turn the steering wheel to the right and disconnect the lefthand link. Remove the two bolts, arrowed in **FIG 1 : 31** securing the steering flexible coupling to the steering column and remove the bolt, arrowed in **FIG 1 : 31**, which secures the earth lead to the cylinder block.

5 Remove the four bolts, two of which can be seen in **FIG 1 : 32**, that secure the steering crossmember to the cowl sides and then turn the steering through its full lock to the right, free the lefthand end of the assembly towards the front, as illustrated in **FIG 1 : 33** and remove the assembly.

6 Disconnect the speedometer drive cable and the link at the gearshift lever. Remove the two bolts, arrowed in **FIG 1 : 34** which secure the gearshift to the transmission case and pull back the control. Hook it to the battery support.

7 Unscrew the two nuts and two bolts, arrowed in **FIG 1 : 35** which secure the mounting pad to the front housing and remove the pad and bracket. Using drift B.V1.31B in the manner shown in **FIG 1 : 36** push the roll pins from the transmission shafts.

8 Fit tool T.AV.247 in the way illustrated in **FIG 1 : 37** in order to avoid the Weiss joint coming out of place and position a jack between the transmission case and lefthand sidemember (see **FIG 1 : 38**). Push the gearbox by means of the jack and free the transmission shaft from the sun wheel. Disconnect the clutch cable, free the bellows and push out the end of the cable from the end stop. Remove the jack and place it on the righthand sidemember. Push the box over and free the transmission shaft from the sun wheel.

9 **The engine must never be lifted by taking the load on the cylinder head bolts.** Position the sling at the upper starter securing point and at the

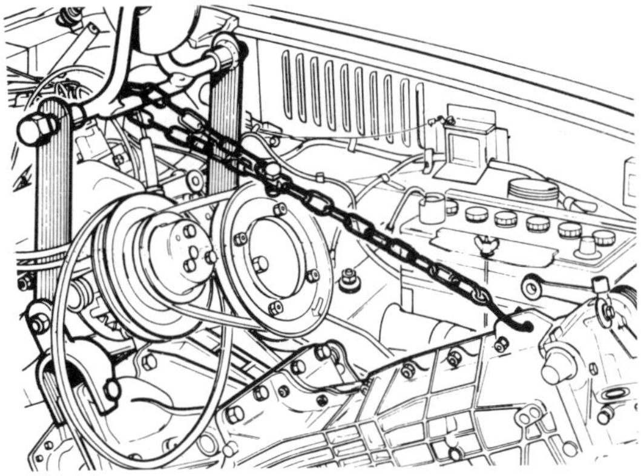

FIG 1 : 39 Lifting out the engine/gearbox

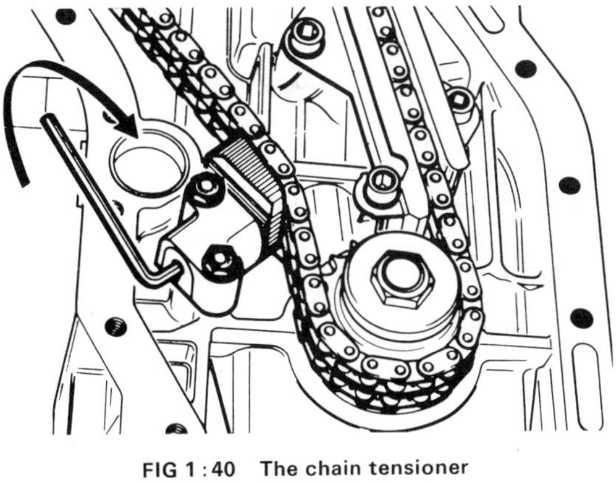

FIG 1 : 40 The chain tensioner

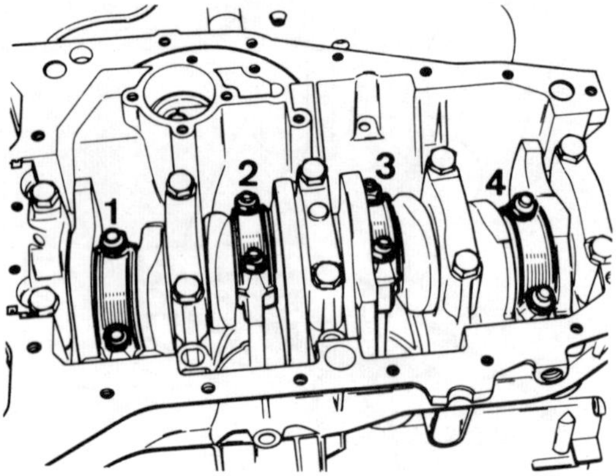

FIG 1:41 Connecting rod markings

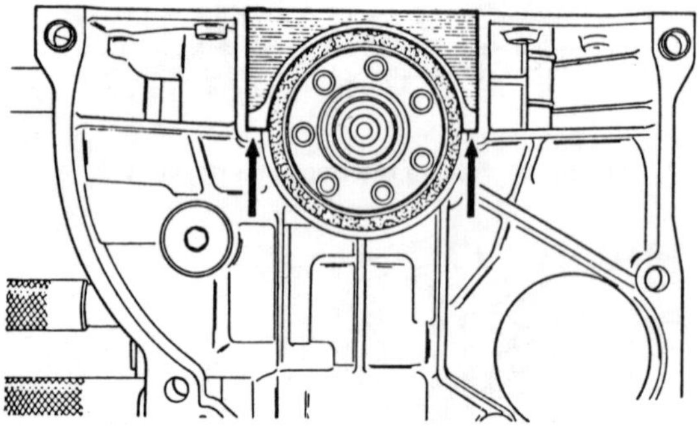

FIG 1:42 Removing the front bearing

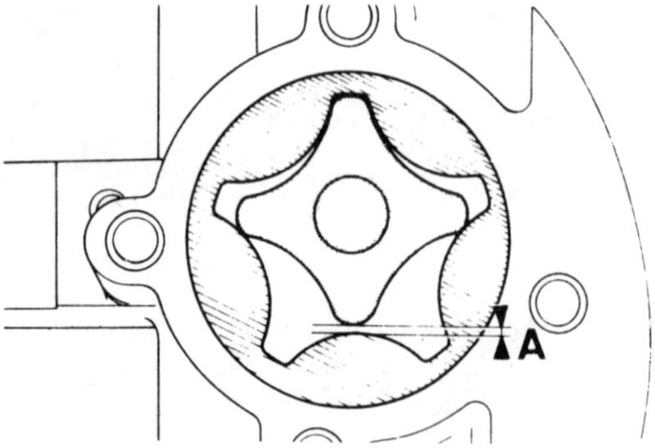

FIG 1:43 Checking inner and outer rotor clearance

Key to Fig 1:43 A Clearance

point where the earth lead was secured to the cylinder block. Take the weight of the engine and then remove the side mounting pad securing bolt from either side.

10 Finally using a chain in the manner shown in **FIG 1:39** lift the front of the gearbox until the assembly is tilted so that it can be freed from the engine compartment. Lift the engine/transmission unit and remove it taking care not to damage the radiator.

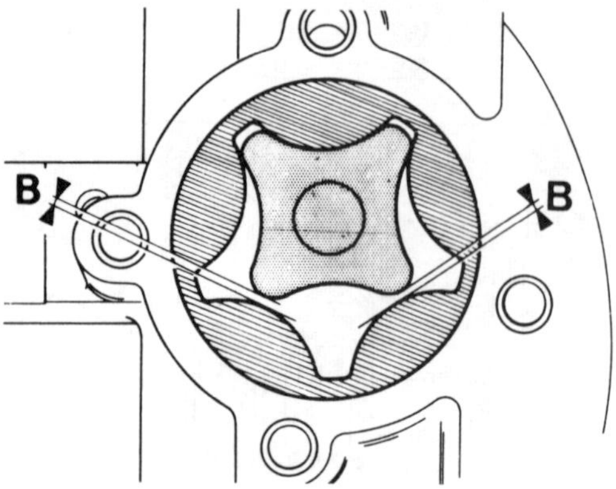

FIG 1:44 Checking lobe clearance

Key to Fig 1:44 B Clearance

11 Remove the starter, the outer flange from the camshaft pulley, the pulley adjusting shims, the belt and the pulley. Unlock and remove the three clutch housing securing bolts on the engine. Separate the gearbox from the engine.

Refitting:

Refit the engine by carrying out the removing operations in reverse ensuring that the clutch shaft splines and sun wheel splines are lubricated **sparingly** with Molykote BR.2 grease, that the leakage hole in the thermostat is towards the top and in-line with the slot in the water pump (see **FIG 1:19**) and that the alternator belt is tensioned until there is a deflection of $\frac{9}{64}$ to $\frac{13}{64}$ inch (3.5 to 5 mm) along its longest run. On completion fill the gearbox with EP.80 oil and the cooling system with coolant.

1:5 Removing the engine (R.1151)

1 Carry out 1 in the previous section. Remove the air filter and the spare wheel carrier crossmember together with the coil. Disconnect the leads from the fan unit to the relay, the temperature switch lead, the hoses at the water pump and remove the radiator.

2 Disconnect the lead from the temperature switch on the cylinder head, the starter leads, the heater hose at the pump, the throttle spring, the throttle link and the throttle cable. Loosen the locknut and unscrew the adjustable end fitting on the rocker arm cover. Remove the starter upper securing bolt, the emission valve capsule with its pipe, the dipstick and its tube, the exhaust pipe clamp and the exhaust pipe lower securing bolt.

3 Disconnect the alternator leads and remove the alternator. Disconnect the fuel inlet pipe at the pump, the fuel return to tank pipe, the heater hose at the cylinder head, the vacuum pipe at the manifold and the oil pressure switch lead.

4 Carry out 4 to 11 inclusive in the previous section.

Refit the engine by carrying out the refitting instructions layed out in the previous section.

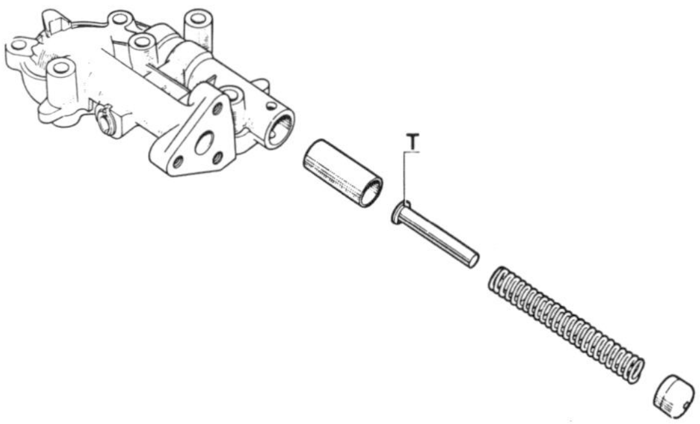

FIG 1:45 The oil pump

Key to Fig 1:45 T Head of the spring guide

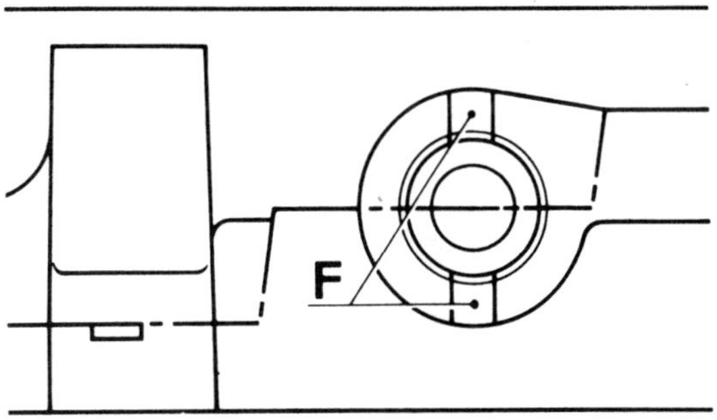

FIG 1:46 The pump slot

Key to Fig 1:46 F Slot

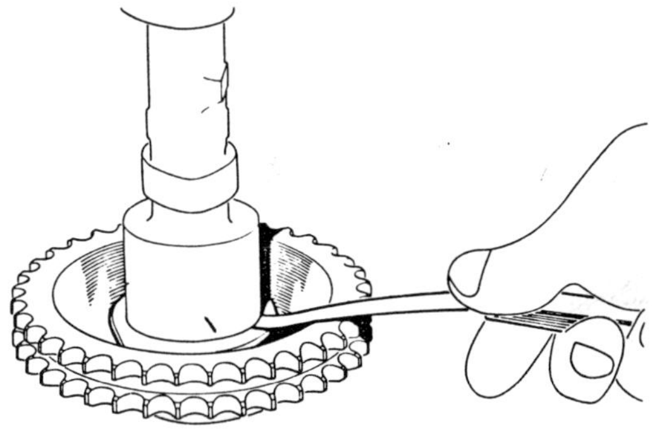

FIG 1:47 Checking the camshaft

1:6 Dismantling the engine

1 Remove the distributor, fuel pump, oil filter, oil pressure switch, lefthand side mounting point, alternator bracket, righthand side mounting point and clutch. On R.1150 models remove the combined exhaust and inlet manifold whereas on R.1151 models the separate inlet and exhaust manifolds will have to be removed as well as the ignition coil.

2 Drain the oil and remove the rocker cover, on R.1151 models also remove the rubber washers and cups in the spark plug counterbores. On R.1150 models unscrew the rocker arm assembly securing nuts and bolts and remove the rocker shaft assembly and pushrods, putting the pushrods aside in the order they were removed. On R.1151 models unscrew the rocker arm adjusting screws and remove the pushrods again put them aside in their correct order.

3 Remove the cylinder head securing bolts, except for the bolt in the centre on the distributor side on R.1150 models. Tap the end of the cylinder head **horizontally** with a hide or plastic hammer in the manner shown in **FIG 1:9**. As the cylinder head gasket is stuck to the cylinder head, the cylinder block and the liners, **it is very important not to lift the cylinder head.** When the head is free slightly lift the cylinder head and remove the tappets putting them aside in their correct order. Remove the cylinder head and on R.1151 models take out the fuel pump plunger.

4 Remove the rubber gasket and fit the liner retaining clamps MOT.12 shown in **FIG 1:9a**. Remove the distributor/oil pump drive pinion and unscrew the three camshaft front bearing securing bolts. Remove the front bearing. Undo the bolts which secure the sump, the oil pump cover securing bolts and remove the oil pump. Take out both rotors.

5 Unscrew the timing gear casing securing bolts and remove the timing gear casing. With regard to **FIG 1:40** insert a 3 mm socket key into the retaining cylinder and turn the key in a clockwise direction until the tensioner is brought away from the pad carrier assembly. Remove the tensioner.

6 Unscrew the crankshaft sprocket retaining bolt and the washer and thrust ring. Remove the lug or lugs which prevent the chain flailing. Undo the two bolts which secure the camshaft flange. Using a suitable pulley extract the camshaft sprocket. Remove the camshaft.

7 Unlock and unscrew the flywheel securing bolts and then remove the flywheel. Check that the connecting rods are correctly marked. Number 1 is at the clutch end and at the opposite side to the camshaft (see **FIG 1:41**). Remove the big-end nuts and lift off the caps and the shells. Mark the crankshaft main bearings with reference to their position on the cylinder block and unscrew the main bearing cap bolts. Remove the bearing caps and shells except for the front bearing.

8 Push out the front bearing in the direction indicated by the arrows in **FIG 1:42** by tapping lightly on its two lower ends. Remove the seal and take out the front bearing side seals. Lift out the crankshaft.

9 Remove the crankshaft main bearing shells and end float flanges. Remove the liner retaining clamps and take out the liner/piston/connecting rod assemblies.

1:7 The engine components

The oil pump:

To remove the oil pump place the vehicle on ramps and drain the engine oil. Unscrew the sump securing bolts and lift off the sump. Undo the pump strainer cover

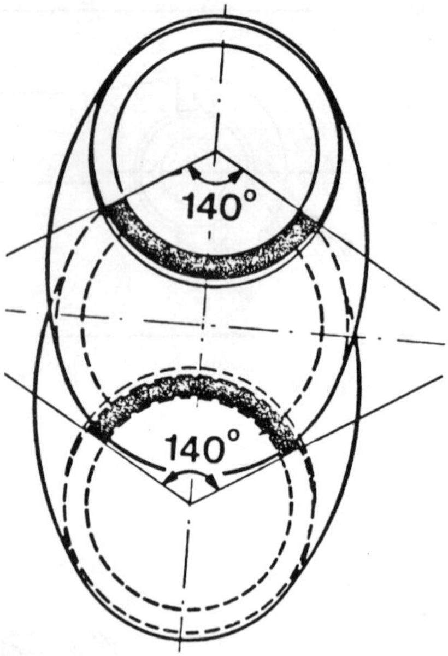

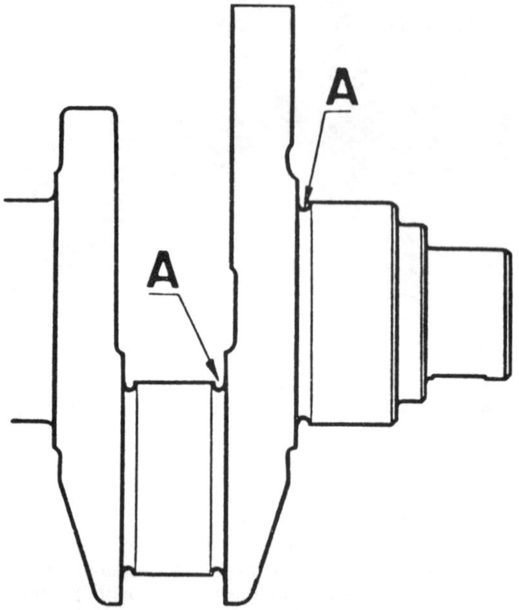

FIG 1:48 The journal undercuts

Key to Fig 1:48 A Undercuts

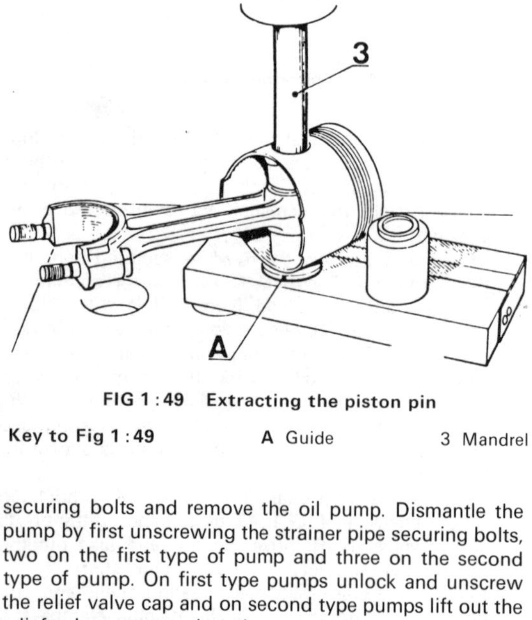

FIG 1:49 Extracting the piston pin

Key to Fig 1:49 A Guide 3 Mandrel

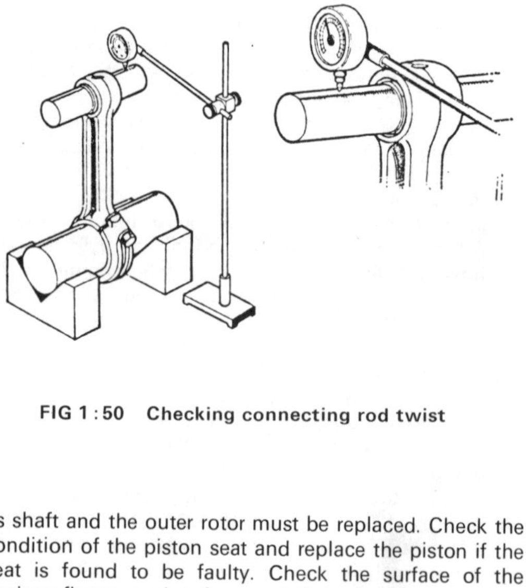

FIG 1:50 Checking connecting rod twist

securing bolts and remove the oil pump. Dismantle the pump by first unscrewing the strainer pipe securing bolts, two on the first type of pump and three on the second type of pump. On first type pumps unlock and unscrew the relief valve cap and on second type pumps lift out the relief valve cup securing pin.

Clean and check all the parts. Examine the inner and outer rotors for wear by placing them in the cylinder block. Check the clearance A in **FIG 1:43** which should be between .002 and .012 inch (.04 to .29 mm) and the clearance B in **FIG 1:44** which should be between .001 and .006 inch (.02 to .14 mm). If the clearances are not within these limits the inner rotor which is supplied with its shaft and the outer rotor must be replaced. Check the condition of the piston seat and replace the piston if the seat is found to be faulty. Check the surface of the strainer flange gasket face and the pump cover gasket face, refacing the strainer flange gasket face and or replacing the pump cover if either is found to be necessary.

If the sump on an R.1150 engine is changed from a flat bottomed one to a curved bottom one, a special repair strainer is available.

On the second type of pump check that the plug, arrowed in **FIG 1:45,** has a hexagon socket in it. If the plug has not, unscrew it and make a slot F in **FIG 1:46,**

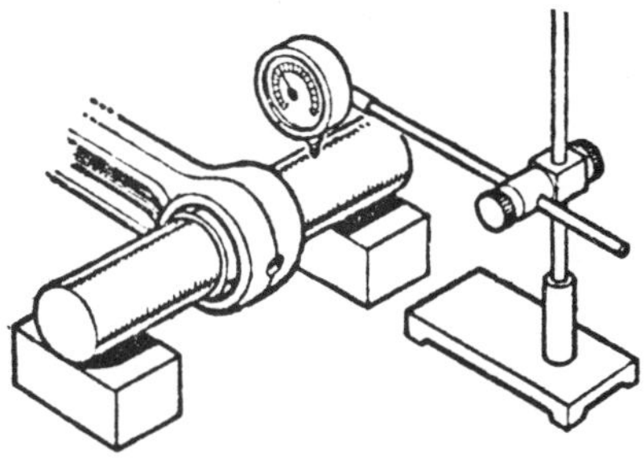

FIG 1 : 51 **Checking connecting rod bend**

$\frac{7}{64}$ inch (2.5 mm) wide and $\frac{5}{64}$ inch (2 mm) deep in the cover. Screw in a hexagon socket plug $\frac{29}{64}$ inch (11.5 mm) long and tighten in position. Pean the metal of the plug into the slot.

Reassemble the pump by placing the piston in the cover followed by the spring guide with the 'T' head inside the piston then finally fit the spring and spring cup. Secure the assembly with the cap or the pin.

Refit the pump by reversing the removal procedure.

Camshaft:

Remove the camshaft by carrying out operations 1 to 6 inclusive of the previous section.

Remove the two pulley drive pins. Check the clearance at the flange (see **FIG 1 : 47**) which should be between .002 and .0045 inch (.05 to .12 mm). This clearance cannot be adjusted so if it is not correct replace the flange To do this press off the sprocket and remove the flange. Fit the new flange and press on a new sprocket taking the load on the first camshaft shoulder. Recheck the clearance.

Note that the sprocket must be replaced by a new one each time it is removed. Do not refit used roll-pins. If the camshaft is replaced the distributor drive pinion must be replaced with it and vice versa. These two parts are sold as a matched set.

Refit the camshaft by following the instructions 8 to 13 inclusive of **Section 1 : 8.**

Crankshaft:

Remove the crankshaft by carrying out sequences 1 to 8 inclusive of the previous section.

Using extractor MOT.11 remove the clutch shaft locating bearing. Clean the crankshaft and pass a steel wire down the lubrication holes.

Examine the crankpins and main bearings for scoring, wear and ovality. If the scoring is deep or if the wear or ovality exceeds .002 inch the crankshaft crankpins and journals will have to be reground. The standard diameter of the crankpins is 1.890 inch (48 mm) whereas the standard diameter of the journals is 2.158 inch (54.8 mm). Repair size shells can be obtained for .010 inch (.25 mm) undercut journals and for .020 inch (.5 mm) undercut journals. The crankpins and journals are roll-hardened and have undercuts in the corners A of **FIG 1 : 48.** If the crankpins are reground, the roll hardening must remain intact over an area of 140 deg. on the crankshaft rotational centre line side.

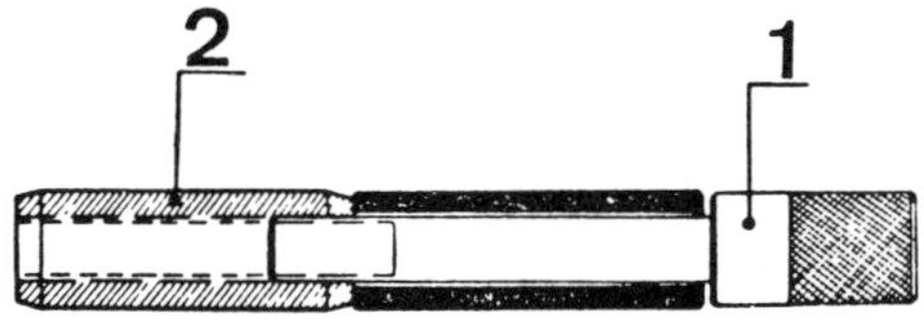

FIG 1 : 52 **The pin positioned on the mandrel**

Key to Fig 1 : 52 1 Mandrel 2 Pin

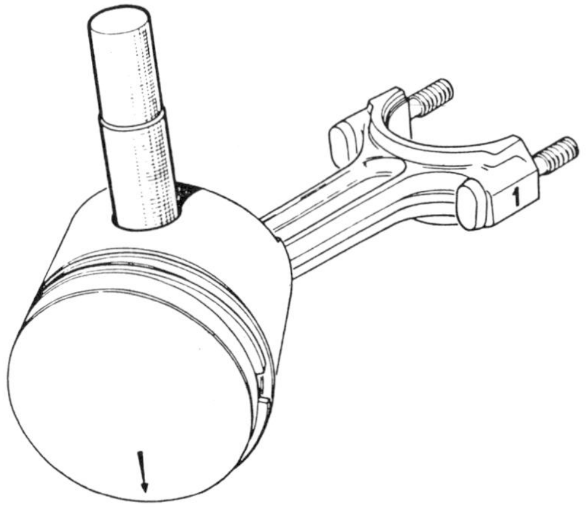

FIG 1 : 53 **The piston positioned correctly on the connecting rod**

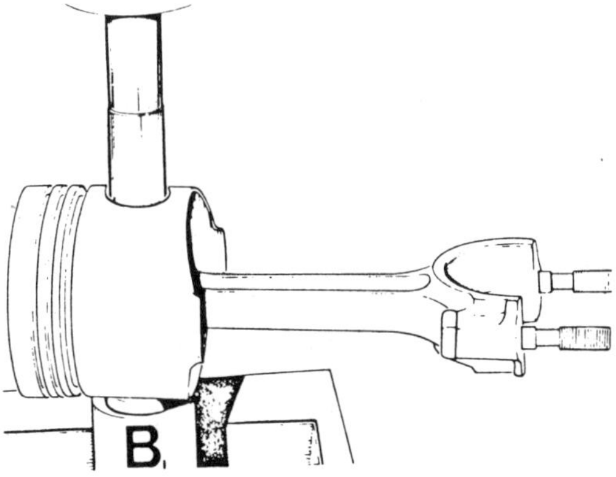

FIG 1 : 54 **Inserting the pin into the piston**

After any necessary renovation has been carried out ensure that the connecting oilways between the journals and crankpins are perfectly clean by forcing paraffin through them and when they are clear inject a thin film of oil in the same manner. If a bearing has 'run' it is essential to clear out the oil pump, pump strainer and all the oilways in the block.

Fit the clutch shaft bearing with the seal towards the

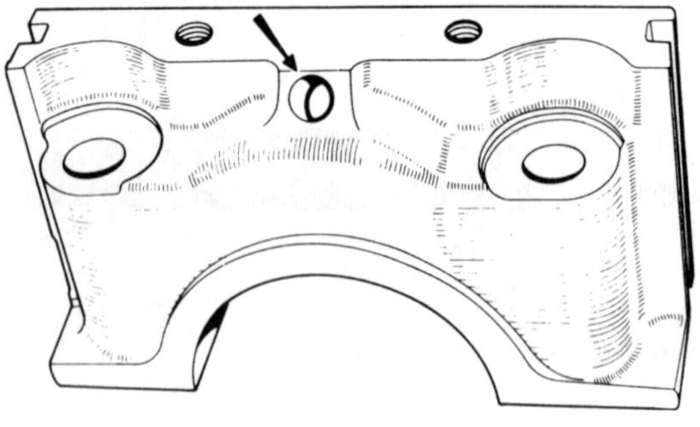

FIG 1:55 The front main bearing cap

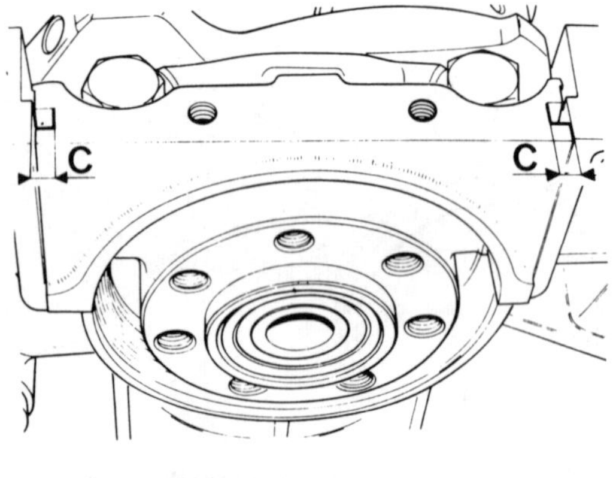

FIG 1:56 The bearing seal locating groove

Key to Fig 1:56 C Clearance

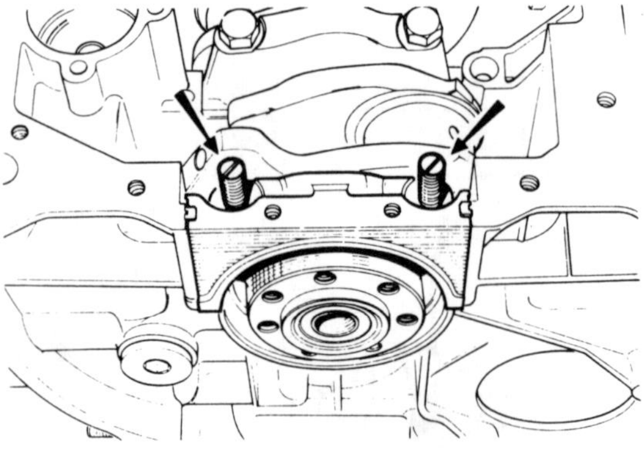

FIG 1:57 Locating studs

outside. As the bearing is supplied pre-greased, it is not to be cleaned. Refit the crankshaft by following sequences 1 to 13 inclusive in **Section 1:8.**

Liner/Piston/Connecting rod assembly:

To gain access to the liner/piston/connecting rod carry out sequences 1 to 9 inclusive of the previous section. Withdraw the piston/connecting rod assembly from the liner and remove the piston rings.

To extract the piston pin from the piston, tool MOT.255 will have to be used. With reference to **FIG 1:49** place the shaft guide A on the support base and using extracting mandrel 3 press out the pin.

Check the condition of each connecting rod and establish whether any rod is twisted or bent. Connecting rod twist can be checked by placing the big-end of the rod around a bar that has the same diameter as the crankshaft crankpin then lay the bar in two 'vee' blocks. Place the dummy checking pin, found in tool kit MOT.255, in the small-end of the rod and place it against two blocks of the **same size** as illustrated in **FIG 1:50.** Using a dial gauge check the height of each end of the piston pin and if one end of the pin is higher than the other the connecting rod is twisted. Checking for connecting rod bend is shown in **FIG 1:51,** a greater reading obtained from one end of the pin indicates that the rod is bent.

Place the connecting rod in a container of water and heat the water until it boils. Ensure that the piston pin turns freely in its piston. Slide the pin onto the inserting mandrel 1 in **FIG 1:52** and then screw the locating guide onto the mandrel until it makes contact with the piston pin. **Do not tighten it.** Lubricate the pin with molykote M55 oil.

With regard to **FIG 1:53** check that the rod is correctly positioned in the piston that is with the arrow of the piston pointing downwards and with the number on the connecting rod big-end facing towards the right, when the crown of the piston is facing towards the operator. Carry out the next sequence of events quickly so that the heat loss is reduced to a minimum. Push the piston pin/mandrel/guide assembly **by hand** into the piston and the connecting rod small-end until the pin makes contact with the connecting rod. Fit the assembly into the inserting guide B, as shown in **FIG 1:54,** ensuring that the spot-face on the piston is correctly located against the guide collar. Press in the mandrel/piston pin/guide assembly until the locating guide makes contact with the bottom of the inserting guide.

Fit an oil control ring, compression ring and 'firing' ring to each piston. Note that as the gaps in all the piston rings are prepared **they must never be adjusted.** Lubricate the piston rings, set their gap at 120 deg. to each other ensuring that the gap in the oil control ring covers an unpierced section of its groove. Refit the piston/connecting rod/liner assemblies by following instructions 5 to 13 inclusive of **Section 1:8.**

1:8 Assembling the engine

1 Fit the main bearing shells **with the lubrication holes** into the cylinder block. Lubricate the bearings and the crankshaft journal and fit the crankshaft in place. Fit the end float flanges to the centre bearing with the machined faces towards the crankshaft. Fit the bearing shells **that have no lubrication holes** to the second, third, fourth and fifth main bearing caps and secure them in place with their bolts, **tighten them finger tight.** When the shells are lubricated do not over-oil them as this can cause a hydrostatic lock which will result in the crankshaft being unable to be rotated.

2 Check the diameter of the oil drain hole, arrowed in **FIG 1:55,** in the front main bearing cap. If this is

found to be .315 inch (8 mm) it must be increased to .472 inch (12 mm). Carefully de-burr the edges of the hole. Fit the shell to the front bearing cap, temporarily fit the front bearing cap and tighten the bolt **finger tight.** With regard to **FIG 1 : 56** measure the dimension C between the cylinder block and the bottom of the bearing seal locating groove. If the reading is less than .197 inch (5 mm) obtain two seals .201 inch (5.1 mm) if it is above .197 inch (5 mm) select two seals .211 inch (5.35 mm) thick. The wider seal has a white colour code. Remove the bearing cap and fit the two side seals to the cap with the groove in the seal towards the outside. Lubricate the shell and the side seals.

3 With reference to **FIG 1 : 57** screw the studs (diameter 10 mm, pitch 150) into the cylinder block, fit two shims between the cylinder block and the seals in order not to damage the seals and then fit the front bearing cap. When the cap is almost in position, remove the shims and fit the bolts. Tighten the bearing cap securing bolts to a torque of 45 lb ft (6.5 mkg). Ensure the crankshaft turns freely.

4 Using a dial gauge check the crankshaft end float which should be between .002 to .009 inch (.05 to .23 mm). If the play is incorrect end float flanges .004 and .006 inch (.1 and 1.5 mm) oversize are available. Fit the flywheel. Apply 'loctite' locking compound to the flywheel securing bolt threads and fit the locking plate and securing bolts. Tighten the bolts to 40 lb ft (5 mkg) torque and then fold over the locking plate folds.

5 Fit the lower seals, identified by a blue code, to the liners and fit the liners into the cylinder block. Check the extent liners project above the cylinder block face using thrust plate MOT.252 and a dial gauge, which should be between .0055 and .0057 inch (.14 to .19 mm). Take the reading on two opposite sides of the liner diameter and if they differ more than .001 inch (.005 mm) turn the liner half a turn and repeat the operation. Seals can be obtained in two different thicknesses .003 inch (.07 mm) which have a blue colour code and .004 inch (.10 mm) which have a red colour code. Mark the position of the liners with reference to the cylinder block so that they may be refitted to the same position on final assembly. Make the marks on the camshaft side. Remove the liners.

6 Lubricate the pistons and using sleeve MOT.227 fit the piston/connecting rod assemblies into their liners. Ensure that the number marked on the connecting rod is on the same side as the reference mark made on the liner. The big-end faces must be parallel with the flats on the top of the liners. Fit the shells to the big-end then fit the connecting rod/piston/liner assemblies in the cylinder block with number one piston at the clutch end, with the arrow on the piston pointing towards the clutch end, with the number on the big-end on the camshaft side and with the mark on the liner in-line with that made on the cylinder block. Fit retaining flanges MOT.12 and turn the engine over.

7 Place the connecting rods on the lubricated crank-pins, fit the big-end caps together with their shells and fit the cap nuts. Tighten the nuts to a torque of 30 lb ft (4.5 mkg). Check that the crankshaft can rotate. Fit the outer and inner rotor to the oil pump

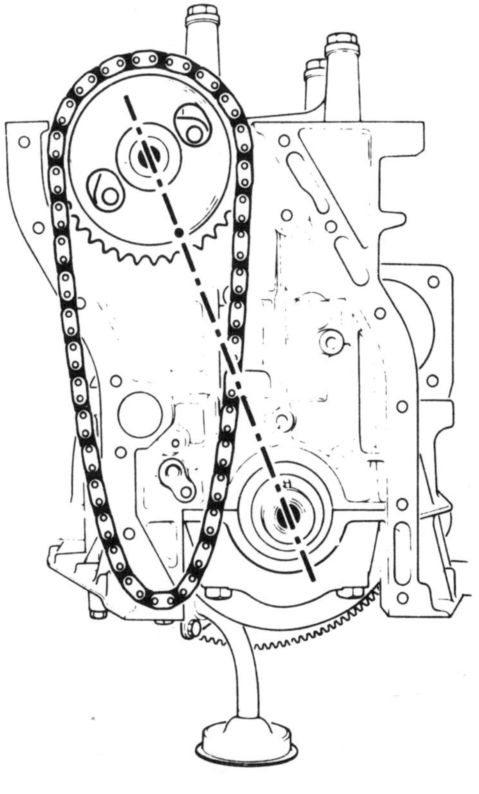

FIG 1 : 58 Aligning the camshaft sprocket

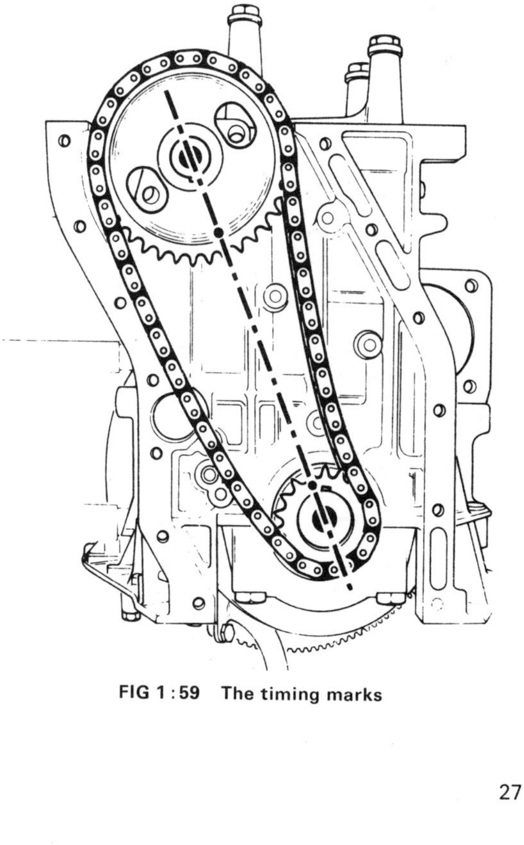

FIG 1 : 59 The timing marks

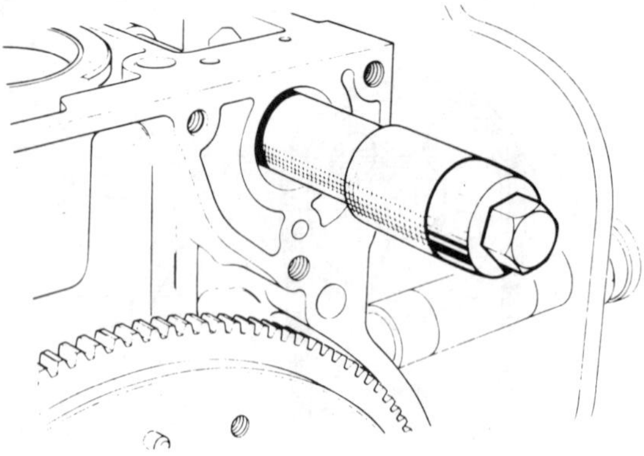

FIG 1:60 Fitting tool MOT.258

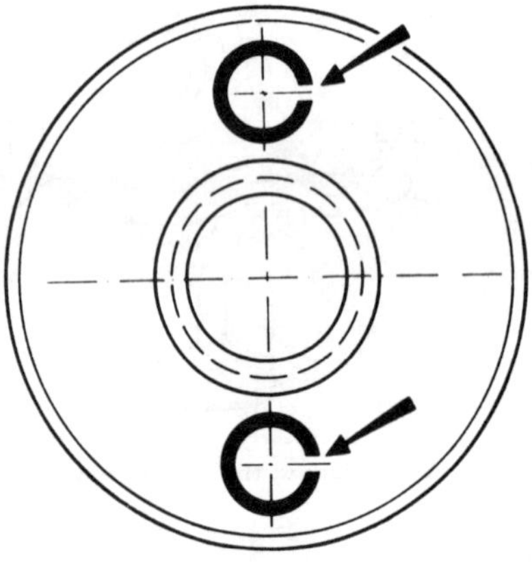

FIG 1:61 The camshaft drive pinions

and then fit the oil strainer cover and secure it.

8 Lubricate the camshaft bearings and fit the camshaft but do not push it fully home. Place the chain over the camshaft sprocket and align the mark on the sprocket with the centre of the crankshaft and the centre of the camshaft (see **FIG 1:58**). Turn the crankshaft to bring the key to the uppermost position then fit the crankshaft sprocket, with the reference marks towards the outside, on the chain. The reference marks on the crankshaft sprocket should be in line with the reference mark on the camshaft sprocket and the centres of the crankshaft and camshaft (see **FIG 1:59**). Fit the spacer, thrust washer and the crankshaft sprocket bolt and tighten it to a torque of 45 lb ft (6 mkg). Fit and tighten the two camshaft flange bolts.

9 Fit the chain tensioner together with its filter and backplate. Tighten the two securing bolts. Insert a .118 inch (3 mm) socket key into the retaining cylinder and turn the key in a clockwise direction until the pad carrier assembly is projected against the chain. Tighten and lock the bolt on the retaining cylinder. Fit the flail limiting lug(s). If one lug is fitted, when the chain is correctly tensioned the lug should be .032 inch (.8 mm) from the chain. If two lugs are fitted place gauge MOT.420 on the chain, push the lugs against the gauge and tighten the securing bolts on the lugs. Remove the gauge.

10 Fit the timing gear casing with its gasket, align the upper edge of the casing with the upper edge of the block then fit and tighten the casing securing bolts. Cut off the two front bearing seals flush with the cylinder block and fit the sump with its gasket. Secure the sump with the appropriate bolts, the two shortest ones being screwed into the front bearing.

11 Fit tool MOT.258 to the camshaft securing it in place by means of the camshaft pulley bolt (see **FIG 1:60**). Fit the camshaft bearing casing together with its paper gasket and secure in place by means of three bolts. Fit the two pins which drive the pulley in the manner shown in **FIG 1:61**. Set the distributor drive pinion as detailed in **Section 1:2** fill the cavity in the the cylinder block with engine oil and finally remove the liner retaining flanges. Fit the cylinder head as detailed in **Section 1:2.**

12 Fit the manifold gasket(s) with the metal face on the cylinder head side then fit the manifold(s) and tighten the securing bolts to 20 lb ft (2.5 mkg) torque. Connect the heating pipes between the bottom of the carburetter and the cylinder head. Fit the clutch mechanism, centralizing the friction disc with mandrel EMB.257.

13 On R.1150 models fit the ignition coil, oil pump drive shaft location coverplate, the side mountings, the oil pressure switch, the dipstick, the oil filter and the fuel pump. On R.1151 models fit the fuel pump aperture coverplate, oil pump aperture coverplate, side mounting pads, oil pressure switch, the oil filter, the distributor, the spark plugs, the rocker arm cover and the fuel pump with its plunger. Connect up the vacuum pipe to the distributor and the carburetter base heater to the water pump.

1:9 Fault diagnosis

(a) Engine will not start

1 No fuel in tank
2 Defective coil
3 Faulty distributor capacitor (condenser)
4 Faulty contact breaker points
5 Ignition wire loose or faulty insulation
6 Water on sparking plug leads
7 Faulty sparking plugs
8 Battery discharged, terminal connection faulty
9 Faulty or jammed starter
10 Sparking plug leads incorrectly positioned
11 Vapour lock in fuel system
12 Defective fuel pump
13 Overchoking or underchoking
14 Leaking cylinder head valve
15 Sticking cylinder head valves
16 Valve timing incorrect
17 Ignition timing incorrect
18 Defective cylinder head gasket

(b) Engine stalls

1 Check 4, 5, 6, 7, 10 and 12 in (a)
2 Retarded ignition
3 Mixture too weak or rich
4 Water in fuel system
5 Incorrect valve clearance

(c) Engine idles badly

1 Check 4, 7, 13, 14, 15, 16, 17 and 18 in (a)
2 Check 2 and 7 in (b)
3 Air leak at manifold joints
4 Air leak in carburetter
5 Incorrect carburetter idle setting
6 Worn valve stems or guides
7 Worn piston ring
8 Weak exhaust valve springs

(d) Engine misfires

1 Check 2, 3, 4, 5, 6, 7, 10, 11, 12, 13, 14, 15, 16, 17 and 18 in (a)
2 Weak or broken valve springs

(e) Engine overheats (see Chapter 4)

(f) Low cylinder compressions

1 Check 14, 15 and 18 in (a), 7 and 8 in (c) and 2 in (d)
2 Worn piston ring grooves
3 Scored or worn cylinder bores

(g) Engine lacks power

1 Check 3, 6, 12, 13, 14, 15, 16, 17 and 18 in (a), 3, 4 and 6 in (b), 7 and 8 in (c) and 2 in (d). Check (e) and (f)
2 Faulty ignition automatic advance
3 Clutch slipping

(h) Burnt valves or seats

1 Check 14 and 15 in (a), 8 in (b) and 2 in (d). Also check (e)
2 Excessive carbon around valve seats and head

(j) Sticking valves

1 Check 6 in (b) and 2 in (d)
2 Bent valve stems
3 Scored valve stem or guide

(k) Excessive cylinder wear

1 Check 13 in (a) and Chapter 4
2 Lack of oil
3 Dirty or contaminated oil
4 Piston rings gummed up or broken
5 Badly fitted piston rings
6 Connecting rod bent

(l) Excessive oil consumption

1 Check 2 and 8 in (c) and check (k)
2 Ring gaps too wide
3 Scored cylinders
4 Oil level too high
5 External oil leaks
6 Ineffective valve stem oil seals

(m) Crankshaft and connecting rod bearing failure

1 Check 3 and 6 in (k)
2 Restricted or blocked oilways
3 Worn journals or crankpin
4 Loose bearing caps
5 Extremely low oil pressure

(n) Internal water leakage (see Chapter 4)

(o) Poor water circulation (see Chapter 4)

(p) Corrosion (see Chapter 4)

(q) High fuel consumption (see Chapter 4)

(r) Engine vibration

1 Loose generator bolts
2 Mounting rubbers loose or faulty
3 Fan blades out of balance
4 Misfiring, see (d)

(s) Low oil pressure

1 Low oil level
2 Fault in oil pressure indication circuit
3 Oil strainer in sump choked
4 Clearance between pump rotors excessive
5 Worn crankshaft bearing
6 Broken relief valve spring
7 Leakage from any oil tight joint or seal

(t) High oil pressure

1 Incorrect grade of oil
2 Faulty relief valve

CHAPTER 2

THE FUEL SYSTEM

2:1 Description

The fuel tank is placed at the rear of the vehicle as far away as possible from the power unit to minimize the risk of fire. The tank fitted to both the R.1150 and the R.1151 have a capacity of 11 gallons.

Fuel in the tank is drawn into the carburetter float chamber by the action of the fuel pump. The pump fitted to both models is termed a 'mechanical' pump as it is driven mechanically by the camshaft. A lobe on the camshaft lifts one end of a lever in the pump body causing the other end of the lever to pull down a diaphragm in the pumping chamber. This action causes a depression in the chamber and fuel at atmospheric pressure, is forced into the chamber via a one-way valve. When the lobe, due to camshaft rotation, moves off the lever, a spring returns the diaphragm so forcing fuel out of the pumping chamber via another one-way valve. The lever is made in two parts so that when the carburetter float chamber, fuel line and pump pumping chamber are full of fuel and thus the diaphragm is held down the inner part of the lever remains stationary and the outer part simply 'idles' on the camshaft lobe. Unfortunately the pump fitted has no means of priming the system externally, so if the carburetter float chamber is empty the engine would have to be turned over a few times before the fuel in the float chamber reaches a sufficient level to allow the engine to start. The fuel pump cannot be dismantled and failure of the pump can only be remedied by fitting a completely new unit.

The carburetter fitted to R.1150 models varies. Models manufactured after 1967 are fitted with a Solex type 35 DITA whereas those made between 1965 and 1966 were fitted with a Solex type 35 DISA. In 1966 all models contained Zenith type 36 IF carburetters.

All R.1151 models are fitted with Weber type 32 DAR carburetters.

2:2 Routine maintenance

Fuel sediment drawn from any garage petrol pump will come to rest on the bottom of the fuel tank and if the fuel level in the tank is allowed to become continuously low this sediment will be drawn into the fuel pump, fuel lines and carburetter float chamber, causing in time, a faulty fuel system or a complete breakdown in the system, therefore it should be routine maintenance to allow the fuel level to become low as infrequently as possible.

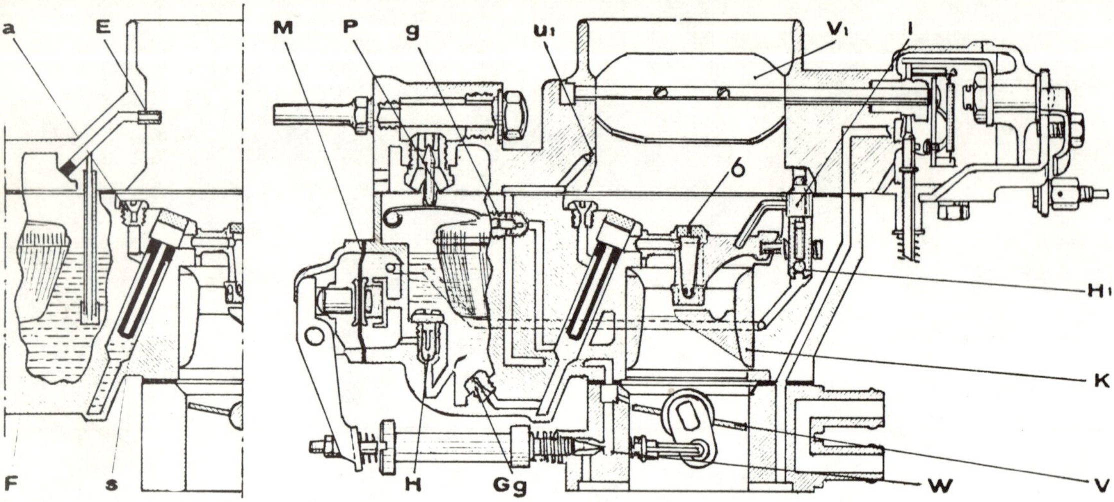

FIG 2:1 **The Solex carburetter type 35 DISA**

Key to Fig 2:1 a Correction jet **E** Econostat **F** Float **Gg** Main jet **g** Idling jet **H/H1** Pump inlet valve **i** Pump injector **K** Choke tube **M** Diaphragm **P** Needle valve **s** Emulsion tube **U1** Calibrated orifice **V** Throttle **V1** Strangler **W** Volume control screw 6 Discharge tube

Very little maintenance can be carried out to the pump accept to occasional check that the pipe connections to the pump are secure and if a filter is fitted to remove and clean it every 6000 miles.

Check the operation of the accelerator and choke control cables and lubricate them with a graphite grease if any signs of sticking occur. Occasionally lubricate all external cams, pivots and levers on the carburetter.

2:3 Solex type 35 DISA and 35 DITA carburetters

Description 35 DISA:

The Solex type 35 DISA carburetter is shown in **FIG 2:1** and works on the air bleed system. With regard to **FIG 2:1** fuel is allowed to pass into the float chamber through the needle valve P until it reaches a level where the float F shuts off the needle valve, at the same time fuel has passed through the main jet Gg and filled the passage in which the emulsion tube is housed. When the starter rotates the flywheel, the descending pistons creates a vacuum which draws air into the carburetter, the air increasing in speed and decreasing in pressure as it flows through the choke tube K. As the fuel in the float chamber is at atmospheric pressure the level in the chamber drops and the level in the emulsion tube passages rises (consider a simple 'U' tube being blown at one end) and fuel spills out of the discharge tube 6 and mixes with the air passing through the choke tube to give a volatile mixture that at the right time is ignited in the cylinder.

As air speed increases so does fuel flow but unfortunately the density of the air does not increase at the same rate and this causes an over-rich mixture as the throttle is progressively opened. This problem is overcome by fitting a correction jet (a). As the throttle is opened, the greater depression felt at the discharge tube causes the fuel level around the emulsion tube to fall, this results in holes in the tube being uncovered and air from the correction jet can enter the uncovered holes and weaken the mixture. The greater the throttle opening, the greater the depression and the more holes uncovered and therefore the greater the weakening.

When the engine is cold less fuel is evaporated and some of the fuel that is evaporated condenses onto the cold manifold walls with the result that a very weak mixture enters the cylinder. To overcome this problem we enrichen the mixture when starting from cold by operating a strangler V1 which restricts the air flow so enrichening the mixture. When the engine fires the sudden increase in depression would quickly flood the engine so the strangler spindle is offset so that directly the engine starts the depression has a greater effect on the larger area of the flap this resulting in the flap opening slightly giving an increase in air flow to prevent the flooding that would otherwise occur.

At slow engine speed the engine depression is insufficient to draw fuel from the discharge tube but the depression at the edge of the throttle V is sufficient to draw fuel so a drilling is placed at this point and air from the calibrated orifice U1 and fuel from an idling passage, the quantity of each being controlled by the pilot jet g, mix and pass out the passage by the edge of the throttle plate in sufficient quantity to enable the engine to run at slow engine speeds.

When the throttle is opened suddenly the air rushes into the cylinders but it is not met with a corresponding rush of petrol because the petrol being heavier that air lags behind. This results in a weak mixture causing a hesitation or 'flat-spot' and in some cases misfiring. To overcome this an accelerator pump is fitted. On small throttle openings a spring behind the diaphragm holds the diaphragm back so allowing fuel into the chamber in front of the diaphragm. When the throttle is opened suddenly an operating rod acts on the diaphragm and forces fuel from the diaphragm chamber via the pump injector into the air stream.

In order to achieve maximum economy the fuel is deliberately set weak at small throttle openings but in order to obtain maximum power at full throttle the mixture must be enriched at full throttle. This enrichment is carried out by the injector tube E which is supplied by fuel from the float chamber and discharges into the main air intake of the carburetter. It operates only when depression has reached a predetermined value.

Description 35 DITA

The only difference between the 35 DITA and 35 DISA carburetters is that an automatic choke control is fitted on the Solex type 35 DITA. With reference to **FIG 2:2,** with the engine cold the tension of the bimetal coil B and spring r keeps the strangler closed. When the engine fires, manifold depression acts on the strangler flap, which has a large and small area due to the spindle being offset and this force together with the force of a piston operating under the effect of the depression on the downstream side of the throttle opposes the combined resistance of the spring r and coil B and opens the strangler by an amount which is controlled by the groove and the calibrated hole machined into the piston. The bi-metal coil is heated by water taken from the cylinder block and as this water becomes hot the coil is heated and due to this heating loses its tension and the combined action of the depression on the piston and on the offset strangler opens and keeps open the strangler.

Some models manufactured after 1967 were fitted with a Solex type 35 DITA 2 and the only difference between this type and the 35 DITA is that a lever, arrowed in **FIG 2:3,** is fitted to operate the strangler manually. The Solex type 35 DITA can be converted to a 35 DITA 2 type by replacing the float chamber cover and fitting the lever.

Removing the carburetter:

If a Solex type 35 DISA is fitted remove the air filter and disconnect the fuel pipe, the vacuum pipe, the accelerator link, the capsule pipe, the choke cable and the accelerating pump lever all of which are arrowed in **FIG 2:4.** Remove the two securing nuts, free the two hooks which retain the carburetter base and remove the carburetter.

To refit the carburetter carry out the removing operations in reverse.

To remove a Solex type 35 DITA, remove the air filter then pinch flat the pipes which enter the choke casing. Disconnect the choke casing input pipe, the outlet pipe from the carburetter base, the fuel pipe, the vacuum pipe, the accelerator link and the capsule pipe all of which are arrowed in **FIG 2:5.** Remove the two securing nuts and remove the carburetter.

Refit the unit by reversing the removal procedure.

Overhauling the carburetter:

Unscrew the setscrews securing the top of the carburetter to the main body and place the top to one side. Operate the throttle quickly and check that a thin stream of fuel is injected from the pump injector I in **FIG 2:1,** then operate the throttle slowly and observe whether only a thin trickle of fuel passes out of the tube. If this sequence of events occurs the accelerator pump and economiser is functioning correctly. If the pump is faulty replace the diaphragm M in **FIG 2:1.**

Reconnect the fuel pipe to the top of the carburetter and holding the needle valve shut against its seat, operate the petrol pump and make sure no fuel comes from the needle valve assembly. If there is a leak unscrew the valve from the top housing and clean it thoroughly. Refit and retest and if a leak still persists a new valve will have to be fitted. Lift out the float, shake it and listen for any fuel in the float which will give a 'tinkling' sound. A

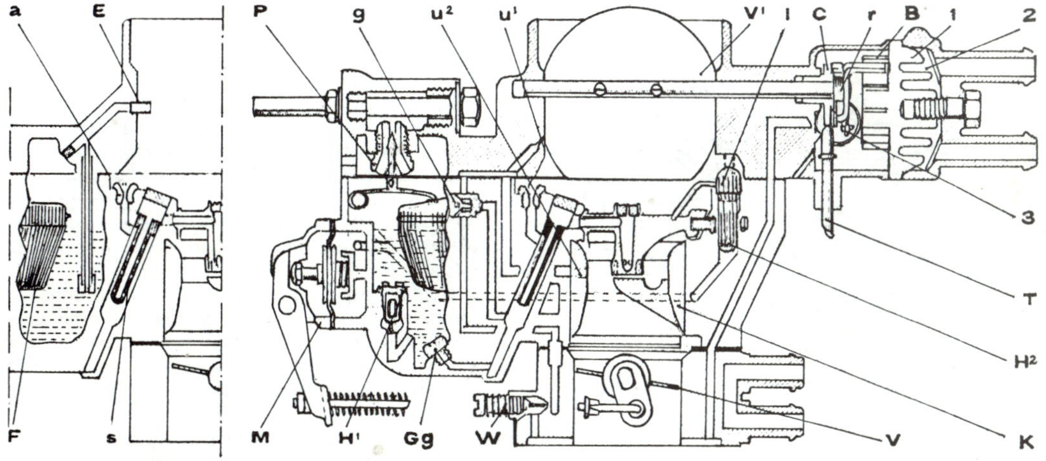

FIG 2:2 The Solex carburetter type 35 DITA

Key to Fig 2:2 **a** Correction jet **B** Bi-metal coil **c** Cam **E** Econostat **F** Float **Gg** Main jet **g** Idling jet **H1/H2** Pump inlet valve **I** Pump injector **K** Choke tube **M** Diaphragm **P** Needle valve **r** Spring **s** Emulsion tube **T** Control rod **U1/U2** Calibrated orifices **V** Throttle **V1** Strangler **W** Volume control screw **1** Body **2** Chamber **3** Lever

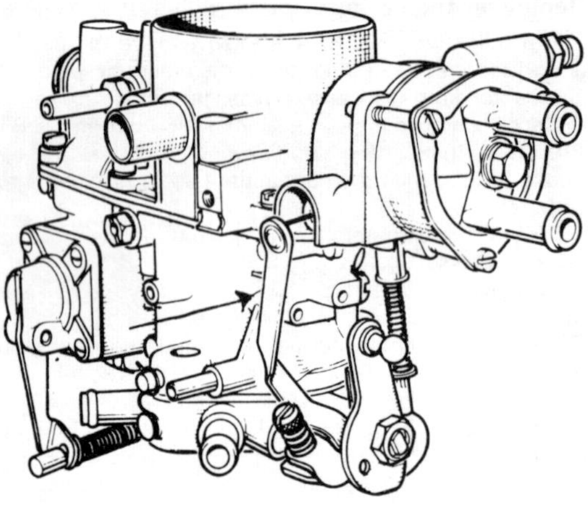

FIG 2:3 The choke lever

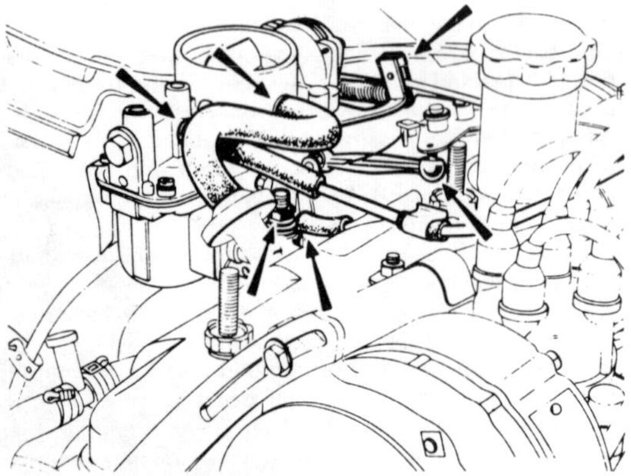

FIG 2:4 The carburetter connections (type 35 DISA)

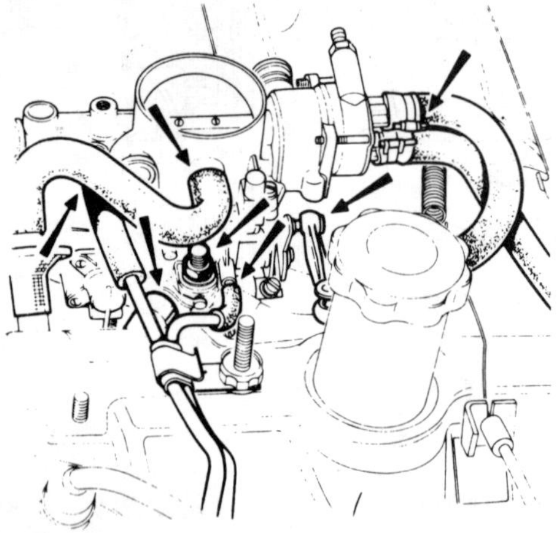

FIG 2:5 The carburetter connections (type 35 DITA)

leaky float must be replaced. With reference to **FIG 2:1** unscrew the main jet Gg, idling jet g and air compensator jet a and ensure that they are all free from obstruction.

Reassemble the carburetter by reversing the dismantling procedure and check that on Solex 35 DITA models the punch mark on the thermostatic spring casing is in direct line with the punch mark on the housing and if it is not so, turn it in a **clockwise** direction until the marks are aligned.

The chart below shows the difference between the jet sizes for each type of carburetter.

Jet settings	*Type 35 DISA*	*Type 35 DITA*
Choke tube	27	26.5
Main jet	140	140
Air compensator	135	155
Idling jet	50	50
Needle valve	1.5 mm	1.7 mm
Float	7.3 gr	7.3 gr
Pump injector	50	50
Pump stroke	5 mm	3 mm

Adjustment:

Care should be taken, before attempting to correct a bad engine idle, that the fault does not lie within the engine itself. Remove the sparking plugs and have them checked as described in **Chapter 3.** Remove the rocker cover and check the valve clearances and adjust them if necessary (see **Chapter 1**). Refit the cover. Before refitting the plugs carry out a cylinder compression check to check for faulty valves, guides, pistons, cylinder head or cylinder head gasket. This check is done by placing a compression gauge with a scale of up to 200 lb/sq inch, ensuring that the rubber end of the gauge is firmly placed in the plug opening so that no possible back leakage can occur. With all the plugs removed and the throttle held in the wide open position turn the engine using the starter motor **after taking off the ignition coil input lead.** Any pressure reading obtained below 110 lb/sq inch indicates that a cylinder head and or engine overhaul is required. Reconnect the coil input lead after refitting the plugs. Examine the distributor for faulty capacitor or contact points, check that the points gap is correct. Check that there is no leak at the manifold to cylinder head or carburetter to manifold gasket as a leak will draw in air causing a weakening of the mixture. Finally ensure that the carburetter is not flooding by checking the needle valve in the manner described in the overhaul part of this section.

Before carrying out idle adjustment on either type of carburetter ensure that no current consuming service, headlights, heater, etc. is in use as the load on the alternator will vary the engine speed.

Start the engine and while it is warming up check that on models containing a 35 DISA type of carburetter the rod 1 in **FIG 2:6** via lever 2 opens the throttle to give a fast engine tick over. When the engine is warmed through close the choke control and check that the rod no longer operates the lever. On models fitted with 35 DITA type of carburetter check the choke flap begins to open as the water temperature rises and is fully open when operating temperature is reached. Fit the air cleaner correctly. Adjust the screw 3 in **FIG 2:6** that operates the throttle. When an idling speed of approximately 650 rev/min has been obtained adjust the mixture screw until the highest possible engine idling speed has been obtained. Finally readjust the throttle screw to bring the engine speed back to between 600 to 650 rev/min. It is essential that the idling speed be maintained between these two limits if the carburetter is to give maximum performance.

2:4 Zenith type 36 IF carburetter

This carburetter was only fitted to 1966 models and is shown in **FIG 2:7.** Compensation is by an air well rather than an emulsion tube as in Solex type carburetters. An accelerator pump, economiser and idling system are fitted and the choke control is operated manually. The carburetter base is heated by hot water this feature assisting the atomisation of the fuel thus giving better burning. The removal and overhauling procedure of the carburetter is very similar to the procedure layed down for the Solex types of carburetters. The jet sizes and positions are shown in **FIG 2:8.** Adjust the carburetter in exactly the same manner as adjustment for Solex carburetters.

2:5 Weber type 32 DAR carburetter

Description:

This carburetter is shown in **FIG 2:9.** During normal running fuel from the float chamber 16 passes through the main jets 15 into the wells 14. This fuel is mixed with the air from the openings in the emulsion tubes 13, the amount of air being governed by the air correction jets 5, and the fuel and air passes out of the nozzles 8 into the cylinders. At full throttle fuel from the float chamber 16, the fuel being controlled by a calibrated orifice 3, mixes with air from the orifice 4 to give the enrichment necessary for full throttle operation.

An idling drilling is situated at the edge of the throttle plate to give an idling mixture at idling engine speed. When the throttle is opened there is a hesitation when the main discharge tube takes over from the idling drilling and to eliminate this hesitation a progression drilling 39 in **FIG 2:10** is fitted. The progression drilling gives extra fuel when the throttle is positioned just past idling position.

On sudden acceleration the fuel increase necessary to eliminate the flat spot that would otherwise occur is provided by a lever and pump. With reference to **FIG 2:11** when the throttles are closed, the position of the lever 44 frees the diaphragm 52 which, through the action of the spring 50 draws fuel from the float chamber through the ball valve 49 Opening the throttles causes the lever 44 to act on the diaphragm 52 this action forcing fuel into the drilling 41 through the delivery valve 45 and the pump jet 46. The spring 51 absorbs the rapid throttle openings and prolongs fuel delivery. Any excess fuel delivered by the accelerator pump is discharged into the float chamber along with the pump chamber vapours, through the duct 47 and calibrated bush 48.

The choke mechanism is of the semi-automatic type. **To switch on when the engine is cold it is necessary to depress the accelerator pedal completely then slowly allow it to return to its normal position.** With regard to **FIG 2:12,** when the pedal is depressed the bi-metallic spring 64 acting through a series of levers keeps the chokes 56 closed. At the same time, again through a series of levers, the main primary throttle 22 is partially opened. In this position the fuel/air ratio delivered is sufficient to start the engine when cold. Directly the engine starts the depression created acts through the ducts 63 and causes the diaphragm 62 by means of lever 60 and rod 61 to partially open the throttles giving the necessary weakening required to keep the engine running. As the engine cooling water warms up it heats up the bi-metallic spring which rotates and progres-

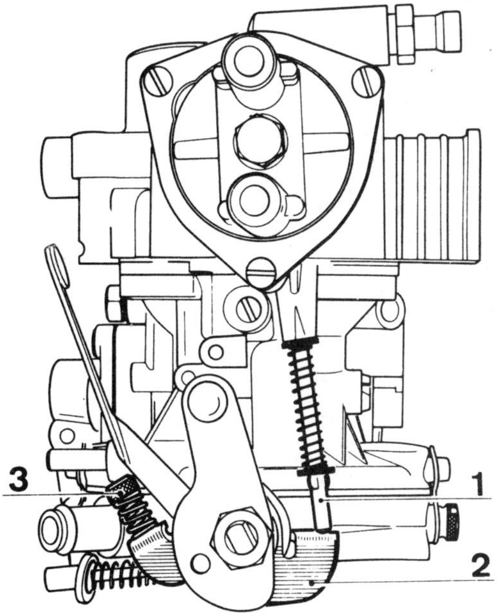

FIG 2:6 The adjusting screw

Key to Fig 2:6 1 Rod 2 Lever 3 Screw

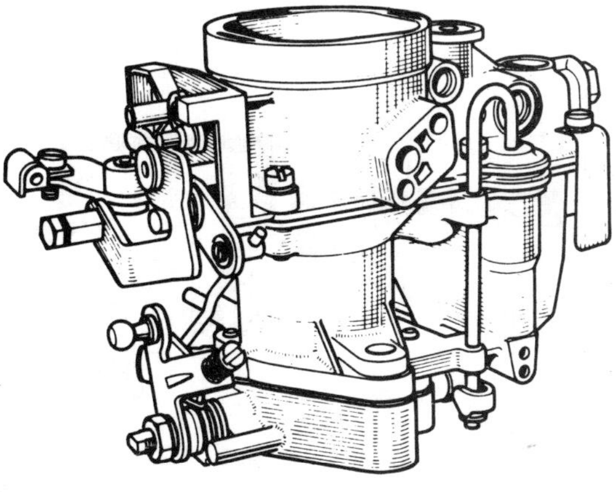

FIG 2:7 The Zenith type 36 IF carburetter

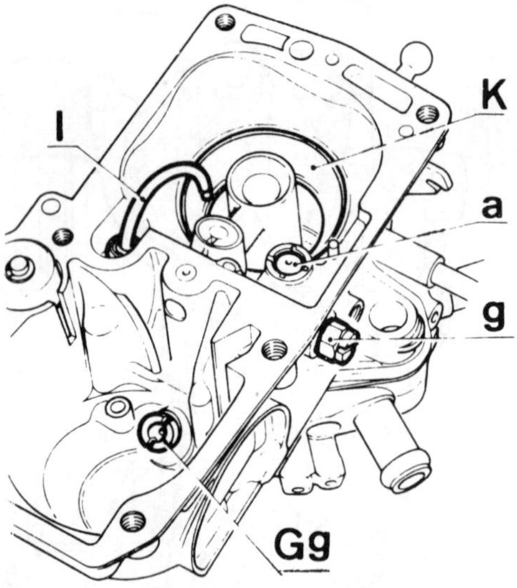

FIG 2:8 The Zenith carburetter jets

Key to Fig 2:8 a Air compensator jet (100) **Gg** Main jet (135) **g** Idling jet (40) **K** Choke tube (27) **I** Pump injector (40)

sively opens the chokes. When running temperature is reached the bi-metallic spring has rotated the lever 60 enough to bring the chokes 56 to the fully open position, this movement also rotating the spring 53 thus allowing closure of the primary throttle 22 down to the normal idling position.

Removal:

To remove the carburetter disconnect the battery and pinch flat the water pipe entering the carburetter base and the outlet pipe from the choke casing. This will prevent water pouring out of the pipes when they are disconnected and save the task of filling and bleeding the cooling system when the carburetter is refitted. Disconnect the throttle link, the fuel pipe, the vacuum pipe and the two water pipes and remove the air filter. Unscrew the four nuts securing the carburetter to the manifold and lift off the carburetter.

Refit the carburetter by reversing the removal operation fitting new carburetter gaskets. After refitting is completed check that the cooling system is full.

Overhauling:

Unscrew the screws securing the top of the carburetter to the main body, disconnect the lever attached to the choke flaps and lift off the top. Check the accelerator

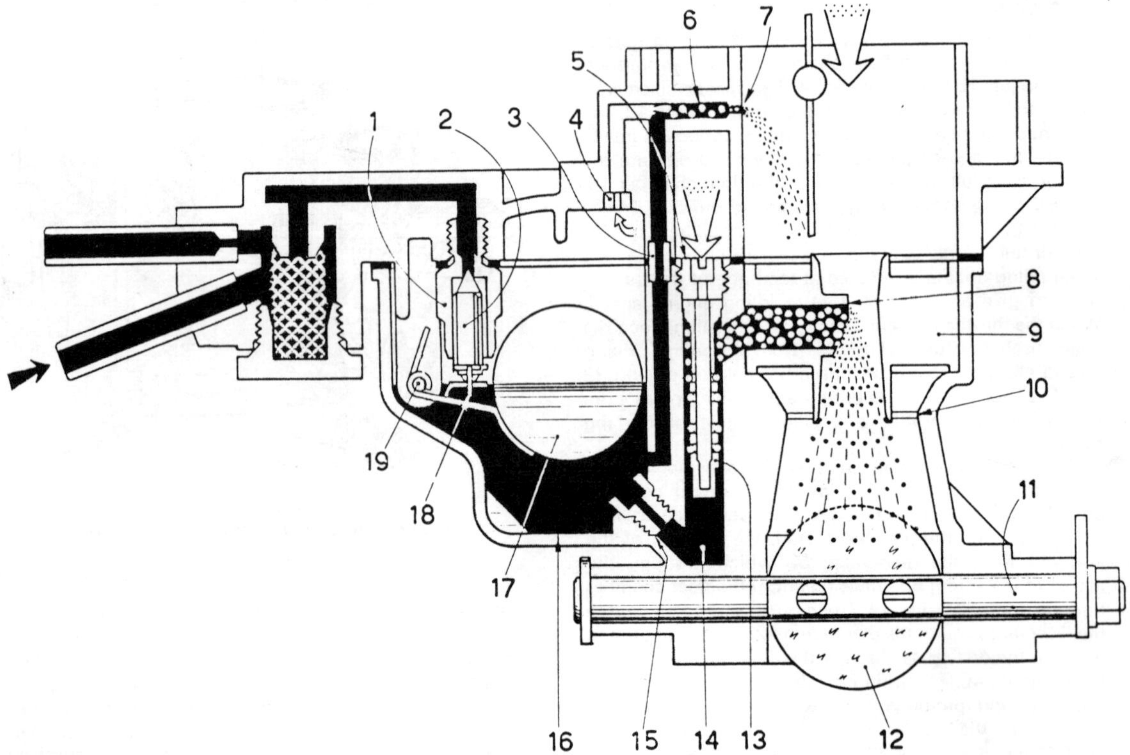

FIG 2:9 The Weber carburetter

Key to Fig 2:9 1 Needle valve 2 Needle 3 Calibrated orifice 4 Calibrated orifice 5 Air compensator jet 6 Duct 7 Calibrated orifice 8 Nozzles 9 Auxiliar/ venturi 10 Chokes 11 Spindle 12 Throttle 13 Emulsion tubes 14 Wells 15 Main jet 16 Float chamber 17 Float 18 Needle tip 19 Spindle

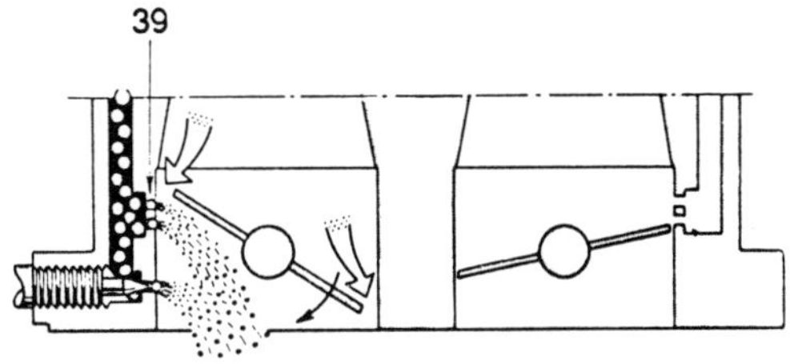

FIG 2:10 Progression drillings

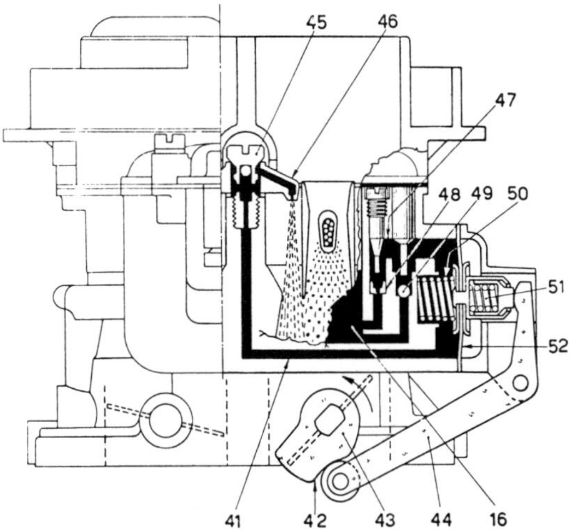

FIG 2:11 Accelerator pump

Key to Fig 2:11 16 Bowl 41 Duct 42 Cam 43 Lever 44 Lever 45 Delivery valve 46 Pump jet 47 Duct 48 Calibrated bush 49 Ball valve 50 Spring 51 Spring 52 Diaphragm

pump and needle valve as layed out in **Section 2:3** replacing the diaphragm and or valve if necessary. Check the float by shaking it, any audible 'tickling' sound means there is fuel inside the float necessitating replacing the float. With regard to **FIG 2:13** unscrew the main jets Gg, air compensating jets a and idling jets g and ensure that they are all free from obstruction.

Assemble the carburetter by reversing the dismantling procedure and check that the punch marks on the thermostatic spring casing is in direct line with the punch mark on the housing and if it is not so turn it in a **clockwise** direction until the marks are aligned.

The chart below shows the difference between the jet sizes of each barrel.

	First barrel	*Second barrel*
Choke tube	24	26
Main jet	140	150
Air compensator jet	190	140
Idling jet	50	80
Needle valve	1.75	1.75

Adjustment:

Carry out the procedure for checking for a fault other than the idling system, this procedure being layed down in **Section 2:3,** before adjusting the carburetter. Warm the engine up and ensure the chokes are fully open. **The idling mixture adjusting screw only operates on the first barrel.** Adjust the throttle screw to give as slow a tick over as possible then adjust the mixture screw to give the highest possible engine idling speed. Readjust the screw that operates the throttle to bring the engine speed back to the slowest engine idling speed that can be obtained without losing engine 'smoothness' or stability.

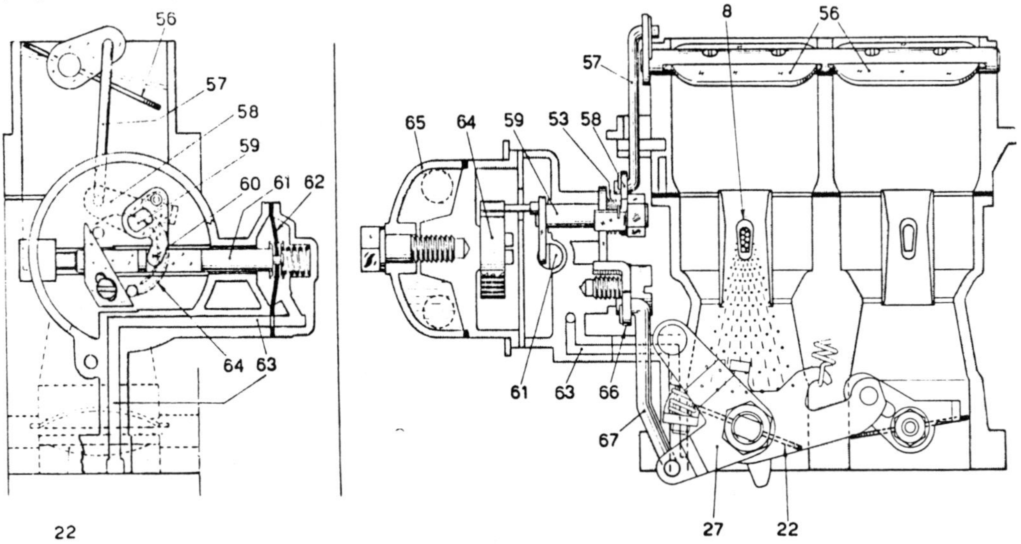

FIG 2:12 Choke mechanism

Key to Fig 2:12 8 Nozzle 22 Throttle 27 Control lever 53 Spring 56 Chokes 57 Rod 58 Lever 59 Spindle 60 Lever 61 Rod 62 Diaphragm 63 Duct 64 Spring 65 Cover 66 Lever 67 Tie rod

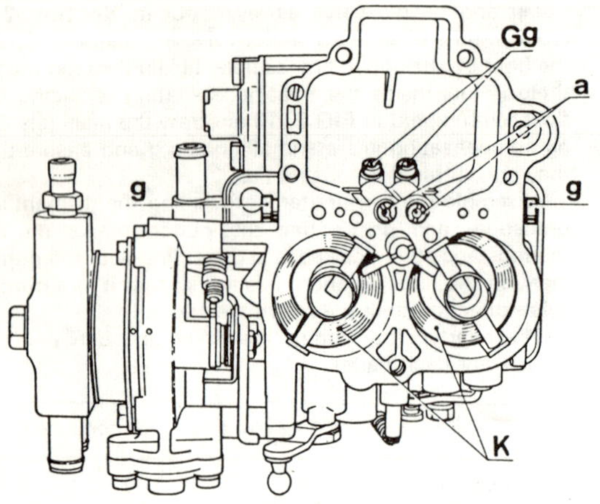

FIG 2:13 The Weber jets

Key to Fig 2:13 **Gg** Main jets **g** Idling jets **a** Air compensator jets **K** Chokes

2:6 Fault diagnosis

(a) Leakage or insufficient fuel delivered

1 Carburetter needs overhauling
2 Fuel pipes blocked
3 Air leak at pipe connections
4 Pump filter blocked
5 Pump diaphragm defective
6 Pump valves sticking or seating badly
7 Fuel vaporizing in pipelines due to heat
8 Needle valve faulty
9 Float punctured

(b) Excessive fuel consumption

1 Carburetter needs overhauling
2 Fuel leakage
3 Sticking choke control
4 Dirty air cleaner
5 Air correction jet partially blocked
6 Excessive engine temperature
7 Brakes binding
8 Tyres under-inflated
9 Idling speed too high
10 Car overloaded

(c) Idling speed to high

1 Incorrect mixture screw setting
2 Carburetter control sticking
3 Diaphragm controlling choke mechanism on Weber carburetters defective
4 Worn throttle plate
5 Air leak at manifold

(d) Noisy fuel pump

1 Loose mounting nuts
2 Air leaks on suction side and or at the diaphragm
3 Obstruction in fuel pipe
4 Clogged pump filter

(e) No fuel delivery

1 No fuel
2 Needle valve stuck up
3 Vent in tank blocked
4 Pump lever broken
5 Pump diaphragm punctured
6 Pipeline obstructed
7 Inlet valve in pump stuck open
8 Bad air leak on suction side of pump

CHAPTER 3

THE IGNITION SYSTEM

3:1 Description

The ignition system produces a spark of approximately 15,000 volts to ignite the mixture in the cylinder. It is also responsible for ensuring that the spark occurs in the right cylinder at the correct time and incorporates means to alter the time of ignition in order to meet the varying conditions that exist at different speeds and loads.

Current from the battery flows to the primary winding of the ignition coil, when the ignition switch is closed, where it sets up a magnetic field in the primary and secondary winding. The current continues to flow across the contact breaker points which are normally closed and then goes to earth. When the engine is turned a rotor in the distributor rotates and causes the points to be opened, this results in the collapse of the magnetic field in both coil windings, the voltage in the secondary winding being much higher due to the fact that it has a greater number of turns of wires. The voltage of the secondary winding being about 15,000 volts is passed from the coil through a high-tension lead between the centre of the coil and the centre of the distributor cap into a carbon brush situated in the centre of the cap. From there it is passed onto the rotor arm and out to the segments in the cap in the order in which the spark will ignite the mixture (i.e. the firing order).

The induced voltage set up in the primary winding is absorbed by the capacitor so preventing this voltage from arcing the points and consequently burning them out. The fact that the induced voltage set up in the primary winding flows to the capacitor also brings about the abrupt collapse of the magnetic field, this quick collapse being essential if the high induced voltage required is to be obtained.

The time taken for the mixture to build up to maximum pressure, after ignition has taken place, is fairly constant. As engine speed increases, due to this fairly constant time factor, it is necessary to ignite the mixture before the cylinder reaches TDC in order that maximum pressure given off by the fuel occurs at TDC.

At the base of the distributor is positioned a pair of bob weights and it is these weights that cause the spark to occur **before TDC.** The weights are attached to a plate, the plate being connected to the distributor cam by two small springs and two small toggles. One spring

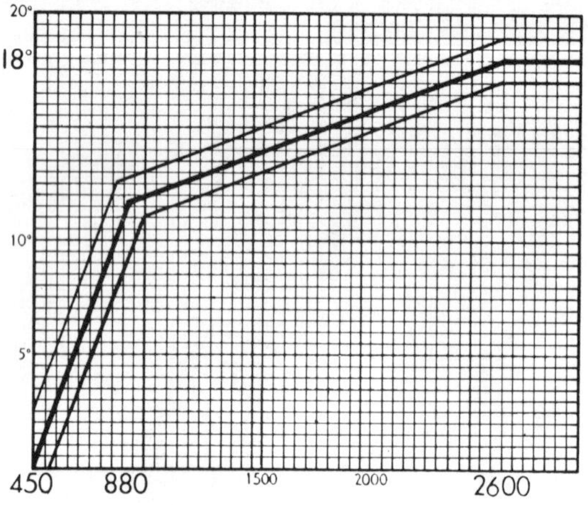

FIG 3:1 Centrifugal advance curve for engines with 8.6:1 compression ratio

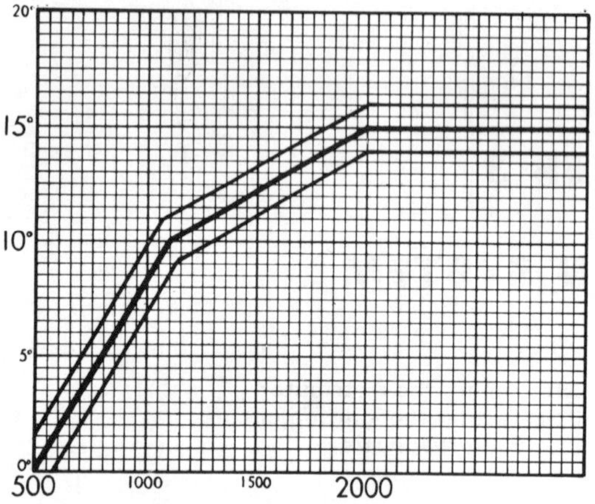

FIG 3:2 Centrifugal advance curve for engines with 7.6:1 compression ratio

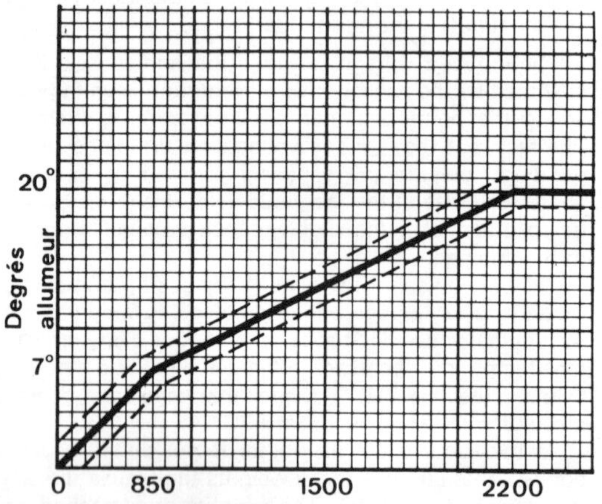

FIG 3:3 Centrifugal advance curve for later engines with 7.6:1 compression ratio

is of fairly high-tension and is called the secondary spring and the other, having a lower spring tension is termed the primary spring. As engine speed increases centrifugal force acts on the weights which results in the weights being moved out, as they do so they cause the cam to be rotated in its direction of rotation, which means the cam opens the points early with the result that the spark occurs early. The graph shown in **FIG 3:1** shows the centrifugal advance curve of distributors fitted to R.1151 engines and to R.1150 engines having a compression ratio of 8.6:1. The advance slope shown in **FIG 3:2** is that of distributors fitted to R.1150 engines having a compression ratio of 7.6:1. New distributors have a different centrifugal advance, the advance curve being illustrated in **FIG 3:3,** but these distributors can be fitted to all engines having a 7.6:1 compression ratio although it must be noted that old distributors cannot be used to replace the new ones.

In order to obtain maximum fuel economy the carburetter is designed to give a weak mixture at part throttle openings. As a weak mixture burns slowly a greater ignition advance is required at part throttle setting. At part throttle the depression in the manifold draws a diaphragm, arrowed in **FIG 3:4,** forward. As the diaphragm is connected via a rod to the contact breaker baseplate the contacts are caused to be moved towards the cam, so further advancing the point at which the spark occurs. At full throttle, because there is no appreciable manifold depression present, a spring behind the diaphragm prevents any spark advance, due to vacuum, taking place so preventing detonation (pinking). The vacuum advance curve for all engines fitted to both the R.1150 and R.1151 models is shown in **FIG 3:5.**

3:2 Maintenance

The contact breaker points should be inspected and removed if necessary at 6000 mile intervals. As the contact points that are fitted are of the self-wiping type they cannot be cleaned but only replaced. To remove the contact set pull the high-tension leads of the sparking plugs noting which lead was on number one plug, a convenient piece of string or coloured tape is a good way in which to mark the lead, unclip the distributor cap and place it out of the way. Lift off the rotor arm and place it somewhere safe to prevent it from becoming broken or cracked. Undo the screw securing the base contact and lift the base contact away. Unscrew the small nut securing the coil lead and remove the lead. Slacken the large securing nut at the side of the distributor body and ease out the contact lead and finally prise away the clip holding the spring contact on its pivot and lift out the spring contact. Fit the new points by reversing the previous procedure.

The points will have to be adjusted after they are fitted and when adjusting the points it is essential that the heel of the spring contact is on the lobe of the cam. If it is necessary to rotate the engine to bring the lobe onto the heel jack up the front road wheel, engage top gear and rotate the wheel until the lobe is on the heel. **It is very important that the engine is only rotated in this way as the manufacturer forbids the use of the camshaft pulley securing bolt to turn the engine.** Slacken the screw securing the base contact and move the base contact until a gap of .018 inch (.45 mm) exists between the contact points. Tighten the screw securely and then recheck the gap as it might have altered whilst the base contact was being secured in place. Operate the rod coupled to the vacuum diaphragm to the maximum vacuum position and with the diaphragm held in this position check the contact points gap, again the clearance should be the same, i.e. .018 inch (.45 mm). If it is not rotate the cam 1 in **FIG 3:4** until the contact points gap is .018 inch (.45 mm) with the diaphragm in both the 'off' and 'fully on' position. Rotate the engine and bring the next cam lobe into contact with the heel of the spring contact and once again recheck the clearance. Repeat this operation with the two remaining lobes. If there is more than .0025 inch (.6 mm) difference between any of the readings obtained the cam must be replaced. It is very important that the recommended contact breaker gap is kept to because during the period of time the contacts are closed the coil builds up its magnetic field and if the clearance is too much this time period will be reduced resulting in poor coil performance. Refit the rotor arm, distributor cap and the sparking plug leads. As number one lead is marked there is no problem as to that lead and by noting the direction of rotation of the rotor arm and knowing that the firing order is 1–3–4–2 fitting the other leads to their correct plugs should present no problems.

The following servicing should be carried out regularly.

1 Clean the distributor cap so that there is no moisture inside the cap. Do not clean off the carbon deposits that form on the distributor segments as doing so will create an undue resistance in the high-tension circuit because of the increased air gap between the segments and rotor arm. Examine the cap for cracks and signs of tracking, this will be denoted by a dull light pencil thin marking alongside a hairline crack, the mark being caused by the spark going prematurely to earth.

2 Inspect the high-tension leads for signs of cracking and renew them if necessary.

3 The functioning of the centrifugal advance should be checked by holding the drive shaft tightly and then turn the rotor arm in the direction of rotation and after ensuring it has turned approximately another 30 deg. from its original position, release it, upon which the rotor should return to its original position without any tendency to stick.

4 Never tape the sparking plug leads together in an attempt to make the leads tidy as the high-tension spark can and will transfer itself to another lead resulting in engine misfire.

3:3 Sparking plugs

The sparking plugs should be removed, cleaned and adjusted at the recommended intervals, but if they are suspected to be the cause of poor performance they should be examined more frequently.

Remove the high-tension lead from the plug top, blow all dirt from the cylinder head around the plugs, then unscrew them. Before cleaning the plugs examine them carefully. Check the type of carbon deposit on the firing end of the plug, this deposit should normally be powdery and range from greyish tan to brown in colour. This kind of deposit is one produced by mixed periods of high speed and low speed driving. If the deposits are white or yellowish they indicate long periods of constant speed driving or a lot of low speed city work. Both these types of deposit are acceptable.

If, however, the plug deposit is black and or wet, oil is entering the combustion chamber either past worn cylinders and piston rings or down defective valve guides. The cure is an engine or cylinder head overhaul, but some relief may be gained by fitting a plug that has a higher temperature range, the plug running hotter will cause the oil deposit to be burnt off.

Around the insulation of the centre electrode a washer, that transfers the heat from the centre electrode to the body of the plug, is fitted. If the washer is placed near the tip of the centre electrode any heat that occurs to the elctrode will quickly be transferred through the washer to the plug body and therefore the plug will operate at a fairly low temperature. If, however the heat transfer washer is placed away from the centre electrode tip, any heat that occurs to the electrode will not be transferred to the plug body quickly with the result that the plug will operate at a higher temperature.

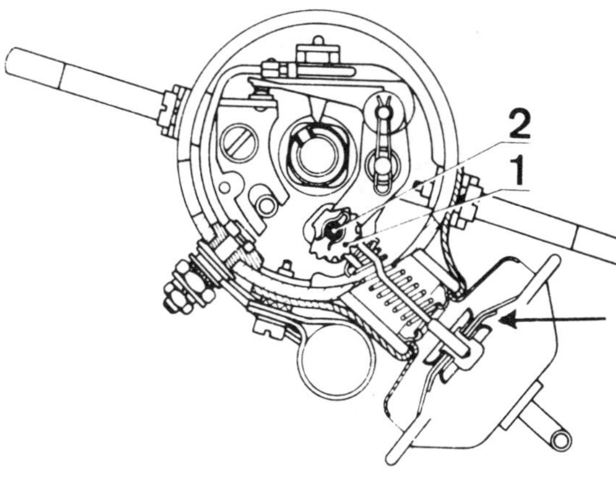

FIG 3:4 The distributor

Key to Fig 3:4 1 Adjuster 2 Pin

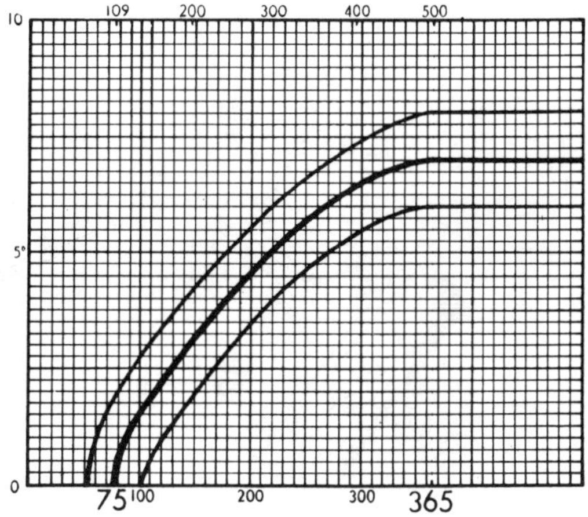

FIG 3:5 Vacuum advance curve

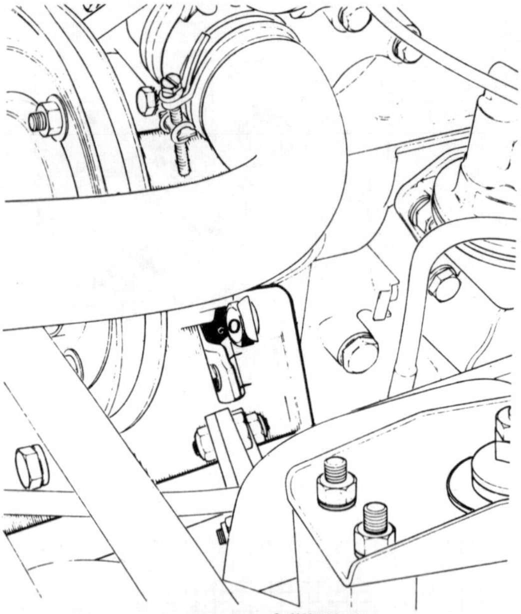

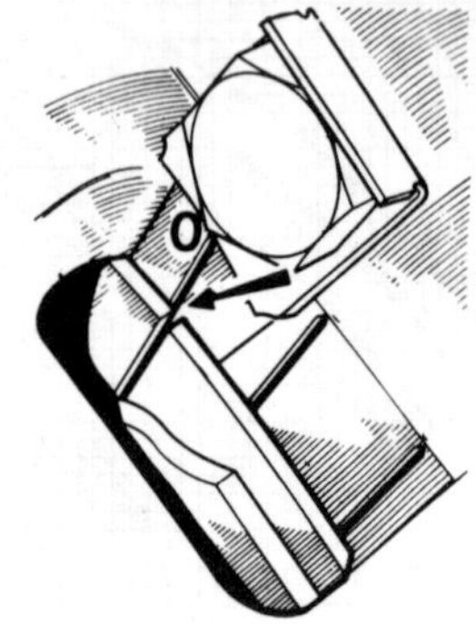

FIG 3:6 The timing marks

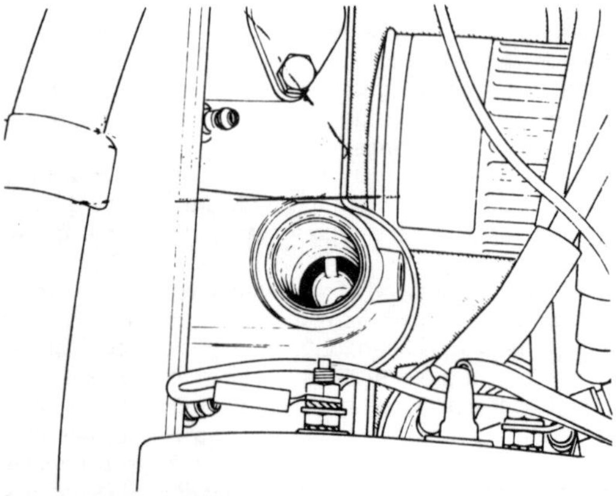

FIG 3:7 Pinion position (R.1150)

Dry, black, flaky deposits are usually the result of running with a rich mixture although defective ignition or excessive idling, which will cause incomplete combustion may also be a cause.

Sparking plugs that are overheated have a white blistered centre electrode and the side (earth) electrode may be badly eroded. This can be caused by inadequate cooling or incorrect ignition timing, but if both of these have been checked and found to be satisfactory, fitting a plug that has a higher temperature range will probably cure the problem.

Give the plugs to a garage that has air-blasting equipment and ask them to carry out a pressure test, this test finds out at what pressure the spark ceases to 'jump' across the plug gap. A sparking plug may be considered satisfactory if it sparks continuously under a pressure of 100 lb/sq inch (7 kg/sq cm).

Set the spark gap to .025 inch (.56 mm) bending only the side electrode if adjustment is necessary to obtain the required setting and clean the gasket seatings in the cylinder head. Inspect the plug gaskets for signs of blowing and check the gasket thickness, if it has been compressed to less than half its original thickness a new one must be fitted. Refit the plugs and tighten them to a torque of 30 lb ft (4.1 kgm).

The distributor:

To remove the distributor lift off the cap and rotate the engine by jacking up a front road wheel, engaging top gear and turning the wheel. **Never turn the engine by using the camshaft pulley nut.** Turn the engine until the heel of the spring contact is on the lobe of the cam with the rotor arm in-line with the segment, in the cap, attached to number one plug lead. Undo the nut securing the input lead from the coil after taking off one of the battery leads as a safety precaution. Mark the lead that goes to number one plug and pull off the high-tension leads to the plugs and ignition coil. Loosen the bolt securing the distributor.

To refit the unit, providing the engine has not been rotated, place it back in the cylinder block with the spring contact on the cam lobe and the rotor arm in-line with number one plug and reverse the removal instructions. If the engine has been turned and thus the timing lost refer to **section 3:5.**

If a distributor is found to be faulty and the fault is not in the contact breaker points or capacitor the unit will have to be replaced as there are no replacement parts available to carry out any internal repairs.

3:5 Timing the distributor

If the distributor and or driving pinion have been removed and the engine rotated the distributor will have to be refitted in the following manner.

1 Unscrew the sparking plugs, in order that the engine can be rotated smoothly, placing them somewhere safe for if they are dropped it is probable that the insulation will be broken resulting in the purchasing of a new plug.

2 Jack up the front road wheel, select top gear and turning the road wheel rotate the engine until the reference mark on the engine flywheel is opposite the zero mark arrowed in **FIG 3:6.** Remove the rocker

cover and check that the pushrods for the inlet and exhaust valves of number four cylinder can be rotated. If the rods cannot be turned rotate the engine one revolution further again aligning the reference mark on the engine flywheel with the zero mark and check that the pushrods can be rotated.

3 With the reference marks aligned and the pushrods of number four cylinder free insert the pinion on R.1150 models so that its smallest offset is on the engine side as illustrated in **FIG 3:7** and on R.1151 models align the offset in the manner shown in **FIG 1:12a**.

4 Fit the distributor and rotate it until the heel of the spring contact is on the cam lobe that brings the rotor arm in-line with the segment, in the distributor cap, that is attached to the lead that goes to the number one plug.

Electrical setting of timing:

Connect a pilot light containing a 12-volt bulb between the distributor input (primary current) and earth (ground) (see **FIG 3:8**) and switch on the ignition. After ensuring that the battery and coil input lead have been reconnected turn the distributor in an anticlockwise direction until the light switches on. At this point cease rotation of the distributor and tighten the distributor retaining clamp. Refit the cap and plug leads in their correct order and finally refit the high-tension lead to the coil.

Stroboscopic timing:

Refit the battery and coil input lead, the distributor cap, plug leads and the coil high-tension lead. Start the engine and with the engine at the correct idling speed (see **Chapter 2**), bring the stroboscopic light near the zero mark arrowed in **FIG 3:6.** Rotate the distributor until the reference mark on the engine flywheel is opposite the zero mark and then switch off the engine. Tighten the distributor retaining clamp then restart the engine and check that the reference marks are still in-line as the distributor could have been moved whilst the retaining clamp was tightened.

3:6 Testing the ignition circuit

Connect a 12-volt test lamp between the coil terminal that contains the distributor input lead and the distributor side terminal. **Switch on the ignition.** If the lamp lights when the contacts are closed, that is when they are together and the lamp goes out when the contacts are open all the components of the low-tension circuit except for the capacitor are in order. To check the capacitor connect the lamp between the two open contacts. No reaction indicates a faulty capacitor.

Should the lamp fail to light there is a fault in the low-tension circuit.

Locating a fault in the low-tension circuit:

Rotate the engine until the contact breaker points are **fully open** then using a 12-volt test lamp check the circuit in the following order. If the circuit is in order the lamp bulb will light.

1 Connect the lamp between the input lead to the ignition switch and earth. No reaction indicates faulty wiring to the switch. **All further tests must be carried out with the ignition switch on.**

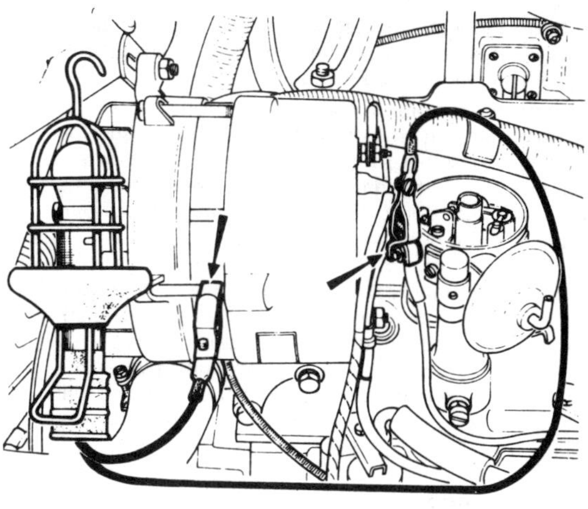

FIG 3:8 Connecting a pilot light

2 Connect the lamp between the output lead from the ignition switch and earth. No reaction indicates a faulty ignition switch.

3 Connect the lamp between the input lead to the coil and earth. No reaction indicates faulty wiring from the switch to the coil.

4 To test the ignition coil primary circuit, disconnect the cable from the lead to the distributor and connect the test lamp between the terminal the lead came off and earth. No reaction indicates a fault in the primary winding of the coil necessitating replacing the coil.

5 Disconnect the cable from the low-tension terminal on the distributor and connect the lamp between the end of this cable and earth. No reaction indicates a damaged cable or loose connections.

6 With the points **open** connect the test light between the points. No reaction indicates the contact breaker points are at fault.

Locating a fault in the high-tension circuit:

It is essential to ensure that the low-tension circuit is satisfactory before any tests on the high-tension circuit are made.

1 Obtain a length of high-tension wire and ensure it is functioning correctly by connecting one end to the battery terminal and the other to one end of a 12-volt bulb test lamp, then connect the other end of the lamp to the remaining battery terminal. The bulb should light.

2 Unscrew the high-tension lead from the centre of the coil and fit the tested high-tension wire. Place the end of the wire that is not in the coil to within $\frac{1}{8}$ inch of the cylinder head and with the **ignition switch on** rotate the engine. A spark should intermittently jump from the free end of the wire to the cylinder head. If no spark is present the secondary winding in the coil is at fault again necessitating a replacement coil being fitted.

3 Refit the original lead to the coil and hold the other end to within $\frac{1}{8}$ inch of the cylinder head and again

with the ignition switched on and the engine rotating note if there is an intermittent spark. The absence of a spark shows the lead is faulty.

4 Remove the distributor cap and place one end of the test high-tension lead onto the carbon brush and the other end to within $\frac{1}{8}$ inch of the cylinder head, rotate the engine with the ignition on, again there should be an intermittent spark. No spark indicates the carbon brush or distributor cap is unsatisfactory.

5 Fit the high-tension test lead to any one of the distributor segments and with the engine switched on, crank it and check there is a spark. If there is no spark the rotor arm or distributor cap is unserviceable.

6 Lastly check any of the normal sparking plug leads against its plug to ensure a spark is present which will indicate that the sparking plugs are in someway faulty.

3:7 Fault diagnosis

(a) Engine will not fire

1 Battery charge low
2 Distributor contact points dirty, pitted or incorrectly adjusted
3 Capacitor faulty
4 Distributor cap dirty, cracked or 'tracking'
5 Carbon brush inside distributor cap not touching rotor
6 Faulty cable or loose connection in low-tension circuit
7 Distributor rotor arm cracked
8 Faulty coil
9 Broken contact breaker spring
10 Contact points stuck open
11 Ignition timing incorrect

(b) Engine misfires

1 Check 1, 2, 3, 4, 6, 7 and 8 in (a)
2 Weak contact breaker spring
3 High-tension plug leads taped together
4 High-tension plug leads loose or going to earth
5 Sparking plug(s) loose
6 High-tension plug and or coil leads cracked or perished
7 Sparking plug insulation faulty
8 Incorrect sparking plug gap
9 Loose capacitor
10 Any loose wire in the ignition circuit

CHAPTER 4

THE COOLING SYSTEM

4:1 Description

The vehicles covered in this manual all have the same type of pressurized cooling system. The reason behind pressurizing the cooling system is to raise the boiling point of the water as the boiling point at normal atmospheric pressure is below the most efficient engine operating temperature. A water pump is fitted to provide a positive circulation of the coolant. The pump receives water from the bottom tank of the radiator and passes it around the cylinder walls. From the cylinder block it rises into the cylinder head until it reaches the thermostat which prevents cold water from passing to the top tank in the radiator. The water is then recirculated until it reaches a high enough temperature to open the thermostat. The thermostat contains a bellows which is filled with a volatile liquid, usually alcohol, and as the water becomes hot the liquid expands causing the bellows to expand, this action opening the thermostat valve which allows water to flow out of the cylinder block. The hot water having passed the thermostat goes into the radiator top tank where it then falls through a series of finned passages. The water being cooled whilst passing down the passages by the cold air pushed through the radiator by the fan when the engine is operating, when the vehicle is stationary and by the oncoming air when the vehicle is in motion.

A spring-loaded valve incorporated in the system pressurizes the system and an expansion tank is fitted so that as the water in the cooling system expands, the excess fluid is passed down the hose into the expansion tank. When the engine cools down and the water temperature drops, a partial vacuum is created in the top tank of the radiator, this vacuum drawing back the coolant that was forced out. With this system there is no necessity for regular topping up but the level of the coolant should be checked occasionally to ensure that there has been no leakage.

4:2 Draining and refilling the cooling system

Draining:

To ensure that the system is fully emptied it must be drained as follows. Place the heating controls in the heating position, loosen the cap on the expansion chamber and remove the expansion chamber valve. Remove the drain plug from the radiator and the coolant will start to run slowly. When it is running out freely, this

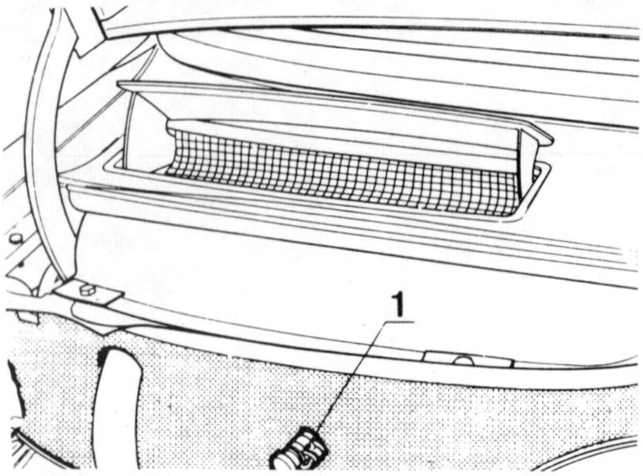

FIG 4:1 The radiator bleed screw

Key to Fig 4:1 1 Screw

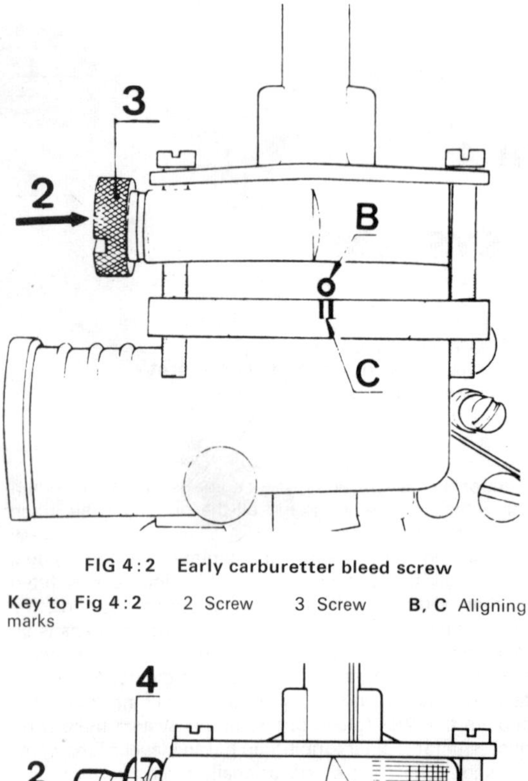

FIG 4:2 Early carburetter bleed screw

Key to Fig 4:2 2 Screw 3 Screw **B, C** Aligning marks

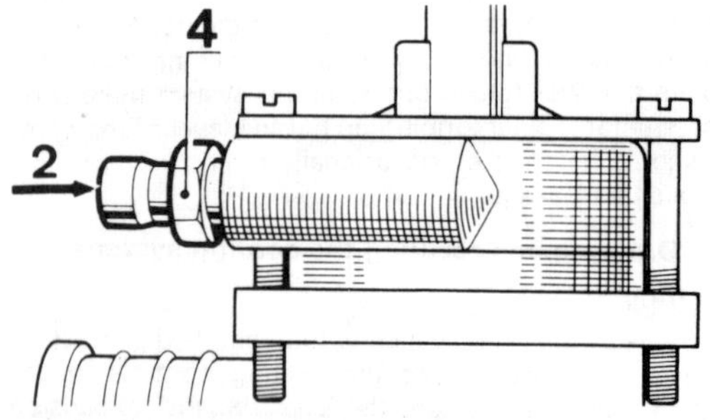

FIG 4:3 Later carburetter bleed screw

Key to Fig 4:3 2 Screw 4 Screw

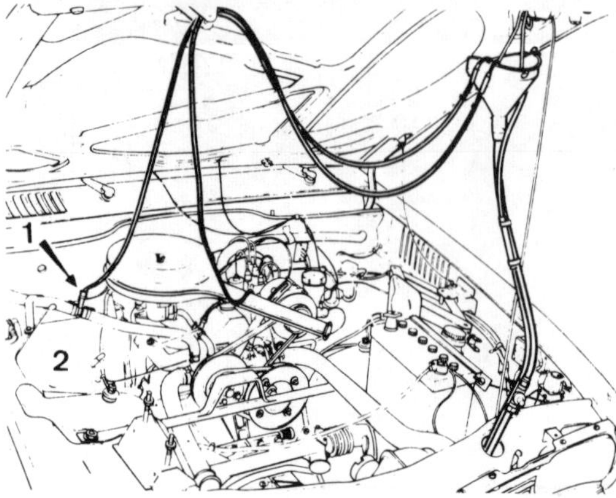

FIG 4:4 Filling the system

Key to Fig 4:4 1 Bleed screw 2 Bleed screw

occurs when the expansion chamber is empty, remove the radiator filler cap. Open the radiator bleed screw which is positioned on the scuttle screen panel (see **FIG 4:1**) and the bleed screw on the carburetter which on 1965 and 1966 models is positioned on the pipe between the base of the carburetter and the cylinder head and on 1967 models on the choke casing. Remove the engine drain plug which is to the left of the fuel pump.

On 1967 model vehicles two types of bleed screw were fitted. The plain screw shown in **FIG 4:2** necessitates removing the bleed screw to fit the bleeding hose whereas the needle valve screw shown in **FIG 4:3** has an end fitting to which the hose can be fitted directly. The needle valve bleeding screw can be fitted to models that have the plain bleeding screw fitted.

Refilling:

Fill the expansion chamber until the fluid reaches the maximum mark then fit the expansion chamber valve and screw down the cap. Fit the end fitting of tool Mot.401 to the radiator (see **FIG 4:4**), and hook the funnel to the bonnet. Place the heating control in the heating position and remove the bleed screws 1 and 2 in **FIG 4:4.** Screw hoses Mot.413 in place of the bleed screws and position the hoses as shown in **FIG 4:4.** Fill the funnel with coolant, open the valve on the device and start the engine. Top up the coolant in the funnel as the system fills and when the fan starts place the two hoses so that the fluid in them flows into a container placed on the ground (see **FIG 4:5**). When the level in the funnel falls, pinch flat the two hoses carrying fluid to the container on the ground and pour the coolant in the container, into which they flow, into the funnel. Repeat the operation.

Never allow the funnel to completely drain to prevent further air entering the system. When there is no further air in the hoses, lift them and allow them to flow into the funnel, then switch off the engine. Allow the engine to cool then close the valve on the apparatus. Disconnect the bleeding hoses and refit the bleed screws without tightening them fully down. Open the valve on the apparatus and allow coolant to flow from the bleed

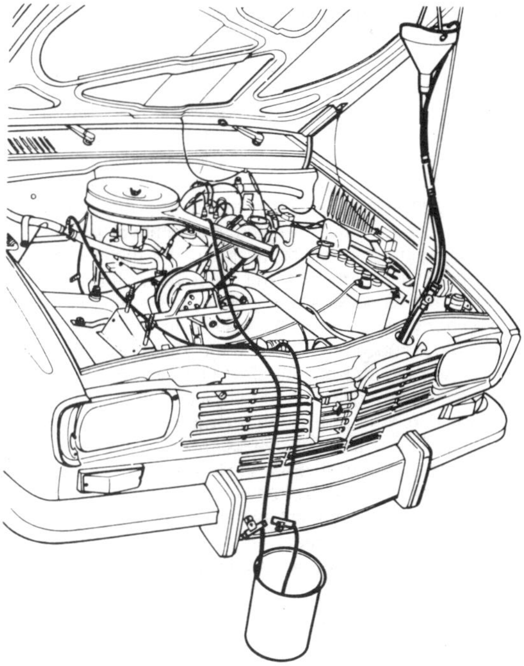

FIG 4:5 Filling the expansion chamber

screws for a short time then tighten down the bleed screws. Close the valve on the apparatus, remove it and fit the radiator filler cap.

4:3 The radiator

To remove the radiator disconnect the battery, remove the spare wheel and drain the cooling system (see **Section 4:2**). Disconnect the radiator hose at the radiator, arrowed in **FIG 4:6,** the motor fan unit leads at the relay and the temperature switch leads at the radiator. Unscrew the radiator securing bolts, arrowed in **FIG 4:6** and remove the radiator together with the hose which is connected to the expansion chamber.

To refit the radiator carry out the removal operations in reverse and then fill the cooling system as detailed in **Section 4:2.**

4:4 The expansion chamber

To remove the chamber take out the spare wheel, pinch flat the hose which flows to the radiator and unscrew the expansion chamber valve cap and remove it. If the cap is stuck use a pin spanner, in the manner illustrated in **FIG 4:7,** to remove it. Unscrew the expansion chamber securing bolt, arrowed in **FIG 4:7,** and remove it.

To refit the chamber, bolt it back in position and tighten the bolt until its retaining spring is coil bound, then loosen it one turn. Fill the expansion chamber to the maximum mark then fit the valve and screw on the cap. Free the hose which leads to the radiator.

The valve must be fitted correctly, otherwise any air leakage past the valve gasket will cause the red warning light on the instrument panel to switch on.

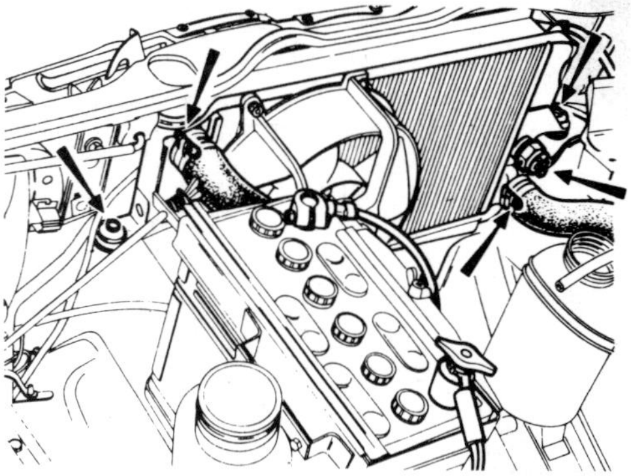

FIG 4:6 Removing the radiator

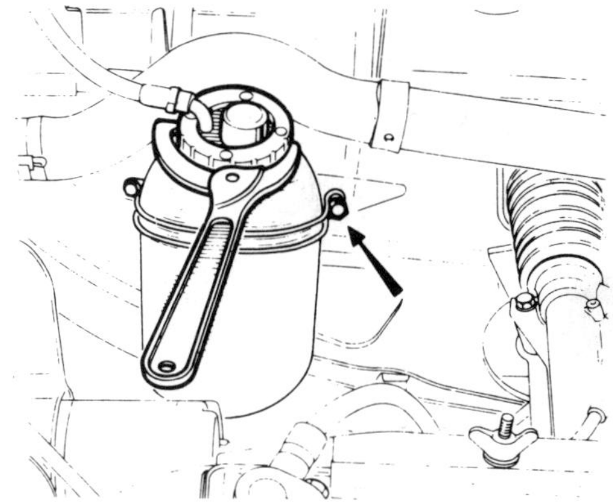

FIG 4:7 The expansion chamber

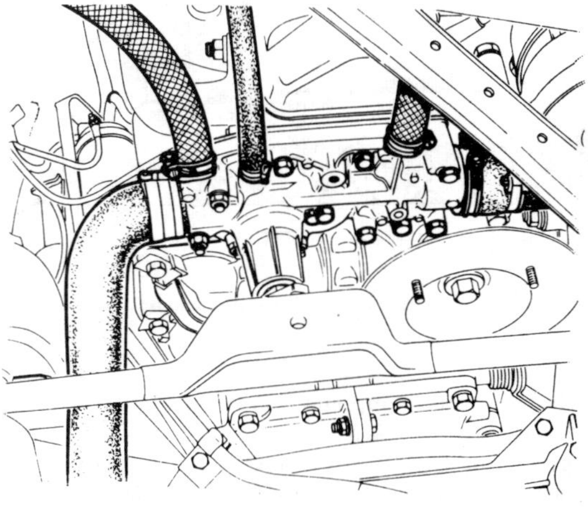

FIG 4:8 The water pump

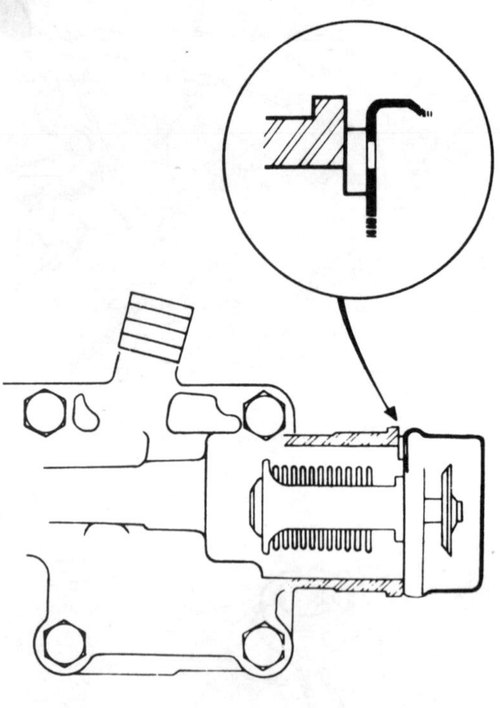

FIG 4:9 Thermostat leak hole

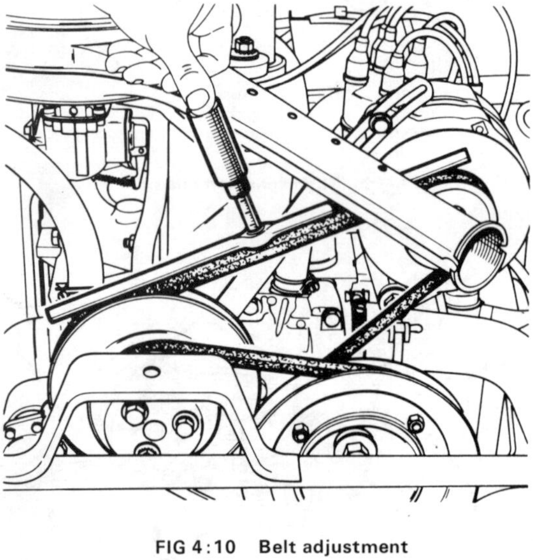

FIG 4:10 Belt adjustment

4:5 The water pump and thermostat

To remove the pump disconnect the battery, remove the spare wheel and drain the cooling system. Remove the outer camshaft pulley flange, the shims and the belt. Loosen the alternator fastenings and remove the belt. Remove the water pump pulley and alternator tensioner belt on the pump. Disconnect the hoses shown in **FIG 4:8** from the water pump and unscrew the pump securing bolts. Using a plastic mallet remove the pump and its backplate.

Check the thermostat valve placed at the water outlet of the water pump is in the closed position. To check the operation of the thermostat, heat a large can of water to boiling point then immerse the water pump unit into the boiling water and ensure that the thermostat valve opens.

Refit the unit by reversing the removal instructions after cleaning the gasket faces. Ensure that the gaskets are fitted dry and that the thermostat leakage hole, shown in **FIG 4:9,** is upwards, opposite the slot in the pump body. When fitting the water pump drive belt slowly tighten the nuts on the outer flange of the camshaft pulley whilst turning the engine. The engine must be rotated by selecting top gear and turning a jacked up road wheel. **Never use the pulley securing bolts to turn the engine.** Check the belt deflection using tool Ele.346 in the manner shown in **FIG 4:10**. The deflection on the alternator belt must be between $\frac{9}{32}$ and $\frac{3}{8}$ inch (.7 to 9.5 mm) and that on the water pump belt between $\frac{3}{32}$ and $\frac{5}{32}$ inch (2.5 to 4 mm). On completion fill the cooling system as detailed in **Section 4:2.**

4:6 Fault diagnosis

(a) Internal water leaks

1 Cracked cylinder head
2 Cracked cylinder block
3 Loose cylinder head nut
4 Faulty cylinder head gasket

(b) Poor circulation

1 Radiator core blocked
2 Engine water passages restricted
3 Faulty water pump
4 Loose water pump belt
5 Low water level
6 Faulty thermostat
7 Perished or collapsed water hoses

(c) Corrosion

1 Impurities in water
2 Infrequent draining and flushing

(d) Overheating

1 Check 4 in (a)
2 Check (b)
3 Faulty ignition timing
4 Defective temperature gauge
5 Low oil level
6 New pistons and cylinder bores
7 Choked exhaust system
8 Binding brakes
9 Incorrect valve timing
10 Weak mixture
11 Defective motor fan unit

CHAPTER 5

THE CLUTCH

5:1 Description

The clutch is fitted in order that the drive between the engine and gearbox can be disconnected primarily to enable the torque from the engine to be transmitted gradually to the gearbox, therefore enabling the vehicle to move off from rest smoothly, and secondly to allow gear changing to take place.

The operation of the clutch mechanism is understood by studying **FIG 5:1**. The clutch pedal movement is transmitted by a cable to the withdrawal fork 1. The fork pivots on the pivot boss of the clutch housing and moves the withdrawal bearing forward. The bearing presses on a ring which is in permanent contact with the diaphragm 2 and pushes the diaphragm inwards causing its outer edge to swing round fixed points 3 which are attached to the cover, the cover being bolted to the flywheel. In this way the diaphragm moves the pressure plate 4 to which it is attached by strips. At this point the clutch friction disc 5 is no longer held between the flywheel and pressure plate so the drive between the engine and the gearbox is therefore disconnected. The clutch is re-engaged by the elasticity of the diaphragm which reassumes its original shape as soon as the pressure at its centre is released.

The driven plate comprises a splined hub connected to a flexible plate by a spring mounting. The annular friction facings are riveted to the plate and damper springs are assembled around the hub to absorb power shocks and torsional vibration.

The diaphragm clutch has several advantages over the conventional type of clutch layout. Due to the simplicity of its construction there are less moving parts and thus less parts to fail in service. Also the diaphragm spring deflection does not increase at the same uniform rate as a coil spring. If for example a coil spring requires 50 lbf to deflect the spring $\frac{1}{4}$ inch it will take 100 lbf to deflect it $\frac{1}{2}$ inch, whereas the pressure required to deflect the diaphragm plate increase uniformly with deflection until the plate straightens then any further deflection requires progressively less pressure. This action means the pedal effort is reduced and due to this reduction a cable operating layout can be used instead of the more complicated hydraulic layout used on most conventional clutch constructions.

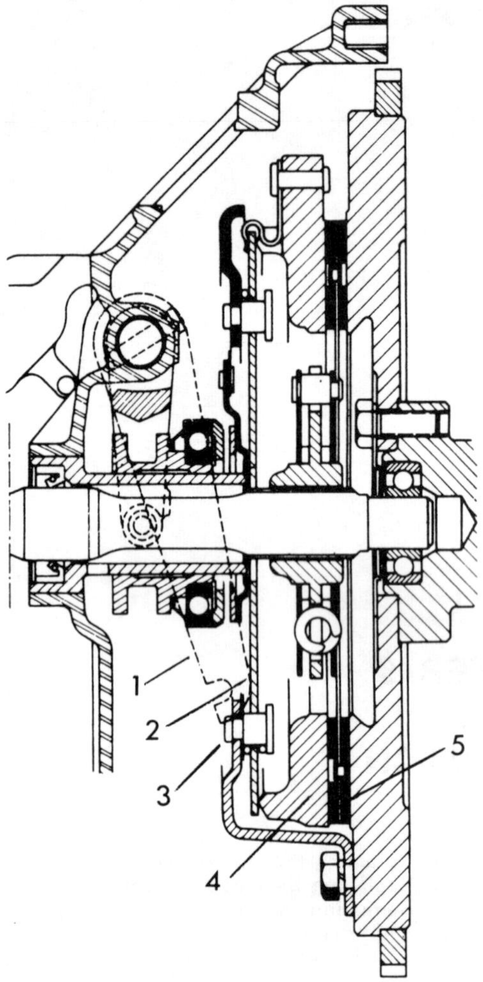

FIG 5 : 1 Clutch mechanism

Key to Fig 5 : 1 1 Fork 2 Diaphragm 3 Rivet 4 Pressure plate 5 Friction disc

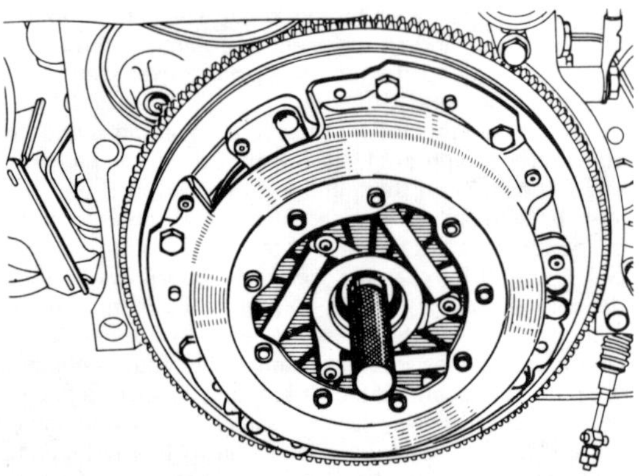

FIG 5 : 2 Using mandrel Emb.257

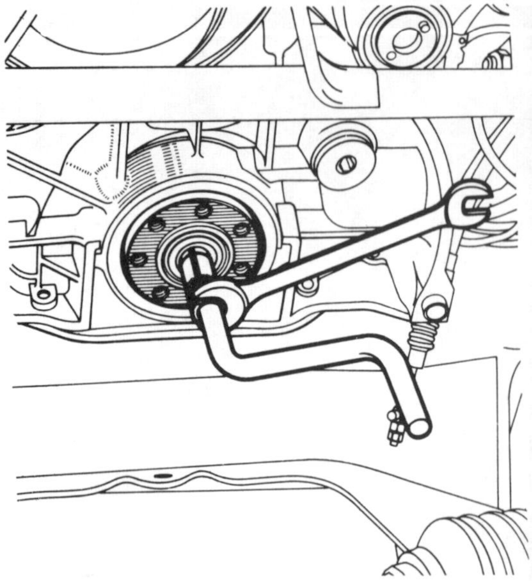

FIG 5 : 3 Extracting the clutch shaft bearing

5 : 2 Removing and refitting the clutch

Removal:

To remove the clutch remove the transmission unit as detailed in **Chapter 6** and mark the position of the clutch mechanism with reference to the flywheel. This is most important as the flywheel and clutch mechanism are dynamically balanced and if the mechanism is placed incorrectly on the flywheel the combined unit will be unbalanced which could result in quite serious engine vibration. Undo the eight bolts securing the pressure plate assembly to the flywheel and lift away the pressure plate and friction disc.

Examination:

Examine the clutch friction disc taking care that no oil or grease comes into contact with the friction facings. If renewal of the friction surfaces of the driven plate become necessary it is essential to install a complete driven plate assembly because if wear has occurred to such an extent to warrant renewing the friction linings, then slight wear will have taken place on the splines and also on the torque reaction springs and their seatings. There is also a question of concentricity involved so it is important that the driven plate be replaced by a standard service unit or by a new unit.

If small quantities of oil gain access to the clutch and find their way onto the driven plate friction faces, they will burn off due to the heat generated by the clutch slipping. This slipping occurs under normal moving away from rest conditions. The burning of this small quantity of lubricant has the effect of gradually darkening the facings, but provided the polish of the facings remains such that the grain of the material can be distinguished clearly, it has very little effect on clutch performance.

Should the driven plate friction facings have a dark

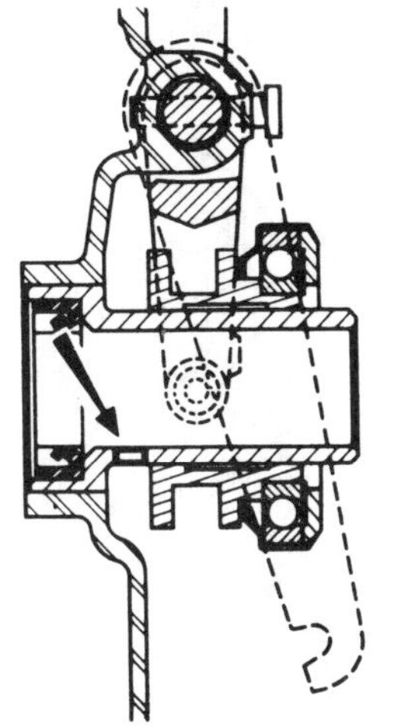

FIG 5:4 Withdrawal pad guide hole

appearance it indicates that the facings have been contaminated by excessive quantities of lubricant and means the plate will, due to an oil leak, have to be renewed. Before reassembling the new plate to the fly-flywheel the cause of the leak must be traced and rectified.

Check that the driven plate is not loose on the splines of the first motion shaft as this will result in noticeable backlash in the clutch. Misalignment of the plate puts undue stresses on the driven plate and may result in the hub braking loose from the plate, with consequent total failure of the clutch. It may also be responsible for a fierce chattering or dragging of the clutch, which makes gear changing difficult. If clutch drag proves to be a persistent difficulty it is advisable to check the flywheel for true with a dial indicator. The dial reading should not vary more than .003 inch (.06 mm) anywhere on the flywheel face.

Check to ensure there is a .315 inch (8 mm) diameter hole at the bottom of the clutch withdrawal pad carrier guide. If there is not, drill one in the manner described in **Section 5:4.**

If the friction face of the flywheel is damaged (scoring, overheating marks, etc.) it must be replaced. **Refacing the clutch friction face on the flywheel is forbidden.**

Refitting:

Fit the friction disc with the offset on the hub towards the transmission unit and position the pressure plate assembly aligning the marks made before dismantling took place. Using mandrel Emb.257 in the manner illustrated in **FIG 5:2** centralize the disc. Slowly screw in the bolts which secure the mechanism and then fully tightening them. Refit the transmission unit in the manner detailed in **Chapter 6.**

5:3 Replacing the clutch shaft bearing

Remove the transmission unit and clutch pressure plate and friction disc. Unlock and unscrew the seven bolts securing the flywheel to the crankshaft. Using extractor

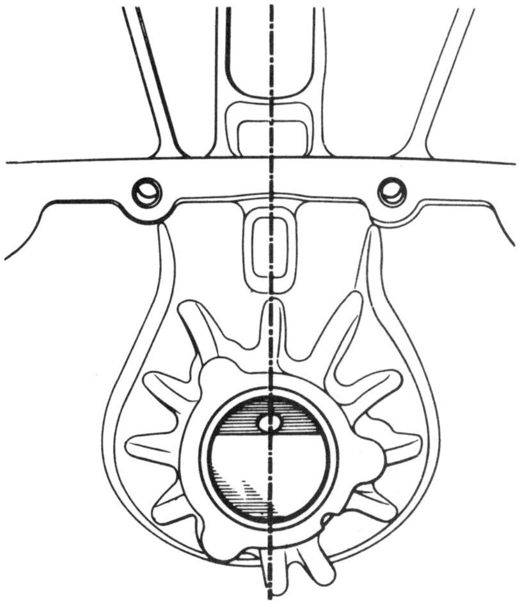

FIG 5:5 Aligning tool Emb.387

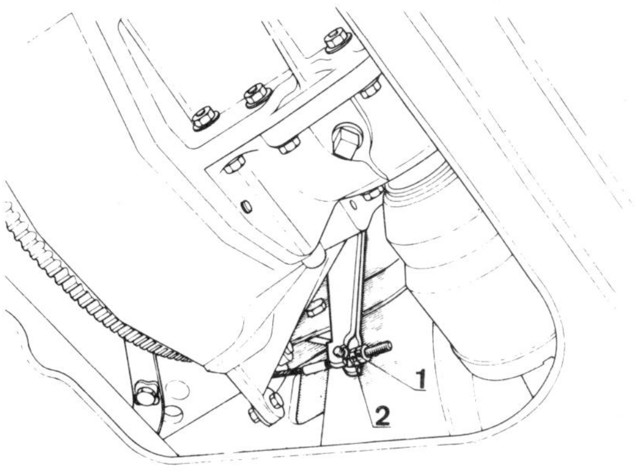

FIG 5:6 Adjusting the clutch clearance

Key to Fig 5:6 1 Locknut 2 Nut

MOT.11 and a spanner in the way shown in **FIG 5:3** extract the bearing. Fit the new bearing with the seal facing towards the outside. Note that the bearing is supplied pre-greased and is therefore not to be cleaned. Refit the flywheel. Tighten the securing bolts to a torque of 40 lbf ft (5 mkg) and lock them by means of the tab washers provided. Fit the clutch pressure and friction plates as layed out in the previous section and refit the transmission unit (see **Chapter 6**).

5:4 Replacing the clutch shaft seal

Remove the transmission unit and separate the clutch housing from the transmission case. This operation is detailed in **Chapter 6.** Remove the clutch shaft seal and

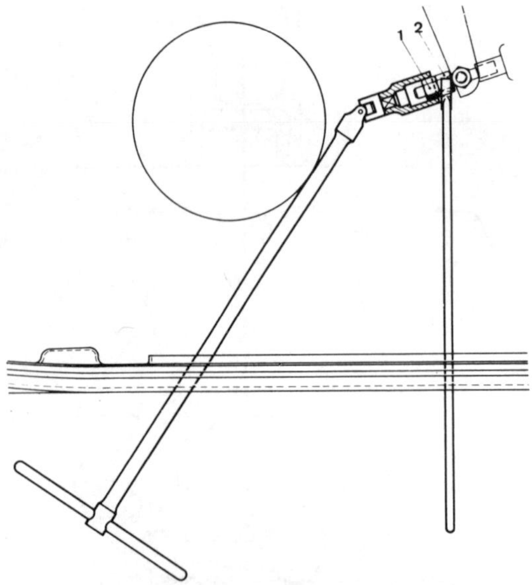

FIG 5:7 Using tools Emb.388 and Emb.389

Key to Fig 5:7 1 Locknut 2 Nut

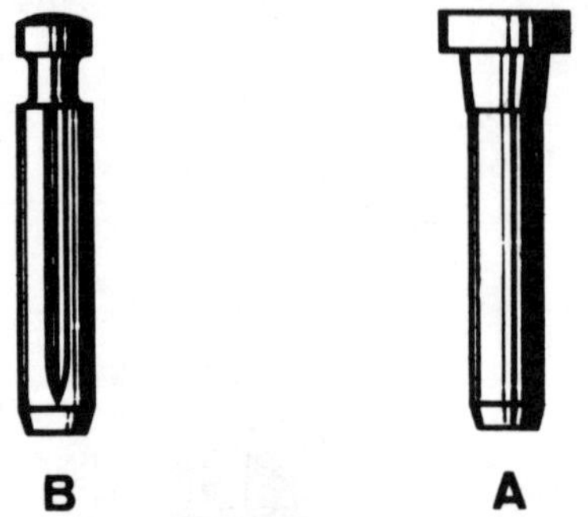

FIG 5:8 Fork retaining pins

Key to Fig 5:8 A Cylindrical pin B Splined pin

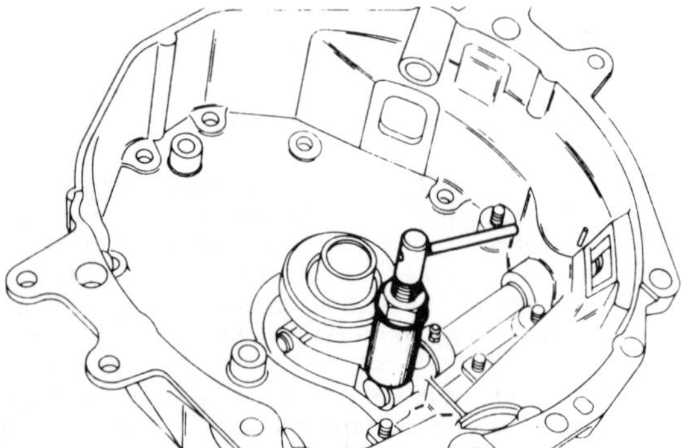

FIG 5:9 Using tool Emb.322 (Emb.384)

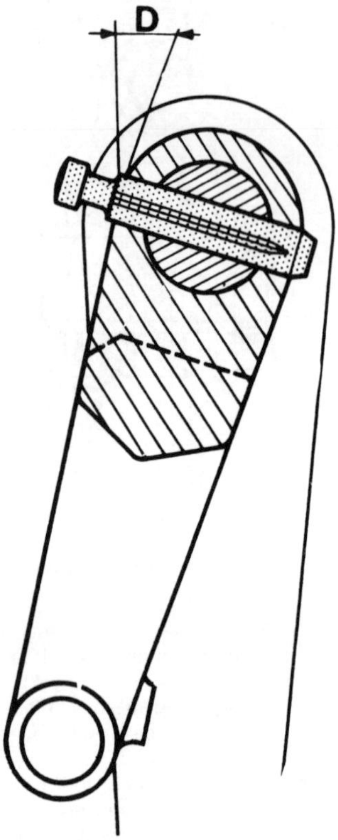

FIG 5:10 Correct positioning of retaining pins

Key to Fig 5:10 D Projection

check to see whether there is a .315 inch (8 mm) hole, arrowed in **FIG 5:4**), at the bottom of the withdrawal pad guide.

If there is no hole place tool Emb.387 inside the guide, position the thrust washer and screw up the retaining nut. Locate the centre of the hole in the tool on the vertical centre-line of the clutch housing (see **FIG 5:5**) and tighten the nut. Move the clutch withdrawal pad as far as it will go forward and hold it in position by means of a spacer. **Slowly** drill the hole using .276 inch (7 mm) diameter drill. Take out the tool and carefully remove the burrs from the edges of the hole.

Fit the new seal with its lip towards the transmission case. Wrap adhesive tape around the splines on the first motion shaft in order than when the clutch housing is fitted to the transmission case the lip on the seal is not damaged. Fit the clutch housing to the transmission case. **Taking off the adhesive strip.** Refit the transmission case (see **Chapter 6**).

5:5 Adjusting the clutch clearance

With regard to **FIG 5:6** loosen the locknut 1 and screw the nut 2 in or out to obtain a clearance of $\frac{5}{64}$ to $\frac{1}{8}$ inch (2 to 3 mm) **at the end of the lever.** Tighten the locknut.

Certain venicles are equipped with a protective engine undertray. On these vehicles open-ended spanner

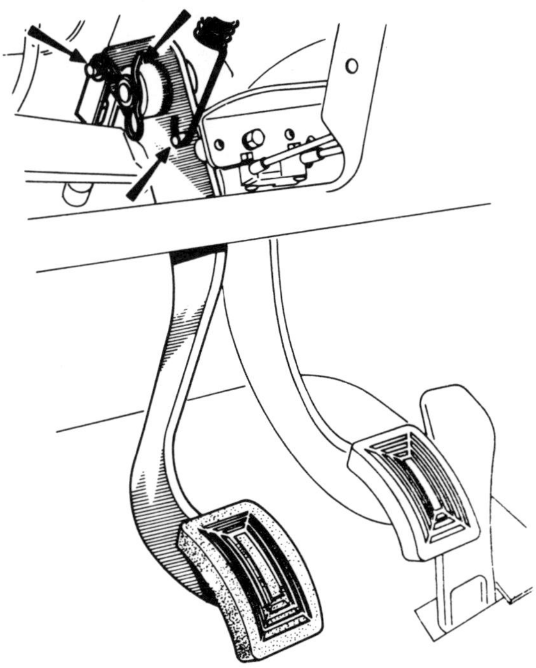

FIG 5:11 The clutch pedal

Emb.389 and knuckle-spanner Emb.388 will have to be used to carry out clutch adjustment. With reference to **FIG 5:7** place the open-ended spanner on the nut 2 and loosen the locknut using the knuckle-spanner. Remove the open-ended spanner and push the knuckle-spanner over both nuts. Screw them in or out until the correct clearance of $\frac{5}{64}$ to $\frac{1}{8}$ inch (2 to 3 mm) **at the end of the lever** is obtained. Tighten the locknut 1 with the knuckle-spanner while holding the nut 2 with the open-ended spanner.

5:6 Replacing the clutch withdrawal pad

To replace the withdrawal pad remove the transmission case (see **Chapter 6**) and remove the fork retaining pins. Two types of pin are fitted, cylindrical, A in **FIG 5:8** and splined, B in **FIG 5:8.** If cylindrical pins are fitted use tool Emb.322 and if splined pins are fitted use tool Emb.384, in the manner illustrated in **FIG 5:9.** Swing the withdrawal fork and remove the withdrawal pad. Lubricate the withdrawal pad guide with 'Molykote BR.2' grease. Fit the new pad, align the holes in the withdrawal fork with that on its shaft and fit the fork retaining pins leaving the correct projection, D in **FIG 5:10**, of $\frac{1}{32}$ inch (1 mm). Refit the transmission case as detailed in **Chapter 6.**

5:7 Removing and refitting the clutch cable

Disconnect the cable at the clutch withdrawal lever, remove the rubber protective cap and push out the cable end fitting from its clamp. From inside the vehicle remove the glove compartment on the lefthand side and unhook the pedal return spring, arrowed in **FIG 5:11.** Remove the pedal retaining clip, arrowed in **FIG 5:11** and free it from its shaft. Disconnect the cable from the pedal and remove it.

To refit the cable carry out the removing operations in reverse and apply compound at the point where the cable passes through the scuttle. Adjust the clutch clearance as detailed in **Section 5:5.**

5:8 Fault diagnosis

(a) Drag or spin

1 Lubricant on driven plate lining
2 Worn driven plate linings
3 Driven plate hub binding on splines
4 Distorted driven plate
5 Damaged pressure plate
6 Damaged diaphragm
7 Damaged driven plate linings

(b) Fierceness or snatch

1 Check 1, 2, 3, 4, 5, 6 and 7 in (a)

(c) Slip

1 Check 1 and 2 in (a)
2 Weak diaphragm
3 Incorrect clutch cable adjustment

(d) Judder

1 Check 1, 2, 3, 4, 5, 6 and 7 in (a)
2 Faulty engine mountings

(e) Tick or knock

1 Badly worn driven plate hub splines
2 Worn release bearing
3 Faulty drive pinion on starter
4 Worn torsion spring(s) on driven plate

CHAPTER 6

THE TRANSMISSION

6:1 Description

A gearbox is fitted to vary the engine torque as the engine torque is insufficient to move the vehicle from rest or enable the vehicle to ascend steep hills. It also has a permanent neutral allowing the engine to be disconnected from the drive wheels in order that the clutch pedal does not have to be held down all the time the vehicle is stationary in traffic and a reverse gear to allow the driver to drive the vehicle backwards.

The crownwheel and pinion serve two purposes. They are the final reduction gears, the reduction in speed giving an increase in torque which allows top gear to be almost a direct drive and they transmit the drive through 90 deg. Bolted to the crownwheel is the differential cage and contained in the cage are two planet wheels which are in mesh with two sun wheels who in turn are splined to the drive shafts. The differential unit allows one road wheel to rotate at a different speed than the other when negotiating a bend, whilst still maintaining a drive to both road wheels.

The transmission unit fitted to both the R.1150 and R.1151 models are of the 336 type and a cross-section view of this unit is shown in **FIG 6:1**. The casing consists of a pressure die cast aluminium housing separated into two parts. The gearbox has four forward gears, all of which are synchronized, a Renault synchronizer being fitted between the first and second speed gear, and a Borg-Warner synchronizer being fitted between the third and top speed gear. One reverse gear is obtained by sliding a gearwheel, which runs free on a shaft, into mesh with a gear on the primary shaft and a gear cut on the outside of the Borg-Warner synchronizer. The crownwheel has 34 teeth and the pinion fitted either has 8 or 9 teeth. If an 8 tooth pinion is fitted the speedometer drive consists of a 6 start worm and a speedometer pinion having 14 teeth whereas the speedometer pinion has 12 teeth when a 9 tooth pinion is fitted.

The clutch plate is splined to the primary shaft and when the plate is trapped between the flywheel and the pressure plate, that is when the clutch is engaged, the rotary motion of the engine is transmitted to the primary shaft and as the secondary shaft gears are in constant mesh with the primary shaft gears to the secondary shaft gears as well.

To obtain reverse gear a spur gear is slid into mesh with

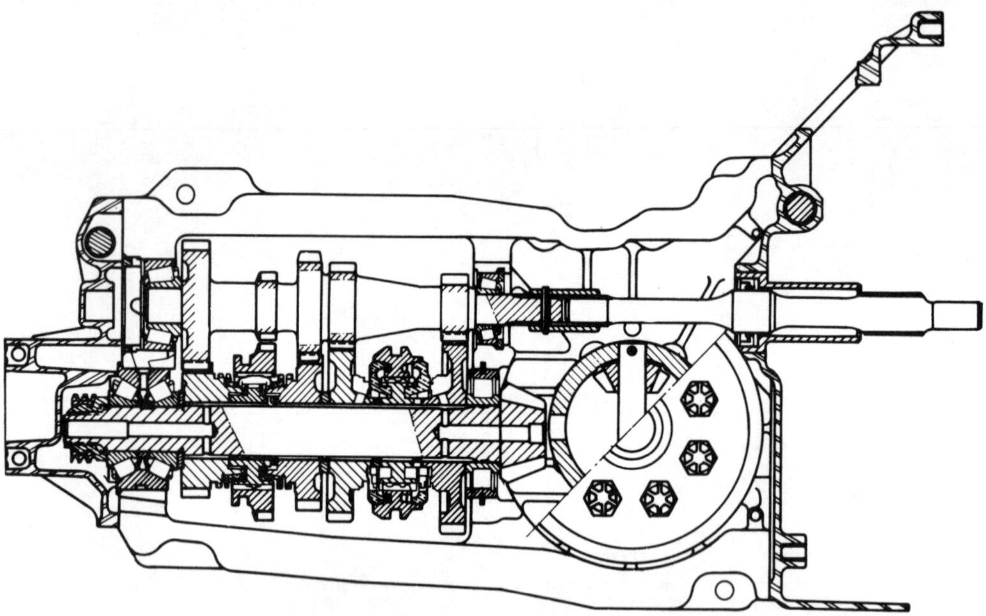

FIG 6:1 The type 336 transmission unit

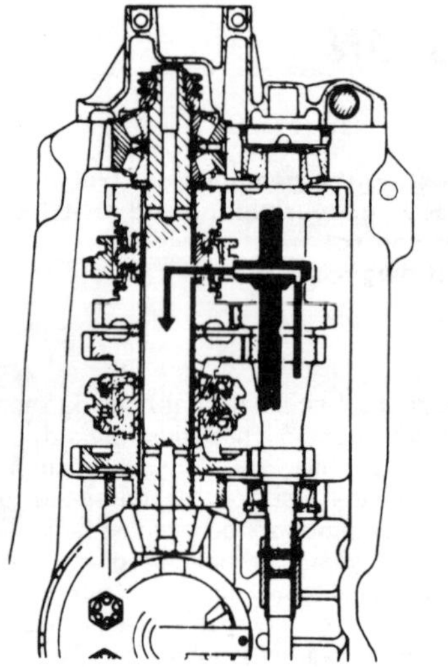

FIG 6:2 Reverse gear position

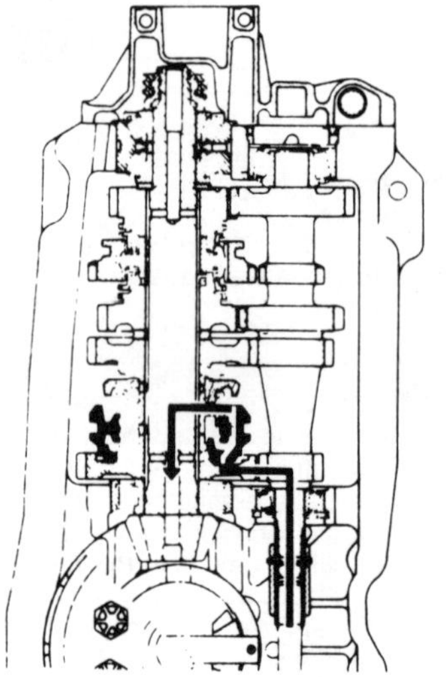

FIG 6:3 First gear position

a spur gear cut on the secondary shaft and a spur gear cut on the outside of the 3rd/4th synchronizer. Drive from the primary shaft is transmitted to the idler gear, from the idler gear to the synchronizer and as this is splined to the secondary shaft, to the secondary shaft onto the crownwheel and pinion. This gear layout is shown in **FIG 6:2** and gives a gear ratio of 3.07:1.

First gear is selected by moving the 1st/2nd synchronizer into mesh with the first speed gear on the secondary shaft (see **FIG 6:3**). Drive between the first speed gears on both shafts is transmitted to the synchronizer and as this is splined to the secondary shaft is naturally transmitted to the secondary shaft. First gear ratio is 3.61:1.

In second gear, the Renault synchronizer is slid into contact with the second speed gear on the secondary shaft. Drive from the second speed gears on the secondary and primary shafts is again transmitted to the secondary shaft via the synchronizer. Second gear ratio is

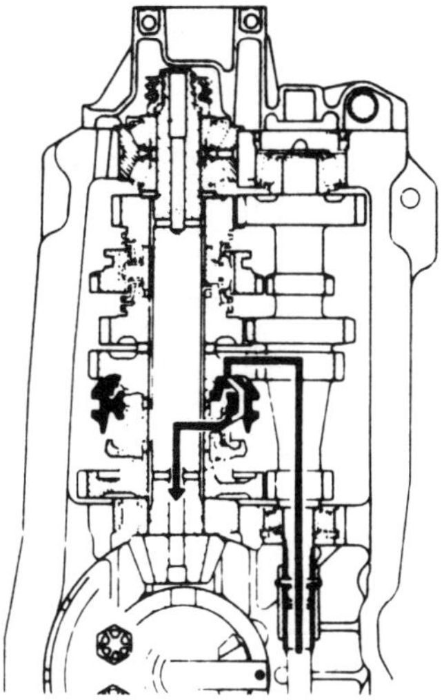

FIG 6:4 Second gear position

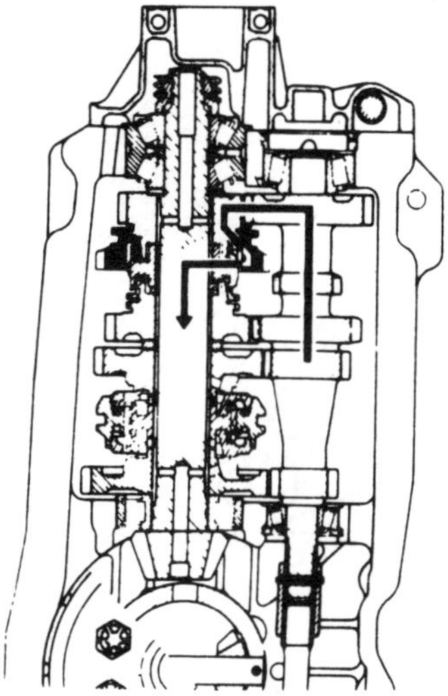

FIG 6:6 Top gear position

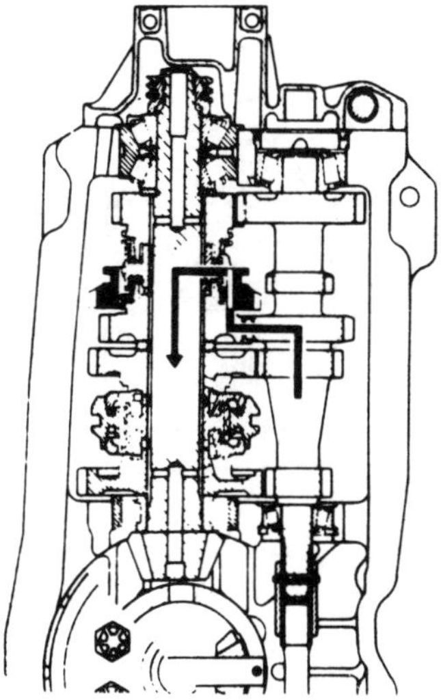

FIG 6:5 Third gear position

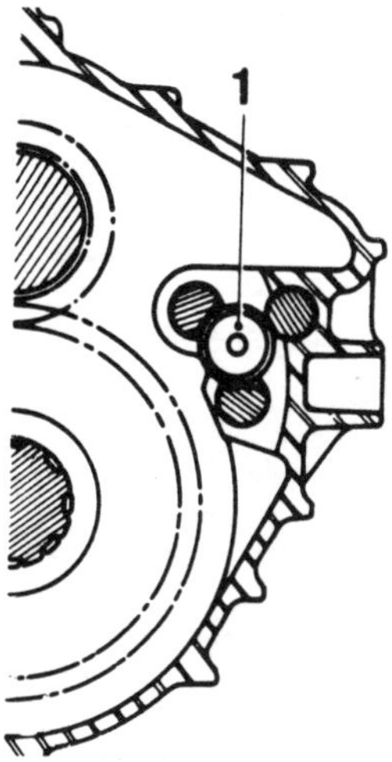

FIG 6:7 The selector rod locking disc

Key to Fig 6:7   1 Disc

2.25:1 and this gear layout is shown in **FIG 6:4.**

To obtain third gear the 3rd/4th synchronizer is made to hold the third speed gear on the secondary shaft (see **FIG 6:5**). The torque produced between the third gears on the primary and secondary shaft is transmitted by the synchronizer to the secondary shaft. Third gear ratio is 1.48:1.

Top gear is obtained by moving the Borg-Warner synchronizer into mesh with the fourth speed gear on the secondary shaft. Engine torque from the primary shaft is transmitted via the fourth speed gears on the primary and secondary shafts to the synchronizer and as this is splined to the secondary shaft onto the secondary shaft to give a ratio of 1.03:1. This gear position is shown in **FIG 6:6.**

In order that the synchronizers and reverse idler gear stay in their neutral positions when not required and when required select fully into mesh, not half in or half out each selector rod is locked, no matter what its position (whether in neutral or with a gear engaged) by a ball and spring. In order that two gears are not selected at the same time a disc 1 in **FIG 6:7** locks the 3rd/4th and 1st/2nd selector rods when reverse gear is engaged, the 1st/2nd and reverse selector rods when either third or fourth gear is engaged and the 3rd/4th and reverse selector rods are locked when either first or second gear is engaged.

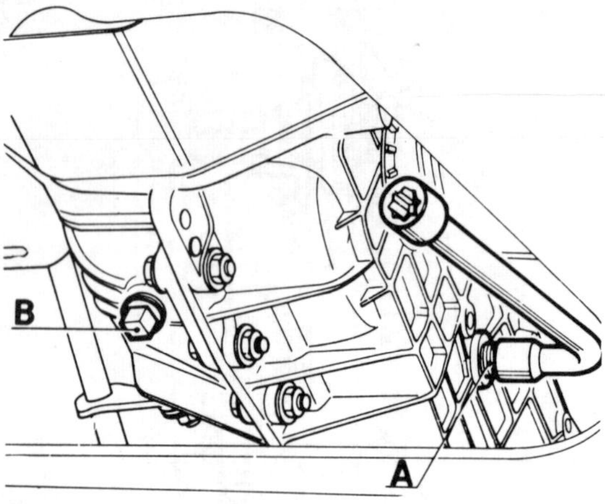

FIG 6:8 The transmission unit drain plug

Key to Fig 6:8 A Refill plug B Drain plug

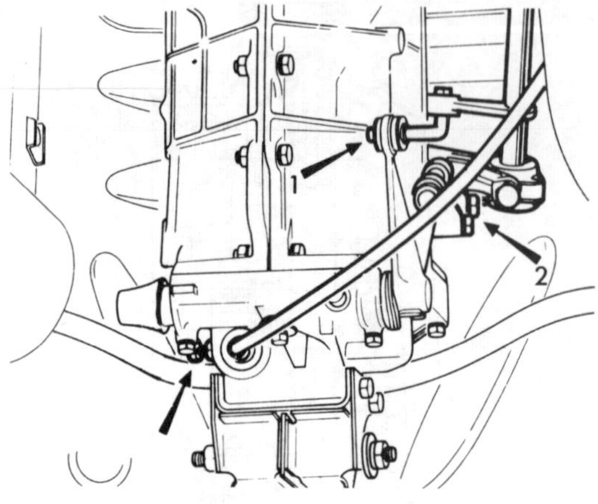

FIG 6:11 The gearshift lever

Key to Fig 6:11 1 Link 2 Bolts

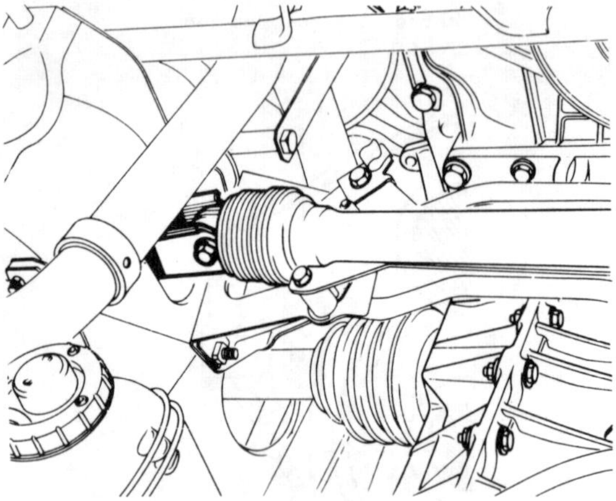

FIG 6:9 Righthand steering link

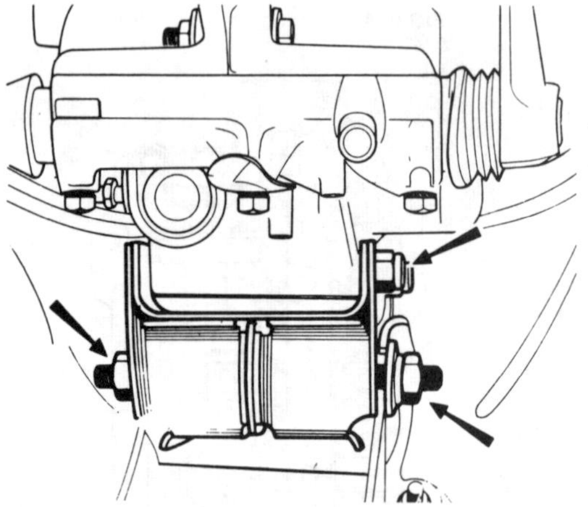

FIG 6:12 Mounting pad

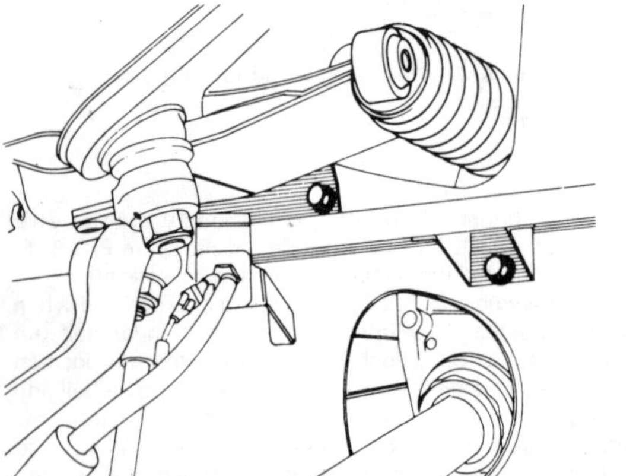

FIG 6:10 Steering crossmember bolts

6:2 Maintenance

The only regular maintenance that can be applied to the transmission unit is to periodically check the level of the oil in the unit and every 24,000 miles to change the oil.

To check the transmission oil level undo the hexagon screw placed on the side of the unit, A in **FIG 6:8** and ensure that the oil is level with the lower edge of the tapped hole the plug was removed from. When checking this level ensure the vehicle is horizontal otherwise an incorrect reading will be obtained. If the oil level is low fill the unit to the required level. Refit and **tighten** the plug.

To change the oil place a container, large enough to hold three pints, under the drain plug B in **FIG 6:8** and undo plug A to allow atmospheric pressure to act on the oil and plug B to allow the oil to drain out. Refit plug B and tighten it then fill the transmission unit with three pints (1.64 litres) of EP.80 gear oil. Refit and tighten plug A.

FIG 6:13 Using drift B.Vi.31B

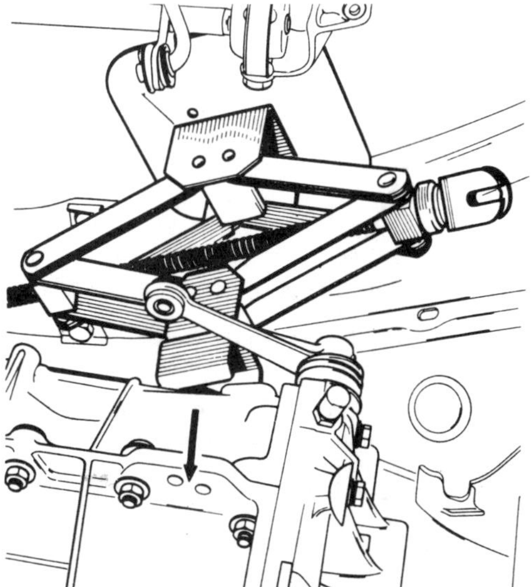

FIG 6:14 Levering the transmission case

6:3 Removing and refitting the transmission case

Removal:

1 Disconnect the battery, drain the oil from the transmission unit and remove the spare wheel, the fan and its casing. Disconnect the feed lead at the battery and detach it from its retaining clip on the steering column. Turn the steering to the left and disconnect the right-

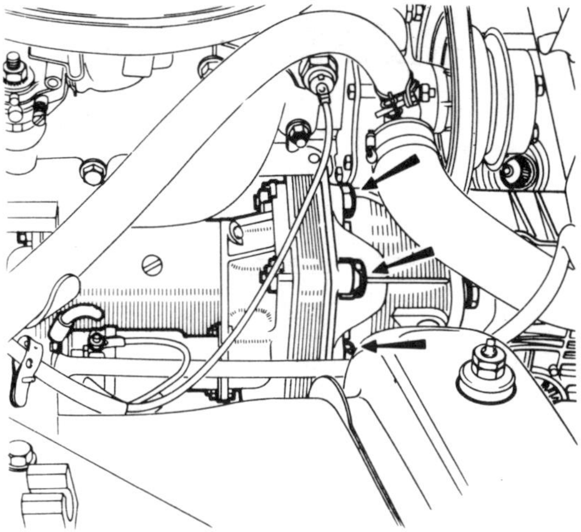

FIG 6:15 Engine to transmission securing bolts

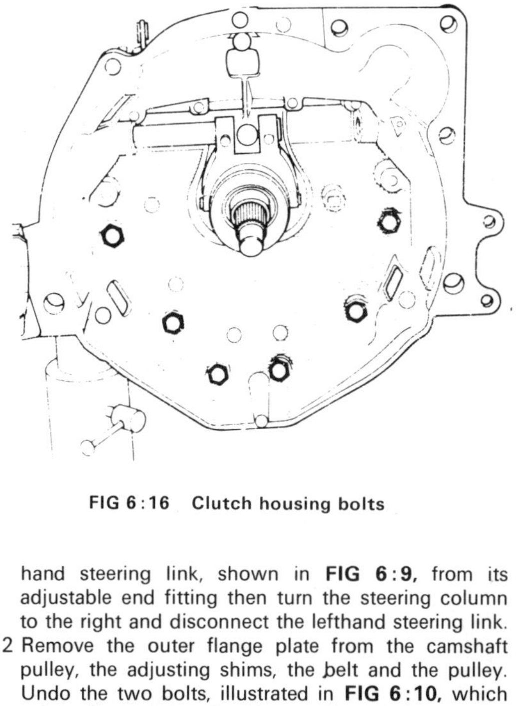

FIG 6:16 Clutch housing bolts

hand steering link, shown in **FIG 6:9**, from its adjustable end fitting then turn the steering column to the right and disconnect the lefthand steering link.

2 Remove the outer flange plate from the camshaft pulley, the adjusting shims, the belt and the pulley. Undo the two bolts, illustrated in **FIG 6:10**, which secure the steering flexible coupling to the steering column and remove the four bolts which secure the steering mechanism crossmember to the cowl sides. Turn the steering to its full lock in the righthand direction and pulling on the lefthand side of the steering crossmember' assembly take out the assembly.

3 Disconnect the speedometer drive cable, the link at the gearshift lever 1 in **FIG 6:11** and unscrew the two bolts 2 which secure the gearshift control to the gearbox. Pull back the control and hook it to the battery support. Undo the two front mounting pad

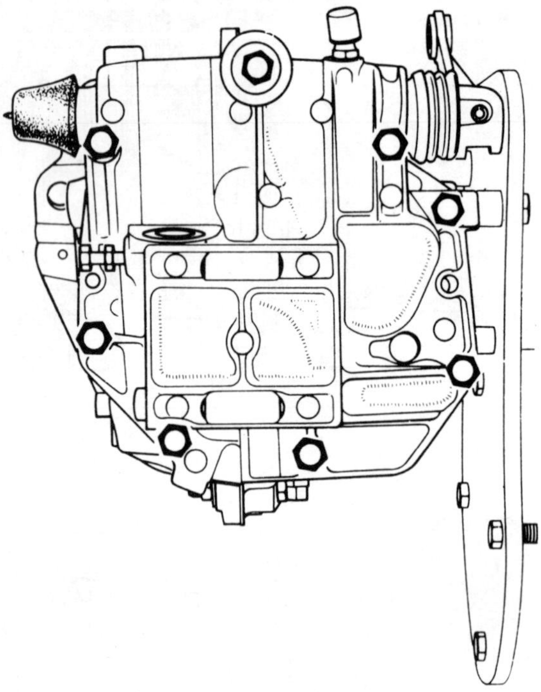

FIG 6:17 Front housing securing bolts

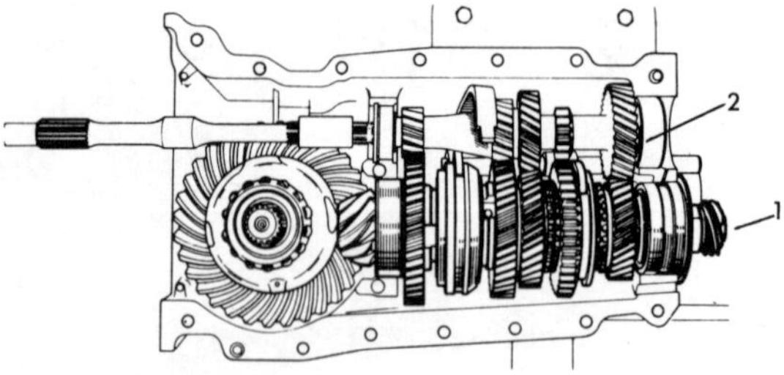

FIG 6:18 The primary and secondary shaft

Key to Fig 6:18 1 Secondary shaft 2 Primary shaft

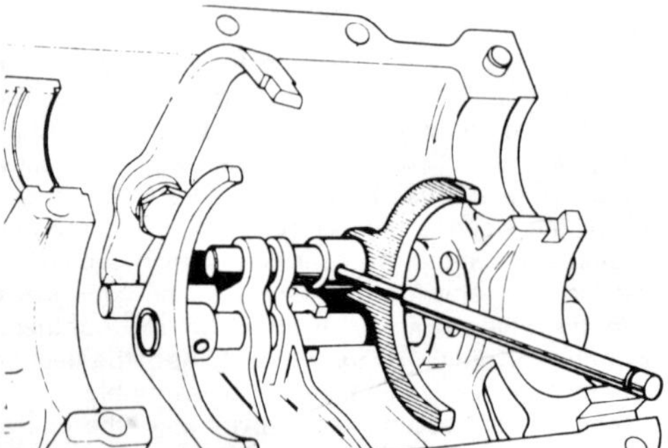

FIG 6:19 3rd/4th shift fork

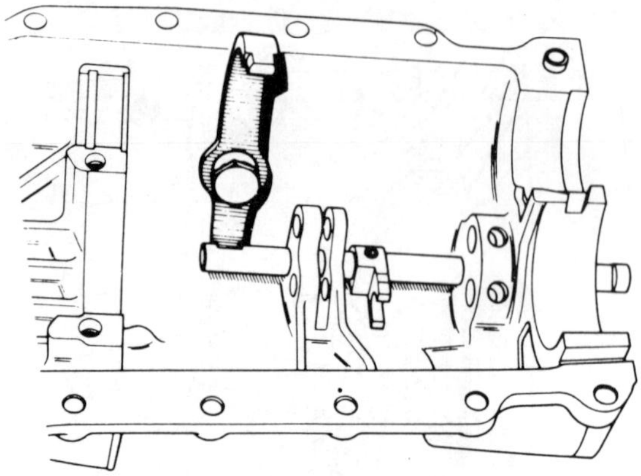

FIG 6:20 Reverse swivel lever

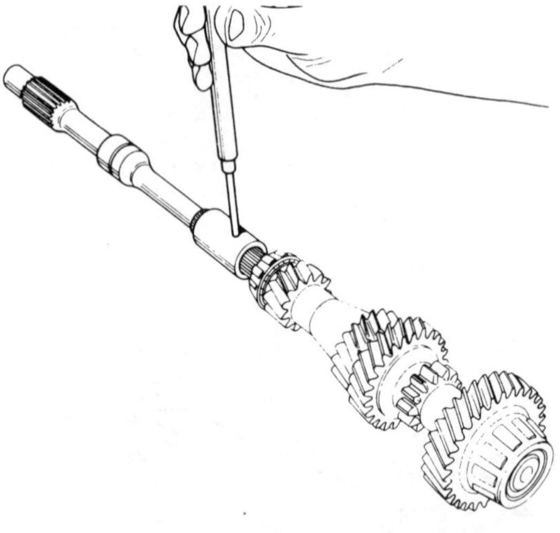

FIG 6:21 Separating the clutch shaft

securing nuts, arrowed in **FIG 6:12,** remove the two bolts which secure the pad bracket to the front housing and then remove the pad and bracket.

4 Using drift B.Vi.31B in the manner shown in **FIG 6:13** remove the roll-pins from the transmission shafts. Fit tool T.Av.247 to the transmission shafts to prevent them becoming disjointed then place a jack between the gearbox and the lefthand sidemember as illustrated in **FIG 6:14.** Push the box to one side using the jack and remove the transmission shaft from the sun wheel.

5 Disconnect the clutch cable and free the dust cover and push the cable end fitting from its clamp. Unlock and unscrew the two bolts which secure the engine to the gearbox on the lefthand side (see **FIG 6:15**), remove the jack and place it on the righthand side. Using the jack push the gearbox over and free the transmission shaft from the sunwheel. Unlock and unscrew the bolts securing the engine to the transmission on the righthand side and the starter securing bolts pulling the starter back as far as it will go. Push

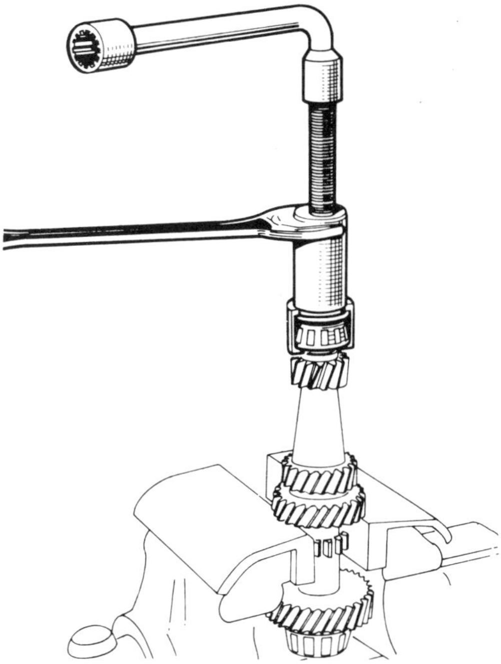

FIG 6:22 Extracting the primary shaft bearings

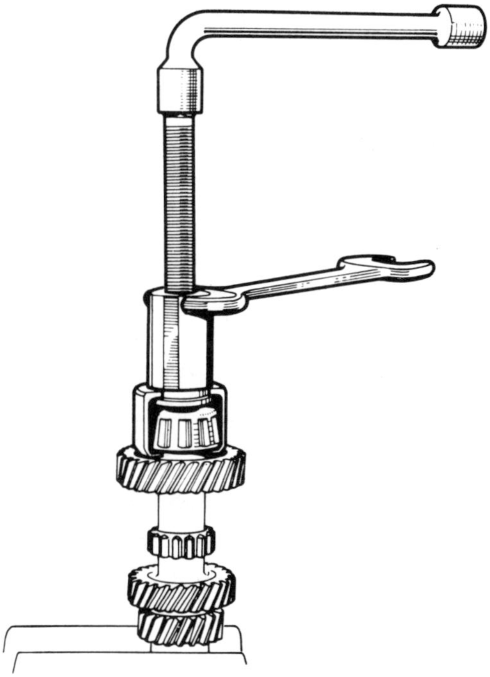

FIG 6:23 Using extractor B.Vi.22

the transmission unit forward to free the clutch shaft then lift the front of the unit, taking care not to damage the radiator and remove the unit vertically.

Refitting:

Refit the unit by reversing the removal procedure taking care to lubricate the splines on the clutch shaft and planet wheels. Ensure that one of the pin holes at the bottom of one of the splines in the transmission shaft is placed inline with the hole on top of one of the sun wheel splines and refit the roll-pins to the transmission shafts using the cranked end of drift B.Vi.31 B.

When fitting the water pump drive belt, slowly tighten the nuts on the outer flange while turning the engine, in order to avoid damage to the belt. **Never use the camshaft pulley retaining bolt to turn the engine.** Rotate the power unit by lifting one drive wheel clear off the ground, engaging top gear and turning the raised wheel in the forward direction.

After completion adjust the clutch clearance (see **Chapter 5**) and fill the gearbox with oil (see **Section 6:2**).

6:4 Overhauling the transmission

Removal:

1 Unscrew the six clutch housing securing bolts (shown in **FIG 6:16**) and remove the clutch housing. Undo the six bolts securing the front housing, the bolts being shown in **FIG 6:17** and remove the front housing. If the differential unit is one where the differential bearings are adjusted by means of nuts, remove the locking plates from the nuts and then loosen and unscrew the nuts.

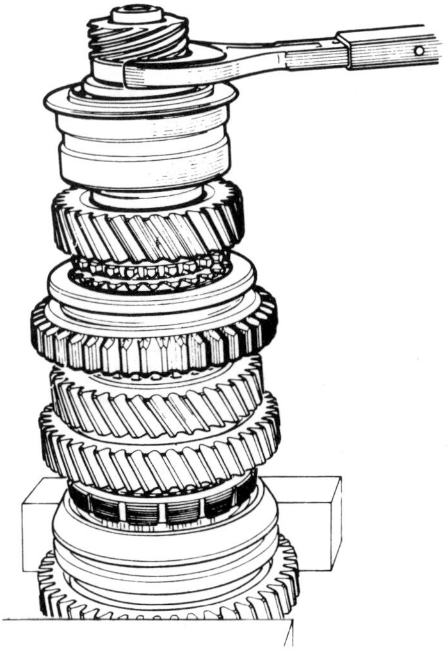

FIG 6:24 The secondary shaft

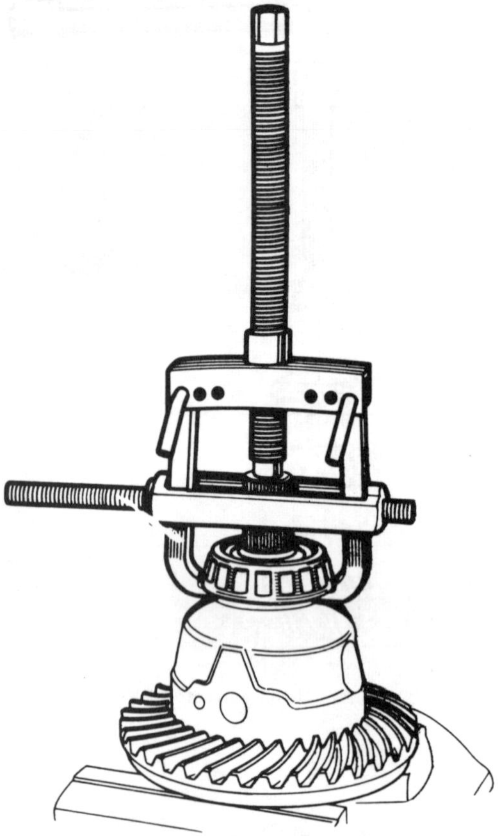

FIG 6:25 Extracting the differential bearings

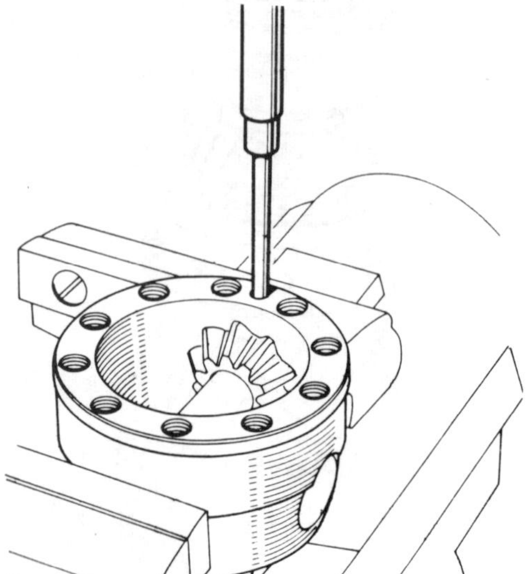

FIG 6:26 Removing the planet wheel shaft roll pin

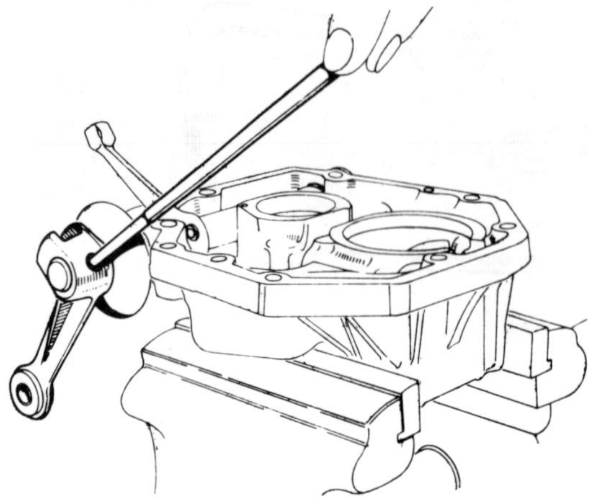

FIG 6:27 Removing the shift lever roll-pin

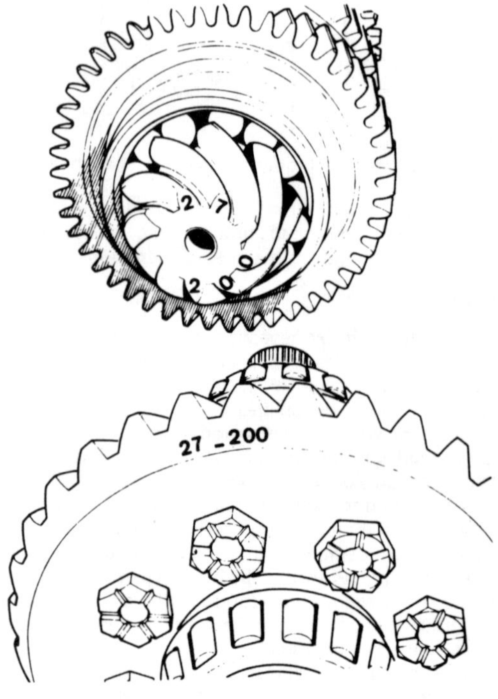

FIG 6:29 The crownwheel and pinion

2 Unscrew the fifteen bolts securing the two half housings and separate the half housings. Remove the spacer and the adjusting shims from the primary shaft bearings. Lift out the secondary gear cluster 1 in **FIG 6:18** and the stud which locks the outer track ring on the double taper roller bearing. On R.1151 models the bearing under the final drive pinion shoulder has only one circlip retaining the outer track ring, so care must be taken to ensure that the bearing assembly does

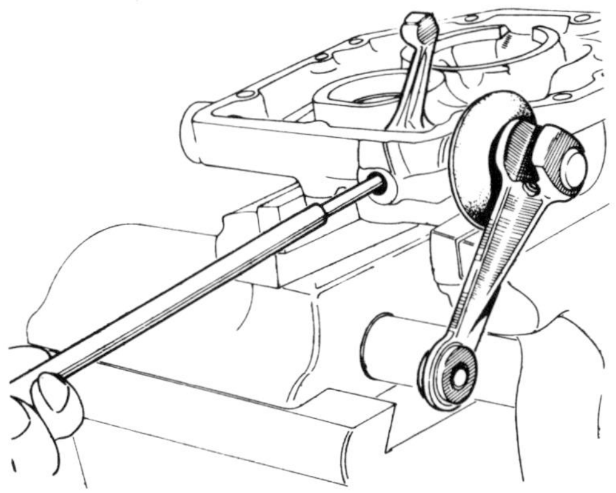

FIG 6:28 Removing the internal shift lever roll-pin

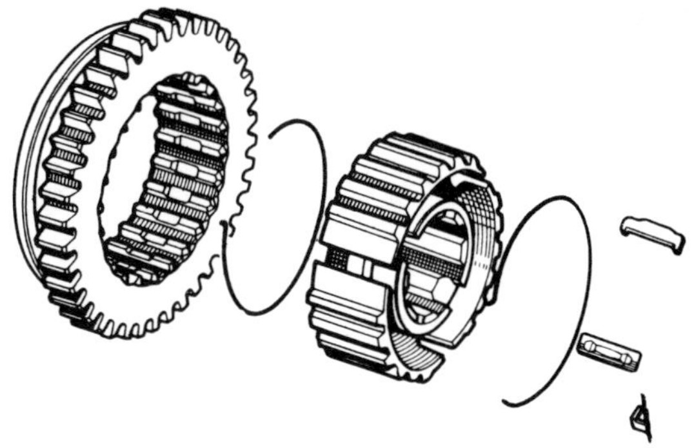

FIG 6:31 3rd/4th speed synchronizer

FIG 6:30 1st/2nd speed synchronizer

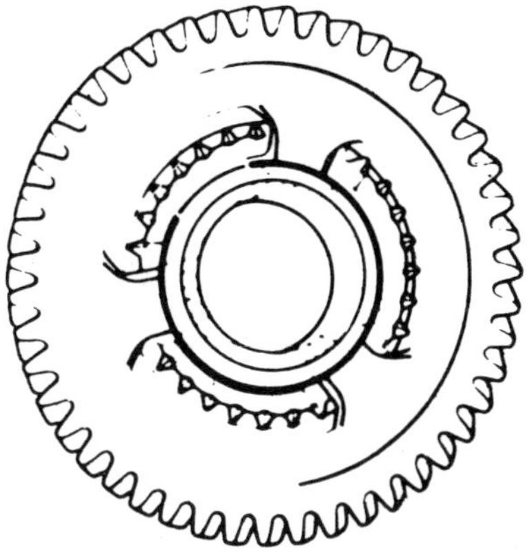

FIG 6:32 Synchronizer spring

not fall apart. Remove the primary shaft 2 in **FIG 6:18.** Remove the differential.

3 Push out the roll-pin from the 3rd/4th shift fork using drift B.Vi.31B in the manner shown in **FIG 6:19.** Remove the shift fork and the shaft, putting aside the locking ball and spring. Lift out the locking disc from between the two shafts. Engage first gear, pull back the reverse shaft as far as it will go towards the control end and push out the roll-pin from the 1st/2nd shift fork using drift B.Vi.31B. Remove the shaft and shift fork again putting aside the locking ball and spring. Unscrew the reverse swivel lever pivot pin (shown in **FIG 6:20**) and take out the swivel lever. Push out the roll-pin from the reverse shift fork until the pin makes contact with the housing, then turn the shaft and free the roll-pin by means of a pair of pliars. Remove the shaft and fork.

4 Remove the circlip retaining the reverse gearwheel assembly and take out the shaft, gearwheel, friction washer and guide. Put aside the locking ball and spring. Take off the bearing track rings and adjusting washers from the primary shaft then separate the clutch shaft from the primary shaft by pushing out the roll-pin by means of drift B.Vi.39 (see **FIG 6:21**).

5 Extract the bearing from the differential end of the primary shaft using extractor B.Vi.22 in the manner shown in **FIG 6:22.** Extract the second bearing by means of extractor B.Vi.22 fitted with shell B.Vi.47 as shown in **FIG 6:23.**

6 Grip the secondary shaft assembly in a vice fitted with safety jaws, engage first gear and unlock the speedometer drive worm using spanner B.Vi.204 in the manner shown in **FIG 6:24.** Unscrew the drive worm and remove the double taper roller bearing, the pinion depth adjusting washer, the fourth speed gearwheel with its ring and the 3rd/4th speed synchronizer sliding gearwheel with its keys. Mark the position of the sliding gearwheel with reference to the hub. Press off the 3rd/4th speed synchronizer hub and remove the gearwheel stop washer retaining key, the third speed gearwheel stop washer, the third speed gearwheel with its ring, the second speed gearwheel stop washer, the second speed gearwheel and its ring, the 1st/2nd speed synchronizer sliding gear-

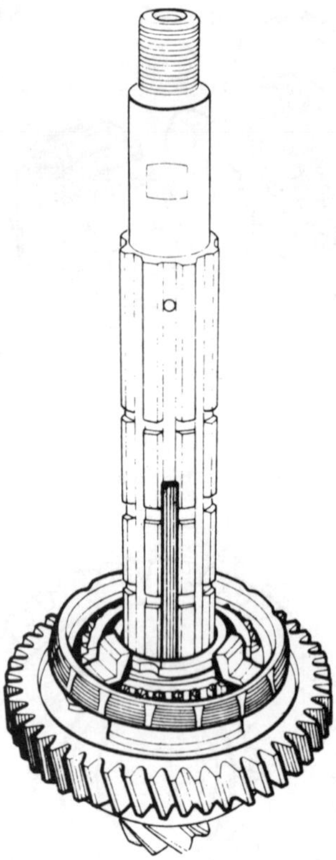

FIG 6:33 First speed gearwheel and its ring

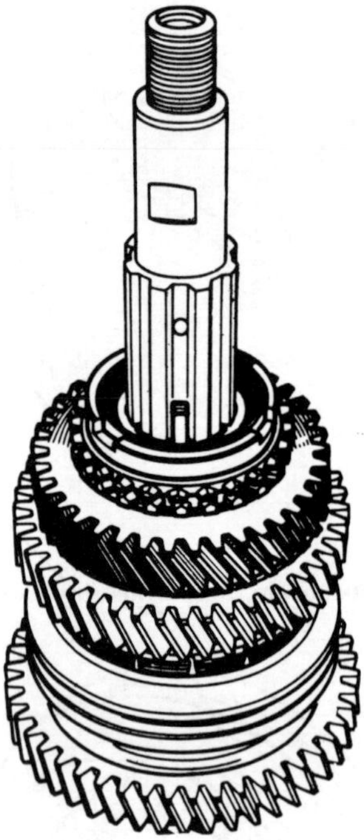

FIG 6:34 Third speed gearwheel and its ring

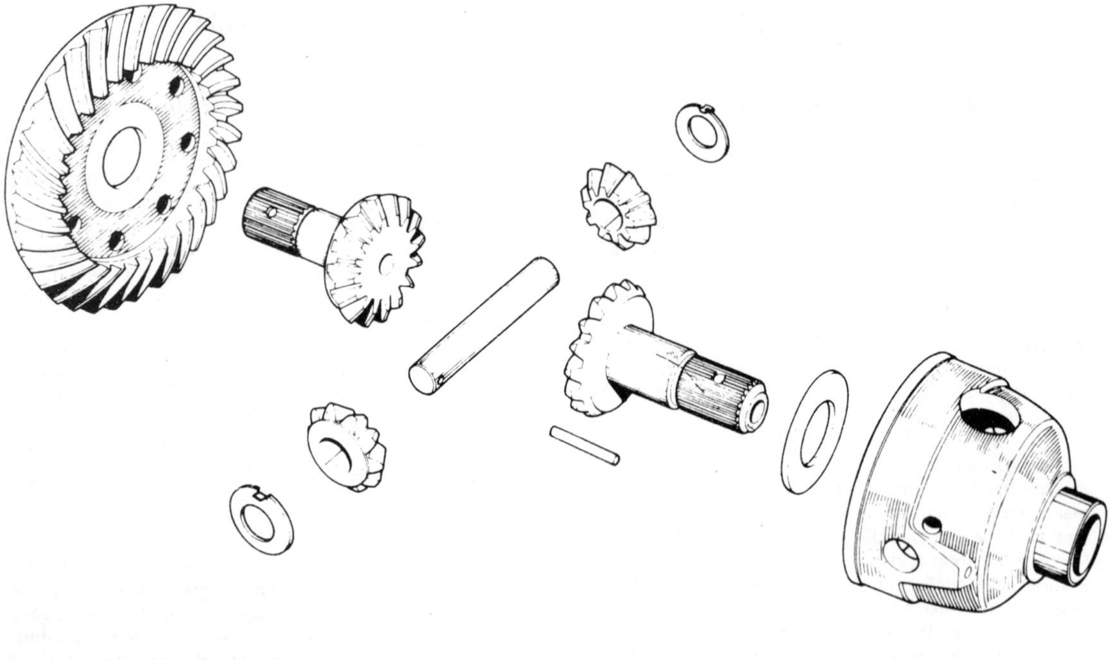

FIG 6:35 The differential

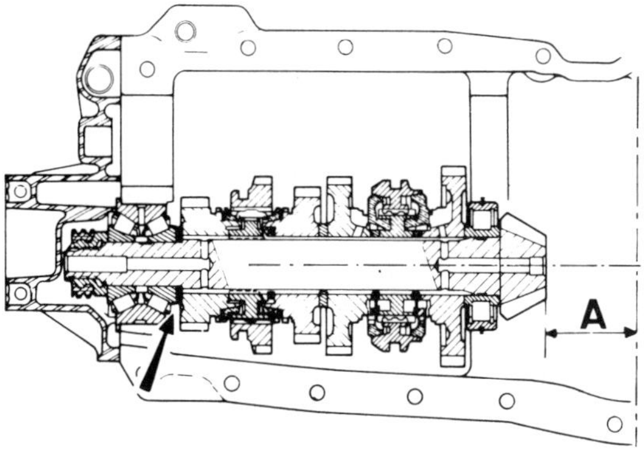

FIG 6:36 Pinion depth

Key to Fig 6:36 A Pinion depth

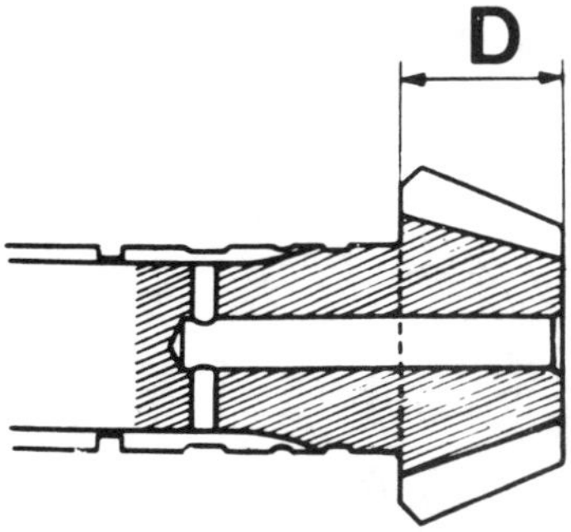

FIG 6:37 Flat face pinion

Key to Fig 6:37 D 1.083 inch (27.5 mm)

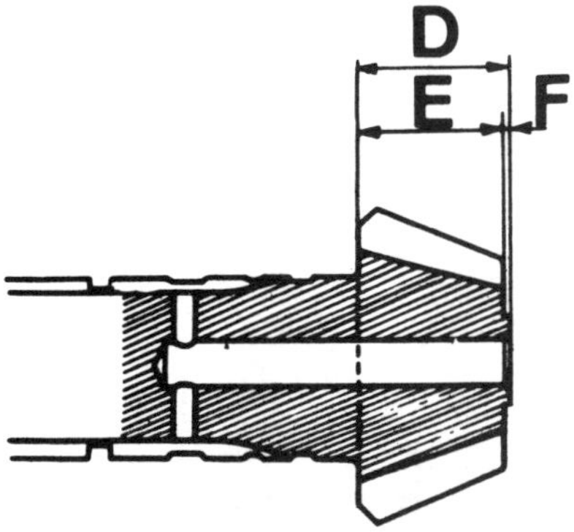

FIG 6:38 Front face with shoulder

Key to Fig 6:38 D 1.083 inch E 1.040 inch F .043 inch

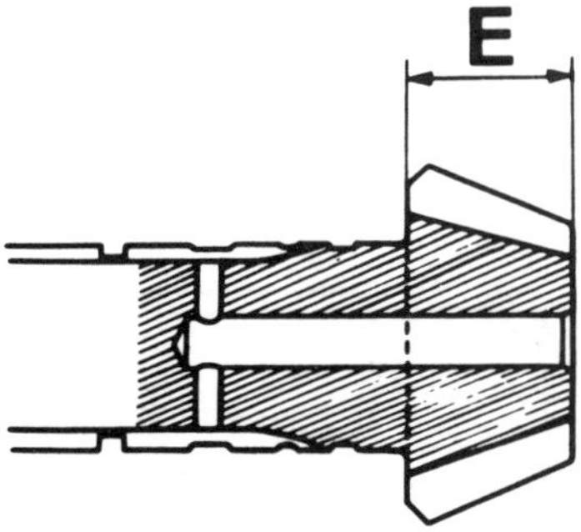

FIG 6:39 Flat face pinion from No. 5998 onwards

Key to Fig 6:39 E 1.040 inch

wheel again mark its position with reference to the hub and the 1st/2nd speed synchronizer hub stop washer. Press off the 1st/2nd speed synchronizer hub. Remove the first speed synchronizer ring, the first speed gearwheel stop washer and the first speed gearwheel. Note that as the roller bearing inner track ring is bonded to the shaft, this bearing cannot be removed.

7 Using tool B.Vi.88 with claws B.Vi.48 remove the differential bearings in the manner illustrated in **FIG 6:25.** To remove the bearing on the crownwheel side, two crownwheel securing bolts will have to be unscrewed to get the claws B.Vi.48 into position. Undo the remaining crownwheel securing bolts **(these are self-locking bolts which cannot be used again)** and lift off the crownwheel. Push out the planet wheel shaft roll-pin in the manner shown in **FIG 6:26** using drift B.Vi.39 for R.1150 models and drift B.Vi.31B for R.1151 models. Separate the various parts.

8 Remove the pinion, the guide and the O-ring from the front housing. Push out the shift lever roll-pin (see **FIG 6:27**) by means of a drift. Unscrew the breather and push out the roll-pin from the internal shift lever through the breather hole by means of a drift (see **FIG 6:28**). Take out the lever, the rubber, the shaft and the internal lever.

Examination:

Thoroughly clean, dry and examine all parts for wear, deterioration and thread damage. Check the half housings for cracks and or distortion at mating surfaces. Examine all bearings for excessive wear, pitting, loose cages and loose fit in their housings. Examine all gear teeth for excessive wear or damage. When renewing a gear it is advisable to renew also its mating gear. Check the rings of the synchromesh units with their mating tapers on the gears. If the rings do not lock on before they contact the edge of the dogteeth on the gear, the ring and possibly the hub must be renewed. Renew pitted or worn locking selector balls and compare the locking ball springs with a new spring and if a spring is shorter it must be replaced. After examination coat all components with transmission oil. **All seals, gaskets, roll-pins and self-locking bolts must be replaced with new ones.**

Reassembling the sub-assemblies:

1 The crownwheel and pinion are lapped together during manufacture they therefore cannot be used separately. Replacing one of these parts automatically

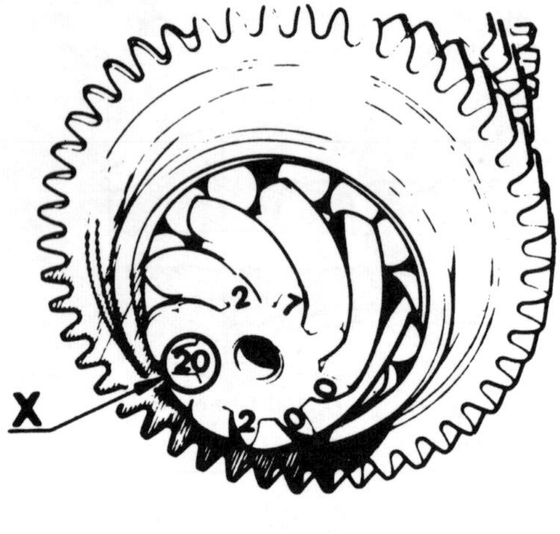

FIG 6:40 Pinion mark

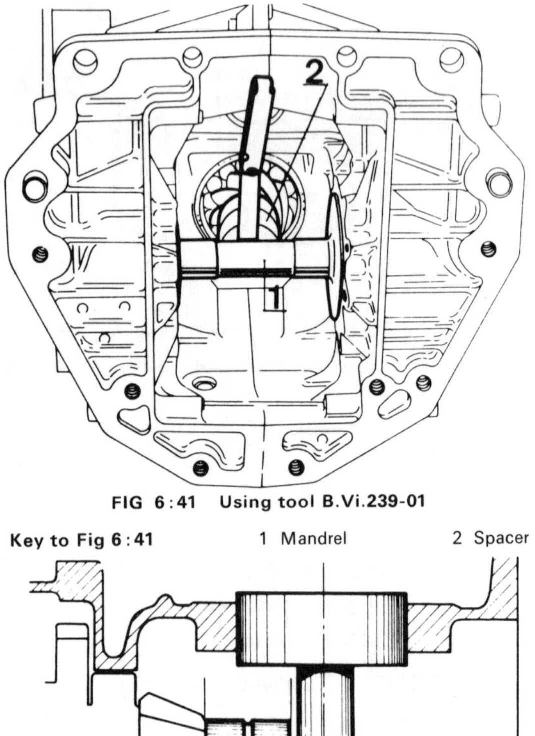

FIG 6:41 Using tool B.Vi.239-01

Key to Fig 6:41 1 Mandrel 2 Spacer

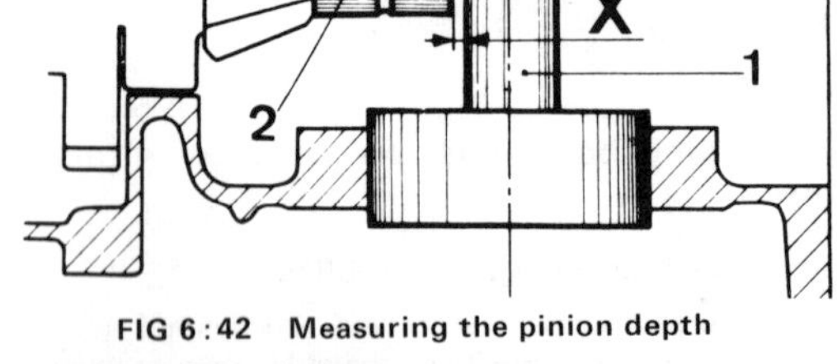

FIG 6:42 Measuring the pinion depth

Key to Fig 6:42 X Clearance 1 Mandrel 2 Spacer

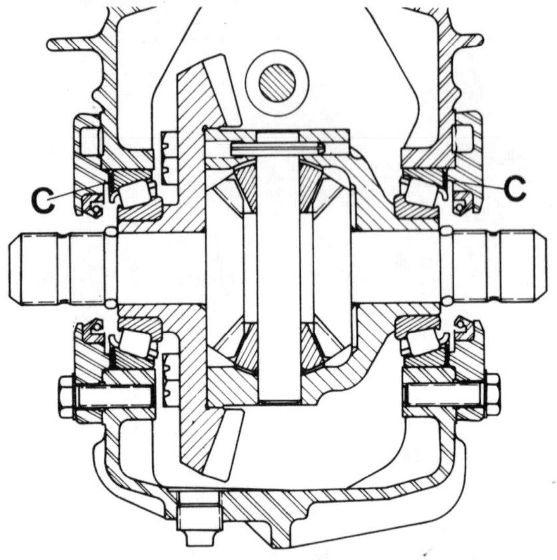

FIG 6:43 Differential bearing adjustment by shims

Key to Fig 6:43 C Shims

involves replacing the other. A common marking (shown in **FIG 6:29**) is inscribed on both the crownwheel and pinion. **Under no circumstances must any notice be taken of other readings on the crownwheel.** The synchronizer hubs are matched with the final drive pinion and therefore if the final drive pinion, crownwheel or roller bearing are damaged replace the crownwheel and pinion assembly. It is as well to note that, at present, the roller bearing is fitted with a circlip on the outlet track ring and this has involved machining a groove in the gearbox housing. A bearing that is not fitted with a circlip can be used in a housing that has a groove, though quite obviously a bearing which has a circlip cannot be used in a housing which has no groove.

2 Using a micrometer (or vernier gauge) measure the dimension across two of the splines on the final drive pinion shaft taking a number of measurements at different points around the splines at the point where the synchronizer hub fits and find the average. There are five different size groups for the final drive pinion shaft and they correspond to five different synchronizer hub size groups. The different sizes are identified by a colour code, the colour mark on the final drive pinion is to be found on the corresponding crownwheel alongside the matching reference and the synchronizer colour code is to be found on the hub.

Final drive pinion dimension

.6516 to .6523 inch (16.55 to 16.57 mm)	White*
.6527 to .6535 inch (16.58 to 16.60 mm)	Red*
.6539 to .6547 inch (16.61 to 16.63 mm)	Blue*
.6551 to .6559 inch (16.64 to 16.66 mm)	Yellow*
.6563 to .6571 inch (16.67 to 16.69 mm)	Green*

**Corresponding final drive pinion and hub colour code*

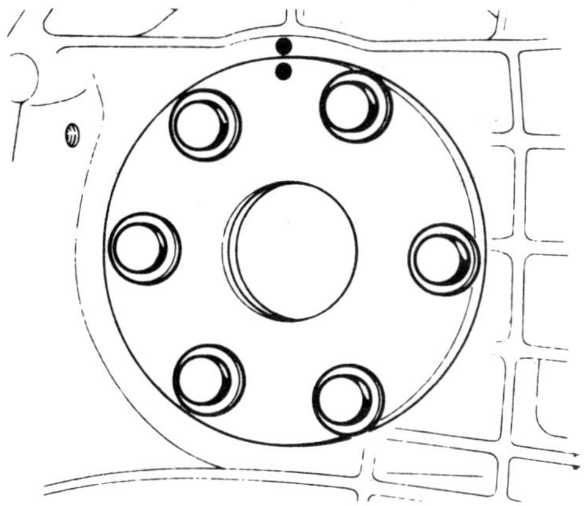

FIG 6:44 Side coverplate reference marks

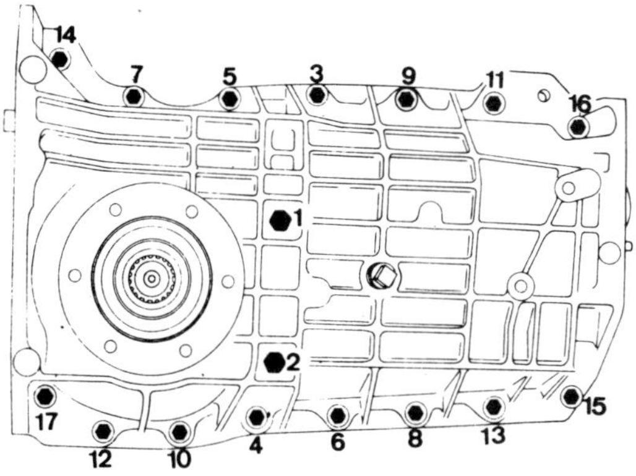

FIG 6:45 Half housing securing bolts

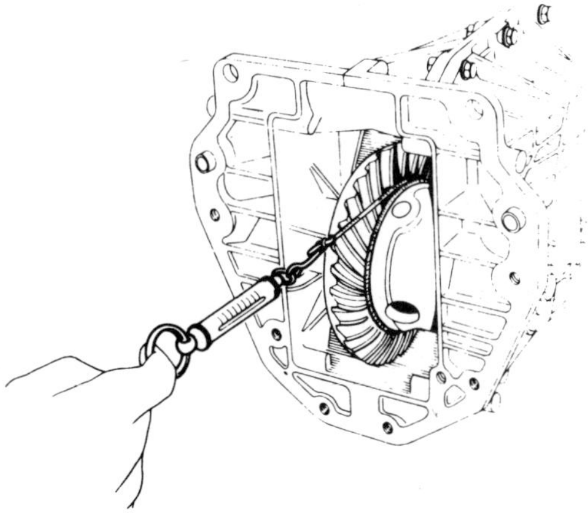

FIG 6:46 Checking pre-load

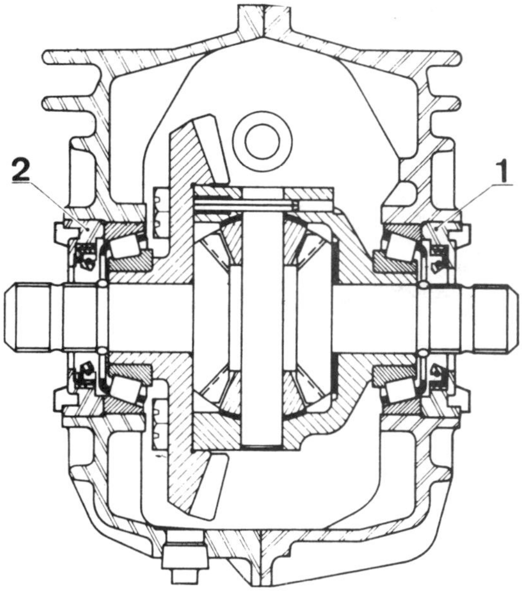

FIG 6:47 Differential bearing adjustment by nuts

Key to Fig 6:47 1 Nut on differential housing side 2 Nut on crownwheel side

3 Once the size group has been determined mark the sliding gearwheel and hub on the 1st/2nd synchronizer (see **FIG 6:30**), before the two parts are separated as the two parts are matched. **The position mark must be made on the second speed gear wheel side so that it can be seen after the hub is fitted.** Place the hub only in an oven and heat it to 250°C (482°F). Give the oven enough time to heat the hub before starting to reassemble the secondary shaft assembly.

4 With regard to **FIG 6:31** place the three keys onto the inner hub of the 3rd/4th synchronizer and insert the two springs so that one end of each of the springs is in one of the keys with the free ends on the opposite side of it. Position the sliding gearwheel with the groove in the sliding gearwheel on the opposite side to the two notches in the hub and the reference mark on the sliding gearwheel in line with the mark on the hub. These reference marks were made during the dismantling procedure (see **FIG 6:6** of the previous part of this section).

5 Place the synchronizer spring on the first speed gearwheel so that it covers the three notches (see **FIG 6:32**). Place the first speed gear and its ring followed by the first speed gearwheel stop washer on the final drive pinion shaft. Turn the stop washer and locate it by means of a dummy key in the manner shown in **FIG 6:33.** The dummy key, which is a washer retaining key with one of its lugs removed, is to be placed in one of the keyways which has an oil hole in it. Take the 1st/2nd speed gearwheel from the oven and place it on the final drive pinion with the part containing the position mark facing towards the second speed gearwheel and with one of the

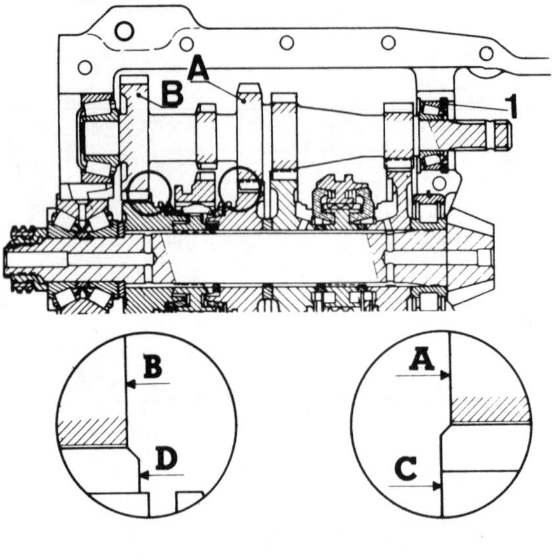

FIG 6:48 Positioning the primary shaft

Key to Fig 6:48 1 Adjusting washers

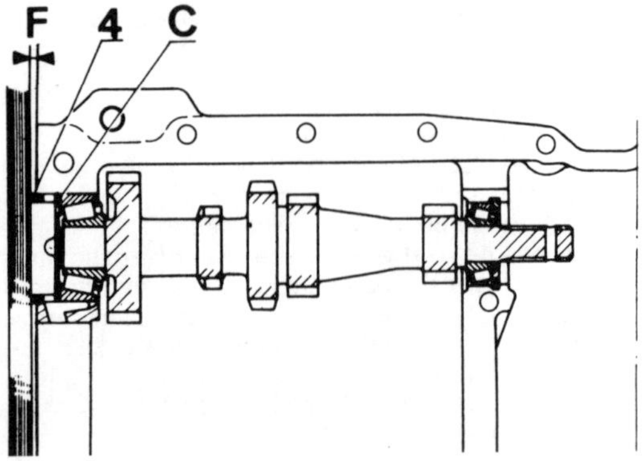

FIG 6:49 Adjusting primary shaft bearings

Key to 6:49 **C** Adjusting shims 4 Spacer **F** Clearance

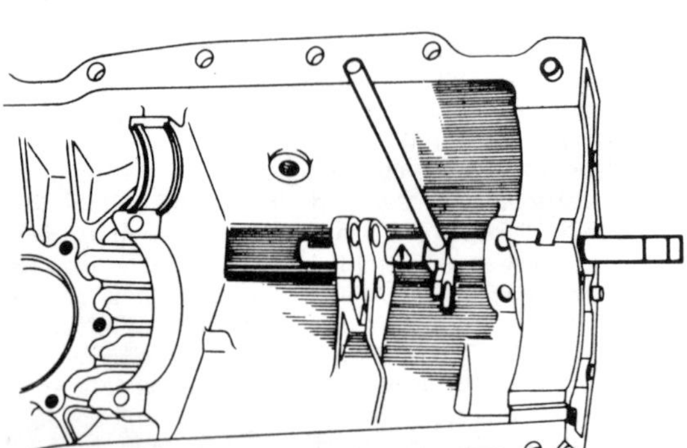

FIG 6:50 Fitting the roll-pin to the reverse shaft

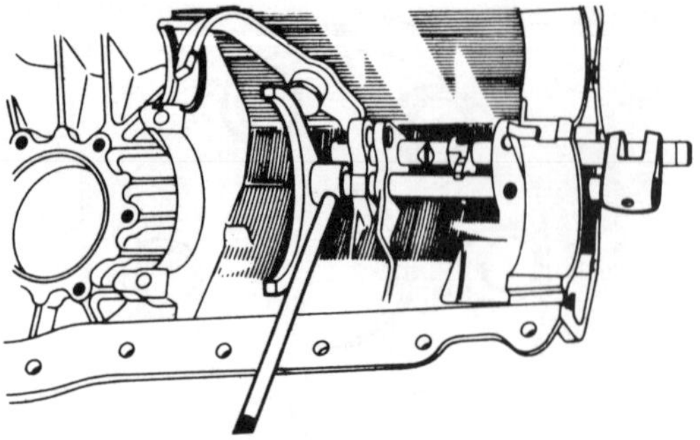

FIG 6:51 Fitting the roll-pin to the 1st/2nd shaft

unsplined portions in-line with the dummy key. Press the hub on the shaft until it makes contact with the stop washer then still holding pressure on the press, hold the synchronizer ring in a central position, with the lugs below the level of the stop washer so as not to damage the spring. When the hub has cooled release the press pressure. Remove the dummy key.

6 Fit the 1st/2nd speed sliding gearwheel with a chamfer on the second speed gearwheel side and with the position reference in-line with that on the hub. Fit the hub stop washer, turning it to align its splines with those on the final drive pinion. Place the synchronizer spring on the second speed gearwheel in the same way as on the first speed gearwheel and position the second speed gearwheel and its ring. Position the gearwheel stop washer, turning it to align its splines with those on the final drive pinion shaft and fit the gearwheel stop washer retaining key in one of the keyways that has an oil hole in it (see **FIG 6:34**).

7 Fit the 3rd/4th speed synchronizer, ensuring that the notches on the hub are on the third speed gearwheel side and that one of the notches is in-line with the retaining key, then press the synchronizer on until it makes contact with the third speed gear wheel stop washer. **Check that the three notches on the synchronizer hub are in-line with the three keys.** Fit the fourth speed gearwheel with its ring, the pinion depth adjusting washer, the double taper roller bearing and the speedometer drive worm. Gripping the secondary shaft assembly in a vice, across the first speed gearwheel, engage first gear and tighten the speedometer drive worm to a torque of 85 lb ft (12 mkg). **Do not lock the worm as pinion depth has still to be adjusted.**

8 With reference to **FIG 6:35** fit the bakelite impregnated washer, with the lubrication groove on the sun wheel side then one of the sun wheels after dipping it in EP.80 oil, in the differential cage unit. Fit the two planet wheel with their friction washers and insert the planet wheel shaft, aligning the hole in the shaft with that in the housing. Fit the roll-pin Immerse the other sun wheel in oil (EP.80) and fit it in the crownwheel. Fasten the crownwheel to the differential cage by means of **new** self-locking bolts and tighten the bolts to a torque of 45 lb ft (6 mkg) for the .394 inch (10 mm) diameter bolts and 80 lb ft (11 mkg) for the

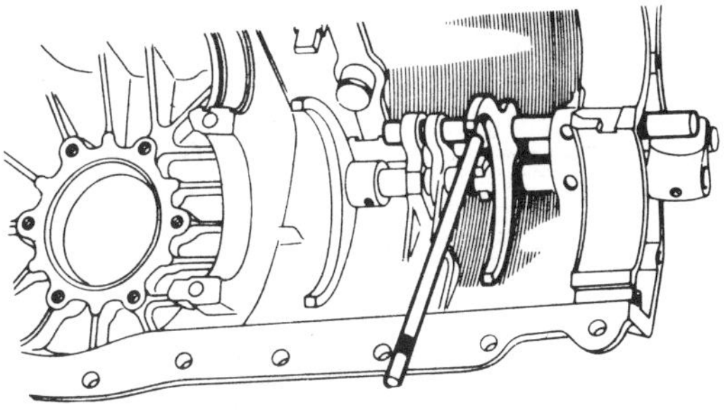

FIG 6:52 Fitting the roll-pin to the 3rd/4th shaft

.434 inch (11 mm) diameter bolts. Press on the differential bearings. Fit the two bearings to the primary shaft by means of a press.

Adjustments:

Before reassembling the gearbox three adjustments have to be carried out:

1 Pinion depth.
2 Adjusting the differential bearings (without play if the original bearings are used again or with pre-load if new bearings are fitted).
3 Adjusting the primary shaft bearings.

Pinion depth:

The final drive pinion is in its correct position when its front face is distance A (see **FIG 6:36**), from the crownwheel centre line. This position is obtained by placing a washer of a suitable thickness between the double taper roller bearing and the shoulder on the secondary shaft.

On the 9 tooth pinion and the 34 tooth crownwheel assemblies two different pinion depths are used. If the pinion has a flat front face (see **FIG 6:37**) and the depth of the pinion D is 1.083 inch (27.5 mm) or if the front face of the pinion has a shoulder on it (see **FIG 6:38**) and the depth of the pinion D is again 1.083 inch (27.5 mm), the pinion depth A is 1.988 inch (50.5 mm). If, however, the pinion has a flat front face and the depth of the pinion is 1.040 inch (26.4 mm) E in **FIG 6:39**, the pinion depth A is 2.032 inch (51.6 mm). **All the 9 x 34 crownwheel and pinion sets supplied as spare parts must be set at a pinion depth of 2.032 inch (51.6 mm).**

On 8 tooth pinion and 34 tooth crownwheel assemblies the pinion depth A must be 9.087 inch (53 mm).

With reference to **FIG 6:40** if a pinion has a number, X, beside the matching reference number it means that the pinion depth is A plus whatever the number stamped on the pinion. For example, if the pinion depth A for the type of pinion shown in **FIG 6:40** was 51.6 mm, then the correct pinion depth for this particular pinion would be 51.6 mm + .20 mm, i.e. 51.8 mm.

To check the pinion depth tool B.Vi.239-01 will have to be used. Fit the secondary shaft to the lefthand half-housing and secure it in place with a number of bolts. Do not tighten the bolts. Temporarily fit the front housing to hold the double taper roller bearing track ring in position then tighten the half-housing securing bolts.

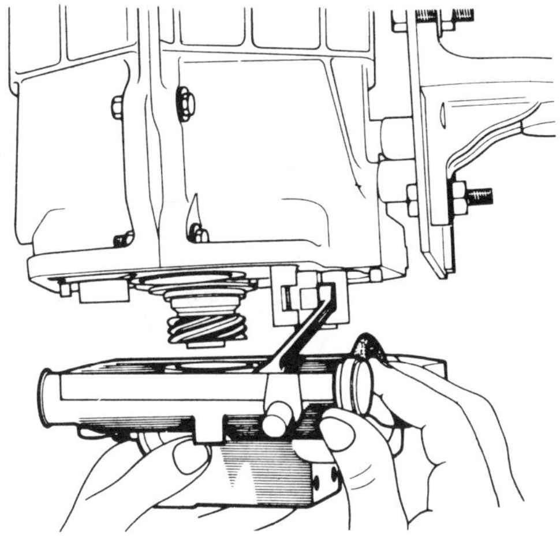

FIG 6:53 Front housing

Fit the mandrel 1 in **FIG 6:41** of tool B.Vi.239-01 and the spacer 2 against the front face of the final drive pinion. Measure, by means of feeler gauges, the dimension X in **FIG 6:42**, between the spacer and mandrel. For 1.988 inch (50.5 mm) pinion depth this distance should be .020 inch (.5 mm) for 2.032 inch (51.6 mm) pinion depth this distance should be .024 inch (.6 mm) and for 2.087 inch (53 mm) pinion depth the distance should be .020 inch (.5 mm). If the dimension measured is greater than it should be replace the adjusting washer, arrowed in **FIG 6:36** with a thicker one and if the measurement is less than that required replace the adjusting washer with a thinner one. Washers are obtainable in thicknesses of .138 inch to .162 inch (3.5 to 4.1 mm) in increments of .002 inch (5/100th mm). When the final adjustment has been obtained, remove gauge B.Vi.239-01, the front housing and the righthand housing. Lift out the secondary shaft assembly and lock the speedometer drive worm.

Adjusting the differential bearings:

If the differential bearings are adjusted by shims C in **FIG 6:43** being placed under the side coverplates proceed as follows:

1 Fit the corresponding bearing track ring to the lefthand half housing **but do not push it fully in.** Fit the adjusting shims removed on dismantling, the paper gasket and the corresponding side coverplate aligning the mark with that on the housing (see **FIG 6:44**). Tighten the side coverplate securing bolts to a torque of 15 lb ft (2 mkg).
2 Fit the differential, together with its bearings, into the lefthand half-housing. Fit the righthand half-housing and secure it to the lefthand half-housing by means of all the bolts. Tighten the bolts in the sequence shown in **FIG 6:45** to a torque of 15 lb ft (2 mkg) for the .276 inch (7 mm) diameter bolts and 20 lb ft (2.8 mkg) for the .315 inch (8 mm) diameter bolts. Fit the bearing track ring to the righthand half-housing **but again do not push it fully in.**
3 If the old bearings are being fitted place the shims

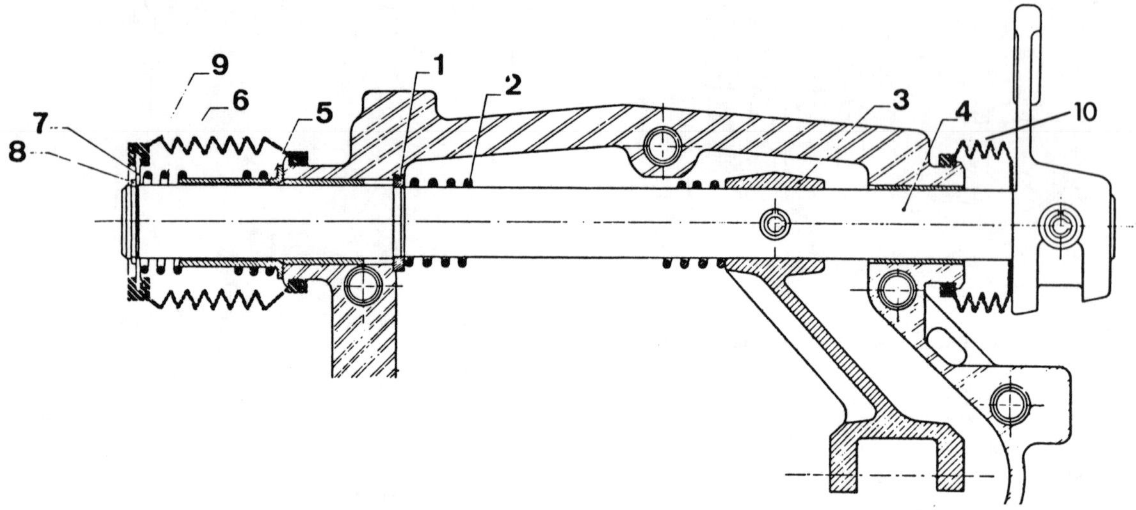

FIG 6:54 Front housing (R.1151 models)

Key to Fig 6:54 1 Washer 2 Spring 3 Shift lever 4 Shaft 5 Cup 6 Spring 7 Washer 8 Circlip 9 Bellows 10 Bellows

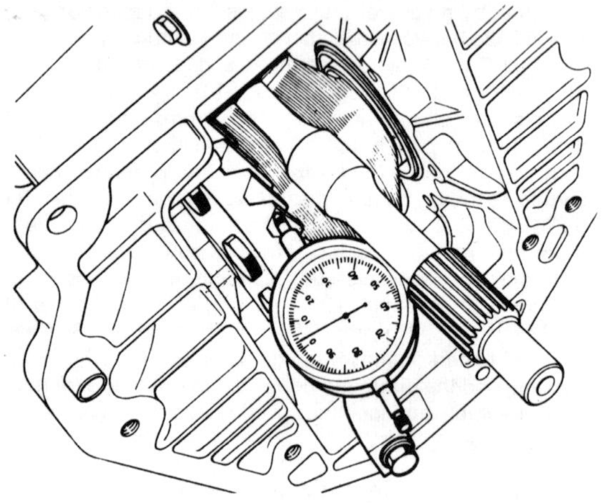

FIG 6:55 Measuring backlash

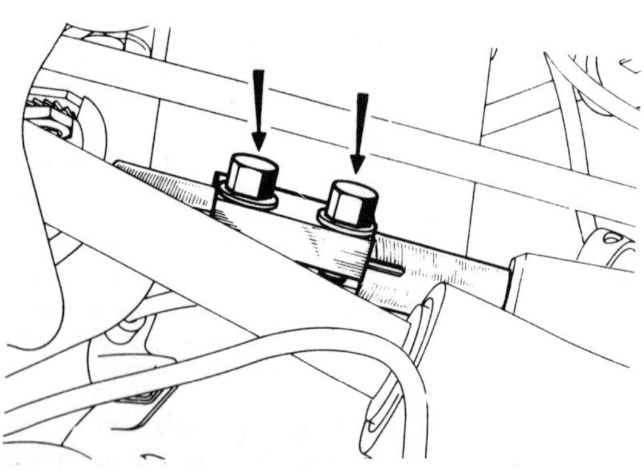

FIG 6:56 Clamp bolts

removed during dismantling under the righthand half-housing track ring, fit the paper gasket and side coverplate again aligning the coverplate mark with that on the housing. Gradually tighten the coverplate securing bolts to bring the track ring near the bearing. If the differential becomes stiff to rotate before the coverplate bolts are fully pulled down, remove shims. If, however, the differential turns too freely after the coverplate bolts are fully tightened down, add shims. The side coverplate bolt tightening torque is 15 lb ft (2 mkg). Shims are available in thicknesses of .004 inch (.1 mm), .008 inch (.2 mm), .010 inch (.25 mm), .020 inch (.5 mm) and .040 inch (1 mm).

4 If new bearings are to be fitted they must be fitted with a certain pre-load. Fit the adjusting shims removed during dismantling under the righthand half-housing track ring, the paper gasket and the side coverplate, again aligning the reference marks. Gradually tighten the side coverplate securing bolts using a spring balance in the manner shown in **FIG 6:46** to check the bearing pre-load. The differential unit should rotate at a load of between 2 to 7 lb ft (.5 to 1 mkg). If the adjustment is not correct increase or reduce the thickness of the shim pack under the righthand half-housing coverplate.

5 When the correct adjustment has been obtained remove the righthand half-housing and the differential Take off the side coverplates and remove the shims **taking great care to remember which pack of shims were fitted to each side.**

If the differential bearings are adjusted by means of screwing nuts in or out the procedure is as follows:

1 Fit the corresponding bearing track ring to each half-housing in such a way that it is slightly below the inner face of the housing, then fit the differential, together with its bearings, into the lefthand half-housing. Fit the righthand half-housing and secure it by means of all its bolts, tightening the bolts in the

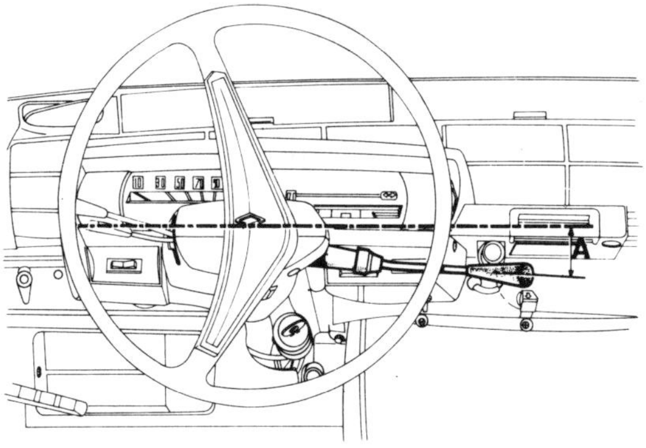

FIG 6 : 57 The column lever vertical position

Key to Fig 6 : 57 **A** Distance

sequence shown in **FIG 6 : 45** to a torque of 15 lb ft (2 mkg) for the .276 inch (7 mm) diameter bolts and 20 lb ft (2.8 mkg) for the .315 inch (8 mm) diameter bolts. Smear the threads of the nuts in the housing with 'Blue-stop N' locking compound. Screw the adjusting nut into each half-housing until it makes contact with the bearing track ring.

2 If the old bearings are being refitted continue to screw in the nuts which push in the bearing track ring taking care to screw in the nut on the differential housing side, 1 in **FIG 6 : 47,** a little more than the one on the other side in order to obtain a crownwheel and pinion backlash which is slightly larger than that required on final assembly. When the differential can be felt to be turning without play, stop screwing in the nuts.

3 If new bearings are to be fitted they must be fitted with a certain pre-load. Again continue to screw in the nuts which push in the bearing track ring taking care to screw in the nut 1 in **FIG 6 : 47** on the differential housing side a little more than the one on the other side. When the differential becomes slightly stiff to rotate, stop screwing in the nuts then using a spring balance in the manner shown in **FIG 6 : 46** check the bearing pre-load. The differential unit should rotate at a load of between 2 to 7 lb (.5 to 1 mkg). If the adjustment is not correct, screw the nut on the differential housing side slightly in or out until the correct adjustment is obtained.

4 Mark the position of the nuts with reference to the housing by means of two punch marks and remove the righthand housing and differential.

Adjusting the primary shaft bearings:

Place the bearing track rings and the adjusting washer removed during dismantling, on the primary shaft. Fit the primary and secondary shaft into the lefthand half-housing. By means of a washer 1 in **FIG 6 : 48,** washers being available in thicknesses of .179 inch (2.5 mm), .089 inch (2.75 mm), .098 inch (3 mm), .108 inch (3.25 mm), .118 inch (3.5 mm) and .128 inch (3.75 mm), obtain an offset A on the primary third speed gearwheel to face C of the secondary shaft third speed gearwheel that is exactly the same offset as that between

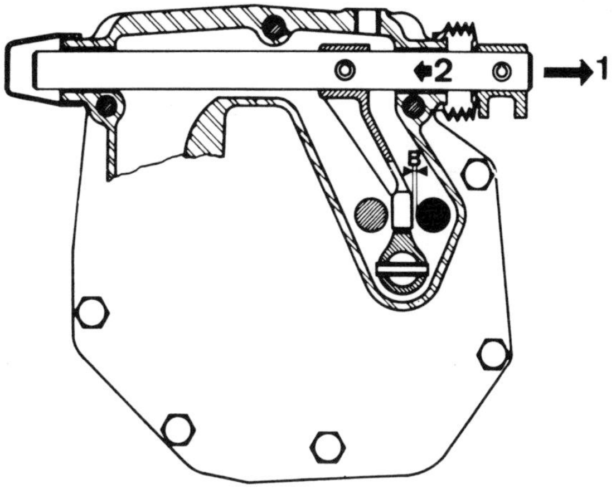

FIG 6 : 58 Shift fork control lever shaft

Key to Fig 6 : 58 1 Direction 2 Direction **B** Clearance

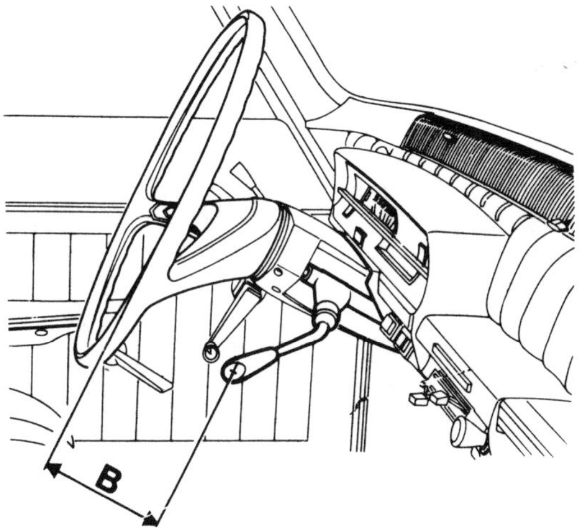

FIG 6 : 59 The column lever horizontal position

Key to Fig 6 : 59 **B** Distance

face B on the primary shaft fourth speed gearwheel to face D on the secondary shaft fourth speed gearwheel. When the correct adjustment has been obtained remove the secondary shaft assembly.

With reference to **FIG 6 : 49** place the righthand half-housing in position without securing it then fit the adjusting shims C removed during dismantling and the spacer 4. Place a rule against the spacer and check the dimension F which should be .008 inch (2 mm). If the adjustment is not correct increase or reduce the thickness of the shim pack C, shims being obtainable in thicknesses of .004 inch (.1 mm), .008 inch (.2 mm), .020 inch (.5 mm) and .040 inch (1 mm). When the adjustment is correct, remove the righthand half-housing and primary shaft. Assemble the clutch shaft to the primary shaft by securing the roll-pin.

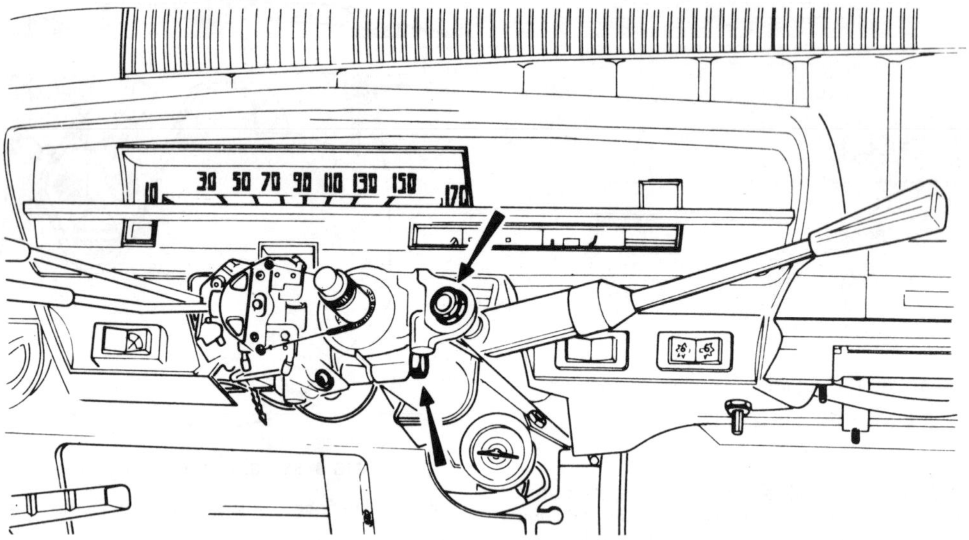

FIG 6:60 Column lever ball joint

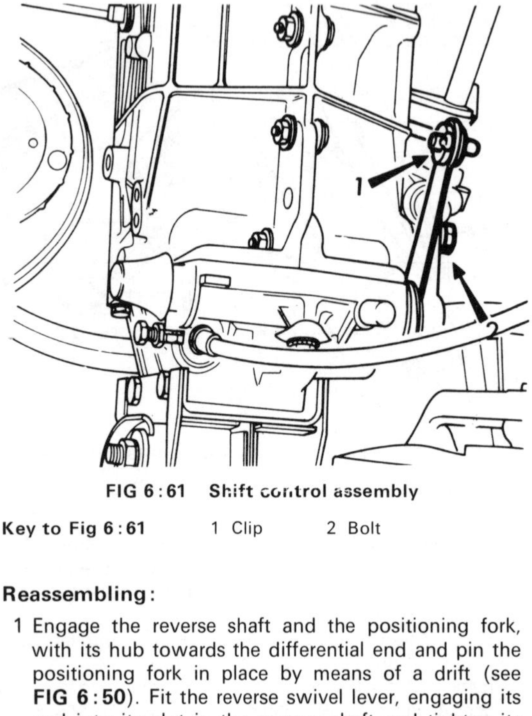

FIG 6:61 Shift control assembly

Key to Fig 6:61 1 Clip 2 Bolt

Reassembling:

1 Engage the reverse shaft and the positioning fork, with its hub towards the differential end and pin the positioning fork in place by means of a drift (see **FIG 6:50**). Fit the reverse swivel lever, engaging its end into its slot in the reverse shaft and tighten its pivot to a torque of 20 lbf ft (2.8 mkg). Fit the 1st/2nd shift shaft locking ball and spring, insert the 1st/2nd shift and fit the 1st/2nd shift fork with the hub towards the control end and pin it in place (see **FIG 6:51**). Fit the locking disc between the shafts. Fit the 3rd/4th shift shaft locking ball and spring. Insert the shaft, fit the shift fork with the hub towards the differential end and pin it in place (see **FIG 6:52**).

2 Fit the locking ball and spring for the reverse shaft into the righthand half-housing. Note there are two springs of different lengths. These are $\frac{3}{4}$ inch (19 mm) and $1\frac{5}{32}$ inch (29 mm) and are not interchangeable. The $\frac{3}{4}$ inch (9 mm) spring is only to be fitted in housings which has no boss on the spring location. Engage the shaft and fit the gearwheel with the hub towards the differential end then fit the friction washer with the bronze face towards the gearwheel. Insert the guide from inside the bore and push the shaft fully in. Fit the gearwheel retaining circlips.

3 Fit the differential, the primary shaft and the secondary shaft assembly to the lefthand half-housing. Smear the half-housing assembly faces with 'Perfect-seal' jointing compound, then fit the righthand half-housing ensuring that the end of the reverse swivel lever is in the slot of the reverse gearwheel shaft. Insert the half-housing securing bolts, but do not tighten them.

4 On R.1150 models fit the internal shift lever, the shaft, the sealing rubber and the lever to the front housing. Pin the external and the internal levers making sure that the split in the roll-pins are square with the centre line of the shaft and that the second pin is fitted inside the first with the split square with the split in the first roll-pin. Screw in the breather and fit the speedometer drive wheel and its guide with an O-ring seal.

5 On R.1151 models, with regard to **FIG 6:54**, fit the protective bellows 10 then place the seat washer 1, the spring 2 and the shaft lever 3 in the housing. Push the shaft 4 through the shift lever ensuring that the slot in the pin is placed square with the shaft. Fit the second pin inside the first with its slot square with the slot in the first. Fit the spring cup 5, spring 6, washer 7, circlip 8 and protective bellows 9. Fit the breather and the speedometer drive wheel and its guide, fitted with an O-ring seal.

6 Fit the primary shaft bearing adjusting shims and the

spacer. Fit the front housing after smearing its gasket with 'Perfect seal' compound, ensuring that the shift lever engages in the slots of the shift fork shafts (see **FIG 6:53**). Secure the front housing in place without tightening down the bolts. Tighten the half-housing securing bolts in the order shown in **FIG 6:45** to a torque of 15 lbf ft (2 mkg) for the .276 inch (7 mm) diameter bolts and 20 lbf ft (2.8 mkg) for the .315 inch (8 mm) diameter bolts. Finally tighten the front housing securing bolts.

7 Carry out the crownwheel and pinion backlash adjustment as layed down at the end of this section. Smear the clutch housing paper gasket with 'Perfect seal' jointing compound. Fit the clutch housing, paying attention not to damage the lip on the oil seal as it passes over the shaft splines. Tighten the housing securing bolts. Note the transmission unit is to be filled with oil after it is refitted to the vehicle.

Adjusting the crownwheel and pinion backlash:

If shims are fitted under the side coverplates proceed as follows. Fit the side coverplate on the differential housing side with its proper gasket and its corresponding shims. Secure it in place and tighten the bolts to a torque of 15 lbf ft (2 mkg). Mount a dial indicator on the housing with its plunger square on one of the crownwheel teeth (see **FIG 6:55**). Fit the side coverplate on the crownwheel side with its paper gasket and corresponding shims and slowly tighten the securing bolts while checking the backlash which should be between .005 and .010 inch (.12 and .25 mm). If the correct backlash has been obtained before the bolts are fully tightened the thickness of the shim pack in the side coverplate is too great. **Remove shims from the crownwheel side coverplate and place them on the differential side.** If the correct backlash has not been obtained after the bolts are tightened down, the thickness of the shim pack in the side coverplate fitted on the crownwheel is too little. **Remove shims from the differential side coverplate and place them on the crownwheel housing side.** When the correct backlash has been obtained, remove the side coverplates, smear the paper gaskets with 'Perfect seal' jointing compound, refit the coverplates and tighten the bolts to 15 lbf ft (2 mkg) torque.

If nuts are fitted against the bearing outer track rings the procedure is as follows. Feel the backlash by hand, if it is clearly too large unscrew the nut 1 in **FIG 6:47** on the differential housing side and screw in nut 2 on the crownwheel side, **by the same amount,** to obtain a smaller backlash before checking it with a dial indicator. Mount the dial indicator on the housing with its plunger square with the flank of one of the crownwheel teeth. Check the backlash which should be between .005 and .010 inch (.12 and .25 mm). If the backlash is excessive, unscrew the nut 1 and screw in the nut 2 **by the same amount.** If there is insufficient backlash, unscrew nut 2 and screw in nut 1 **by the same amount.** When the correct backlash has been obtained, lock the nuts by means of the locking plates.

6:5 Adjusting the gearshift control

On all models except 1968 models engage second gear and check that the steering column shift lever and

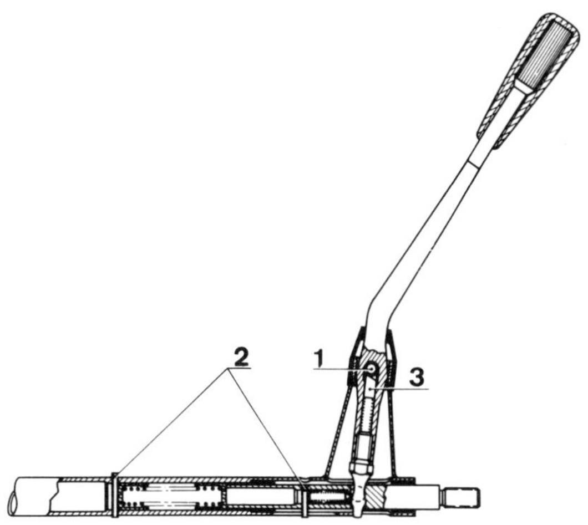

FIG 6:62 Tube lever assembly

Key to Fig 6:62 1 Roll-pin 2 Roll-pins 3 Plunger

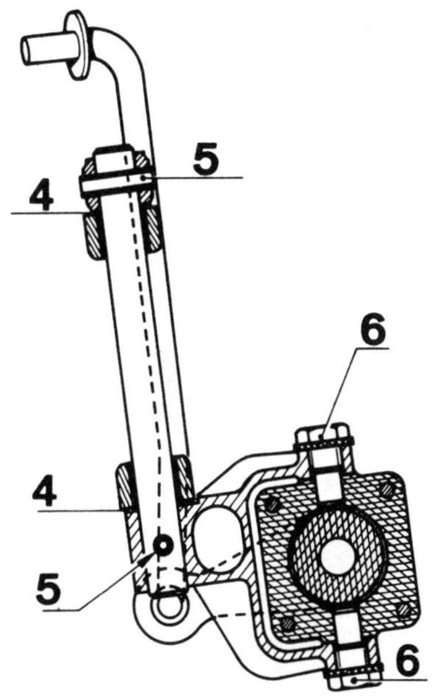

FIG 6:63 Shift control adjusting washers

Key to Fig 6:63 4 Adjusting washer position 5 Roll-pins 6 Bolts

the lever on the transmission case are both in the second gear position. Loosen the two bolts, arrowed in **FIG 6:56,** on the clamp which secures the two parts of the gearshift tube together. Operate the steering column lever a number of times in order to fully free the two parts of the tube. Check that the lever on the transmission case is still in the second gear position and if it is not return it to its

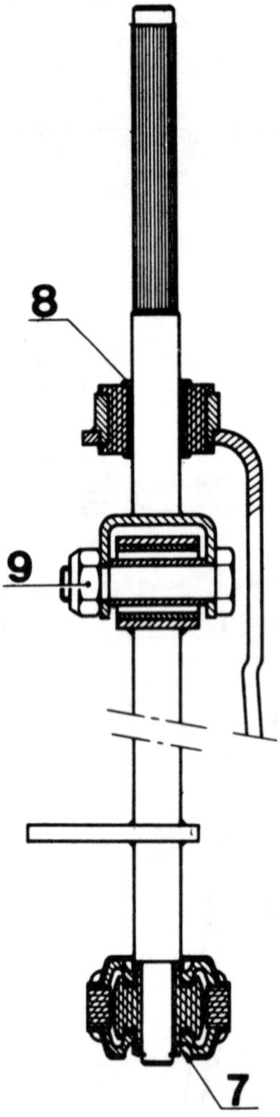

FIG 6:64 **Shaft bearing bushes**

Key to Fig 6:64 7 Adjusting washer position 8 Bushes 9 Bolt

correct position. Move the steering column lever towards the rear in order to bring it to the 1st/2nd gear position against the reverse detent and then move it vertically so that its end is $1\frac{1}{2}$ inch (38 mm) see A in **FIG 6:57**, from a horizontal line passing through the centre of the steering wheel. Get an assistant to hold the lever in this position. Move the shift fork control lever shaft on the transmission case in the direction shown by the arrow 1 in **FIG 6:58,** the lever will come into contact with the reverse shaft. Return the lever in the opposite direction (in the direction shown by arrow 2 in **FIG 6:58**) in order to obtain a clearance of $\frac{3}{64}$ inch (1 mm) B between the lever and the reverse shaft. Hold the shaft in this position. With the lever on the steering column and the lever on the transmission case both in their correct positions, tighten the two bolts, arrowed in **FIG 6:56,** on the gearshift clamp. Check that the gears select and engage correctly.

On 1968 models engage top gear and check that the lever on the transmission case is in top gear. Loosen the two bolts on the clamp which fasten the two halves of the shift control tube together (see **FIG 6:56**). Operate the shift lever on the steering column a number of times in order to free the two halves of the tube and ensure that the lever on the transmission case is still in the top gear position. Place the steering column lever in the vertical position shown in **FIG 6:57** and then move it along the steering column centre line so that its end is a distance $3\frac{23}{32}$ inch (94 mm) B in **FIG 6:59**, from the top edge of the steering wheel. Holding the lever in this position and with the lever on the transmission case in top gear position, tighten the two bolts on the clamp. Check that the gear selects and engages correctly.

6:6 Removing, overhauling and refitting the gearshift control

Removal:

Disconnect the battery, remove the steering wheel embellisher and steering wheel. Take off the horn and lighting switch housing, mark the position of the horn and lighting switch bracket with reference to the steering column and remove the bracket securing bolt and the locknut on the gearshift lever ball joint, both of which are arrowed in **FIG 6:60.** Loosen and unscrew the two bolts, arrowed in **FIG 6:56,** on the clamp which secures the two halves of the gearshift tube together then pull back the horn and lighting switch bracket to free the shift lever and swing the shift lever round the centre of the steering column tube. Remove the tube lever assembly by freeeing it at the clamp, the clip which secures the link to the lever 1 in **FIG 6:61** and the two bolts 2 which secure the shift control to the housing. Remove the shift control assembly.

Overhauling:

The tube lever assembly cannot be repaired and if damaged must be replaced by a new assembly. The roll-pins and the lever rubber cover, however, can be replaced. When replacing the roll-pins with regard to **FIG 6:62** ensure that the slit in the pin 1 is parallel with the shift lever centre line and that the slits in the roll-pins 2 are parallel with the steering column centre line. Check that the inclined plane on the plunger 3 is correctly positioned.

The shift control at the transmission case end can be dismantled. On reassembling fit an adjusting washer 4 in **FIG 6:63** so that there is no end play of the shaft, washers being obtainable in thicknesses of .004 inch (1 mm), .006 inch (.15 mm) and .008 inch (.2 mm). Smear the washers with SI.33 grease. Correctly position the roll-pins 5 so that their slits are square with the pivot pin longitudinal centre line and tighten the bolts 6 to a torque of 10 lbf ft (1.5 mkg). With reference to **FIG 6:64** fit an adjusting washer at point 7 so that there is no end play in the hinge. Washers are available in .004 inch (.1 mm) and .008 inch (.2 mm) thicknesses, again smear the washers with SI.33 grease. Do not grease the bearing bushes 8 and do not tighten the pivot bolt 9 until the shaft control assembly is refitted.

Refitting:

Carry out the removal instructions in reverse, tightening the ball joint until it moves in its housing without play, then tighten the locknut Tighten the nut 9 in **FIG 6:64** to a torque of 20 lbf ft (2.5 mkg). Adjust the shift control as layed out in **Section 6:5.**

6:7 Fault diagnosis

(a) Jumping out of gear

1 Broken locking spring behind selector rod locating ball
2 Excessively worn groove in selector rod
3 Worn synchromesh coupling dogs
4 Fork to selector rod securing pin loose

(b) Noisy transmission

1 Insufficient oil
2 Excessive end float of secondary shaft
3 Incorrect end float of primary shaft
4 Incorrect loading on differential bearings
5 Incorrect backlash
6 Worn or damaged gear teeth
7 Worn or damaged bearing(s)
8 Incorrect grade of oil

(c) Difficulty in engaging gear

1 Incorrect clutch cable adjustment
2 Defective clutch
3 Worn synchromesh rings
4 Damaged synchromesh hubs
5 Bent selector rod
6 Bent selector fork
7 Incorrect grade of oil

(d) Oil leaks

1 Damaged joint washers
2 Warped half-housings
3 Worn or damaged oil seals
4 Faulty joint face on one of the castings

CHAPTER 7

THE SUSPENSION AND HUBS

7:1 Description

The front wheels are independently suspended and the loading is absorbed by torsion bars. Two types of torsion bar are in use, the length of them both is $40\frac{3}{4}$ inch (1.035 m) the difference being that the diameter of one is .685 inch (174 mm), whereas the other is .716 inch (18.2 mm). The small diameter bar is used on vehicles that will be used in countries that have good roads whereas the larger diameter types are used when poor road conditions are to be expected. The torsion bar is splined at each end, 24 splines being used at the suspension arm end and 23 splines being employed at the anchor casing end. Double acting hydraulic dampers and override pads are fitted, the dampers dampening out any undue spring oscillation. The front suspension assembly is shown in **FIG 7:1**.

The rear suspension, shown in **FIG 7:2**, again uses torsion bars their length being $40\frac{9}{32}$ inch (1.023 m), slightly shorter than those used on the front suspension. The diameter is .850 inch (21.6 mm) except on 1968 models when the bars are of a slightly larger diameter of .886 inch (22.5 mm). The torsion bars are again splined at each of their ends, there being 30 splines at the suspension arm end and 28 splines at the anchor casing end. Again double-acting dampers and override pads are fitted.

The righthand and lefthand bars differ in the direction in which the pre-stressing operation is carried out during manufacture and for this reason each bar has an identification mark to determine whether it is a righthand or lefthand torsion bar. On early models the righthand bar had a red dab whereas the lefthand one had a dab of yellow paint. On current models righthand bars are either stamped with the letter D or have three indentations on the chamfer which protects the bar centre drilling whereas lefthand torsion bars are stamped with the letter G or contain two indentations on the chamfer which protects the bar centre drilling.

In order to bring the underbody height as near as possible to the correct figure and to evenly distribute the wheel loading on the wheels of any given axle, reference marks are made on the torsion bars and on the various suspension components. The marks are in the form of a drill mark that is made at each end of the torsion bar on the centre line of one of the splines crests (see **FIG 7:3**) and on the centre line of one of the spline bottoms on the anchor casings and the front or rear suspension arms (see **FIG 7:4**). On the first vehicles made, the casing and suspension arm had two reference marks on them, a drill point mark and an asterisk. On these models only the drill

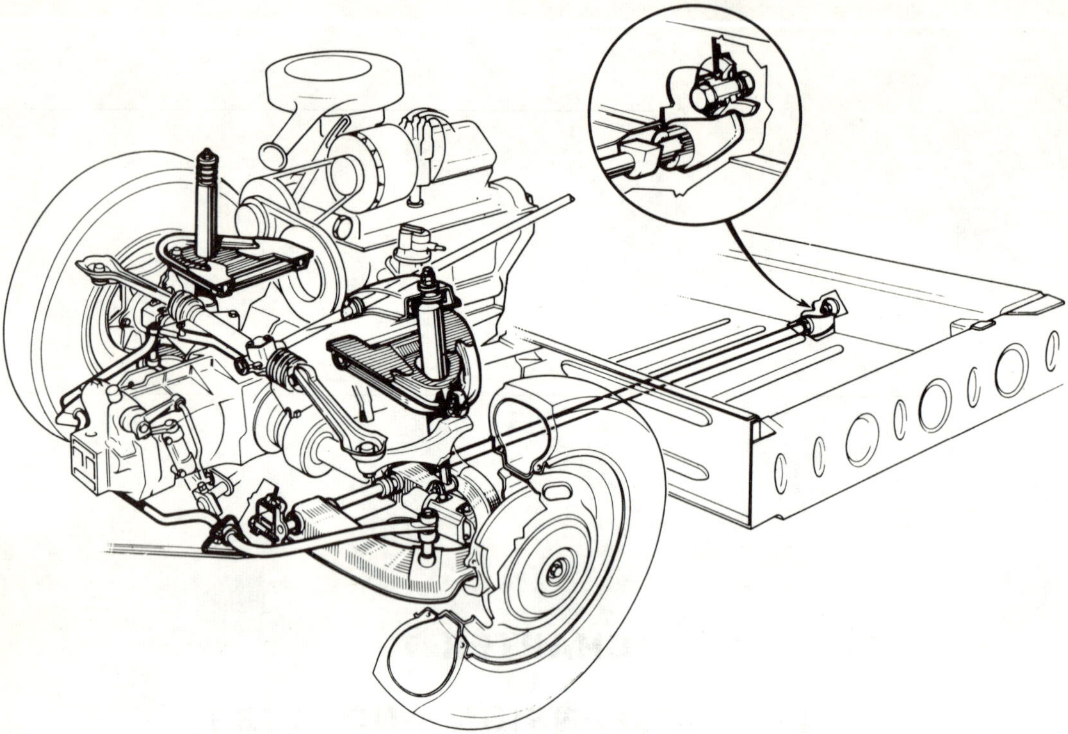

FIG 7:1 The front suspension

FIG 7:2 The rear suspension

point mark is to be used as a reference. On good road vehicles the front and rear torsion bar reference marks must be aligned with the reference marks on the anchor casings and on the suspension arms. On poor road vehicles the front torsion bar reference mark must be offset five differential splines with reference to the marks on the front anchor casing and on the front suspension arm and the rear torsion bar reference mark must be offset six differential splines with reference to the marks on the rear anchor casings and rear suspension arms. **If a torsion bar is offset by a certain number of differential splines the other bar must be offset by the same number so that the two bars operate under the same torsional conditions.**

Torsion bar adjustment:

The underbody height is to be measured with the vehicle empty but with its fuel tank full and all other fluids topped up. Check the tyre pressures are correct and ensure the vehicle is on a horizontal surface. The dimensions are to be measured between the floor and sidemembers at the wheel centres.

Underbody height	*Front*
$7\frac{7}{8}$ inch (200 mm)	Good road bar with 145 x 355 radial tyres
$8\frac{7}{8}$ inch (225 mm)	Poor road bar with 155 x 14 radial tyres
$8\frac{11}{16}$ inch (220 mm)	Good road bar with 155 x 14 conventional tyres Poor road bar with 145 x 14 radial tyres
$7\frac{11}{16}$ inch (195 mm)	R.1151 models
	Rear
$10\frac{1}{4}$ inch(260 mm)	Good road bar with 145 x 355 radial tyres
12 inch (305 mm)	Poor road bar with 155 x 14 radial tyres
$10\frac{5}{8}$ inch (270 mm)	Good road bar with 155 x 14 conventional tyres
$11\frac{13}{16}$ inch (300 mm)	Poor road bar with 145 x 14 radial tyres
$11\frac{1}{4}$ inch (285 mm)	Poor road bar with 155 x 14 radial tyres on vehicles after 170400
$10\frac{1}{16}$ inch (255 mm)	R.1151 models

To increase the height of the front of the vehicle rotate the nut in **FIG 7:5** towards the inside of the vehicle. After adjustment, tighten the bolt. To increase the height of the rear of the vehicle with regard to **FIG 7:6** turn the head of the bolt 1 which operates the cam 2 on the nearside rear torsion bar towards the front of the vehicle and on the offside rear bar towards the rear of the vehicle (i.e. on both sides in an anticlockwise direction). After adjusting, tighten the Nylstop nut on the end of the bolt 1.

Should adjustment by this method not bring the underbody height to the correct setting moving a front torsion bar through one differential spline will alter the height at the front on good road vehicles $\frac{1}{8}$ inch (3 mm) and on poor road vehicles $\frac{5}{32}$ inch (4 mm). Moving a good or poor road rear torsion bar through one differential spline will alter the height at the rear by $\frac{15}{64}$ inch (6 mm).

It is possible however, even if the underbody height is correct, for the torsion in the bars to be out of balance and therefore for different reactions to apply on the two wheels of any given axle assembly, giving the vehicle defective road holding. It is therefore essential that the wheel loadings be checked after adjustment of underbody height has been carried out to any torsion bar. Checking the wheel loadings requires the use of six special tools simultaneously and for this reason will have to be carried out by an authorized Renault dealer.

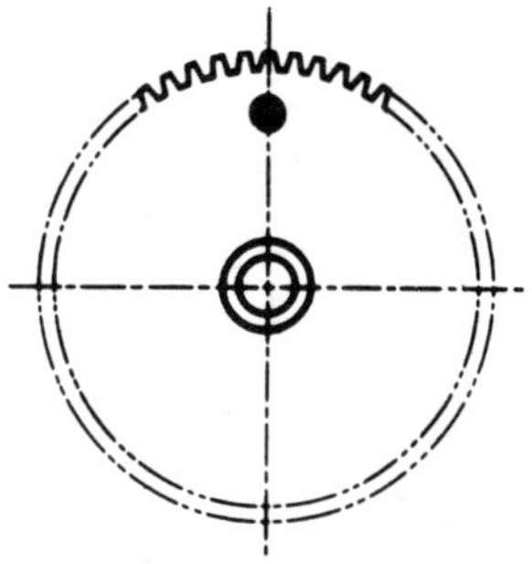

FIG 7:3 Torsion bar reference marks

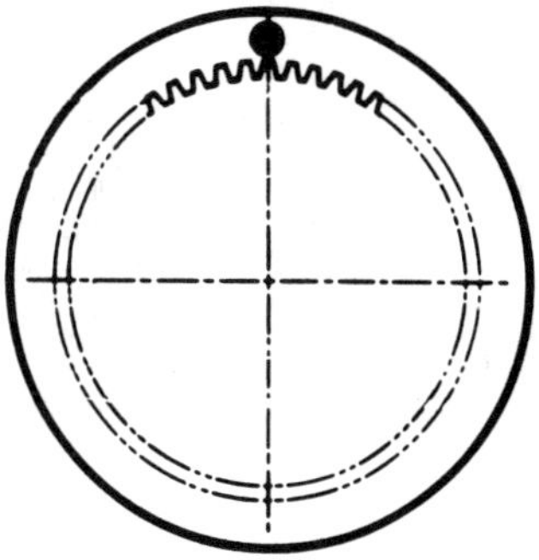

FIG 7:4 Anchor casing reference marks

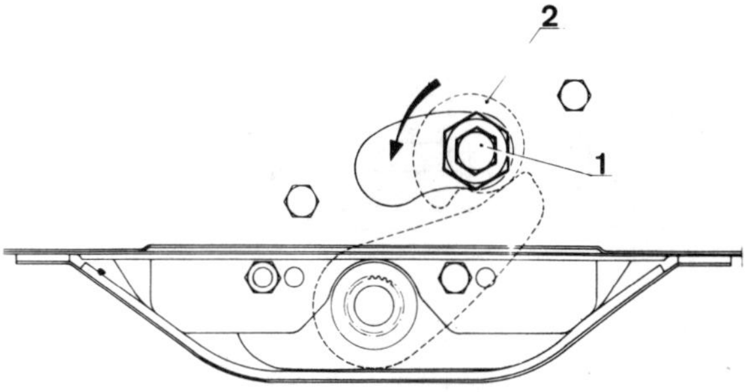

FIG 7:5 Front torsion bar adjustment

Key to Fig 7:5 1 Nut 2 Cam

7:2 Front suspension

Dampers:

To remove the front dampers simply undo the upper and lower damper securing nuts. This must never be carried out when the wheels are hanging free. Refit the damper by carrying out the removal instructions in reverse after smearing the lower pivot point with 'Hatmo 806.661' grease. If Allinquant dampers are fitted in place of De Carbon ones a spacer $\frac{23}{64}$ inch (9 mm) long and washer $\frac{5}{64}$ inch (2 mm) thick, 2 and 3 in **FIG 7:7**, must be placed on the side of the securing point nearest the rear of the vehicle. If a pair of Alliquant dampers are replaced by De Carbon dampers the spacer and washer must be removed. The

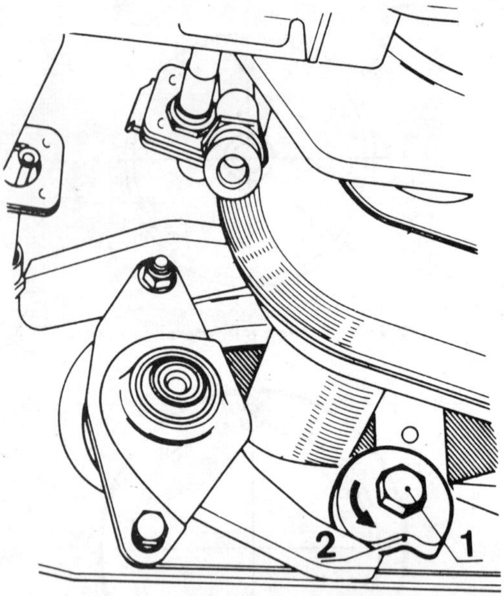

FIG 7:6 Rear torsion bar adjustment

Key to Fig 7:6 1 Nut 2 Cam

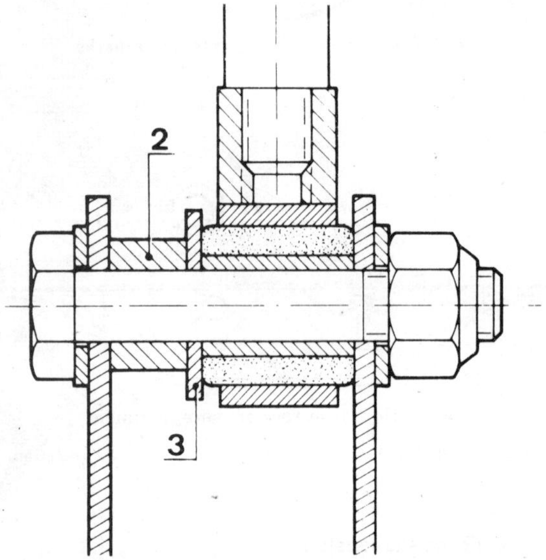

7:7 Modifications to dampers

Key to Fig 7:7 2 Spacer 3 Washer

new Alliquant dampers are strengthened at their lower fastening points and as a result the washer and spacer are removed from their fitting.

Anti-roll bar:

To remove the bar with regard to **FIG 7:8** disconnect the anti-roll bar from the lower suspension arm, separate the bearing by taking out the two adjusting bolts 1 and remove the bearing by taking out the three securing bolts 2. Take off the offside front wheel and undo the two nuts retaining the transmission case to its front mounting bracket. Using a jack, lift the transmission case until it makes contact with the steering crossmember and push out the anti-roll bar towards the right, its end will have to pass over the transmission shaft. Refit the unit by carrying out the removing operations in reverse.

To replace a front anti-roll bar silentbloc bush separate the two bearing half caps and take out the bush. Fit a new one, with the slot in line with the joint between the two bearing half clamps.

Torsion bar:

Remove the bar by jacking up the side concerned and placing it on an axle stand so that the road wheel is not touching the ground. Remove the bars protective cap then with reference to **FIG 7:5** loosen the nut 1 from inside the vehicle and by means of a spanner return the cam 2 to zero by turning it towards the outside of the vehicle. Fit tool Sus.234 into the torsion bar anchor bush and taking the load of the torsion bar on tool Sus.234 unscrew the two securing bolts from inside the vehicle under the floor. Before freeing the torsion bar from the casing, mark the top of the spline opposite the position marking on the anchor casing (see **FIG 7:9**) then remove the casing. Push the bearing inwards without freeing it from the suspension arm and again mark the bar with reference to the suspension arm as shown in **FIG 7:10**.

Refit the bar by first smearing the splines with 'Hatmo 806.661' grease then fit the bar in the suspension arm aligning the reference marks made during dismantling. If a new torsion bar is to be fitted read the notes relating to the torsion bar reference marks in **Section 7:1**. Fit the anchor casing to the bar again aligning the reference marks made during dismantling and with regard to **FIG 7:11** insert the stud 1 into its location 2. Fit a spring washer and nut without tightening it. Place tool Sus.234

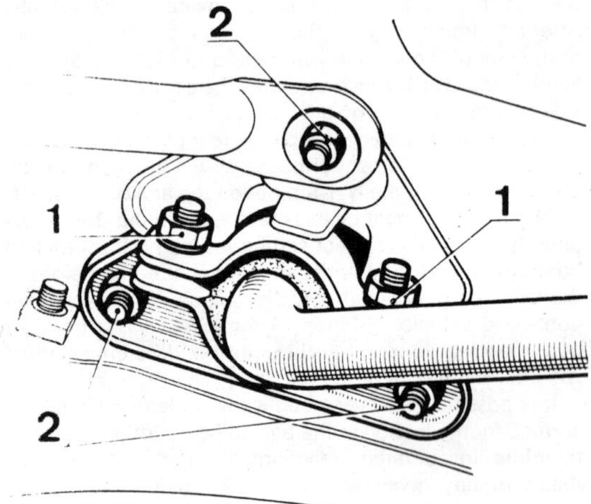

FIG 7:8 Front anti-roll bar

Key to Fig 7:8 1 Adjusting bolts 2 Securing bolts

in the torsion bar anchor bush and apply tension to the bar, in order to secure the anchor casing to the cross-member with the two bolts inside the vehicle and the one bolt underneath the floor. Lower the vehicle onto its wheel and carry out torsion bar adjustment as layed out in **Section 7:1**.

7:3 Rear suspension

Anti-roll bar:

To renew the anti-roll bar silentbloc bushes, with reference to **FIG 7:12** take out the bolt 2 and the two bolts 1. Free and remove the bush and fit the new one, with its slit in line with the bearing joint. Secure the bush in place.

To remove the anti-roll bar remove the bolt 2 and bolts 1 (see **FIG 7:12**) securing one end of the bar in a silentbloc bush and repeat this sequence on the other end of the bar. Disconnect the brake limiting valve at its nut and the anti-roll bar at its end. Remove the bar. Refit the bar by carrying out the removing operations in reverse. On completion connect and adjust the brake pressure limiting valve (see **Chapter 10**).

Dampers:

To remove a damper fitted to the rear, disconnect the upper part of the damper from inside the vehicle, place the side concerned on an axle stand, remove the wheel and remove the damper lower securing point. Refit by reversing the removal sequence.

If a pair of Allinquant dampers are fitted in place of a pair of De Carbon dampers the spacer fitted between the damper and suspension member which will be $\frac{19}{32}$ inch (15 mm) long must be replaced with one that is 1 $\frac{1}{32}$ inch (26 mm) long. On the other hand if a pair of De Carbon dampers are fitted in place of a pair of Allinquant ones the spacer, whose width will now be 1 $\frac{1}{32}$ inch (26 mm), must be replaced by one which is $\frac{19}{32}$ inch (15 mm) in width.

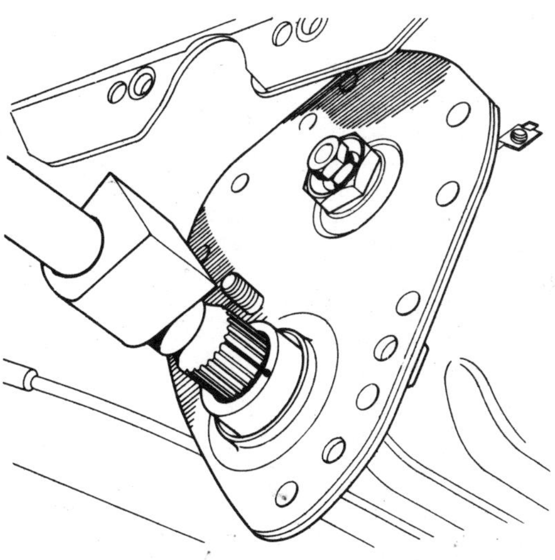

FIG 7:9 Torsion bar alignment

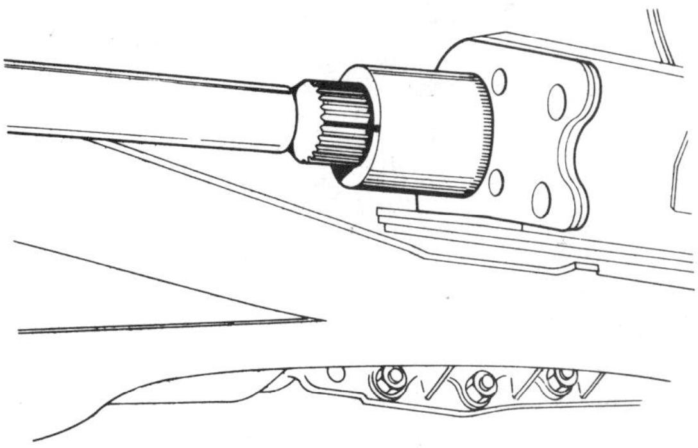

FIG 7:10 Suspension arm reference marks

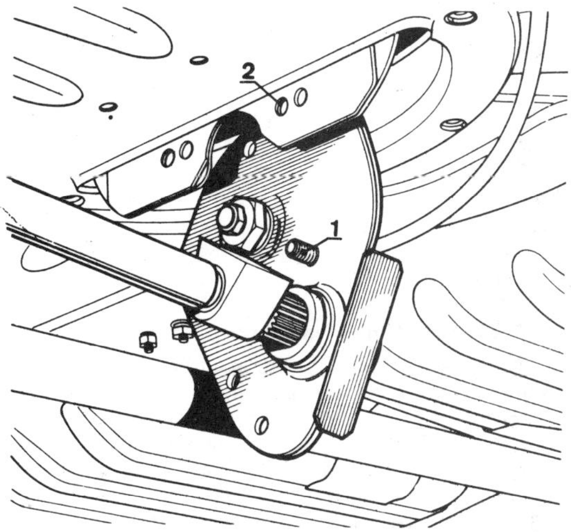

FIG 7:11 Anchor casing stud

Key to Fig 7:11 1 Stud 2 Hole

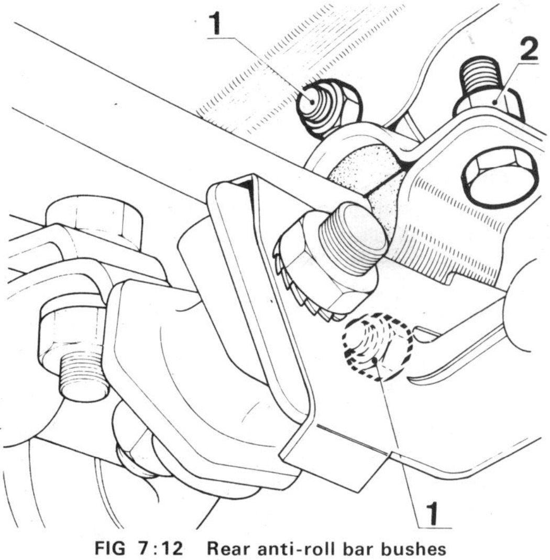

FIG 7:12 Rear anti-roll bar bushes

Key to Fig 7:12 1 Bolts 2 Bolt

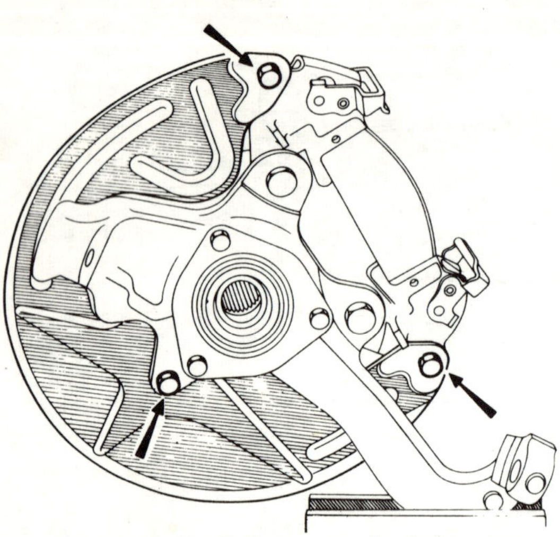

FIG 7:13 Deflector securing bolts

Torsion bar:

The operation of removing rear torsion bars can only be done when the two suspension arms are disconnected from their securing bolts, and for this reason is dealt with in **Chapter 8**.

7:4 Front hub/disc assembly

To remove a front hub/disc assembly remove the road wheel, the hub nut and washer, the brake caliper **without disconnecting its hose**, the steel sheet deflector and the brake caliper bracket then using a suitable hub extractor draw off the assembly. Separate the hub from the disc by unscrewing the three assembly securing bolts after marking the disc with reference to its position on the hub.

Reassemble the hub to the disc aligning the position marks made during dismantling and tighten the three securing bolts to a torque of 35 lb ft (6 M.da N). Fit the hub assembly onto the stub axle and tighten up the hub nut to 90 lb ft (12 M.da N). Fit the brake caliper bracket without omitting the adjusting shims and the sheet steel deflector. Secure the brake caliper in position and refit the road wheel.

Front bearings:

To remove the outer bearing take off the hub/disc assembly as detailed previously and using a suitable puller extract the bearing. Press the new bearing into place using a tube $1\frac{7}{16}$ inch (36 mm) in diameter. Refit the hub by following the instructions layed out in the previous sub-section.

To extract the inner bearing remove the stub axle carrier (see **Chapter 8**) then gripping the carrier in a vice, **fitted with safety jaws**, remove the three deflector securing bolts arrowed in **FIG 7:13**. Unscrew the two bolts securing the caliper bracket and remove the bracket together with its adjusting shims. Remove the rear bearing coverplate and using a press and a ring with a diameter of $3\frac{15}{32}$ inch (88 mm), press out the bearing. Press in the new bearing with the lip on the seal towards the outside then push it in on the press by means of a tube with an outside diameter of $2\frac{11}{16}$ inch (68 mm). Refit the rear bearing coverplate, the caliper bracket with its adjusting shims and the deflector. Refit the stub axle carrier by following the procedure layed down in **Chapter 8**.

7:5 Rear hub/drum assembly

To remove a hub/drum assembly jack up the appropriate side and place it in a safety stand. Remove the road wheel and grease cap. Remove the pin securing the hub nut and unscrew the locknut and the hub nut. Take off the hub washer and using a suitable hub extractor withdraw the hub/drum assembly. To refit the assembly carry out the removing sequence in reverse ensuring that the seal is in position, that the bearings are in good condition and that the bearings and the space between them contain sufficient grease. After fitting the hub, tighten the hub nut to a torque of 25 lb ft (3 M.da N) while rotating the drum, then loosen it by a quarter of a turn. Secure tool T.Av.235 to the hub, gently tighten the screw on the tool to take up any end play then remove the tool. Using a dial gauge check the bearing end play which should be between .002 and .004 inch (0.06 and 0.09 mm). If necessary screw the nut in or out to obtain the adjustment. Finally fit the sheet steel locking plate, splitpin the nut and three-quarter fill the hub plug with grease. Adjust the brakes (see **Chapter 10**) and refit the road wheel.

To replace the rear bearings, remove the drum which will automatically give access to the front bearing. To extract the rear bearing place the half shells of tool Rou.370 around the bearing and hold them together with a retaining ring. Place a large soft metal washer on the stub axle, to protect it, and using tool MOT.490 pull off the bearing.

If a new thrust washer (placed behind the bearing) is to be fitted, heat the washer before fitting it to the shaft as it is a tolerance fit.

7:6 Fault diagnosis

(a) Wheel wobble

1 Incorrect tracking
2 Worn hub bearing(s)
3 Defective suspension arm(s)
4 Worn suspension swivel joints
5 Loose wheel fittings

(b) 'Bottoming' of suspension

1 Incorrect torsion bar
2 Incorrect torsion bar setting
3 Torsion bar weak
4 Low tyre pressures
5 Rebound rubbers missing

(c) Heavy steering

1 Low tyre pressures
2 Incorrect steering geometry
3 Suspension swivel joints seized

(d) Excessive tyre wear

1 Incorrect tracking
2 Suspension geometry incorrect
3 Incorrect wheel loadings

(e) Excessive rolling

1 Check 3 in (a); 2 and 3 in (b) and 2 and 3 in (d)
2 Anti-roll bar broken or fixings loose

CHAPTER 8

THE FRONT AND REAR AXLES

8:1 Description

The front axle layout is shown in **FIG 8:1**. The stub axle is held to the upper and lower suspension arms by ball joints, and the suspension arms hinge on flexibloc and fluidbloc bushes. The kingpin inclination is 13 deg., the castor angle is set at 2 deg. 40 minutes $\pm$ 1 deg. whereas the camber angle is 45 minutes. The wheels are also set an $\frac{1}{8}$ inch (3 mm) in to one another as when the vehicle is moving along the road the wheels tend to be forced out slightly, this adjustment is known as toe-in. The kingpin inclination, castor and camber angles and toe-in can only be checked using expensive equipment and for this reason the checking of these angles will have to be undertaken by a service station.

The rear axle consists of two suspension arms suspended by means of two parallel torsion bars, this arrangement allowing each rear wheel to be independent of the other. An anti-roll bar is fitted between the two arms and rear suspension arm travel is limited by rubber pads situated on the dampers. If abnormal tyre wear is noted the rear axle specifications can be checked using a set of equipment that is available at any Renault Main Dealer. The rear wheel toe-in is set at $\frac{5}{32}$ inch (4 mm) and this can be checked using the same tool that is used to check the front axle toe-in.

8:2 Replacing an upper and lower front suspension arm

Upper front suspension arm:

To remove an upper suspension arm jack up the vehicle, place the side concerned on a safety stand and remove the road wheel. Remove the damper, unscrew the upper suspension ball joint nut and using tool T.Av.50-1 extract the ball joint. Unscrew the two suspension arm securing nuts, arrowed in **FIG 8:2** and lift away the suspension arm.

The alignment of the arm can be checked using tool T.Av.418. Examine the fluidbloc bushes and if they are damaged, replace the entire suspension arm.

Fit the suspension arm in place, smear the securing bolts with 'Molykote BR.2 grease' and secure the arm in place by tightening the arm securing bolts to a torque of 30 lb ft (4.2M.da N). Fit the upper ball joint and tighten the ball joint nut to 25 lb ft (3 M.da N) torque. Refit the damper. Have a garage check the castor angle and toe-in.

Lower front suspension arm:

To remove a lower front suspension arm, jack up the vehicle, place the side concerned on an axle stand and remove the road wheel. Unscrew the hub nut and washer

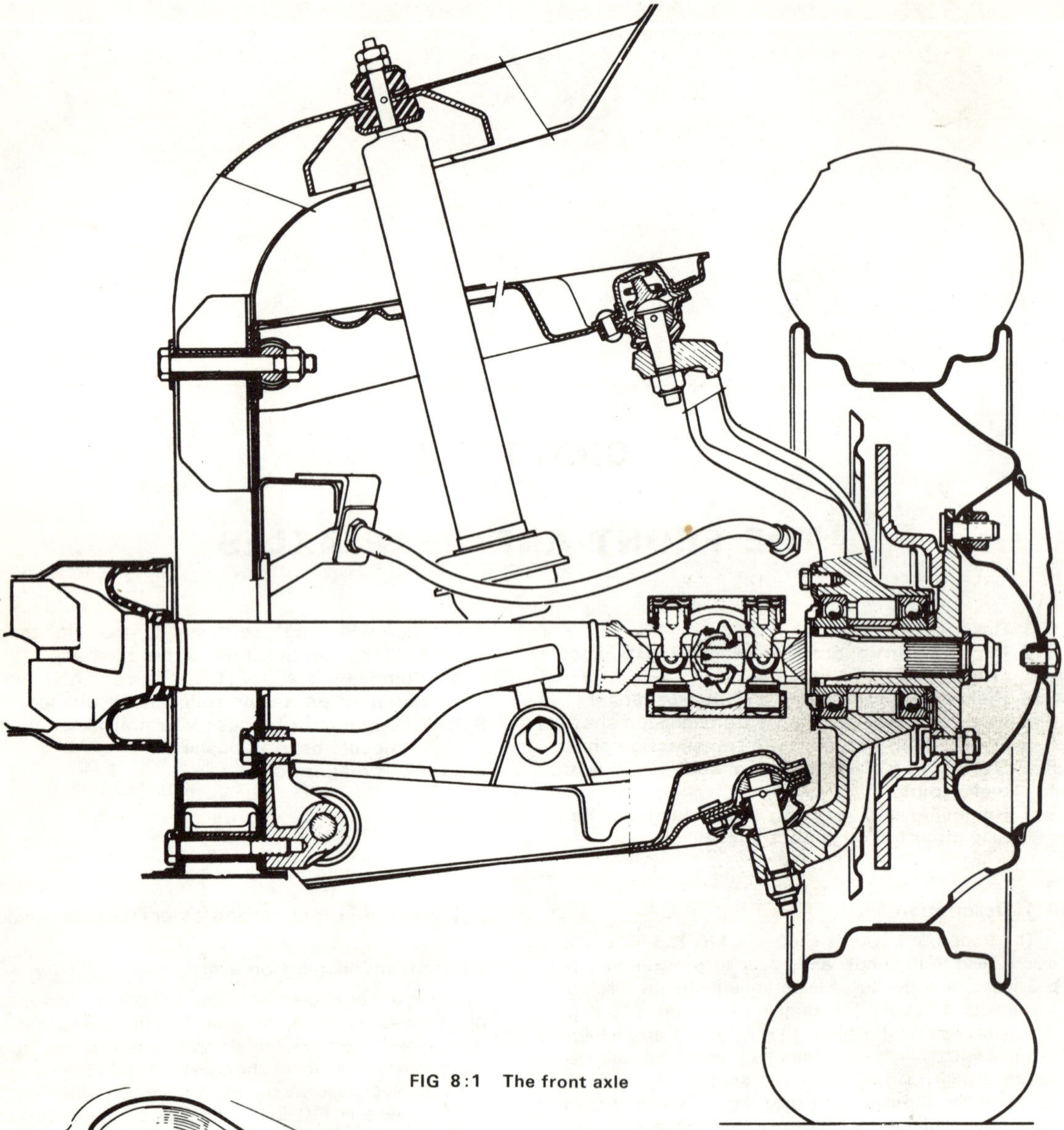

FIG 8:1 The front axle

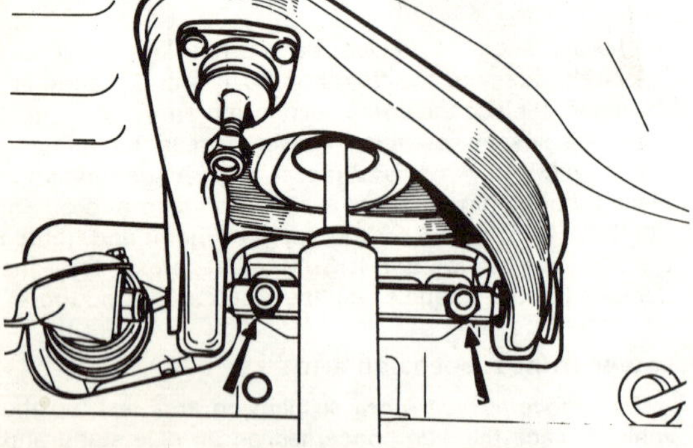

FIG 8:2 Upper front suspension arm securing nuts

and remove the brake caliper **without disconnecting its hose**. Using a small diameter drift push through the pins on the Bendix Weiss joint (see **FIG 6:13, without removing them entirely**. Fit the tool T.Av.205 to the transmission shaft (see **FIG 8:3**) and retaining tool T.Av.247 for those Bendix Weiss joints with metal casings, or the tool which is supplied with the new transmission shaft for Bendix Weiss joints with rubber bellows. **When dismantling never allow the joint to pass through a greater angle than 45 deg.** Return the underbody height adjusting cam to zero and take off the anchor casing protective cap (see **Chapter 7**). Insert tool Sus.234 into the torsion bar anchor bush, mark the position of the torsion bar with reference to the suspension arm and the anchor casing and then remove the torsion bar as detailed in **Chapter 7**. Remove the damper pivot pin at its lower end and unscrew the anti-roll bar bolt. Disconnect the lower ball joint using tool T.Av.237-01 and unscrew the bolts which secure the lower suspension arm. Free the arm from the chassis using a hub extractor pull out the transmission shaft without removing it fully, then lift the hub disc assembly and free the lower suspension arm from the stub axle carrier.

A lower front suspension arm can be checked using tool T.Av.417. If the suspension arm bearings are damaged replace the entire suspension arm.

To refit the arm place the suspension arm ball joint in the carrier and position the other end against the chassis fitting any castor angle shims, that were removed during dismantling, under the rear bearing. Smear the bolts with 'Molykote 806.377' grease and tighten them to a torque of 30 lb ft (4.2 M.da N). Fit the transmission shaft by means of tool T.Av.236 followed by B.V1.31 and fit the Weiss joint pin in position. Refit the damper pivot pin and the anti-roll bar bolt ensuring that the cups are fitted the right way round. Fit tool Rou.436 to the hub and tighten the nut to 30 lb ft (4.2 M.da N) torque. Fit the torsion bar in position following the reference marks (see **Chapter 7**), then fit the brake caliper. Have the castor angle, toe-in, underbody height and wheel load distribution checked.

From vehicle 9380 onwards the between centre dimension of the lower suspension arm front hinge point bearing was increased by $\frac{3}{16}$ inch (4 mm). In cases where old suspension arms are fitted to new bodywork components with regard to **FIG 8:4** elongate hole 'A', in a downwards direction, by $\frac{3}{16}$ inch (4 mm) and make a plate following the directions given in **FIG 8:5** out of .060

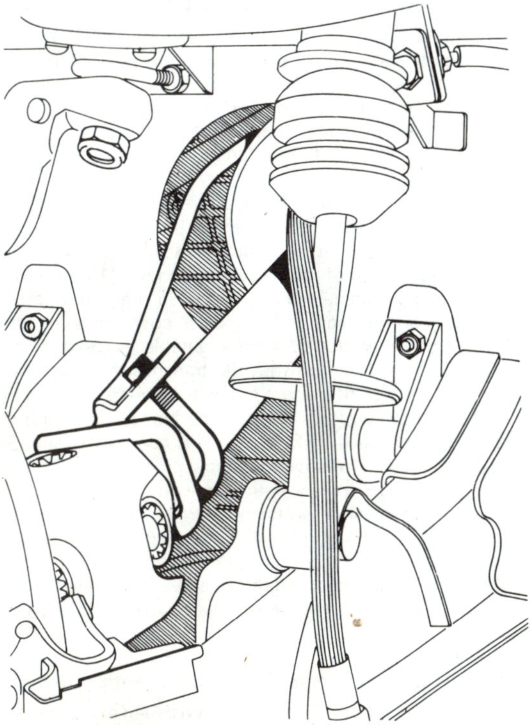

FIG 8:3 Using tool T.Av.205

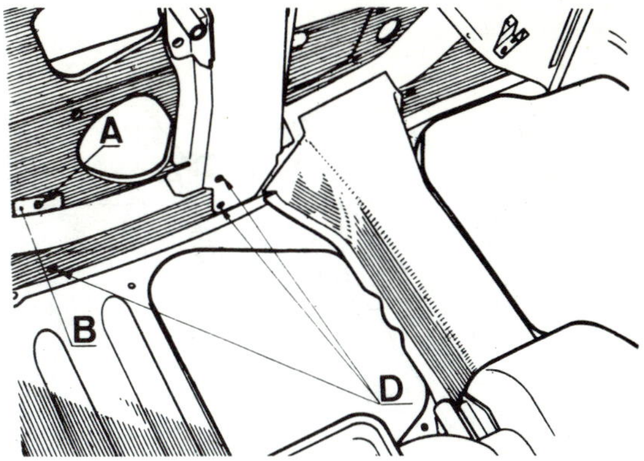

FIG 8:4 Modifying bodywork

Key to Fig 8:4 **A** Hole **B** Plate **D** Hole

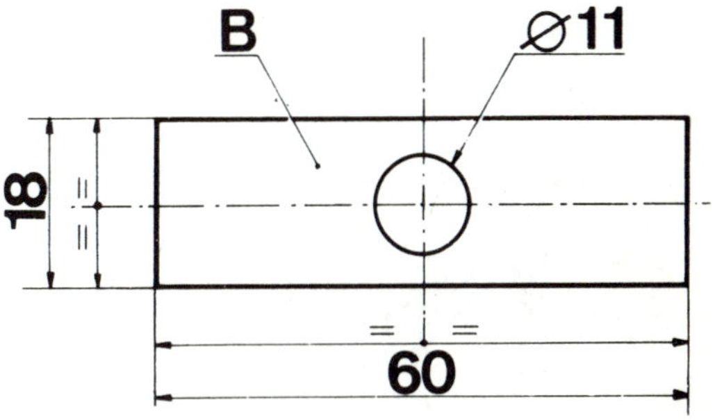

FIG 8:5 Modification plate

Key to Fig 8:5 **B** Plate 11 11 mm ($\frac{7}{16}$ inch) 18 18 mm ($\frac{45}{64}$ inch) 60 60 mm ($\frac{3}{8}$ inch)

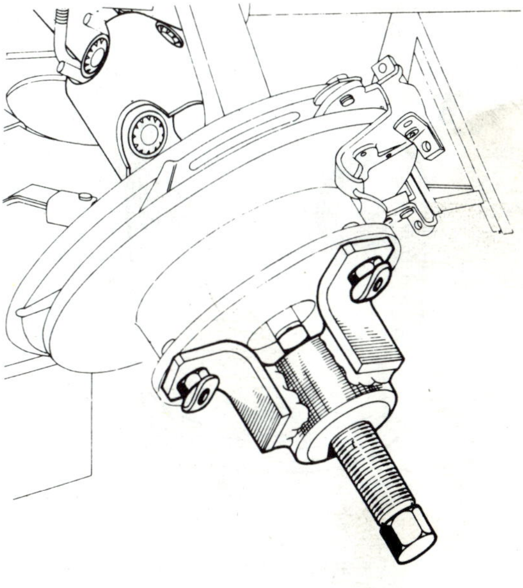

FIG 8:6 Tool T.Av.235

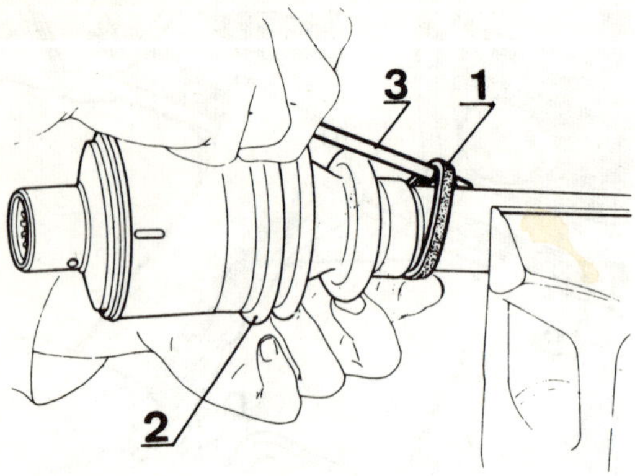

FIG 8:7 Removing the transmission shaft ring

Key to Fig 8:7 1 Ring 2 Bellows 3 Rod

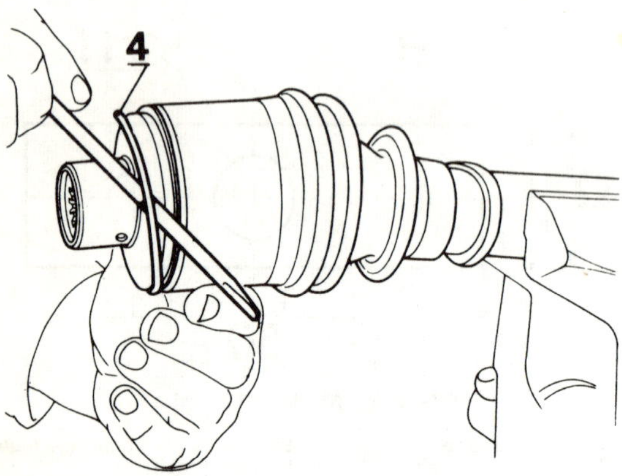

FIG 8:8 Removing the snap ring

Key to Fig 8:8 4 Snap ring

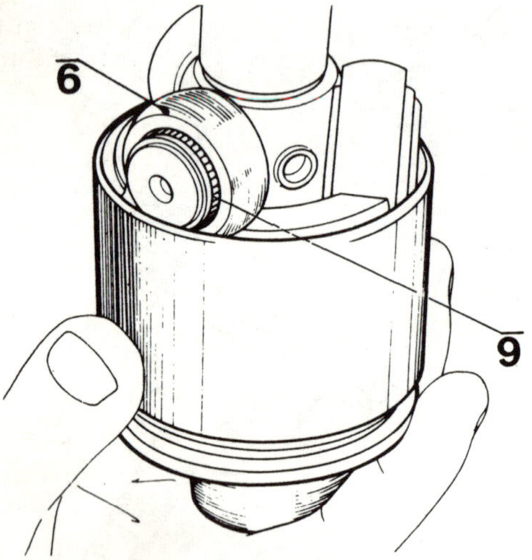

FIG 8:9 The spider yoke

Key to Fig 8:9 6 Yoke 9 Rollers

inch (1.5 mm) sheet steel and weld the plate on the inside of the sidemember. If new suspension arms are fitted to an old type body, make a hole, elongated by $\frac{3}{16}$ inch (4 mm) in an upwards direction, starting at hole 'A'. Again make a plate to the dimension given in **FIG 8:5** and weld the plate on the inside of the sidemember.

8:3 Removing and refitting a stub axle carrier

To remove a stub axle carrier jack up the side concerned, place it on an axle stand and remove the road wheel. Remove the hub nut with its washer and the brake caliper **without disconnecting the hose**. With regard to **FIG 6:13** partially push out the roll pins then fit tool T.Av.205 and retaining tool T.Av.247, in the manner shown in **FIG 8:3**, for Weiss joints with metal casings or the tool supplied with new transmission shafts for shafts with Weiss joints protected by rubber bellows. Disconnect the upper suspension and steering ball joints. Using a suitable puller push out the transmission shaft as illustrated in **FIG 8:6**. Disconnect the lower ball joint and remove the stub axle carrier.

Dismantling of the carrier is carried out in **Chapter 7**. The alignment of a stub axle carrier can be checked using tool T.Av.403.

To refit the carrier connect the stub axle carrier to the upper and lower suspension arms. Reconnect the steering link and fit the transmission shaft into the stub axle carrier. Tighten the upper and lower ball joint nuts, refit the shaft roll pins, the brake caliper and the hub nut with its washer. Refit the road wheel and have the wheel alignment checked.

8:4 Removing and refitting a transmission shaft

To remove a shaft jack up the side concerned, place it on a safety stand and remove the road wheel and the hub nut with its washer. Drain the transmission case and remove the brake caliper **without disconnecting its hose**. Push out the roll pin from the Bendix Weiss joint (see **FIG 6:13**) and fit tool T.Av.247 and T.Av.205 to the shaft. Again if the shaft has a rubber bellows, fit the retaining tool which is supplied with new transmission shafts. Disconnect the steering link and the upper suspension ball joint. Free the shaft from its sun wheel and using a piece of rubber tubing $\frac{19}{32}$ inch (15 mm) long whose inside diameter is $1\frac{3}{8}$ inch (35 mm), protect the area where the transmission case cover housing seal locates on the Weiss joint. Fit a suitable hub extractor to the hub drum and push out the transmission shaft.

To refit the shaft place it in position in the sidemember refit it to the stub axle carrier ensuring, whilst doing so, that the sheet steel deflector remains correctly positioned on the stub axle. Remove the rubber protective end fitting, smear the shaft splines with 'Molykote 806.377' grease and engage the shaft on the sun wheel. Refit the roll pins using a small diameter drift. Reconnect the suspension ball joint, the steering ball joint, the hub nut with its washer and the brake caliper. Remove tool T.Av.247 and T.Av.205 and refill the transmission case. Refit the road wheel.

8:5 Overhauling a spider type transmission shaft

Grip the shaft in a vice **fitted with safety jaws** and free the ring 1 in **FIG 8:7** and the snap ring 4 in **FIG 8:8**.

Using a sharp knife cut away the rubber bellows and ring. Free the spider yoke 6 in **FIG 8:9** taking care not to remove the rollers 9 from their respective trunnions, because the trunnions, needles and rollers are selectively assembled during manufacture, if the spider is not to be renewed. Wrap adhesive tape around the rollers and wipe as much of the grease away from the spider assembly as possible but never dip it in cellulose thinners or any similar cleaner. Clean the inside of the yoke using thinners. If the spider is to be renewed, using a press remove the spider from the transmission shaft.

To reassemble the shaft, position the new spider on the splined shaft with the chamfer towards the transmission tube end and push the spider onto the shaft using a soft metal mallet until the chamfer makes contact with the shoulder on the tube. Make three locking punch marks at 120 deg. to each other with a pin punch, knocking the metal of the splines onto the hub of the spider (see **FIG 8:10**). Obtain tool T.Av.410, lubricate the rods of the tool over their entire length then fit the rubber ring (1 in **FIG 8:11**). Slide the bellows over the spider in the manner shown in **FIG 8:12** and fit it into the grooves in the shaft. Put half the quantity of grease contained in the appropriate tube obtained from a Renault dealer, **never use any other type** and after placing the other half of the grease in the yoke, and having removed the tape from the original spider if a new one was not fitted, position the yoke in front of the spider. Slide the rubber bellows over the yoke until the bellows enters the groove in the yoke.

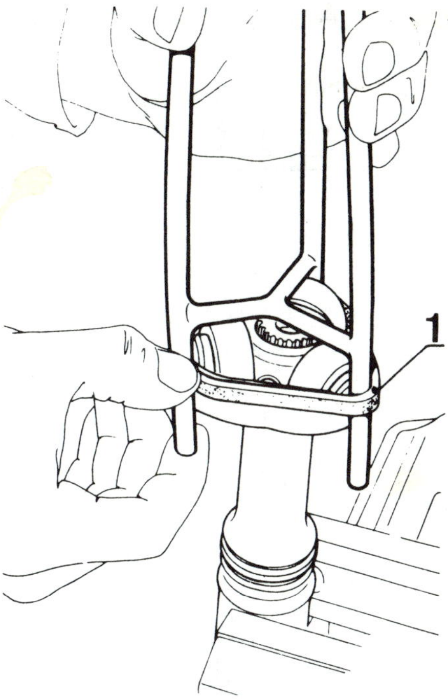

FIG 8:11 Fitting the transmission shaft ring

Key to Fig 8:11 1 Ring

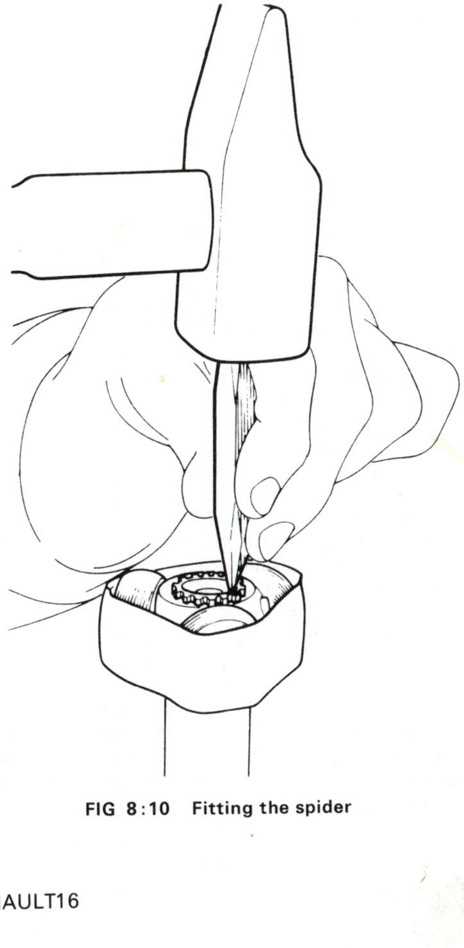

FIG 8:10 Fitting the spider

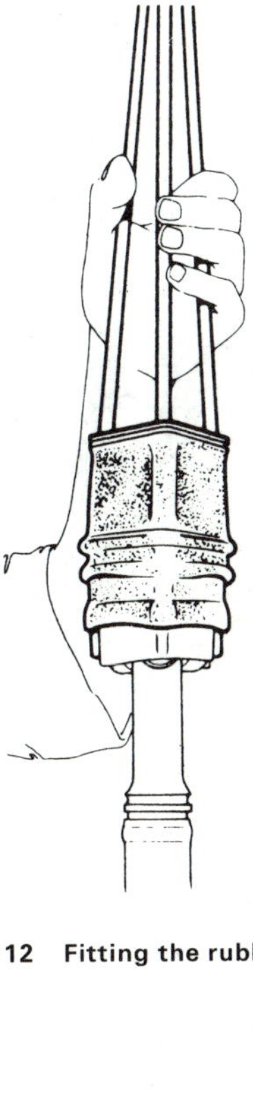

FIG 8:12 Fitting the rubber bellows

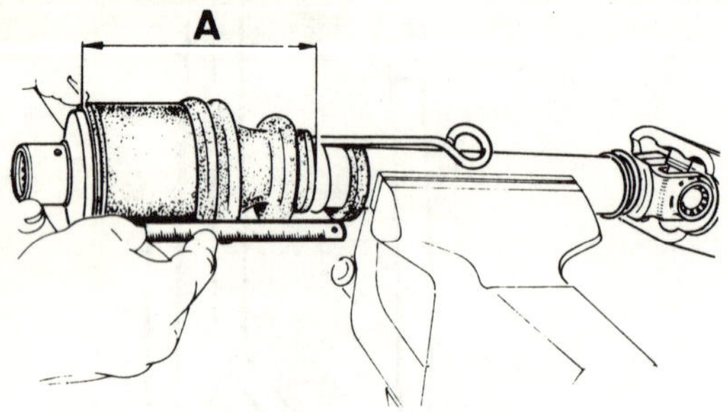

FIG 8:13 Adjusting the bellows

Key to Fig 8:13 A 5¾ inch (146 mm)

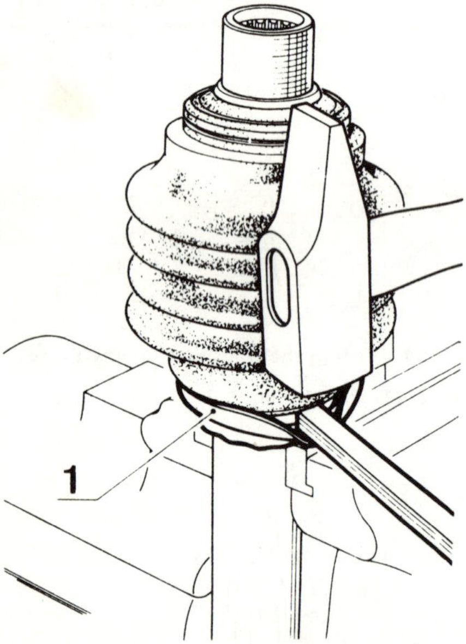

FIG 8:14 Removing a bellows clip

Key to Fig 8:14 1 Clip

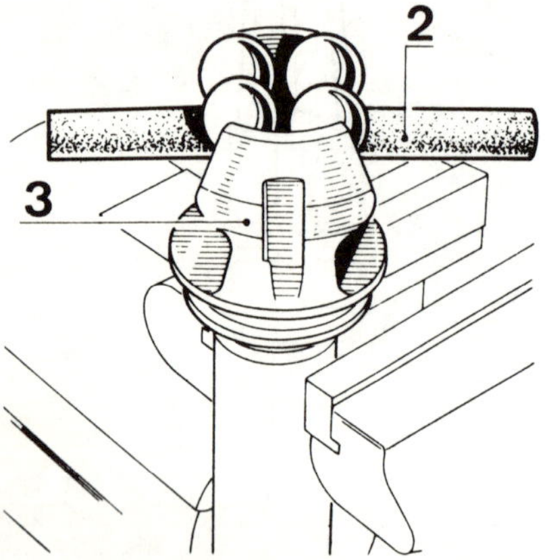

8:15 Assembling the Weiss joint

Key to Fig 8:15 2 Tube 3 Yoke

Fit a new ring (4 in **FIG 8:8**), insert a rod between the bellows and shaft, to allow the air to escape and extend or push in the spider joint until dimension 'A' in **FIG 8:13** is 5¾ inch (146 mm). Remove the rod and fit the rubber ring (1 in **FIG 8:7**).

Under no circumstances should any one vehicle be fitted with a spider type transmission shaft on one side and a Weiss joint transmission shaft on the other side.

8:6 Overhauling a transmission shaft fitted with a Weiss joint

To dismantle the shaft grip the shaft in a vice **fitted with safety jaws** then remove the clips (1 in **FIG 8:14**), using a square bar and a hammer. Cut off the bellows, lift off the upper yoke and remove the four balls. Clean the yokes and balls and check the condition of the ramps and balls. The ramps should show no sign of pin holing, seizure marks, large areas of discoloration, cracks and have no deep depressions. If any part is excessively worn replace the entire transmission shaft.

To reassemble the shaft place a piece of rubber tube (2 in **FIG 8:15**) whose diameter is approximately .383 inch (10 mm) in the yoke 3 and place the four balls in line with their ramps. Fit the upper yoke and remove the rubber tube while pushing the upper yoke into position. Using tool T.Av.51 in the manner shown in **FIG 8:12** push on the new bellows and place it on its grooves. Fit a new lower clip, pull back the bellows and pour in the quantity of oil contained in kit number 8.705.580. Compress the bellows until the edges of the bellows are 4$\frac{7}{16}$ inch (113 mm) away from one another. Fit the upper securing clip. Fit the joint retaining tool before refitting the shaft.

8:7 Removing and refitting a rear lefthand half axle mounted on rubber bushes

Removal:

Jack up the side concerned and place it on an axle stand and with regard to **FIG 8:16** disconnect the hand-brake cable at the sleeve 1. Push back the cover 2 and take out the other end of the cable from its securing clamp. Disconnect the brake line at the union on the chassis and taking the load off the suspension arm with a jack, unscrew the damper at the bottom. Undo the nut which locks the underbody height adjusting cam and with reference to **FIG 8:17**, remove the two bolts which secure the inner bearing 4, the three bolts which secure the exhaust silencer 5 and the brake pressure limiting valve adjusting strip bolt 6. With regard to **FIG 8:18** bring the adjusting cam to zero and remove the anchor casing bolts 'A', the two bolts which secure the anti-roll bar bearings 'B'. Disconnect the anti-roll bar from the suspension arm and pull it back as far as it will go towards the rear. Remove the suspension arm outer bearing nuts (arrowed in **FIG 8:19**), and apply pressure by means of a lever 1 to make removing the two bolts easier. Free the bearing by pulling it towards the rear and turn the inner bearing through 90 deg. and pull it as far as it will go towards the rear, then remove it. **This sequence of operations must be carried out to remove a rear lefthand torsion bar.**

Check the suspension arm with tool T.Av.93.

Refitting:

Engage the inner bearing in the aperture in the sidemember. Push the suspension arm while passing the outer bearing between the righthand suspension arm tube and the floor, then engage the outer bearing on the end of the sidemember. Refit the anchor casing to the torsion bar, following the position reference marks (see **Chapter 7**) and secure the casing whilst applying load to the torsion bar. Secure the anti-roll bar bearings to the anchor casing and the righthand sidemember and refit the handbrake cable, brake pressure limiting valve, adjusting strip and brake line. Secure the exhaust silencer in position and adjust the handbrake (see **Chapter 10**). Bleed the braking system (see **Chapter 10**), adjust the underbody height (see **Chapter 7**) and adjust the brake pressure limiting valve (see **Chapter 10**).

Replacing the rubber bushes:

To replace an inner bush saw the $\frac{7}{32}$ old bush out and fit the new one by means of a press. The outer bush is a force fit on the suspension arm and is secured to the outer bearings by six tabs folded into the six slots in the bearing. Fold out of the way the six tabs then saw the rubber bush to free it from the suspension arm tube. Press in the new bush securing it in place by means of the six tabs.

Never fit a needle roller bearing in place of an outer bush. If an outer needle roller bearing is required a new type suspension arm which is already fitted with a bearing outer bush must be fitted.

8:8 Removing and refitting a rear righthand half axle mounted on rubber bushes

To remove the rear righthand half axle the lefthand half axle must be disconnected therefore start the dismantling operation by carrying out the removal instruction layed out in **Section 8:7**, but do not remove the rear lefthand half axle. Bring the adjusting cam on the righthand half axle to the zero position by turning it towards the left (see **FIG 8:20**). Remove the anchor casing, disconnect the handbrake cable at the swivel lever, the brake hose and the damper at the bottom. Remove the suspension arm outer bearing securing bolts (see **FIG 8:19**) applying pressure with a lever in order to make their removal easier. Free the inner bearing from the sidemember, push back the suspension arm as far as it will go towards the rear of the vehicle, straighten up the inner bearing and pull out the rear righthand suspension arm. Remove the arm.

Check the suspension arm using tool T.Av.93.

Replace the rubber bushes in the manner described in **Section 8:7**.

To refit a rear righthand half axle, fit the righthand half axle and pull it back towards the rear of the vehicle and engage the second half axle in the sidemember aperture. Secure the outer bearing in place by fitting the outer bearing securing bolts, aligning the holes with the holes in the sidemember by means of a lever passed into the bearing. Tighten the bolts to 32 lb ft (4.5 M.da N) torque. Fit the anchor casing to the torsion bars, following the position marks (see **Chapter 7**). Refit the lefthand half axle as layed out in **Section 8:7**. Secure the anti-roll bar to the suspension arms and connect the dampers. Secure the exhaust silencer in position and reconnect the brake

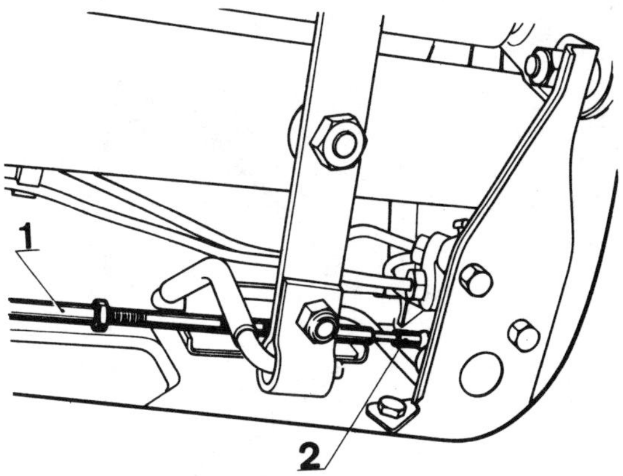

8:16 Handbrake cable sleeve

Key to Fig 8:16 1 Sleeve 2 Cover

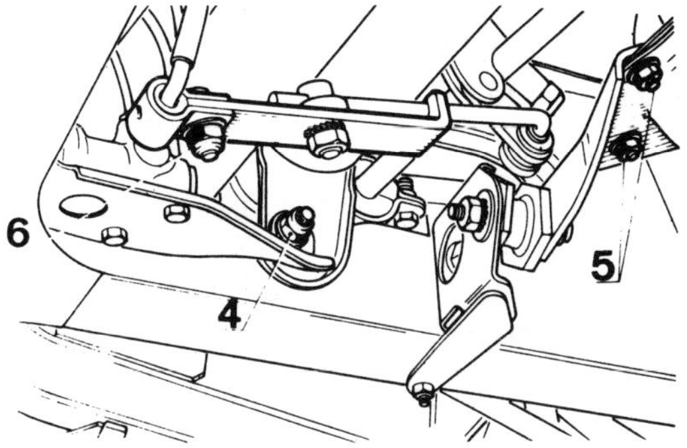

8:17 Securing bolts

Key to Fig 8:17 4 Inner bearing 5 Exhaust silencer 6 Strip bolt

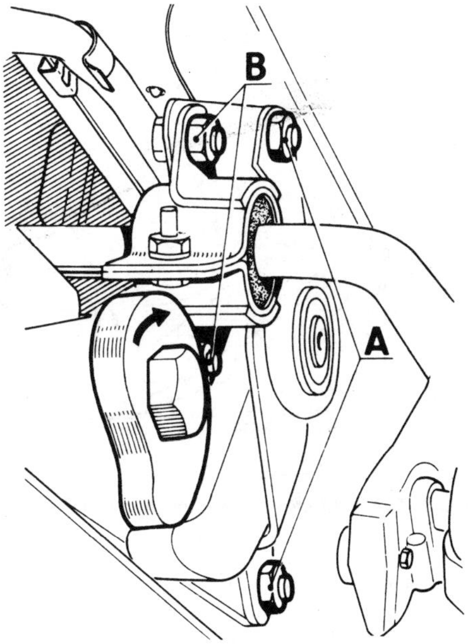

8:18 Adjusting cam

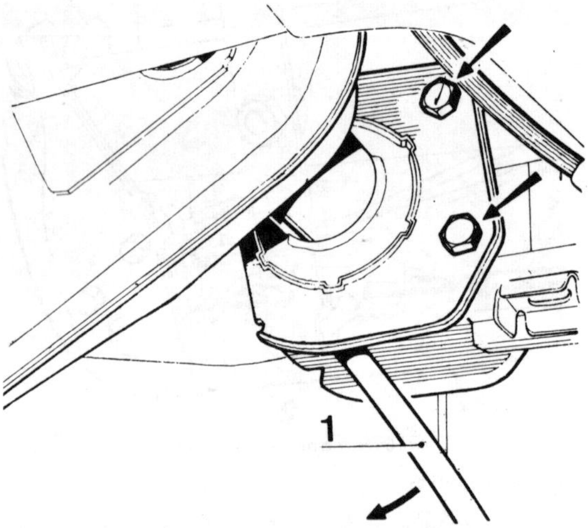

8:19 Outer bearing nuts

Key to Fig 8:19 1 Lever

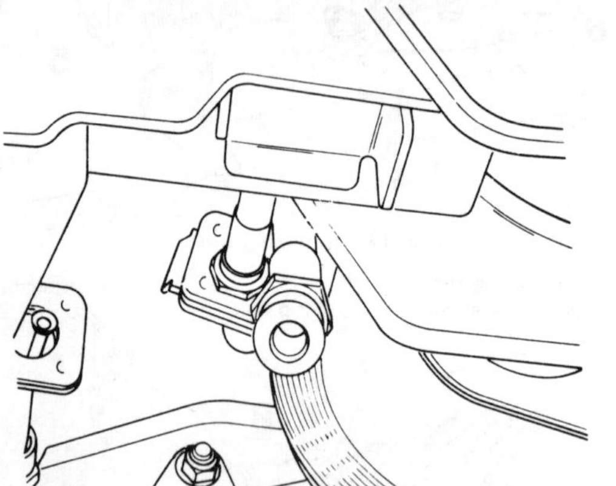

FIG 8:20 Adjusting cam (righthand rear half axle)

lines and brake pressure limiting valve adjusting strip. Bleed the brakes and adjust the handbrake (see **Chapter 10**) and adjust the underbody height (see **Chapter 7**). Adjust the brake pressure limiting valve (see **Chapter 10**).

8:9 Removing and refitting the rear half axles mounted on needle roller outer bushes

To remove the rear lefthand axle (see **Section 8:7**). To remove the rear righthand axle (see **Section 8:8**), but as the torsion bar only locates the suspension arm in a sideways direction, before anchoring the torsion bar in position the suspension arm must be positioned laterally. To do this after bolting the outer bearing to the side-member, insert tool T.Av.386-01 and by means of a hook (E in **FIG 8:21**) hook the suspension arm to the gusset G so that it is approximately 45 deg. to the horizontal. Pull or push the suspension arm so that it engages freely in the fork of tool T.Av.386-01 and leave the tool in position until the suspension arm is fully fitted.

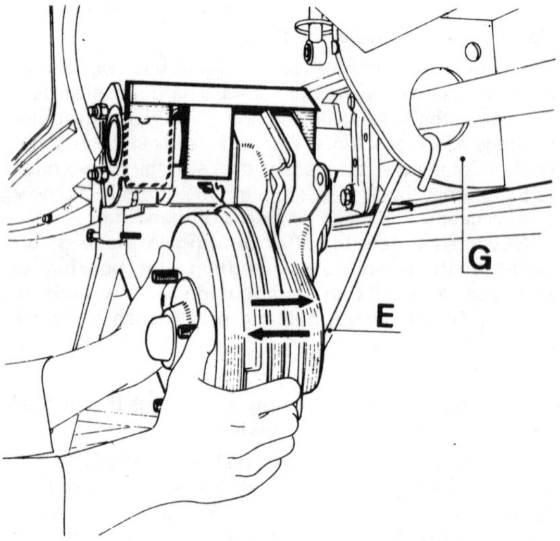

8:21 Aligning the suspension arm

Key to Fig 8:21 E Hook G Gusset

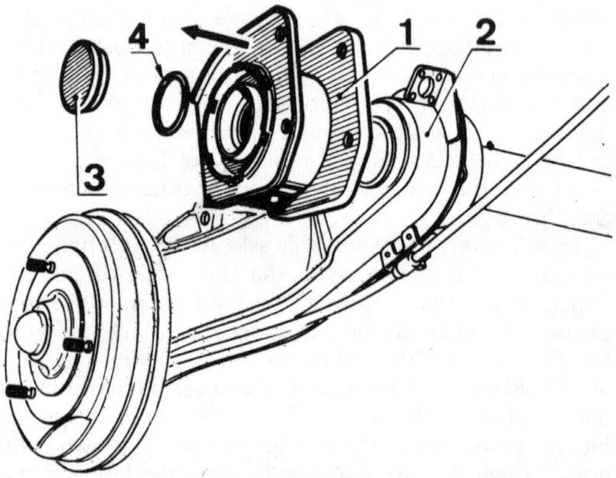

FIG 8:22 Needle roller bearing

Key to Fig 8:22 1 Bearing 2 Arm 3 Plug 4 Seal

8:10 Overhauling rear suspension arms mounted on needle roller bushes

With regard to **FIG 8:22** take out the bearing 1 from the arm 2 and remove the plastic plug 3 and the O-ring seal 4. Replace the entire outer bearing assembly.

If the fluidbloc bush on the inner bearing is damaged replace the complete inner bearing assembly.

If the rear suspension arm is to be replaced remove the outer ring supplied with the fluibloc bush on the inner bearing, if damaged replace the complete inner bearing assembly.

If the rear suspension arm is to be replaced remove the outer ring supplied with the fluibloc bush and fit the bearing directly into the tube on the arm.

If the outer ring on the fluibloc bush is damaged saw it, taking care not to score the tube. Lift the edge of the ring and take it out with a pair of pliers. Press the new ring on the tube leaving $\frac{5}{32}$ inch (4 mm) proud.

8:11 Fault diagnosis

(a) Wheel wobble

1 Incorrect toe-in
2 Worn hub bearings
3 Defective suspension arm bushes
4 Worn suspension ball joints
5 Loose wheel fixings

(b) Bottoming of suspension

1 Defective torsion bars
2 Incorrect torsion bar spline setting
3 Rebound rubbers worn or missing

(c) Heavy steering

1 Incorrect camber angle
2 Incorrect castor angle
3 Incorrect kingpin inclination
4 Tight or seized suspension ball joints

(d) Excessive tyre wear

1 Check 1 in (a)
2 Check 1, 2 and 3 in (c)

(e) Rattles

1 Check 3, 4 and 5 in (a)
2 Steering arm connections loose
3 Anti-roll bar fixings loose

(f) Excessive rolling

1 Tyre pressures too high
2 Check 1 in (b) and 3 in (e)

CHAPTER 9

THE STEERING GEAR

9:1 Description

The steering box used is of the rack and pinion type, a cross-sectional view of the unit being shown in **FIG 9:1**. The rack which is basically a bar with a series of teeth is connected via steering links to the two front wheels. In mesh with the rack teeth are the pinion teeth, the pinion being connected to the steering wheel via the steering column. Rotation of the steering wheel causes the pinion to move the rack to the right or left, the rack in turn moving the wheels to the right or left. After considerable usage the rack and pinion teeth become worn necessitating in their replacement. As the steering box main components are only the rack, pinion and casing the manufacturer, quite wisely, consider the small extra cost to stock a replacement unit worth paying for that convenience of not having to dismantle and assemble the steering box, for this reason only replacement units can be obtained. The reduction ratio of the box is 23:1 and the total number of steering wheel turns is 4. The steering ball joints are sealed units and therefore cannot be repaired and are connected to the steering mechanism by steering links and pins. The steering link for the righthand is different from that for the lefthand so be careful not to intermix the two. Other information that might prove useful is that the overall length of the rack is 21½ inch (546 mm), the steering wheel diameter is 16⅛ inch (410 mm) and the turning circle between kerbstones is 32 ft 10 inch (10.00 m) and overall is 34ft 9 inch (10.60 m).

9:2 Setting up the steering centre point

Fit tool Dir.229 between the end of the steering box and the locking nut on the steering end fitting (see **FIG 9:2**). If the tool is not available operate the steering until the distance between the end of the steering box and the steering end fitting, locking nut at the steering pinion end is $3\frac{3}{32}$ inch (78 mm). The steering wheel spokes should, in this position, form two equal angles from the horizontal on either side of the centre as shown in **FIG 9:3**. If this is not the case reposition the wheel in the manner described in **Section 9:7**.

9:3 Removing and refitting the steering mechanism

Removal:

Jack up the front of the vehicle and place it on safety stands. Disconnect the battery and remove the front and spare wheels. Disconnect the steering link ball joint on the

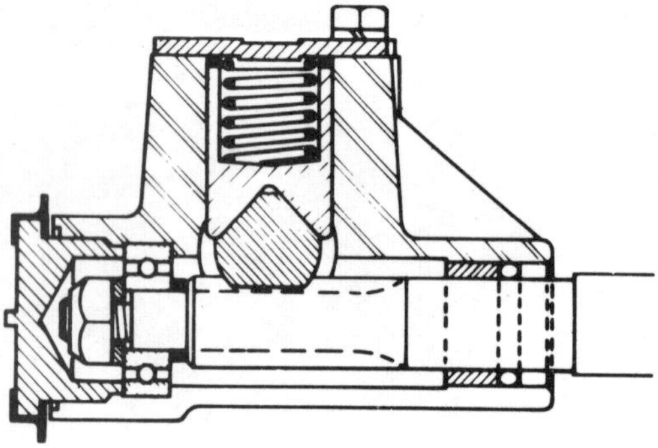

FIG 9:1 The steering box

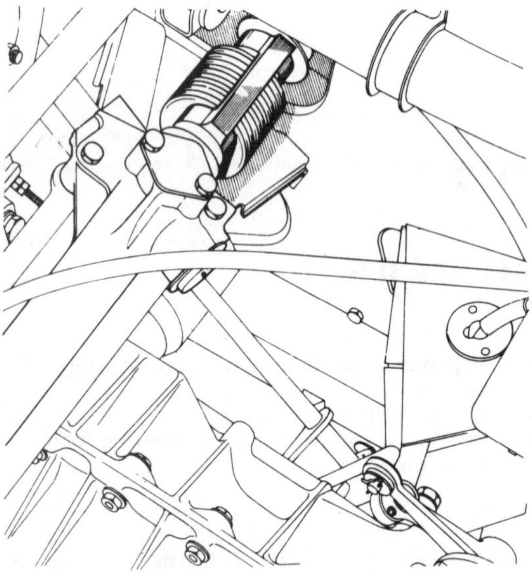

FIG 9:2 Tool Dir.229 in position

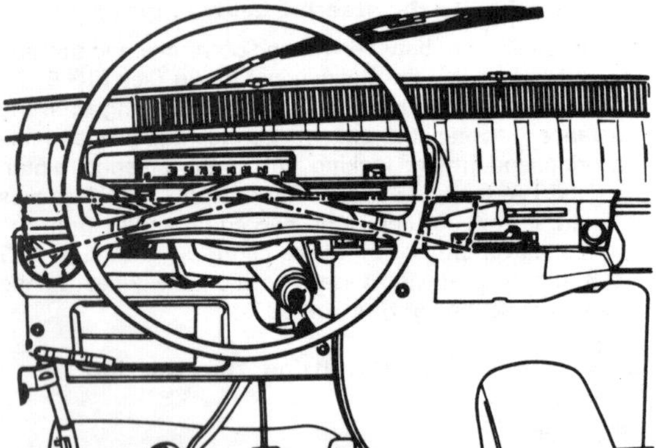

FIG 9:3 Correct steering wheel position

righthand side and the steering link pin on the lefthand side at the rack adjustable end fitting. Undo the two flexible coupling securing bolts (arrowed in **FIG 9:4**) and unscrew the four bolts again arrowed in **FIG 9:5** securing the steering box to the crossmember. Remove the steering box assembly by turning the wheels as far as they will go to the right in order to permit the link end fitting to be freed. Put aside any steering box height adjusting shims that may be fitted.

On R.1151 models the steering box position has been lowered by removing $\frac{13}{64}$ inch (5 mm) from the steering box bosses consequently, on early vehicles whenever replacing a steering box, only new type boxes are to be used.

Refitting:

Refit the box with any height adjusting washers that were removed and secure in place by tightening the four securing bolts 20 lb ft (2.5 M.da N) torque. Establish the steering centre point (see **Section 9:2**) and refit the flexible coupling securing bolts. Tighten the bolts to 10 lb ft (1.5 M.da N) torque. Refit the steering link pin and ball joint and tighten them both to a torque of 30 lb ft (4 M.da N). Refit the front and spare wheels, reconnect the battery, jack up the vehicle and remove the safety stands.

Have a service station check the toe-in. If tracking equipment is available to the operator when tightening the locknut (2 in **FIG 9:6**) hold the steering link so that the link pin and the end fitting 1 are in the horizontal plane. This is essential as it permits the steering and the rack ball joint to operate under the correct conditions.

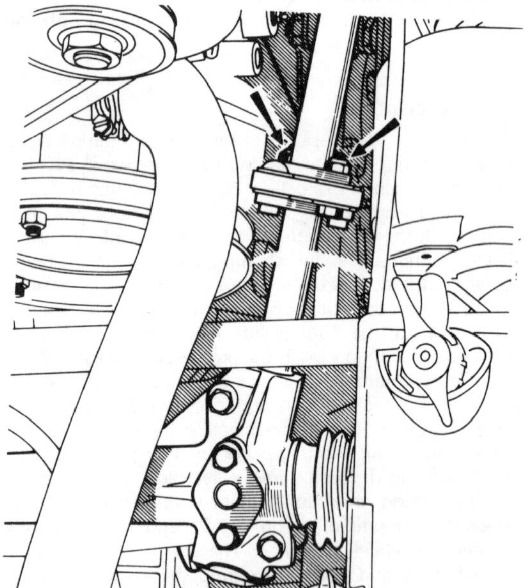

FIG 9:4 Flexible coupling securing bolts

9:4 Removing and refitting a steering link

To remove a steering link jack up the side concerned, place it on a safety stand and remove the road wheel. Disconnect the steering ball joint at the stub axle and the link on the rack adjustable end fitting. Remove the link.

Refit a link by reversing the removal procedure tightening the steering link ball joint and steering link pin to 30 lb ft (4 M.da N) torque. Have a service station check the wheel alignment.

The links are not identical, therefore they must not be mixed. **FIG 9:7** shows the difference between the links.

9:5 Removing and refitting the steering column

Removal:

Disconnect the battery, place the steering lock in the garage position and remove the steering wheel (see **Section 9:7**). Remove the horn and lighting switch housing and disconnect the direction indicator switch return spring. Remove the horn and lighting switch securing bolt and free the switch from the steering column. Mark the position of the clamp with reference to the steering column tube and remove the bolt (1 in **FIG 9:8**), which secures the gearshift clamp. Loosen the gearshaft rod ball joint (2 in **FIG 9:8**) by freeing the clamp on the steering column.

Free the under tray and after marking the five leads (arrowed in **FIG 9:9**) to the steering lock and the two leads, again arrowed in **FIG 9:9**, from the stop switch, disconnect the leads. Disconnect the clutch and brake pedal return spring, remove the clip and take off the clutch pedal. Free the cable cover (arrowed in **FIG 9:9**) from its stop on the pedal assembly bracket. Remove the steering universal joint pin (1 in **FIG 9:10**) at the pedal assembly end and the steering column upper fastening (2 in **FIG 9:10**). Free the shaft and disconnect the speedometer drive cable. Remove the two lower securing bolts on the steering column and free the steering column.

The steering column can be removed by taking out the bolts which secure the tube to the flexible coupling instead of the pin from the universal joint. In this case, take care that you do not damage the scuttle grommet when the flexible coupling flange is pulled through it. When refiting, tighten the flexible coupling bolts to a torque of 10 lb ft (1.5 M.da N).

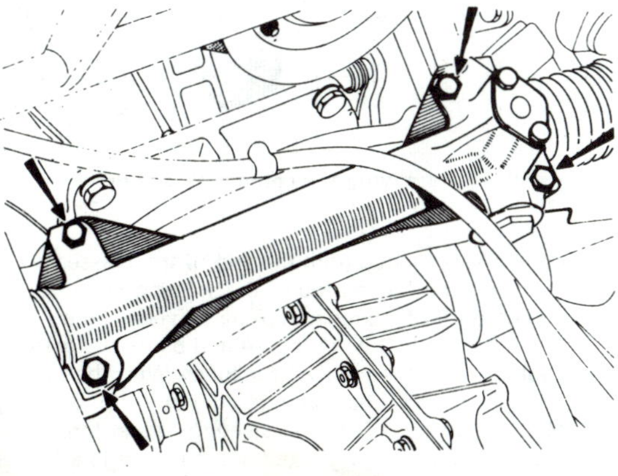

9:5 Steering box securing bolts

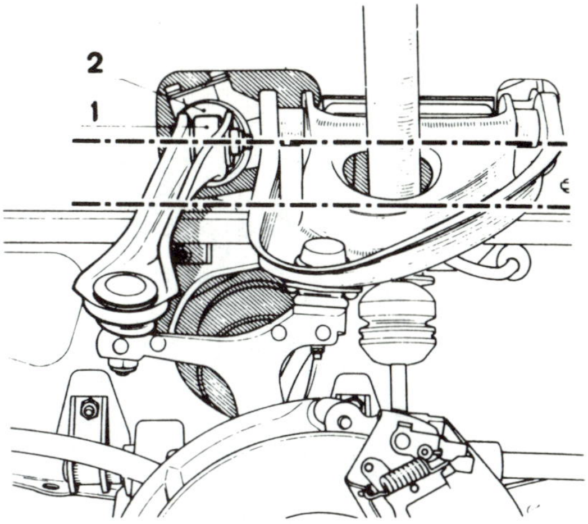

FIG 9:6 Adjusting wheel alignment

Key to Fig 9:6 1 End fitting 2 Locknut

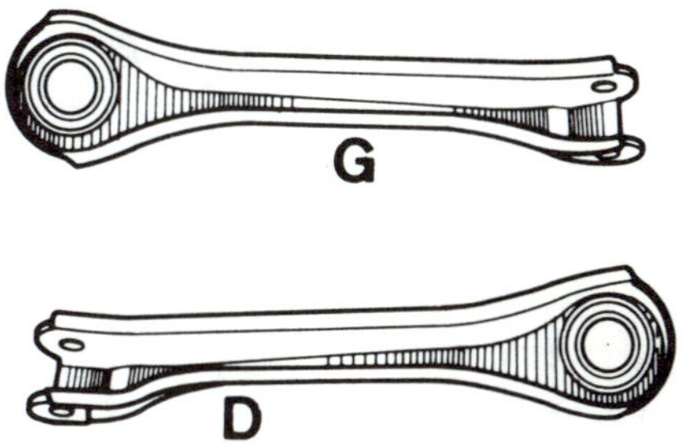

FIG 9:7 Steering links

Key to Fig 9:7 **G** Lefthand link **D** Righthand link

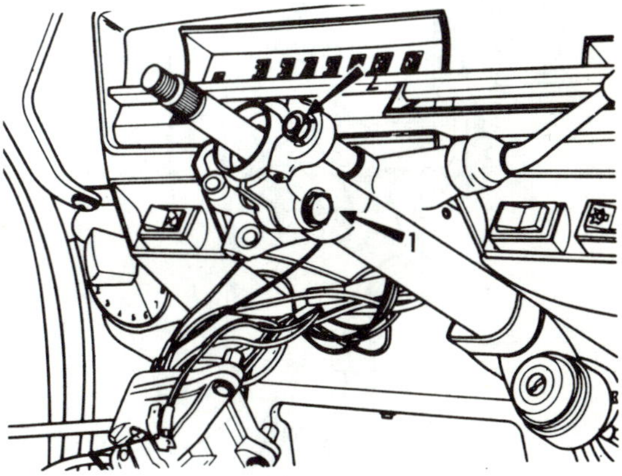

FIG 9:8 Gearshift and ball joint

Key to Fig :8 1 Bolt 2 Nut

Refitting:

Carry out the removing operations in reverse smearing the column lower securing clamp with sealing compound and ensuring that the column upper securing

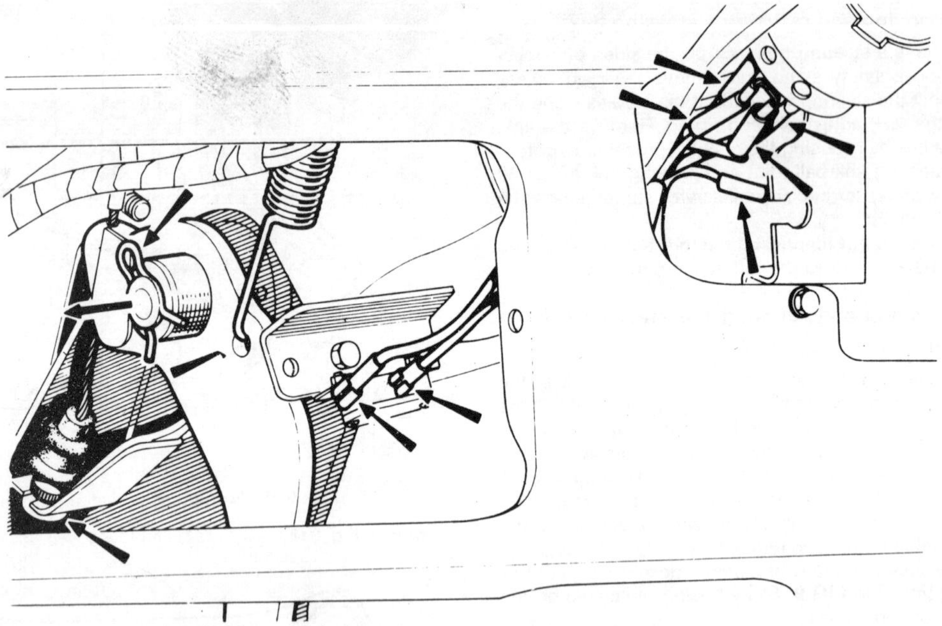

9:9 Removing the steering column

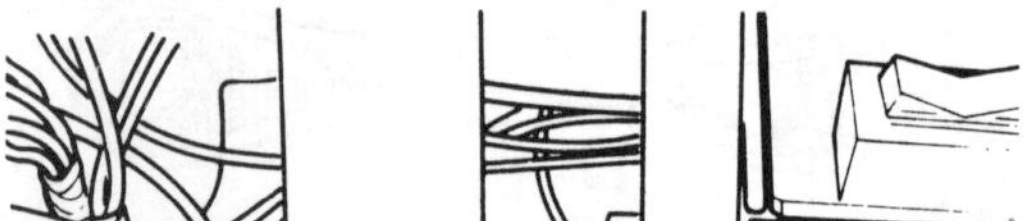

FIG 9:10 Steering column securing bolts

Key to Fig 9:10 1 Bolt 2 Bolt

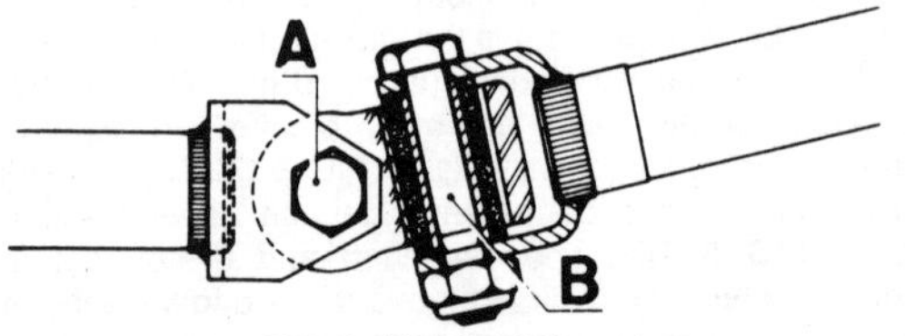

FIG 9:11 Steering pins

Key to Fig 9:11 A Pin B Pin

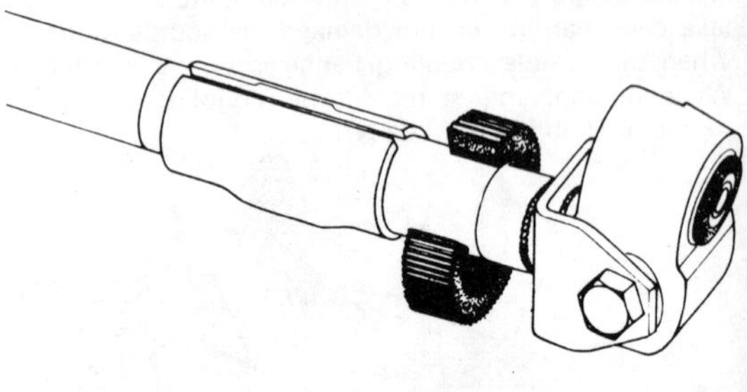

9:12 Removing the column outer bush

clamp is not tightened until the end of the reassembling operations. After having found the steering centre point (see **Section 9:2**), connect up the universal joint.

With regard to **FIG 9:11**, pins A and B must be greased and tightened in the following manner. With the rack in the straight-ahead position tighten pin A to 30 lb ft (4 M.da N) torque. Turn the steering wheel through a quarter of a turn to the right and tighten pin B to a torque of 30 lb ft (4 M.da N).

Check and adjust if necessary the clutch and master cylinder clearance (see **Chapter 5**), the gearshift control (see **Chapter 6**) and the stop switch (see **Chapter 10**). Check all the electrical services operated by the horn and lighting switch.

9:6 Replacing the steering column locating bushes

Remove the steering column (see **Section 9:5**), remove the pedal shaft and put aside the brake pedal. Tap **lightly**, with a soft metal or hide hammer, on the end of the steering column tube until the tube is free. With regard to **FIG 9:12** open the split bush and remove it. Remove the circlip which retains the bush at the steering wheel end and by means of a mandrel with an outside diameter of $1\frac{1}{32}$ inch (26 mm) extract the bush in the manner shown in **FIG 9:13**.

Push in the new bush using the mandrel employed in extracting the old bush and fit the bush retaining circlip. Insert the tube into the steering column and position the split bush on the tube. Place the two half shells of tool Dir.231 on either side of the steering column tube and bring them into contact with the bush and the clevis. Whilst holding the bracket and the two shells, push in the bush (see **FIG 9:14**). **Ensure that the bushes are correctly positioned between the two dishings** (see **FIG 9:15**). Fit the pedal to the steering column bracket and refit the steering column.

Under no circumstances are the steering column bushes and the steering column tube to be greased on refitting.

9:7 Aligning the steering wheel

To remove the steering wheel, unscrew the two screws positioned under the steering wheel which secure the embellisher and undo the steering wheel retaining nut. Extract the steering wheel by means of tool Dir.372.

Set up the steering centre point (see **Section 9:2**) and refit the wheel by reversing the dismantling procedure. Tighten the steering wheel retaining nut to 35 lb ft (5 M.da N) torque.

9:8 Removing and refitting the steering lock

To remove the lock disconnect the battery, place the steering lock in the garage position and remove the key. Mark the leads going to the lock, then disconnect them. Remove the two bolts which secure the steering bracket and press on the locking ball. Slightly free the cartridge in an upwards direction then by means of a scriber point, press on the locking tab and take out the steering lock whilst maintaining pressure on the tab.

Refit the unit by first placing the steering wheel in the garage position and then by carrying out the removing operations in reverse. Check that the lock and switch operate correctly.

9:9 Fault diagnosis

(a) Wheel wobble

1 Unbalanced wheels and tyres
2 Slack steering ball joints
3 Incorrect steering geometry
4 Excessive play in pinion
5 Faulty suspension
6 Worn hub bearings

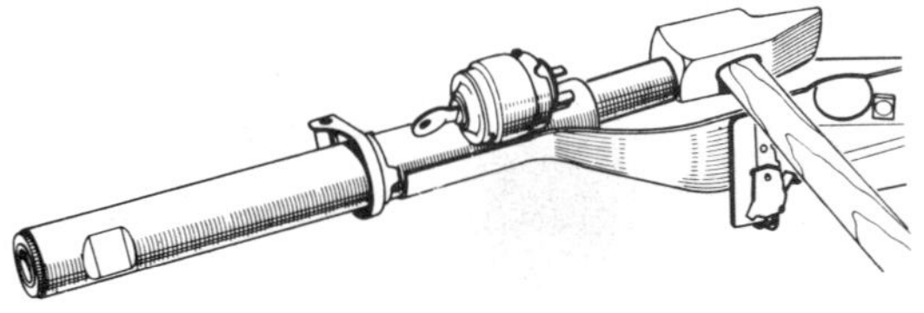

FIG 9:13 Removing the column inner bush

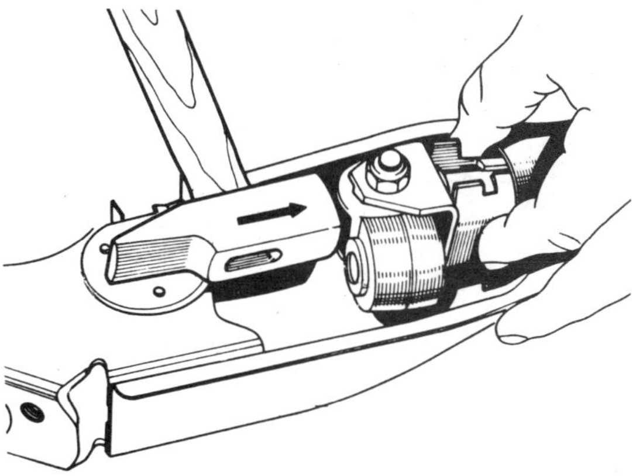

FIG 9:14 Fitting a new outer bush

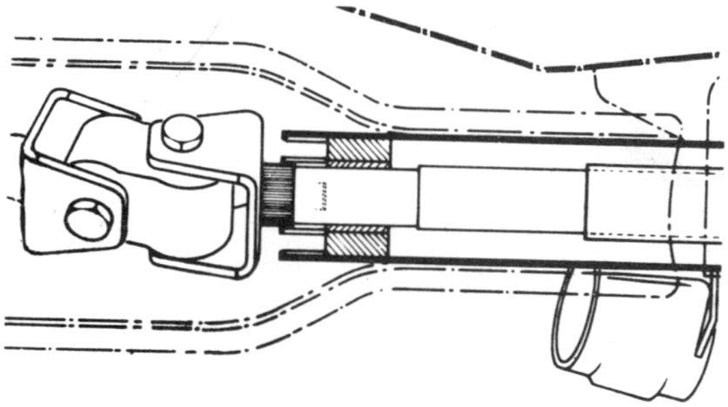

FIG 9:15 Aligning the bushes

(b) Wander

1 Check 2, 3 and 4 in (a)
2 Uneven tyre pressures
3 Uneven tyre wear

(c) Heavy steering

1 Check 3 in (a)
2 Very low tyre pressures
3 Siezed swivel joints
4 Wheels out of track
5 Steering pinion end play incorrect
6 Inner steering column bent
7 Column bushes tight

(d) Lost motion

1 Loose steering wheel, worn splines
2 Worn rack and pinion teeth
3 Worn steering ball joint
4 Worn swivel hub joint
5 Slack pinion bearing

CHAPTER 10

THE BRAKING SYSTEM

10:1 Description

The braking system fitted to the R.1150 model comprises a master cylinder operated by a brake pedal via a thrust rod the master cylinder having a reservoir of brake fluid. Flexible brake lines placed between the body and suspension units feed fluid from the master cylinder to the front disc brake caliper units and the rear wheel cylinders. A cable mechanism also fitted to the rear brakes give both an emergency brake in the event of a failure in the fluid system and a parking brake.

R.1151 models have an identical layout except that a servo vacuum unit is fitted to the master cylinder to increase the pressure of the brake fluid in the lines thus giving a greater braking force.

It is worthwhile to note that disc brakes do not give a better or more powerful braking force, they are fitted because the arrangement ensures that the braking material is cooled more efficiently and therefore the disc brake layout is less likely to fade (brake fade is when the coefficient of friction between shoe/pad and drum/disc is reduced due to heat).

A brake pressure limiting valve is fitted to stop the rear brakes locking up during violent braking. Under normal braking the pressure in the line is not sufficient to compress a spring placed behind a plunger in the unit and so fluid passes to both the front and rear brakes. If the pedal is operated sharply the pressure in the line will rise above the pressure setting of the spring in the limiting valve and thus will be sufficient to move the plunger and spring back. This movement will cause the plunger to seal the opening to the rear brakes and therefore only the front brakes will receive the increased fluid pressure.

When the pedal is operated the pressurized fluid from the master cylinder, this fluid being further pressurized by the servo unit on R.1151 models, acts on the pistons in the caliper units and the pistons in the wheel cylinders pushing on one hand the pads into the disc and on the other hand the shoes into the drum. When the pressure is released the pistons in the calipers move away from the disc owing to the effect of the O-ring which, in re-assuming its original shape, returns the piston to its release position and the pistons in the wheel cylinders are pushed back in place by the brake shoe return springs.

To ensure effective braking under all circumstances a very small clearance between the brake pads and the disc must be maintained and for this reason the caliper comprises an automatic take-up system.

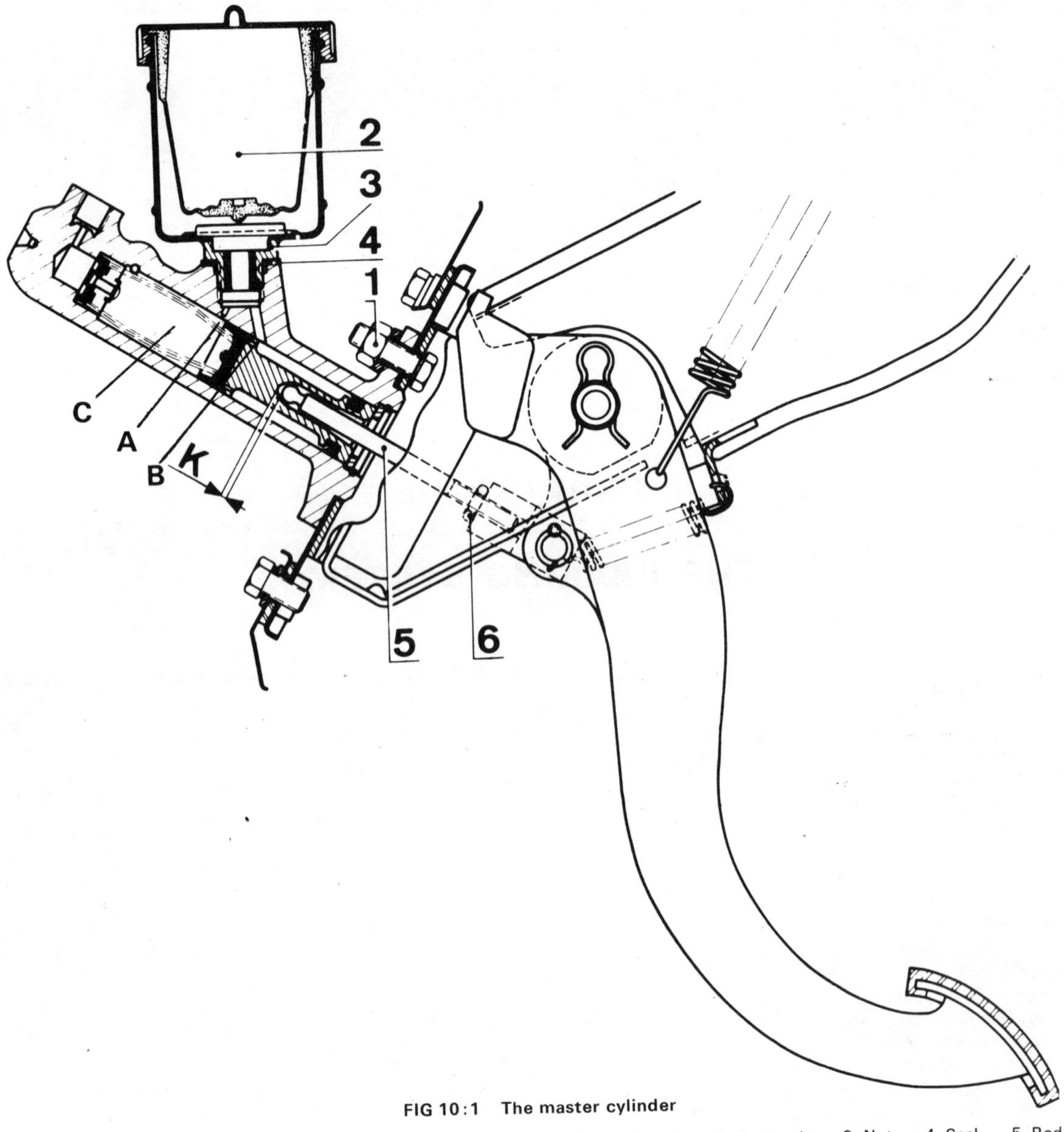

FIG 10:1 **The master cylinder**

Key to Fig 10:1 **A** Bypass port **B** Main feed port **C** Chamber 1 Nut 2 Reservoir 3 Nut 4 Seal 5 Rod 6 Nut

The master cylinder fitted is of the residual pressure type, the layout of the components in the master cylinder ensures the pressure of the fluid in the brake lines is at all times under pressure this has the advantage that it prevents entry of air when the pedal is released in the event of a leak. With regard to **FIG 10:1** operation of the pedal causes the piston to be moved forwards the pistons initial movement covers the bypass port A any further movement forces fluid into the line resulting in the pads/shoes contacting the disc/drum. During this action fluid from the main feed B has passed into the area around the piston 9 in **FIG 10:2**. If the piston reaches the end of its travel before the shoes contact the drum (excessive clearance between shoe and drum) a quick release of the pedal will cause the piston to return quickly which will create a depression in the main chamber C in **FIG 10:1** causing fluid to flow through the feed holes in the piston and over the main cup 10 in **FIG 10:2** to recharge the cylinder. If the pedal is depressed again this extra fluid will be passed into the line causing further movement of the shoes. When the pedal is released the caliper O-rings and shoe return springs cause the fluid to be passed back

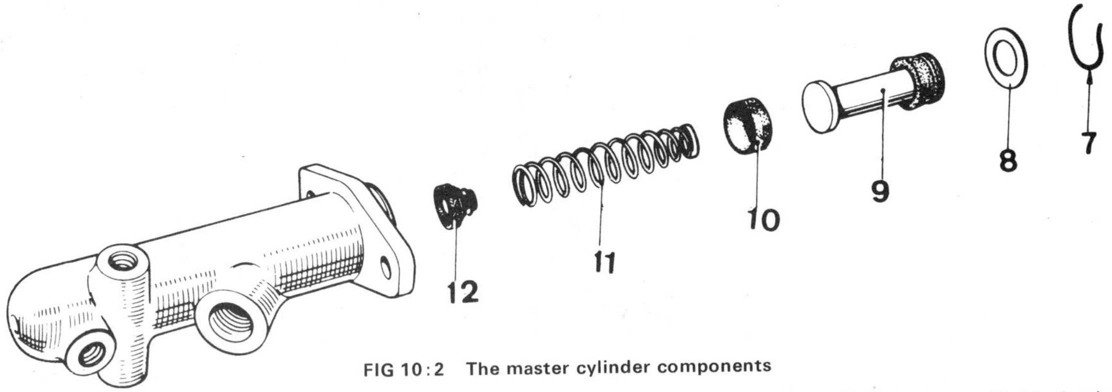

FIG 10:2 The master cylinder components

Key to Fig 10:2 7 Clip 8 Washer 9 Piston 10 Sealing cup 11 Spring 12 Check valve

to the cylinder, any excess fluid returning to the reservoir via the bypass port. The check valve 12 in **FIG 10:2** will stop the return of the fluid until the returning pressure is greater than the pressure of the spring 11 in **FIG 10:2.** Directly the pressure in the line drops below the spring pressure the check valve will stop any more fluid passing back into the cylinder, therefore the pressure in the line is always just below the pressure of the spring 11 in **FIG 10:2** (approximately 8 lb/sq inch).

10:2 Bleeding the system

Check that the level of brake fluid in the brake reservoir is high and ensure that at no time during the bleeding operation the fluid level falls below at least half an inch above the bottom of the reservoir. Start bleeding at the wheel cylinder furthest away from the master cylinder, that is to say the N/S/R wheel cylinder and complete the operation at the nearest caliper.

Fit a piece of hose over the bleed screw and allow the other end of the hose to be immersed **below** the level of a quantity of fluid placed in a clean, clear jar. Open the bleed screw by turning it with a spanner and then get an assistant to press the pedal quickly if bleeding a caliper unit or slowly if bleeding a wheel cylinder. When the pedal is fully depressed close the screw and then ask the assistant to **slowly** release the pedal. Repeat this sequence of operations until no more air bubbles emit from the bleed hose. On completion, that is after having bled all four units top up the fluid in the master cylinder to the correct height.

10:3 Overhauling the master cylinder

Removal:

Unscrew the top off the reservoir and using a suitable syringe draw off the brake fluid from the reservoir. Disconnect the brake hose from the master cylinder and plug it to prevent entry of dirt. Unscrew the two nuts 1 in **FIG 10:1** securing the master cylinder and lift away the master cylinder.

Overhauling:

Remove the reservoir 2 in **FIG 10:1** by unscrewing the nut 3. Using a suitable pair of circlip pliers remove the snap ring 7 in **FIG 10:2** and take out the retaining ring 8, the piston 9, the sealing cup 10, the spring 11 and check valve 12. Clean all the parts in methylated spirits and then check them replacing any parts that show signs of wear with genuine spares only.

Reassemble the cylinder in the reverse order of dismantling dipping the parts in brake fluid which conforms to the standard marked on the brake fluid reservoir. Ensure all the parts slide freely.

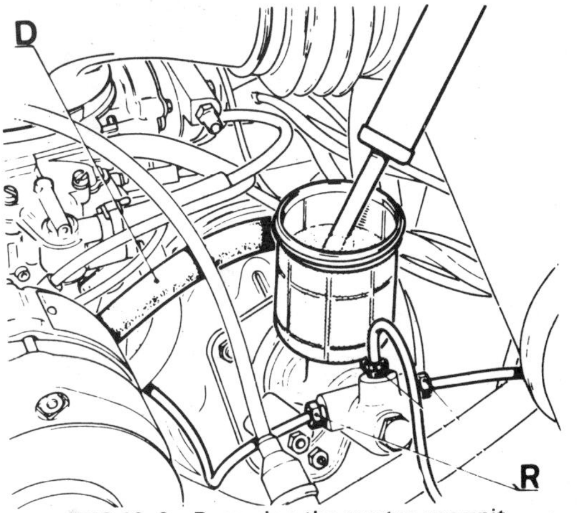

FIG 10:3 Removing the master-vac unit

Key to Fig 10:3 **R** Pipelines **D** Hose

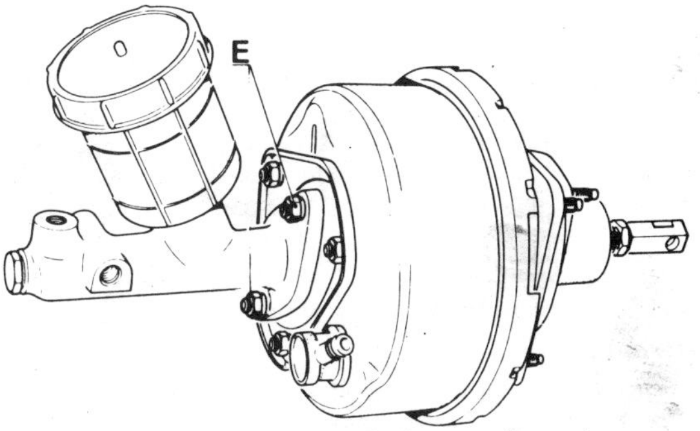

FIG 10:4 Master cylinder securing nuts

Key to Fig 10:4 **E** Nuts

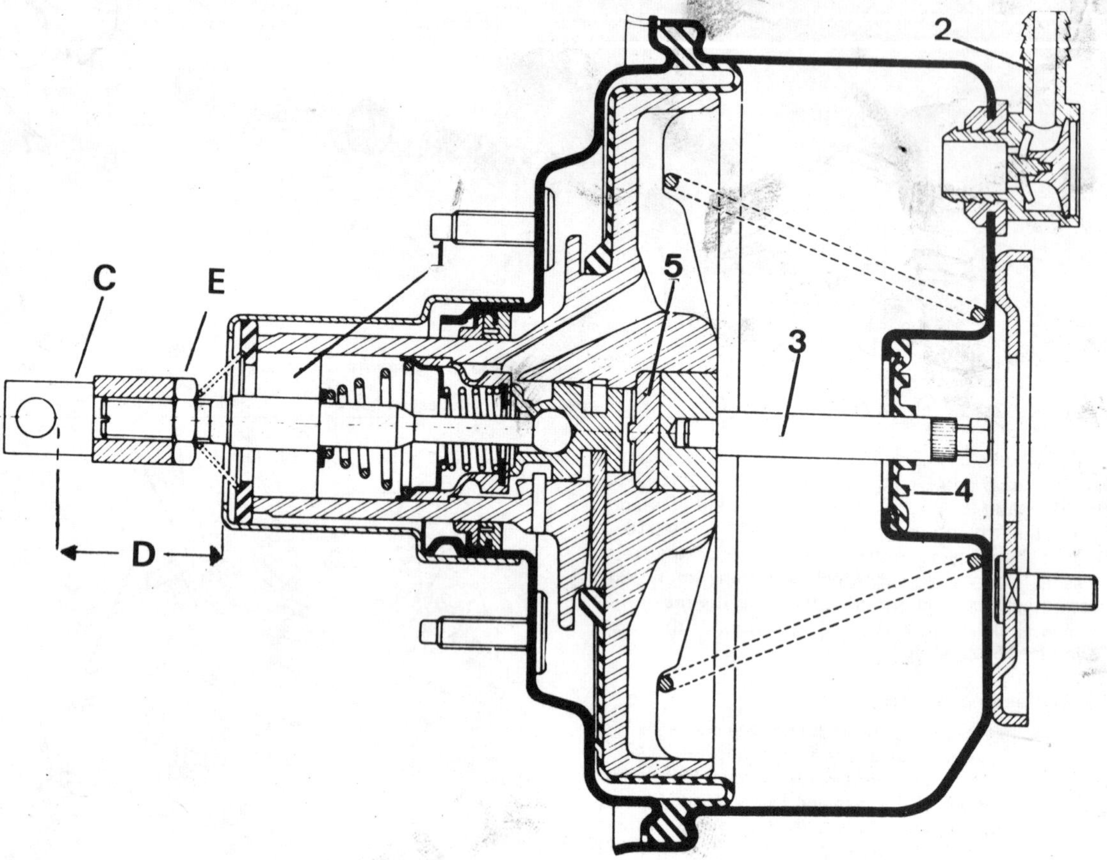

FIG 10:5 Master-vac unit

Key to Fig 10:5 1 Air filter 2 Non-return valve 3 Thrust 4 Diaphragm 5 Plate **C** Clevis **E** Locknut **D** Dimension

Refitting:

Carry out the removing operations in reverse ensuring that when refitting the reservoir, the seal 4 in **FIG 10:1** is replaced. Adjust the master cylinder clearance by loosening the locknut 6 in **FIG 10:1** and then turn the thrust rod 5 until the clearance K is $\frac{1}{64}$ inch (.5 mm). Tighten the locknut 6. Bleed the braking system as detailed in **Section 10:2.**

10:4 Overhauling the master-vac unit

Removal:

Disconnect the battery and using a suitable syringe draw off the brake fluid from the reservoir. Remove the air filter and with regard to **FIG 10:3** unscrew the three rigid brake lines R on the master cylinder and disconnect the vacuum hose D from the engine. Remove the pin from the clevis which connects the brake pedal to the thrust rod, remove the clevis, unscrew the two securing nuts on either side of the brake pedal and remove the master-vac unit. Undo the two nuts E in **FIG 10:4** securing the master cylinder to the master-vac unit and lift away the master cylinder.

Overhauling:

The master cylinder is overhauled in the exact manner as the cylinder fitted to R.1150 models (see **Section 10:3**). With regard to **FIG 10:5** pull the non-return valve 2 to free it from its rubber sealing washer and check the non-return valve by sucking and blowing. It should allow air to be drawn in but not to be blown in. Replace any defective parts. Loosen locknut E on clevis C and unscrew the clevis. Remove the air filter thrust spring and take out the filter 1. Clean it with compressed air or replace it depending on its condition. Incidentally both the non-return valve and the air filter can be replaced without removing the master-vac unit. Remove the flange H in **FIG 10:6** and in order not to damage the sealing diaphragm the rigid portion of the thrust rod should be protected by adhesive tape. Remove the sealing diaphragm and replace it if necessary. **Never remove thrust rod 3 as reaction plate 5 may fall into the vacuum compartment if the rod is removed.**

Reassemble by placing the diaphragm in the master-vac after first greasing the thrust rod 3 in **FIG 10:5** and guide it with a $1\frac{1}{2}$ inch (40 mm) diameter tube to avoid the diaphragm framework coming out of place. Place

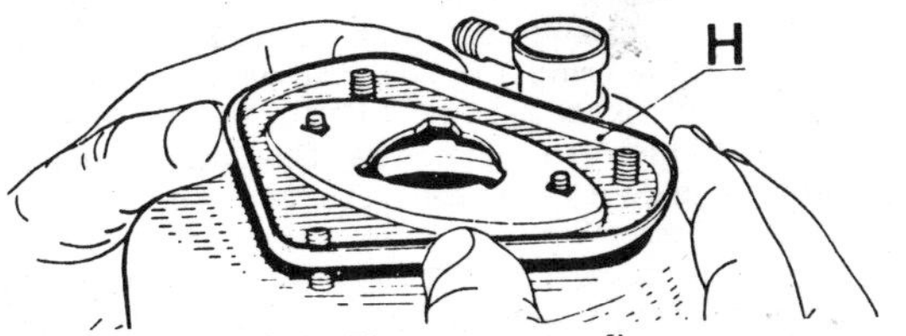

FIG 10:6 The master-vac flange

Key to Fig 10:6 H Flange

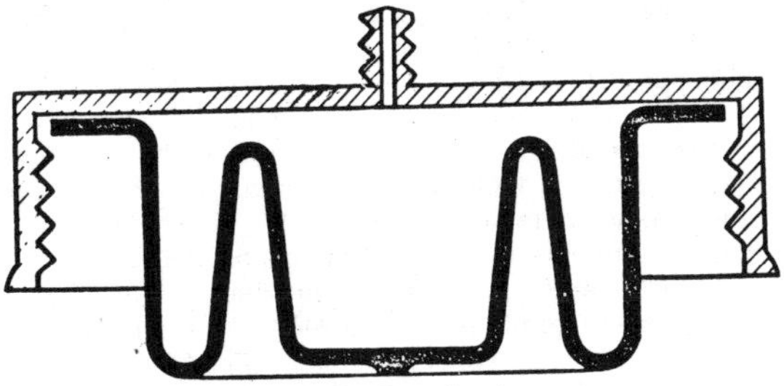

FIG 10:7 Cap diaphragm

the flange in such a position that it does not foul the non-return valve, fit the washers and screw up all the nuts without fully tightening them. Centralize the flange and then tighten the nuts. Complete reassembling by reversing the remainder of the dismantling procedure but when refitting the air filter and the clevis, check before tightening locknut E in **FIG 10:5** that dimension D is 1⅝ inch (42 mm) as the position of the brake pedal is determined by this dimension.

Refitting:

Refit the master-vac securing nuts, refit the clevis securing the brake pedal to the thrust rod and pin it. Reconnect the three brake lines, vacuum hose and battery and refit the air filter. Adjust the master cylinder clearance by turning the nut at the end of the thrust rod 3 in **FIG 10:5** and check that the dimension between the end of the thrust rod 3 and the master cylinder locating face on the master-vac unit is .288 to .236 inch (6.2 to 6 mm). Bleed the braking system as described in **Section 10:2** and fit the reservoir cap placing its diaphragm in the shape shown in **FIG 10:7**.

10:5 Removing and refitting a brake pedal

To remove the pedal with reference to **FIG 10:8** disconnect the brake pedal and clutch pedal return spring, open and remove the pivot pin from the master cylinder rod 1, remove the clip 2 and pull the pedal shaft 3 towards the right. Push out the roll-pin 4 and remove the brake pedal 5.

Refit the pedal by reversing the removal operations, smearing the pedal assembly shaft with grease before reassembling. Check and adjust if necessary the brake pedal free travel (see **Section 10:3**).

10:6 Overhauling a caliper:

Removal:

Using a suitable rubber bung, plug the reservoir outlet passage B in **FIG 10:1**, jack up the side concerned, place it on a safety stand and remove the road wheel. On R.1150 models remove the pins 13 in **FIG 10:9** which secure the swing clamps, tilt the swing clamps 14 and free the caliper by pulling it towards the rear. On R.1151 models remove the clips A in **FIG 10:10**, slide keys B in **FIG 10:11** to one side, free the caliper from the caliper bracket and disconnect the pad wear warning light lead. On both models, with regard to **FIG 10:12** remove the union screw D, the clip C and unscrew the hose B. Remove the caliper.

Follow these instructions, **without disconnecting the feed hose** to renew brake pads. The pad thickness can be checked by measuring the amount of pad on the

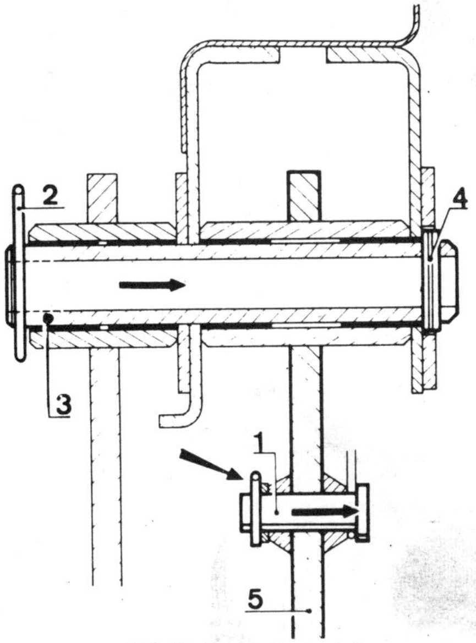

FIG 10:8 Brake pedal

Key to Fig 10:8 1 Rod 2 Clip 3 Shaft 4 Roll-pin 5 Pedal

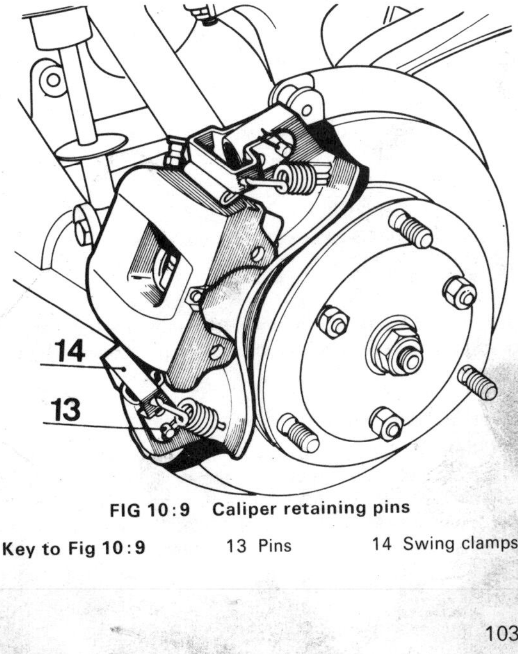

FIG 10:9 Caliper retaining pins

Key to Fig 10:9 13 Pins 14 Swing clamps

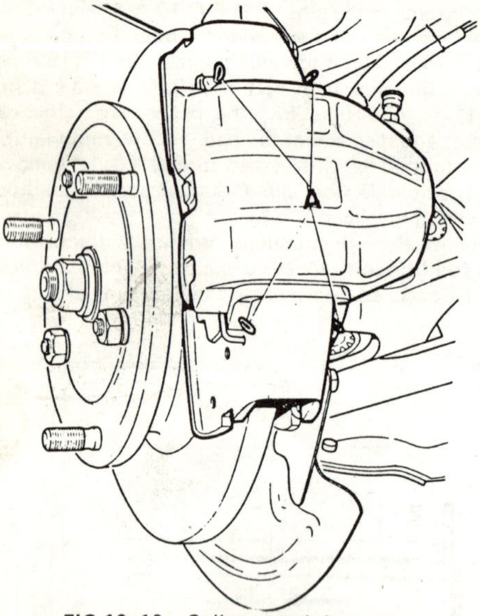

FIG 10:10 Caliper retaining clips

Key to Fig 10:10 A Clip

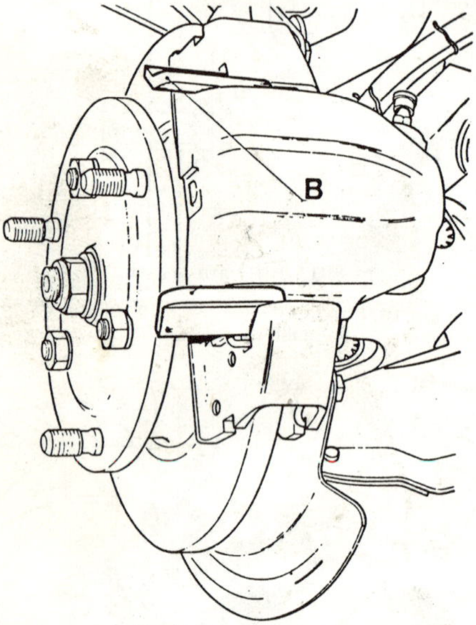

FIG 10:11 Caliper keys

Key to Fig 10:11 B Keys

piston side is recessed with reference to the caliper bracket. This recess dimension should not exceed $\frac{13}{64}$ inch (5 mm).

Overhauling:

Carefully clean the outside of the caliper with **methylated spirits** after plugging the hose tapping. With reference to **FIG 10:13** remove the cap 3, unscrew the nut 2 whilst holding the end of the shaft 6 with a screwdriver and push out the piston 4 by pressing it on shaft 6.

Take out the O-ring seal or the square section seal. from its groove using a flexible strip with well rounded edges in the manner shown in **FIG 10:14. It is absolutely forbidden to dismantle the wear take-up system inside the piston.** The two parts form an inseparable assembly.

Clean the caliper and piston by first cleaning them in a bath of trichlorethylene using a stiff brush, then give them another clean in a bath of clean trichlorethylene and finally clean them in methylated spirits until all traces of trichlorethylene are removed.

Examine the piston and if any scoring, traces of corrosion or roughened areas are visible replace the components. If the seal groove in the caliper has excessive corrosion the entire caliper must be replaced.

Lubricate the caliper bore and groove with brake fluid, fit a new seal **of the same type** as that which has been removed again lubricating the seal with brake fluid. With reference to **FIG 10:15** hold the piston 4 fitted with its seal 7 in a vertical position with the thread of the shaft 6 upwards and gently push the piston into the bore using the thumbs in the manner illustrated in **FIG 10:16. Never tap in the piston in an attempt to insert it as damage might occur to the O-ring or square section**

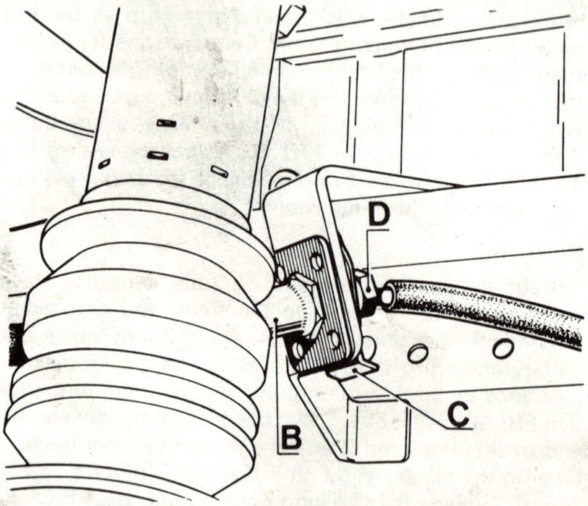

FIG 10:12 Brake hose connections

Key to Fig 10:12 B Hose C Clamp D Screw

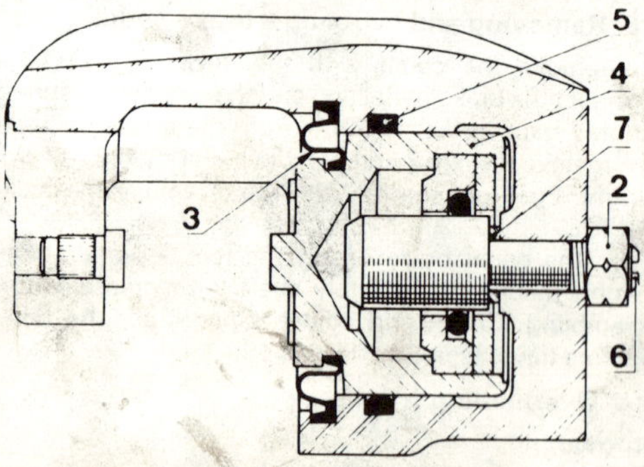

FIG 10:13 The caliper

Key to Fig 10:13 2 Nut 3 Cap 4 Piston
5 Seal 6 Shaft 7 Seal

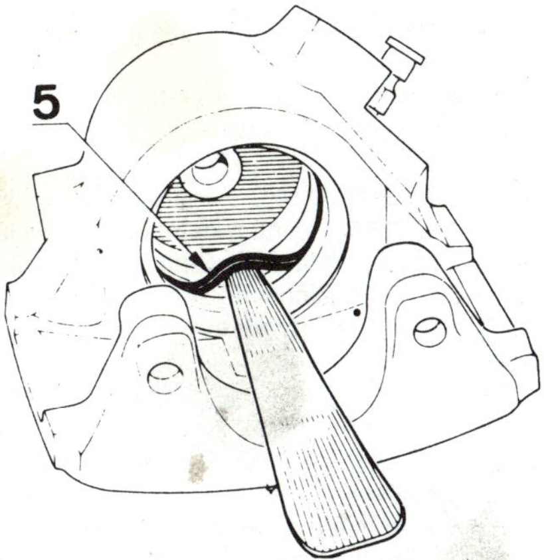

FIG 10:14 Removing the caliper seal

Key to Fig 10:14 5 Seal

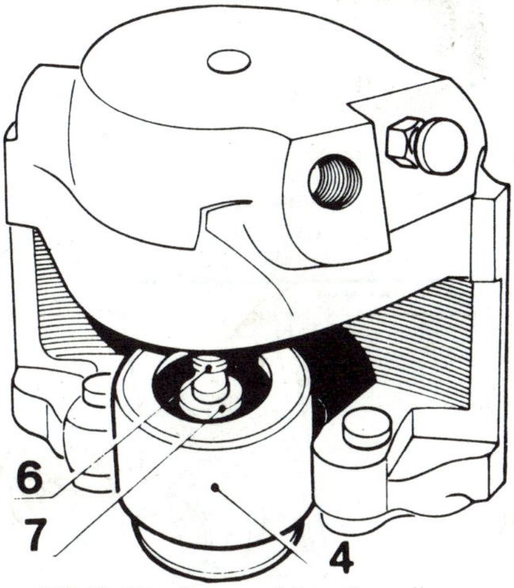

FIG 10:15 Reassembling the caliper

Key to Fig 10:15 4 Piston 6 Shaft 7 Seal

seal. Refit the nut on the piston shaft and tighten it to a torque of 10 lb ft (1.5 m.da.N). With regard to **FIG 10:17** position the reference mark P on the bleed screw side.

To test the caliper fit a union Fre.374 and tool Fre.12A (see **FIG 10:18**). Connect an air hose to the union and immerse the caliper into a tank of methylated spirits. Apply 5 lb/sq inch (.3 bar) pressure to the caliper and move the piston in and out by operating the screw on tool Fre.12A backwards and forwards half a turn. Move the piston ten times in order to expel the air in the caliper seal groove and then repeat the operation at pressures of 10 lb/sq inch (.7 bar), 15 lb/sq inch (1.0 bar), 20 lb/sq inch (1.2 bar), 25 lb/sq inch (1.5 bar) and 30 lb/sq inch (2 bar). If the caliper leaks, which will be detected by a thin stream of bubbles rising to the surface of the fluid, it is to be dismantled again. If the piston is the original one replace it and if it is a new one replace the caliper. Retest and when the caliper is serviceable smear the periphery of the piston with Spagragh grease 806.149. Fit a new protective cap. To make bleeding easier fill the caliper with brake fluid through the hose tapping.

Refitting:

Screw in the brake hose using a new copper seal and on R.1150 models fit the brake pads into the caliper, the caliper into the bracket after having checked that the brake pad thrust springs R in **FIG 10:19** are in position on the caliper bracket then tilt the caliper swing clamps onto the caliper and fit the swing clamp pins, pinning them in place. On R.1151 models insert one end of the caliper between the spring and the key locating face on the caliper bracket, engage the other end of the caliper by compressing both springs, fit the first key then insert a screwdriver into the second key locating area, press the screwdriver down, fit the second key, fit the four clips with the flat part towards the caliper bracket and finally connect the wear warning light lead to the brake pad. On both models place the brake hose, without any strain on it, in front of the retaining lug with the front suspension released and the steering in the straight-ahead position. If the notches do not align with each other turn the hose end fitting to the next notch following the direction shown by the arrows in **FIG 10:20** and **FIG 10:21.** Fit the hose retaining clamp, screw the brake pipe union onto the hose and bleed the system as detailed in **Section 10:2**.

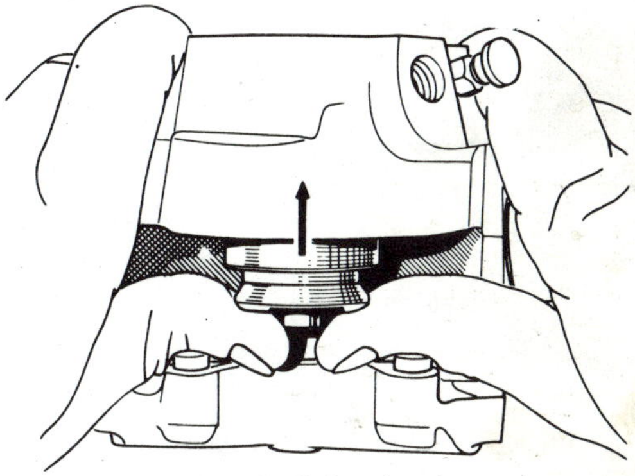
FIG 10:16 Refitting the piston

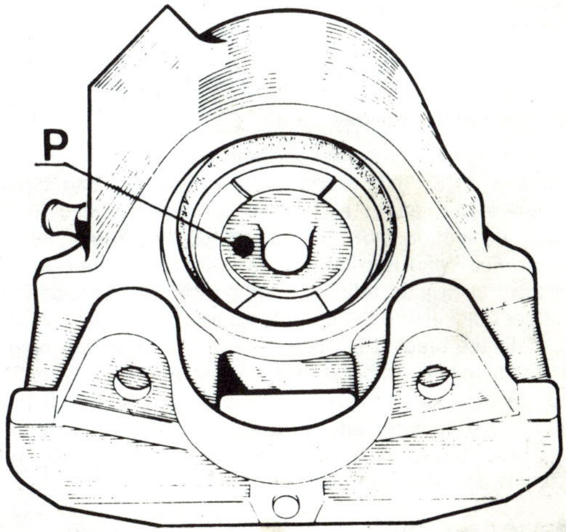

FIG 10:17 Caliper piston reference mark

Key to Fig 10:17 P Reference mark

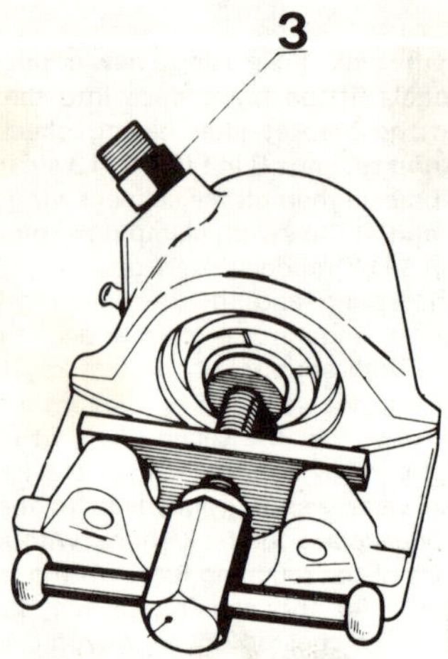

FIG 10:18 Tool Fre.12A in position

Key to Fig 10:18 3 Union

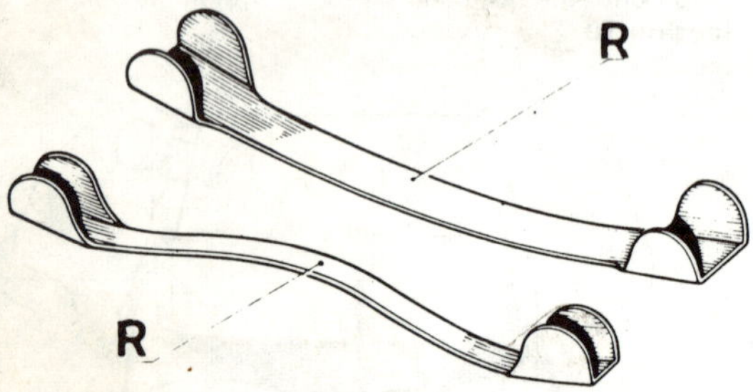

FIG 10:19 Brake pad thrust springs

Key to Fig 10:19 R Springs

With regard to **FIG 10:22** dimension A has been increased from $1\frac{3}{8}$ inch (34.5 mm) to $1\frac{7}{16}$ inch (37 mm). If a new type caliper is fitted as a replacement to an old type it is essential to fit a new type reservoir. Never try to fit new type brake pads to old type calipers.

10:7 Brake caliper bracket and deflector

Brake caliper bracket:

To remove a brake caliper bracket jack up the vehicle, place it on an axle stand and remove the road wheel. Remove the caliper and brake pads as detailed in the previous section. With regard to **FIG 10:23** unscrew the two bolts F and two bolts E. Remove the caliper bracket putting aside any adjusting shims that are between the caliper bracket and the stub axle carrier.

Refit the bracket by carrying out the removing operations in reverse. Check that clearance A and B in **FIG 10:24** are both between $\frac{3}{32}$ and $\frac{1}{8}$ inch ($2.5 \pm .5$ mm), fitting or removing adjusting shims which are available in three thicknesses .059 inch (1.5 mm), .079 inch (2 mm) and .099 inch (2.5 mm) until they are.

Brake deflector:

To remove a brake deflector unscrew the two bolts which secure the deflector to the caliper bracket and undo the bolt which secures the deflector to the stub axle carrier.

Refit the deflector by carrying out the removal sequence in reverse.

10:8 Girling disc brakes

From March 1968 a certain number of vehicles were and still are being fitted with Girling disc brakes. It is essential that only Michelin No. 7.700.502.304 and Dunlop No. 8.559.582 tyres are used with this brake arrangement.

Replacing the brake pads:

Jack up the vehicle, place it on a safety stand and remove the road wheel. With reference to **FIG 10:25** press on strip A to free the two pins B, remove clip C and take out the two pins. Pull out the brake pads.

To fit the new pads using two screwdrivers as levers return the caliper pistons after drawing out some of the fluid in the master cylinder reservoir. Fit the new pads by reversing the removal procedure.

Overhauling a caliper:

To remove the caliper plug the reservoir bottle, jack up the vehicle, place it on an axle stand and remove the road

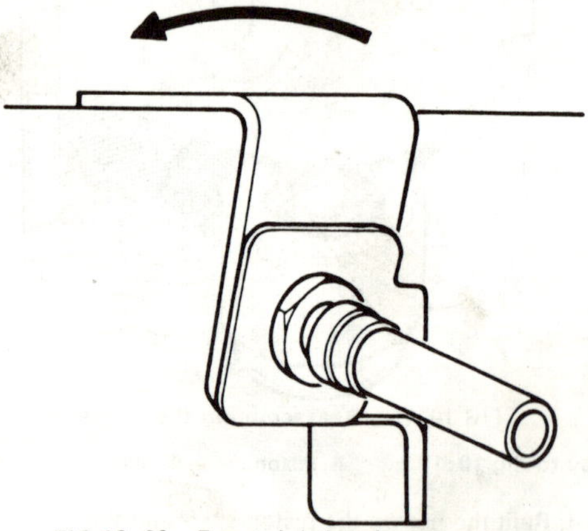

FIG 10:20 Front righthand arrangement

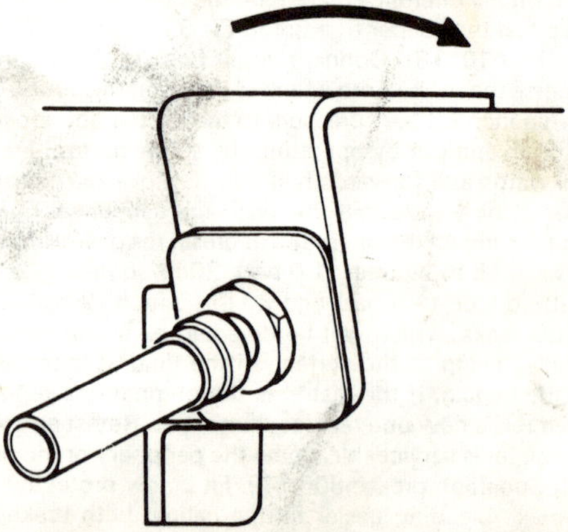

FIG 10:21 Front lefthand arrangement

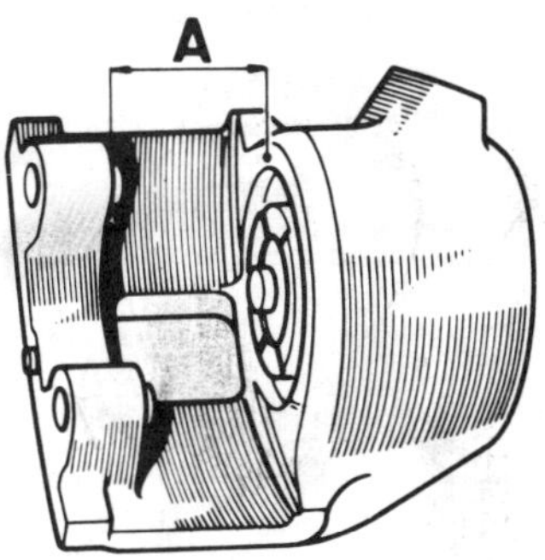

FIG 10:22 **Modified caliper**

Key to Fig 10:22 A Dimension

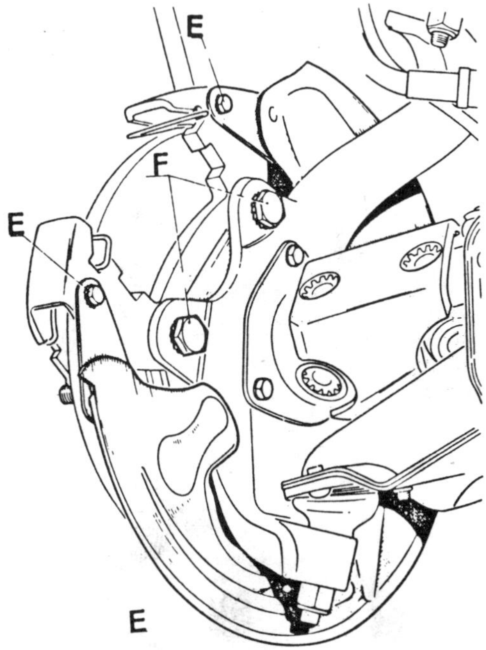

FIG 10:23 **Removing a brake caliper bracket**

Key to Fig 10:23 E Bolts F Bolts

wheel. Disconnect the rigid brake line from the brake hose and loosen the hose at the caliper. Unscrew the two bolts securing the caliper, free the caliper from the brake and unscrew the hose from the caliper.

To dismantle the caliper remove the pads as detailed previously, free the moving clevis on the caliper and slide it out. With regard to **FIG 10:26** remove plastic piston guides 1 and snap rings 2 which retain the dust rubbers. Remove the two cylinder dust rubbers then using compressed air **gently** push the pistons out. Clean all the components in methylated spirits and check for scoring inside the bore or on the pistons which would make replacement of the entire caliper necessary.

Assemble the unit by first lubricating all the parts with brake fluid then with reference to **FIG 10:27** fit pistons A with the counter bores towards the outside, the dust rubbers B and snap rings C.

Refit the unit by reversing the removal sequences tightening the hose to 15 lb ft (2 m.da.N) torque and align the hose in the manner described in **Section 10:6.**

10:9 Removing and refitting a brake drum and disc

Brake drum:

To remove a drum, take off the hub nut plug, remove the splitpin, undo the locknut and hub nut and remove the thrust washer. Using a suitable extractor, extract the brake drum.

Refit by reversing the removal operations.

Disc:

To take off a disc undo the hub nut and remove the washer. Remove the deflector (see **Section 10:7**) and

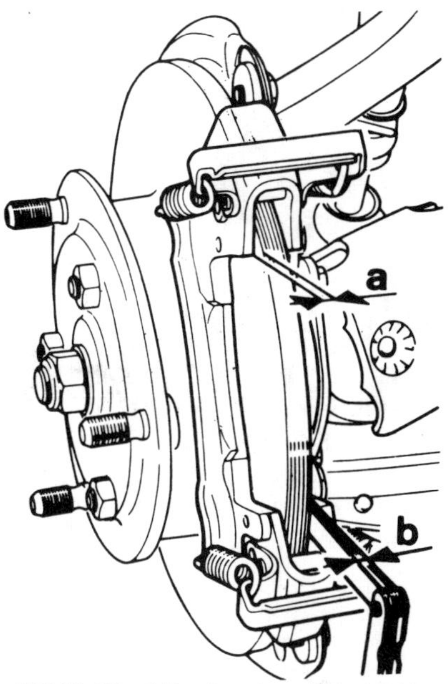

FIG 10:24 **Adjusting the caliper bracket**

Key to Fig 10:24 A Clearance B Clearance

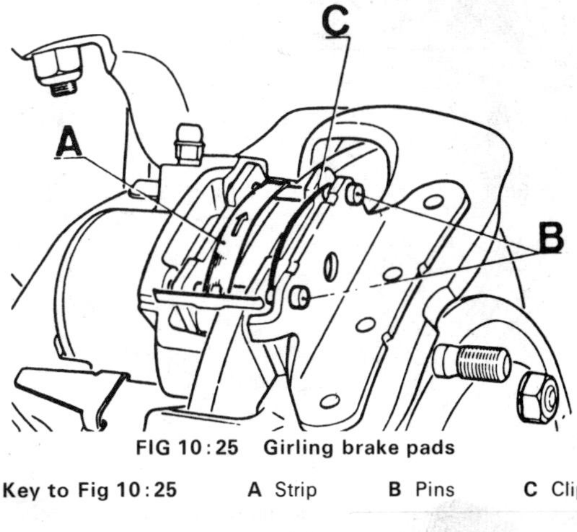

FIG 10:25 **Girling brake pads**

Key to Fig 10:25 A Strip B Pins C Clip

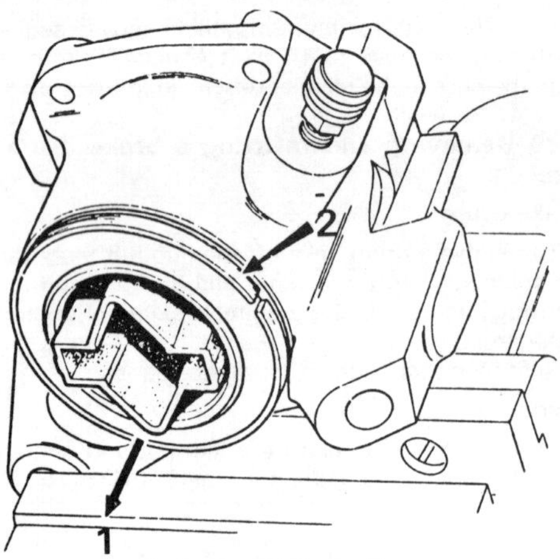

FIG 10:26 Girling caliper

Key to Fig 10:26 1 Piston guide 2 Snap ring

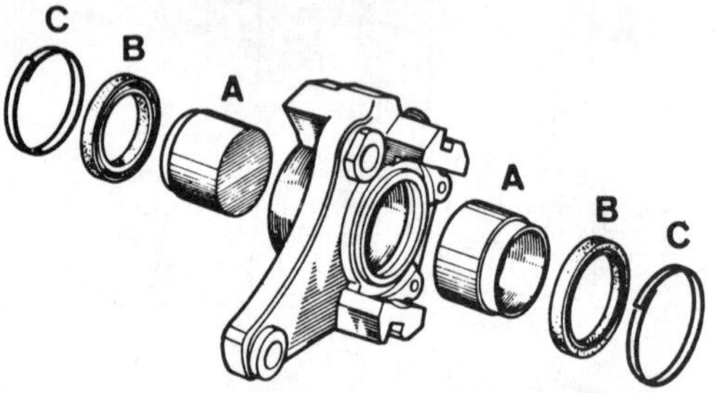

FIG 10:27 Girling caliper components

Key to Fig 10:27 **A** Piston **B** Seal **C** Snap ring

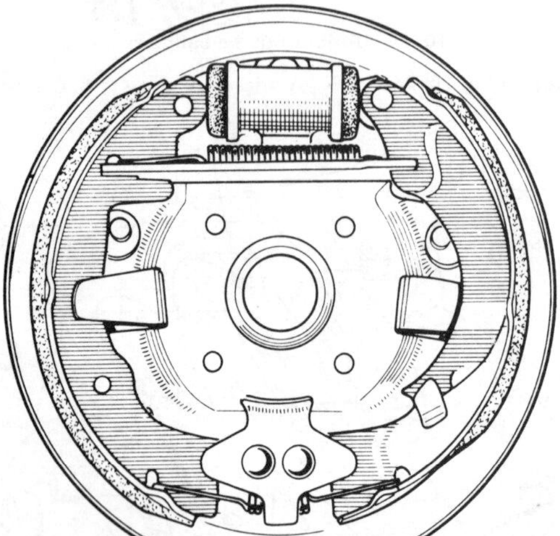

FIG 10:28 Early model Bendix rear brakes

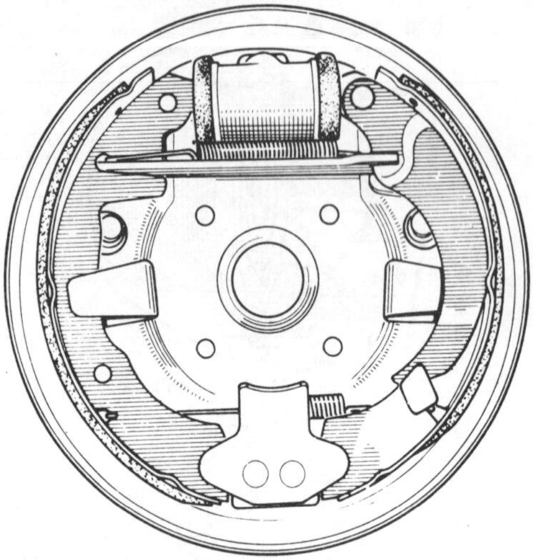

FIG 10:29 Later model Bendix rear brakes

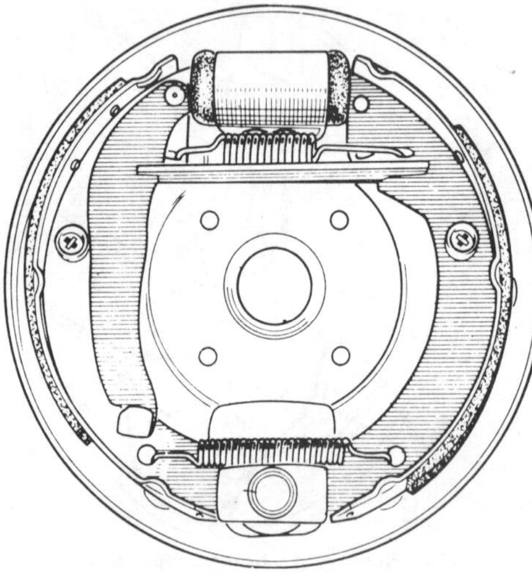

FIG 10:30 Girling rear brakes

caliper (see **Section 10:6**). Secure tool T.Av.235 without its screw on the three wheel securing nuts and fit extractor Rou.378 against the stub axle carrier placing and positioning it bottom first. On R.1151 models as a larger disc is fitted, some metal will have to be ground away from the inside of the 'legs' of tool Rou.378. Secure the centre screw of tool Rou.378 into tool T.Av.235 not forgetting to place a washer under the nut of tool Rou.378. Extract the disc by tightening the nut of tool Rou.378.

Refit the unit by engaging the hub together with the outer bearing and the spacer in position on the stub axle splines and screw tool T.Av.236 onto it. Align the assembly with the stub axle and tighten it to finish fitting the assembly. Remove tool T.Av.236 and fit a new hub nut and washer, tightening the hub nut to 90 lb ft (12 m.da.N) torque.

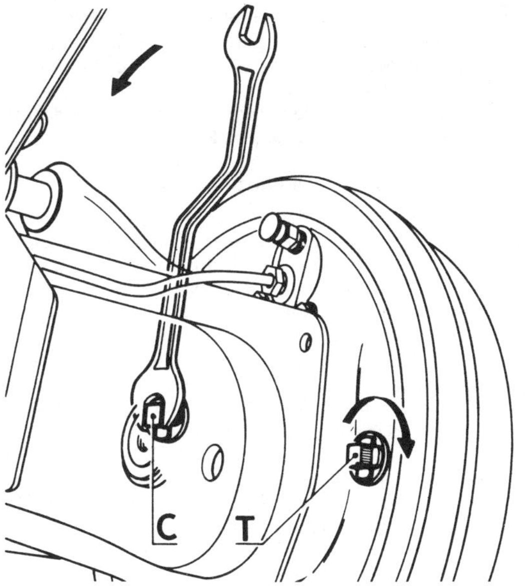

FIG 10:31 **Bendix brake adjuster**

Key to Fig 10:31 **C** Adjuster **T** Adjuster

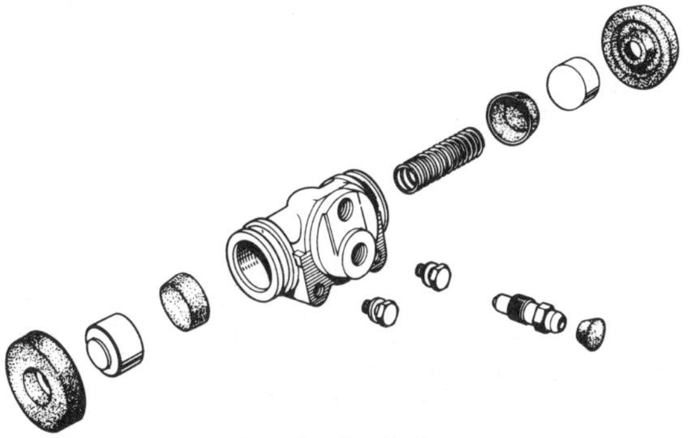

FIG 10:32 **The wheel cylinder components**

10:10 Replacing the rear brake linings

Three types of rear brake layout are used these are shown in **FIGS 10:28, 10:29 and 10:30.** To remove the rear brake linings remove the drum as detailed in the previous section, take off the upper return spring, then tie a piece of wire around the wheel cylinder to stop the pistons coming out. Disconnect the handbrake cable, remove the clips securing the brake shoes and pull back the shoes to free the upper plate. Take out the shoes and the lower return spring.

Refit the shoes by carrying out the removing operations in reverse. Cover the clips on the brake anchor plate side, with sealing compound. On completion adjust the brakes (see **Section 10:11**).

All the linings on any given axle are to be replaced at the same time, and identical grade linings are to be used on all the shoes. If the brake drum has been machined to eliminate scoring the other drum must be machined to the same amount. On the Girling brakes, the brake shoe retaining clips have been replaced by a rod, a spring and two metal caps.

10:11 Adjusting the rear brakes

On Bendix layouts, with reference to **FIG 10:31** turn the adjusting squares C and T in the direction shown by the arrows using a suitable spanner until the brake shoes make contact with the drum. Turn them in the opposite direction until the wheels turn freely.

On Girling arrangements turn the adjuster square in a clockwise direction until the brake linings make contact with the drum, then turn it in the opposite direction until the wheels turn freely.

10:12 Overhauling a wheel cylinder

To remove a wheel cylinder take off the brake shoes as described in **Section 10:10,** disconnect the pipe union on the wheel cylinder and remove the two bolts securing the cylinder to the anchor plate.

The wheel cylinder components are shown in **FIG 10:32**. Inspect the parts, any parts showing signs of

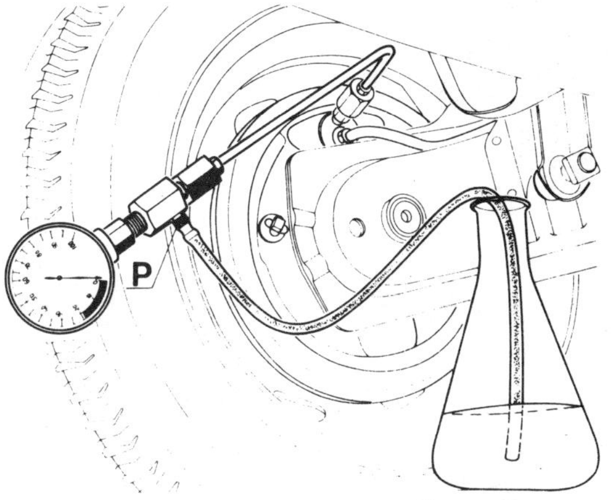

FIG 10:33 **Checking the cut-off pressure**

Key to Fig 10:33 **P** Bleed screw

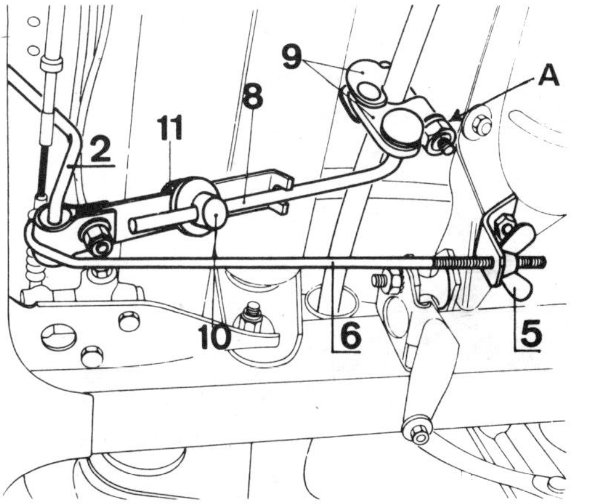

FIG 10:34 **Adjusting the cut-off pressure**

Key to Fig 10:34 2 Bearing 5 Nut 6 Tool Fre.282 8 Link 9 Clamp 10 Screw 11 Nut **A** Nut

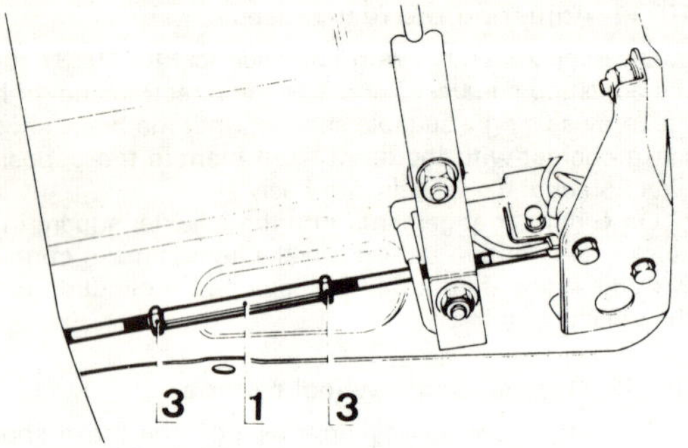

FIG 10:35 Adjusting the handbrake

Key to Fig 10:35 1 Sleeve 3 Nuts

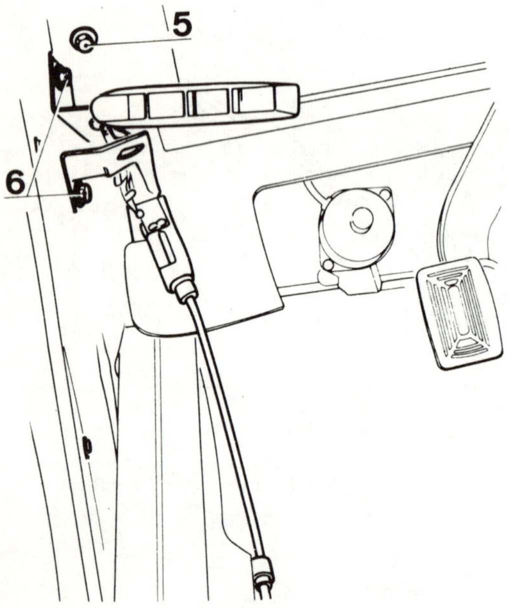

FIG 10:36 Removing the handbrake control

Key to Fig 10:36 5 Bolt 6 Bolt

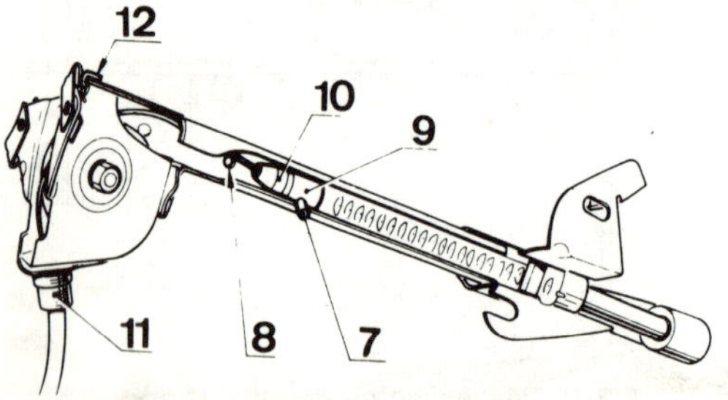

FIG 10:37 The handbrake control lever

Key to Fig 10:37 7 Pin 8 Hole 9 Ring 10 Clamp 11 Stop 12 Clip

wear or distortion must be replaced by genuine spares only. Immerse the pistons and the cups in brake fluid and reassemble in the order shown in **FIG 10:32.**

Refit the cylinder by reversing the removal procedure on completion bleed the braking system (see **Section 10:2**) and adjust the brakes (see **Section 10:11**).

10:13 Brake pressure limiting valve

To check the cut-off pressure connect the pressure gauge Fre.214 to one of the rear wheel cylinder bleed screws, bleed the system by means of screw P in **FIG 10:33** and then with the fuel tank filled and a person sitting in the driving seat press on the brake pedal and note the cut-off pressure which should be 385 to 470 lb/sq inch (30 $\pm$ 3 bars) for R.1150 vehicles fitted with Girling brakes, 415 to 485 lb/sq inch (34 $\pm$ 5 bars) for R.1151 models and 430 to 515 lb/sq inch (33 $\pm$ 3 bars) for R.1150 models with Bendix brakes.

To adjust the cut-off pressure, with reference to **FIG 10:34** check that the clamp 9 is correctly tightened on the anti-roll bar, loosen the locknut 11, hook tool Fre.282 (6) into the lower spring bearing 2 and the exhaust silencer and operate screw 5 until the correct pressure is obtained then tighten the nut 11. Remove tool Fre.282 and the pressure gauge. Refit the bleed screw and bleed the system (see **Section 10:2**).

Early models were fitted with a control rod in place of the adjustable link 8 in **FIG 10:34** and adjustment of these units is obtained by unscrewing nut A on the clamp 9.

When fitting a new brake pressure limiting valve in place of an old one ensure that the pipe from the master cylinder is fitted to the port situated in the plane on the plug side.

10:14 Adjusting the handbrake

To adjust the handbrake loosen the nuts 3 in **FIG 10:35** and turn the sleeve 1 until the shoes make contact with the drum then unscrew the sleeve until the wheels turn freely. Lock the nuts 3.

10:15 Replacing the handbrake control lever and cables

Control lever:

Release the handbrake and disconnect its clevis. Remove the lefthand glove compartment and the securing screws under the wing. With reference to **FIG 10:36** undo the screw 5 and screw 6. Position the pin 7 in **FIG 10:37** inline with hole 8 and push it out by means of a pin punch through hole 8. Slide the ring 9 along the rod, free the cable clamp 10, take out the cable cover end stop 11 and clip 12.

Refit the lever by reversing the removing operations. On completion adjust the handbrake and cover the outer securing bolts with sealing compound.

Cables:

To remove the cable first carry out all the removal instructions layed out in the previous sub-section. Unscrew the nuts 3 in **FIG 10:35** and sleeve 1 and free the cables from their supports and the cable cover end clamp. Remove the brake drum (see **Section 10:9**) and free the end of the cable from the lever on the brake shoe.

Push back the cable cover from its clamp on the anchor plate.

Refit the cables by carrying out the removing operations in reverse. Adjust the handbrake (see **Section 10:14**) and apply compound to the points where the cables enter the anchor plate.

10:16 Fault diagnosis

(a) Spongy pedal

1 Leak in the system
2 Worn master cylinder
3 Fluid level in master cylinder reservoir tank very low
4 Air in the fluid system

(b) Brakes pull or lock to one side

1 Distorted or loose disc/drum
2 Contaminated or mixed pads/linings
3 Worn suspension or steering units
4 Faulty caliper unit
5 Seized handbrake cable or lever
6 Faulty wheel cylinder

(c) Scraping noise when brakes applied

1 No lining material left on pad(s)
2 Rear shoe(s) down to the rivets

CHAPTER 11

THE ELECTRICAL SYSTEM

11 :1 Description

The 12-volt electrical equipment incorporates compensated voltage control for the charging circuit, which incidentally should be adjusted on a specified test bench. The wiring on R.1150 models is divided into nine harnesses; an engine harness, a chassis harness, a horn and lighting switch harness, an instrument panel harness, a rear harness, an interior light harness, a luggage compartment light harness, a positive starter lead harness and a negative starter lead harness. The wiring on R.1151 models is divided into eight harnesses; an engine harness, a rear harness, a horn and lighting switch harness, an interior light harness, a lefthand window winder harness, a righthand window winder harness, a positive starter lead harness and a negative starter lead harness.

Plug mouldings are soldered onto the ends of each lead and the mouldings will only fit into their corresponding connectors so preventing any wrong connection from being made.

The alternator is mounted on the lefthand side of the cylinder block and is driven by an endless belt from the crankshaft pulley. A rotatable mounting enables the belt tension to be adjusted. Two types of 12-volt battery are used, a Tudor and Fulmen and two types of starter motor are used; a Ducellier 6183 and Paris-Rhone D.8.E71.

Above a certain temperature the engine is cooled by a motor fan unit which is automatically switched on and off to suit the engine temperature. The system consists of the motor fan which is basically a 12-volt electric motor, a relay which feeds current to the battery from the fan and a MOSTA temperature switch which automatically switches the fan on and off to suit the engine temperature.

On R.1151 models a Bosch two speed windscreen wiper is fitted. On the same models electric motors are fitted to operate the window winders and sun roof. All these motors are protected by a thermal cut-out which switches off the feed if the current flow becomes too great and if the cut-out operates wait approximately ten seconds for it to return to its normal position. Again on R.1151 models the smokers requisite compartment is fitted with a light which operates at the same time as the instrument panel light, the rear window is fitted with a heating element which removes any frost or mist, a warning light being incorporated in the circuit to show that the heater is in operation and two iodine vapour headlights which come into use when the lighting switch

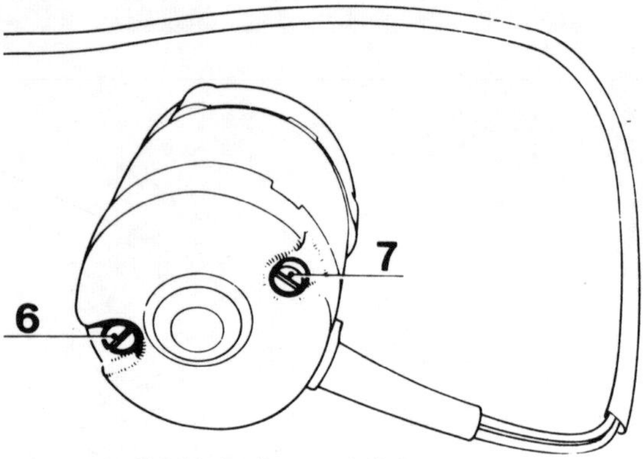

FIG 11 : 1 Rear end plate screws

Key to Fig 11 : 11 6 Screw 7 Screw

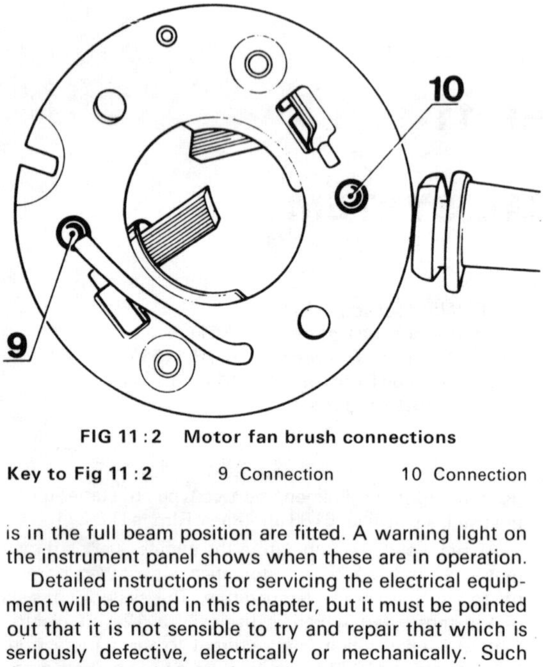

FIG 11 : 2 Motor fan brush connections

Key to Fig 11 : 2 9 Connection 10 Connection

is in the full beam position are fitted. A warning light on the instrument panel shows when these are in operation.

Detailed instructions for servicing the electrical equipment will be found in this chapter, but it must be pointed out that it is not sensible to try and repair that which is seriously defective, electrically or mechanically. Such equipment should be replaced by new units which can be obtained on an exchange basis.

11 : 2 The battery

The battery fitted to both models is a 12-volt acid type, having six cells each consisting of a group of positive and negative plates immersed in a solution of sulphuric acid and distilled water (electrolyte).

The battery has three functions:

1 To supply current to the various components when the alternator is not in use, i.e. starter motor, lights, etc.
2 To provide a constant supply of current to the electrical equipment when the consumption of the electrical equipment exceeds the output of the alternator.
3 To control the voltage of the electrical supply system.

The battery and its surrounding parts should be kept dry and clean, particularly the tops of the cells, as any dampness could cause a leakage between the securing strap and the positive battery terminal which will result in a partially discharged battery. Clean off any corrosion from the battery bolts, strap and tray with diluted ammonia, afterwards painting the affected areas with anti-sulphuric paint. Check the terminal posts and if they are corroded remove the cables and clean the posts with diluted ammonia then smear them with petroleum jelly before remaking the connection. High electrical resistance due to corrosion of the terminal posts is often responsible for lack of sufficient current to operate the starter motor. Check that the battery top(s) are not cracked as this might cause leakage of electrolyte and subsequent corrosion. Maintain the electrolyte level above the cell plates and **always add acid to water.**

Test the condition of charge of the battery cells using a hydrometer. Make certain that the float is free, immerse the tube below the level of electrolyte, depress the bulb then slowly allow the bulb to expand, this action drawing electrolyte into the hydrometer. Be careful not to draw in too much and check the reading at eye-level. If the level of the electrolyte is too low for a hydrometer reading to be taken, top-up with distilled water and recharge the battery for 30 minutes before taking another reading.

The indications from the readings are as follows:

For climates below 80°F (27°C)		
Cell fully charged	—	1.27 to 1.29
Cell about half charged	—	1.19 to 1.21
Cell completely discharged	—	1.11 to 1.13
For climates above 80°F (27°C)		
Cell fully charged	—	1.21 to 1.23
Cell about half charged	—	1.13 to 1.15
Cell completely discharged	—	1.05 to 1.07

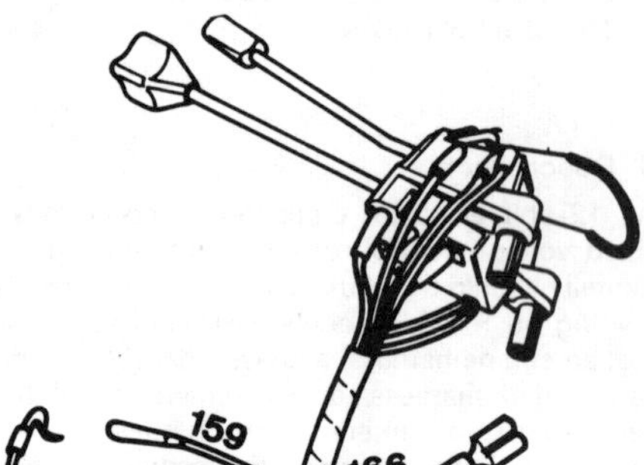

FIG 11 : 3 Horn/lighting switch wiring

These figures are given assuming an electrolyte temperature of 60°F (16°C). If the temperature of the electrolyte exceeds this add .002 inch to the reading for each 5°F or 3°C rise and if the temperature is lower than 60°F (16°C) subtract .002 from the reading for each 5°F or 3°C drop.

All six cells should read approximately the same. If one differs radically from the rest an internal fault is indicated. If the battery is in a low state of charge it should be recharged by first removing the battery from the vehicle and then placing it on a wooden bench coated with an anti-sulphuric paint. Remove the cell top(s) and put the battery on a charger at 5 amps until all cells are gassing freely and the reading of the electrolyte has shown no further rise in four hours. **Never use a naked light near the battery when it is gassing as the hydrogen gas given off is highly explosive.**

11:3 Motor fan unit

Checking the fan unit with the ignition switch on:

1 Connect a 12-volt test lamp between terminal 5 on the relay and earth. If the light fails to light check the lead which connects the battery to terminal 5. If the light lights check the relay coil feed system.

2 Connect the lamp between the positive on the regulator and earth. No light indicates a fault between the voltage regulator and the ignition switch. If the bulb burns check the lead which connects the regulator to terminal 4.

3 Connect the pilot light between terminal 4 and earth. If the light fails to light replace the lead and if it does light check the relay coil.

4 Connect the test lamp between number one relay terminal and earth. If the bulb does not light replace the relay. If the light does light check the motor feed harness and motor.

5 Remove the lead which connects terminal 2 on the relay to earth and short-circuit the two terminals on the temperature switch. If the motor turns replace the switch, if it does not check the lead connecting terminal 2 on the relay to the temperature switch, the lead connecting the switch to terminal 3 on the relay and the relay earth.

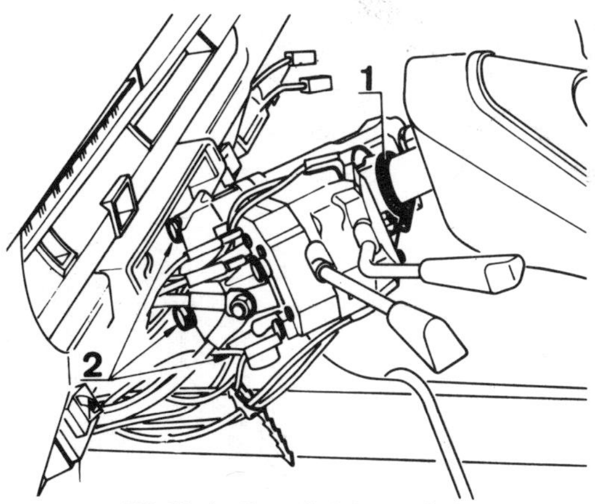

FIG 11:4 Horn/lighting switch

Key to Fig 11:4 1 Return spring 2 Screws

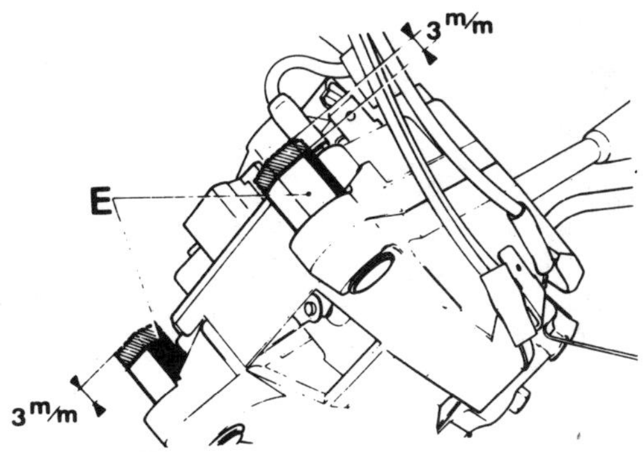

FIG 11:5 Modification to nuts

Key to Fig 11:5 E Nuts

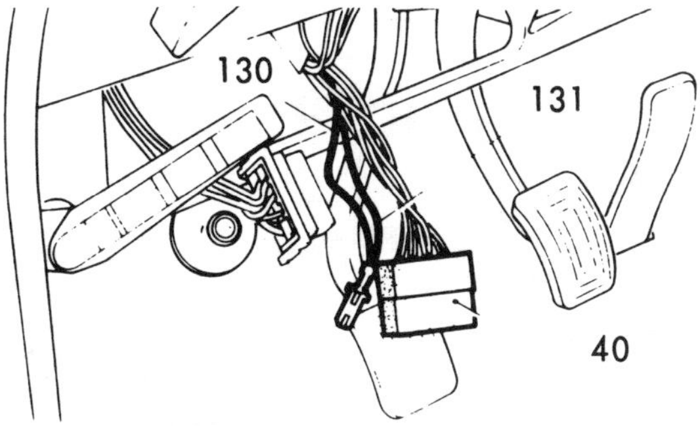

FIG 11:6 Modifications to wiring

Key to Fig 11:6 130 Wire 131 Wire 40 Block

Removal:

Disconnect the battery, mark the two leads which feed the motor fan unit so that they are not connected to the wrong terminals when refitting and then disconnect these two leads from the control relay. Undo the four bolts which secure the fan to the radiator and lift the unit away.

Refit by reversing the removal instructions.

Overhauling:

Unscrew the nut securing the fan to its drive shaft, **note that it is a lefthand thread** and then remove the fan forwards. Unscrew and remove the screws which fasten the support to the motor unit and then unscrew the two screws 6 and 7 in **FIG 11:1** which secure the rear end plate to the body. Remove the end plate and pull back the brush carrier plate and unsolder the brush leads at soldering points 9 and 10 in **FIG 11:2** if the brushes are to be replaced.

Reassemble the unit by carrying out the dismantling instructions in reverse.

11:4 Horn and lighting switch

Removal:

Remove the two protective half-shells on the horn and lighting switch and the glove compartment. Disconnect the two plug blocks 40a and 44a in **FIG 11:3**, leads 158, 159 and 166 and the brake pad warning light. Free the harness from the dashboard and free the direction

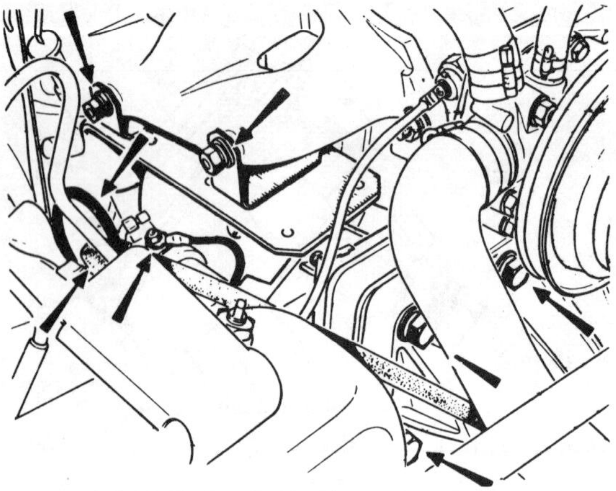

FIG 11 : 7 Removing the starter motor

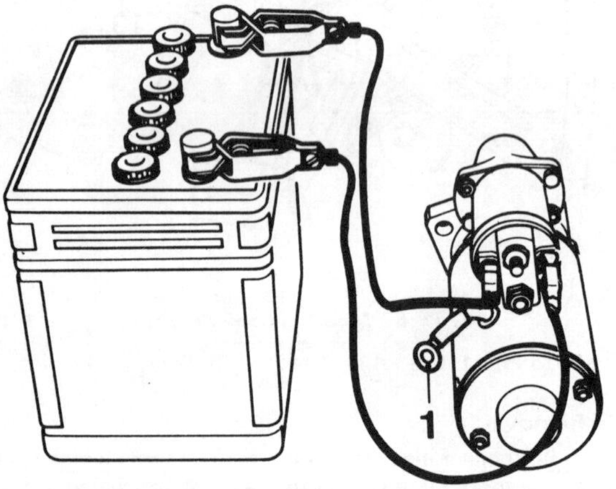

FIG 11 : 8 Testing the starter motor

indicator return spring 1 in **FIG 11 : 4.** Remove the three screws 2 which secure the horn and lighting switch to its support and free the horn and lighting switch.

Refit by reversing the previous instructions.

Modification:

When replacing the horn and lighting switch on vehicles previous to 17.749 the nuts E in **FIG 11 : 5** must have $\frac{1}{8}$ inch (3 mm) removed from the top of them and the leads 130 and 131 (see **FIG 11 : 6**) on plug 40 must be crimped together so that the town and road horns operate simultaneously.

11 : 5 The starter motor

Data:

Brush length:	$\frac{35}{64}$ inch (14 mm)
Minimum brush length:	$\frac{7}{16}$ inch (8 mm)
Commutator diameter:	$1\frac{7}{16}$ inch (36.5 mm)
Minimum commutator diameter:	$1\frac{11}{32}$ inch (34 mm)
Depth of commutator insulation undercut:	.020 inch (.5 mm)
Clearance between front stop and pinion:	.099 inch (2.5 mm)

Removal:

On R.1151 models, with regard to **FIG 11 : 7** remove the protective panel and on both models disconnect the starter feed leads. Remove the locks from the three bolts arrowed in **FIG 11 : 7** and unscrew the three bolts which secure the starter to the clutch housing. On R.1151 models remove the dipstick tube and then on both models remove the starter.

Refit the starter by reversing the removal procedure.

Overhauling:

As replacement parts are very difficult to obtain and special tools are required for adjustment when re-assembling it is recommended that the starter motor be

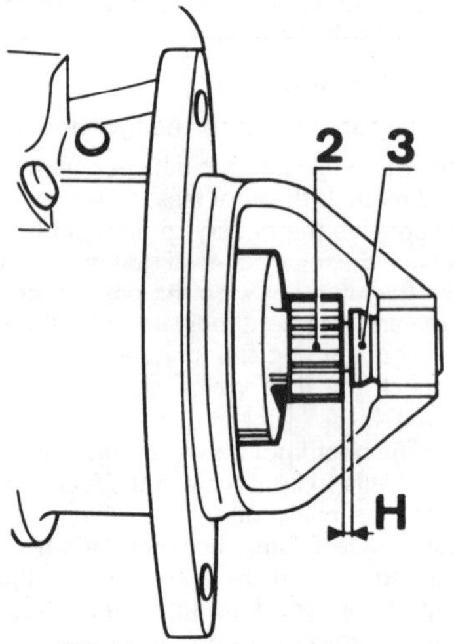

FIG 11 : 9 Pinion clearance

Key to Fig 11 : 9 2 Pinion 3 Stop **H** Clearance

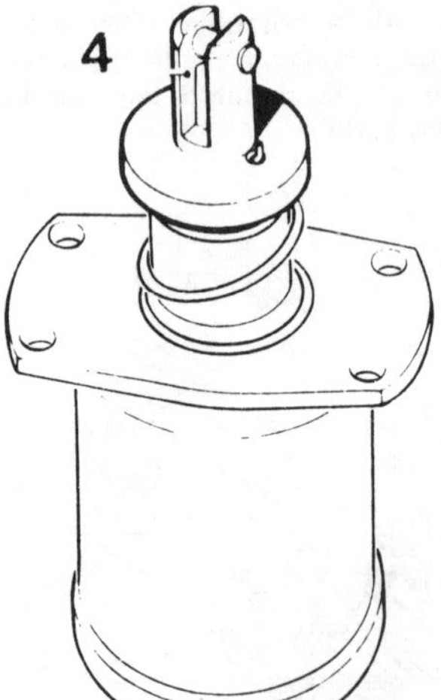

FIG 11 : 10 Pinion adjusting fork

Key to Fig 11 : 10 4 Fork

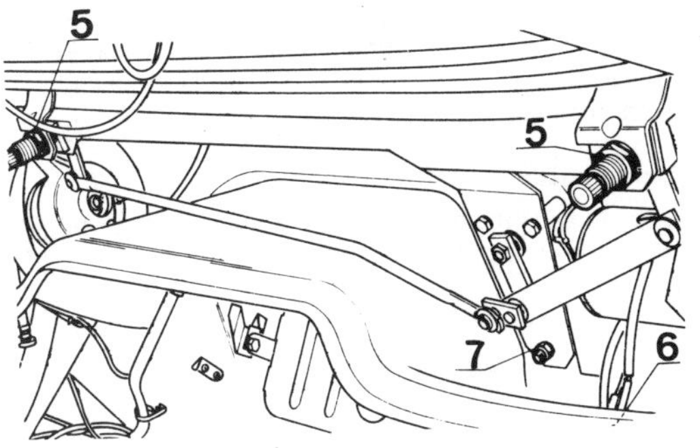

FIG 11 :11 Removing the wiper mechanism

Key to Fig 11 :11 5 Nuts 6 Plate 7 Securing point

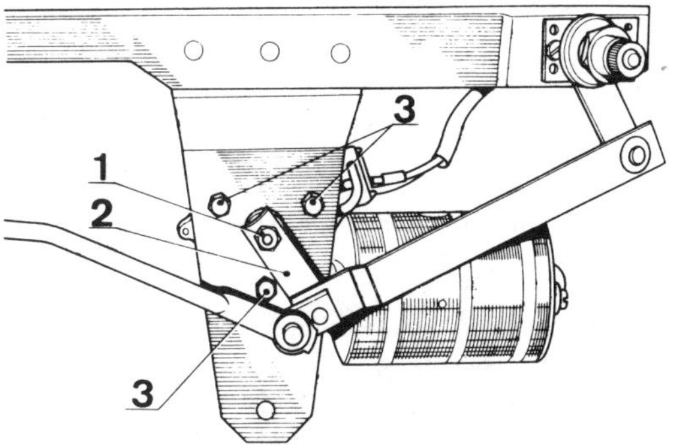

FIG 11 :12 Removing the wiper motor

Key to Fig 11 :12 1 Bolt 2 Link 3 Bolts

replaced as a complete unit. Before, however, changing the starter motor the connection between the core and fork can be checked and adjusted if necessary. To do this connect the starter to a battery in the manner shown in **FIG 11 :8** noting that the field coil feed terminal 1 must not be connected up, and this will bring the pinion 2 in **FIG 11 :9** into its operating position. The clearance H in **FIG 11 :9** should be between .020 and .099 inch (.5 and 2.5 mm) and if the clearance is not correct, remove the switch and screw the fork end 4 in **FIG 11 :10** in or out to obtain the correct clearance.

11 :6 Windscreen wipers

Removal:

Remove the windscreen wiper arms and unscrew the nuts which secure the two bearings. Remove the scuttle grill (see **Chapter 12**). Mark the feed leads and with regard to **FIG 11 :11** disconnect them from the connection plates 6. Loosen the two bearing securing nuts 5 and remove the third securing point 7. Slide the backplate ½ inch towards the righthand side of the vehicle in order to release it from its mounting slides and remove the plate from its location.

Refit by carrying out the removing operations in reverse.

Overhauling:

With reference to **FIG 11 :12** remove the centre bolt 1 and disconnect the drive link 2. Unscrew the three bolts 3 and the five screws which secure the gear train casing coverplate. Remove the plate and wheel. Unscrew the two tie-bolts and remove the end plate, brush carrier plate and armature. Unsolder joints 13 in **FIG 11 :13** if the brushes are to be replaced.

Reassemble by carrying out the above operations in reverse.

11 :7 Instrument panel (R.1151)

To remove the panel remove the switches and two half-shells and unscrew the two securing screws by passing a screwdriver through the apertures (see **FIG 11 :14**). Pull on the panel visor, disconnect the panel light rheostat and remove the visor. Unscrew the three panel securing bolts arrowed in **FIG 11 :15** and the speedometer drive cable. Disconnect both blocks.

Refit by carrying out the removing operations in reverse.

11 :8 Window winder motor (R.1151)

Window winder counter balance:

To remove the counter balance disconnect the motor feed leads, remove the winder mechanism (see **Chapter 12**) and this will give access to the counterbalance.

When reassembling, check that links A and B in **FIG 11 :16** are correctly in line. If they are not, feed the motor with two leads connected to a 12-volt battery and if it does not move in the correct direction, switch over the leads.

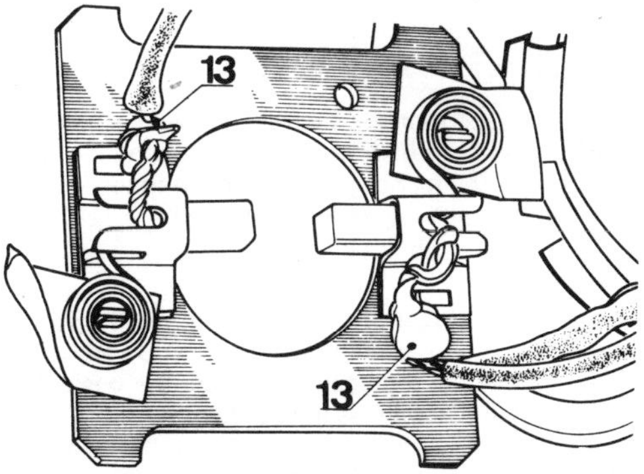

FIG 11 :13 Wiper motor brush connections

Key to Fig 11 :13 13 Joints

FIG 11 :14 Removing the instrument panel

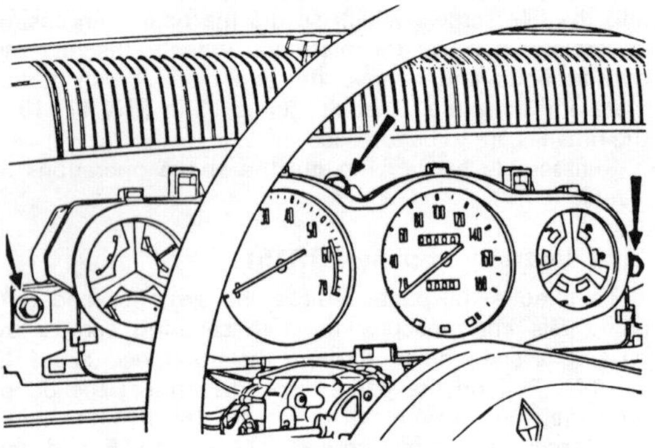

FIG 11 :15 Instrument panel securing bolts

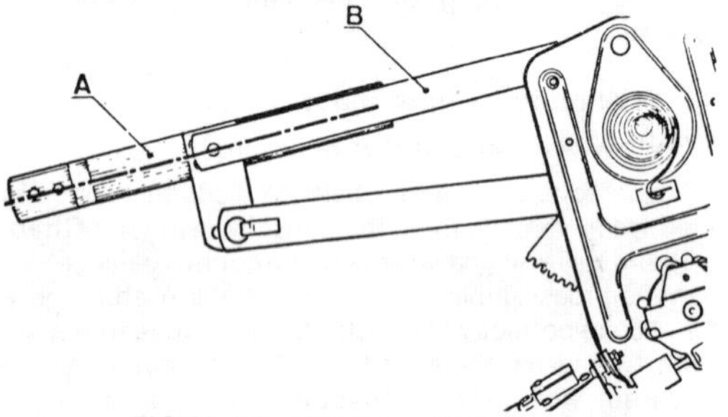

FIG 11 :16 Window winder links

Key to Fig 11 :16 **A** Link **B** Link

The motor:

To remove the motor, unscrew the two securing nuts and free the shaft from its bush after removing the winder mechanism in the manner detailed in **Chapter 12.** If the motor is defective it can only be replaced.

Reduction gear:

Remove the winder unit as described in **Chapter 12,** unscrew the three securing screws, arrowed in **FIG 11 :17** and free the reduction gear from the bush. Again a defective unit can only be replaced.

11 :9 Sun roof motor (R.1151)

The motor:

To remove the sun roof motor slightly pull back the roof to gain access to the screws, disconnect the battery and unscrew the motor embellisher securing screws and remove the embellisher by pulling it back. Disconnect the feed leads, unscrew the guide bearing securing screws and pull them back. Unscrew the motor securing screws, slightly lift the roof and take out the motor. Push out the pin arrowed in **FIG 11 :18** and if the motor is defective, replace it with a new one.

To refit the motor carry out the removing operations in reverse.

Track and friction pads:

Remove the sun roof (see **Chapter 12**) and pull on the tab with a pair of pliers to free the track. Check that the control surfaces are in good condition and if they are not, clean them or replace the part. Check the friction pad switch connections and ensure that the return spring operates correctly and that the pads are both parallel.

Drive belt:

To replace the belt remove the embellisher by unscrewing its securing screws, turn the motor and remove the belt.

11 :10 Fault diagnosis

(a) Battery discharged

1 Terminal connections loose or dirty
2 Short in any circuit
3 Alternator not charging
4 Regulator or cut-out unserviceable
5 Battery defective
6 Fan belt slipping

(b) Insufficient charging current

1 Check 1, 3, 4 and 6 in (a)

(c) Battery will not hold charge

1 Low electrolyte level
2 Battery plates sulphated
3 Electrolyte leakage from cracked casing or top sealing compound
4 Plate separators defective

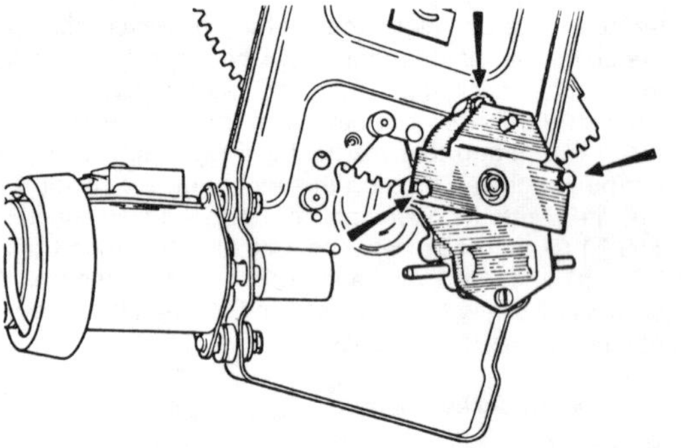

FIG 11 :17 Reduction gear

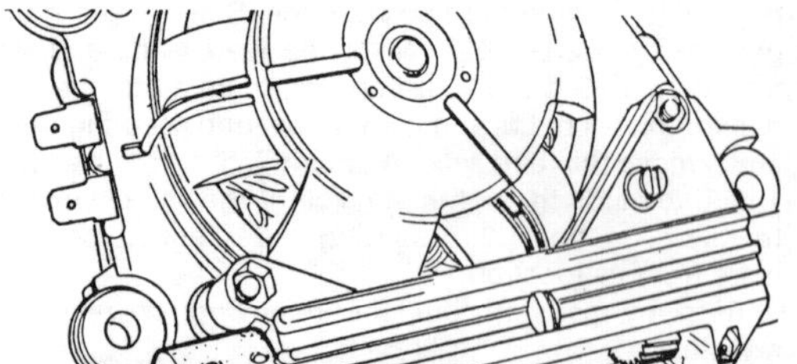

FIG 11 :18 Securing pin

(d) Battery overcharged

1 Regulator needs adjusting

(e) Alternator output low or nil

1 Check 6 in (a)
2 Alternator unserviceable

(f) Starter motor lacks power or will not operate

1 Battery discharged
2 Loose starter cable connections
3 Starter switch faulty
4 Starter motor faulty
5 Engine abnormally stiff
6 Pinion jammed in flywheel ring gear

(g) Starter motor rough or noisy

1 Mounting bolts loose
2 Damaged pinion or flywheel gear teeth

(h) Lamps inoperative or erratic

1 Battery low, bulbs burnt out
2 Faulty earthing of lamps or battery
3 Lighting switch faulty, loose or broken connections

CHAPTER 12

THE BODYWORK

12:1 Front door (R.1150)

Removal:

To remove a front door get an assistant to support the door then using a suitable sized drift push out the door hinge pins.

Dismantling:

With reference to **FIG 12:1** make a hook then by means of the hook compress spring R in **FIG 12:2** and remove the winder handle. Unscrew the two screws securing the arm rest and remove the interior door handle which is secured by either a screw or a roll-pin. Using a screwdriver covered with a protective material (see **FIG 12:3**) remove the interior door trim by pushing the screw-driver into a bottom corner between the door body and trim panel. Free the sealing panel and remove the window winder mechanism assembly. With the window in the upper position, remove the three nuts which secure the backplate and then tilt the plate downwards, inside the body, to free the two rollers from the bearings 6 in **FIG 12:4** on the window bottom 7. Remove the window winder, then lower the window tilting it with the corner downwards and remove it. With regard to **FIG 12:5** remove the outer wiper C and inner wiper B which are secured by clips.

Refit by reversing the dismantling procedure.

On 1967 models two trim pieces were fitted and they are both, like the one trim piece on earlier models, secured by clips.

12:2 Front door (R.1151)

Removing the mechanism:

With reference to **FIG 12:6** align the roller arm 23 with the upper mechanism 24 and unscrew the three nuts 25. Free the assembly by pushing it inside the door and then remove the lower counterbalance to free rollers 26 and 26 bis. Hold the window in an upper position by means of adhesive tape 27, tilt the counterbalance and take the unit out through the aperture in the door body. Note that the feed cable is secured by three welded clips 29.

Refitting and adjusting:

Insert the window winder into the door body, position the window at the height shown in **FIG 12:6** and place the fixed roller into the lower window slide. Position the

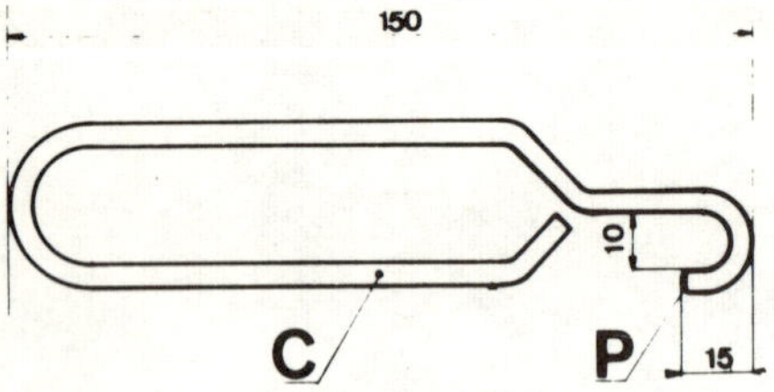

FIG 12:1 Hook

Key to Fig 12:1 C Handle P Chamfer

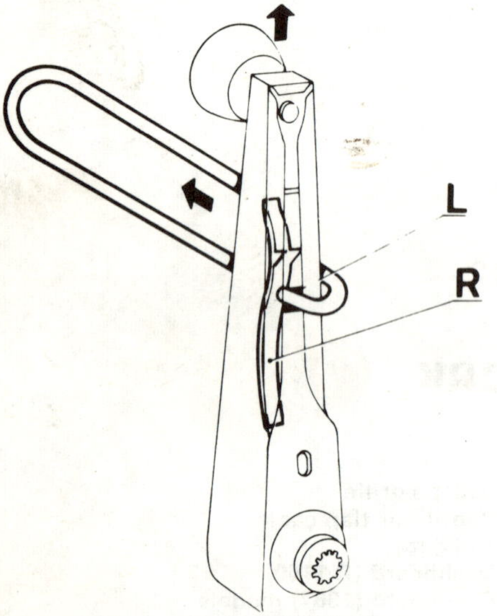

FIG 12:2 Removing winder handle

Key to Fig 12:2 L Hook R Spring

plate with the securing studs 25 in **FIG 12:6** projecting from the door body then screw on the nuts without tightening them. Fit removable roller 26 bis (see **FIG 12:6**), connect up the feed leads and check the window alignment. The window can be straightened by first loosening the nut 30 in **FIG 12:7** then aligning the window and finally tightening nut 30 and the height of the window can be adjusted by means of the adjusting stop 31 in **FIG 12:8** so that the window is placed at the same height as the upper edge of the door body, do not forget after adjustment to lock nut 32. After adjustment has been completed tighten the three nuts 25 in **FIG 12:6**.

12:3 Front door lock

With reference to **FIG 12:9** fit the outer door handle 13 together with its seal 14 and the lock, engaging the plunger in the door aperture. Allow the lock to hang inside (see **FIG 12:10**) then swing the lock through half a turn (see **FIG 12:11**) and finally swing it through a quarter of a turn in the opposite direction to place the plunger in its location as shown in **FIG 12:12.** Fit the inner plate 17 in **FIG 12:13** passing it behind the window slide (arrow) until lever L in **FIG 12:14** comes over the lug M. Secure the lock and plate together. With regard to **FIG 12:15** fit the remote control to the inside door hinge 18, the plate being secured by two screws 9 and then fit clip G to the door body. Check the mechanism and then tighten screws 9. The plunger is secured to the lock by a small hollow rivet (see R in **FIG 12:16**).

12:4 Rear door

Removal:

Unscrew the three screws securing the upper hinge, get an assistant to support the door then using a suitable sized drift push out the door hinge pins.

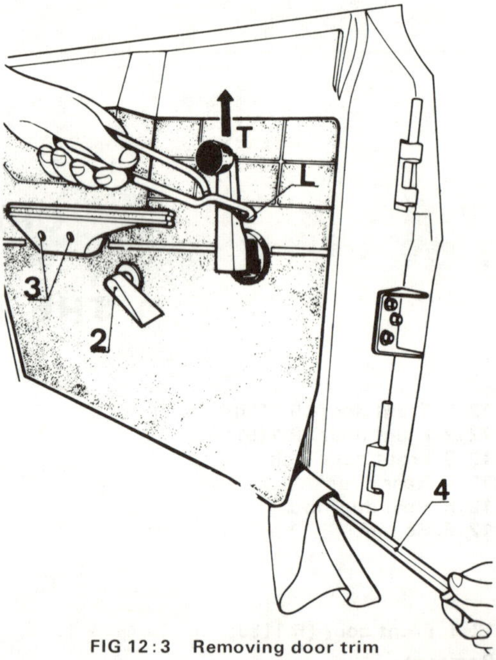

FIG 12:3 Removing door trim

Key to Fig 12:3 4 Screwdriver 3 Screws 2 Handle L Hook T Direction

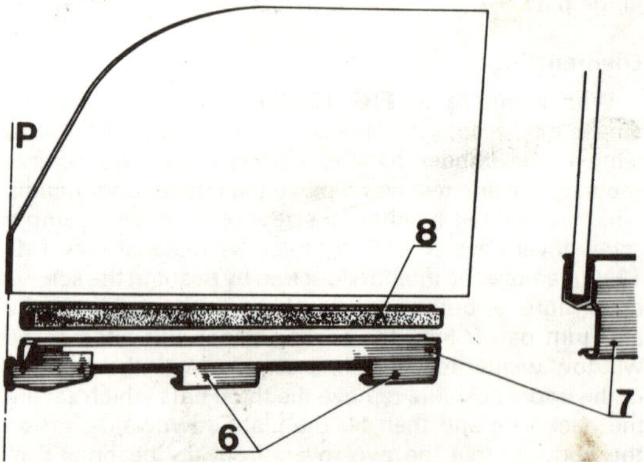

FIG 12:4 Front window

Key to Fig 12:4 P Flush 6 Bearing 7 Window bottom 8 Rubber

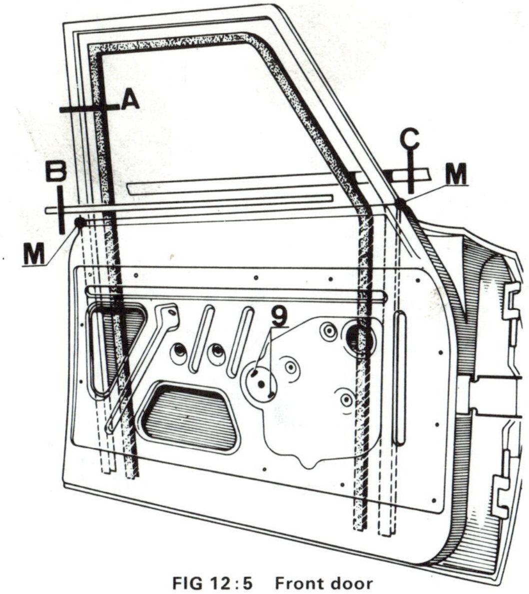

FIG 12:5 Front door

Key to Fig 12:5 B Wiper C Wiper M Compound

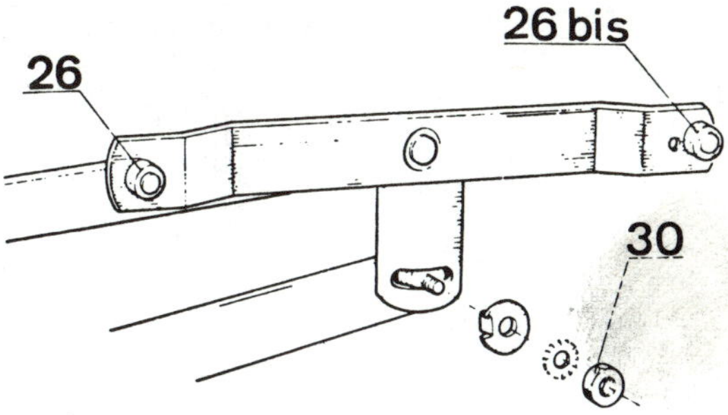

FIG 12:7 Swivel adjustment

Key to Fig 12:7 26 Roller 26 Bis roller 30 Nut

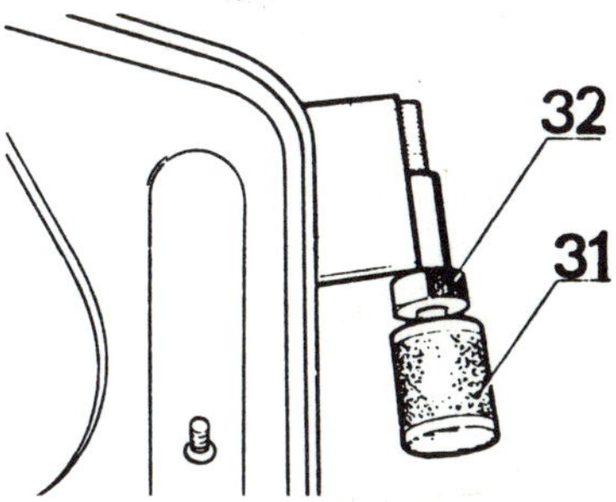

FIG 12:8 Adjust stop

Key to Fig 12:8 31 Stop 32 Locknut

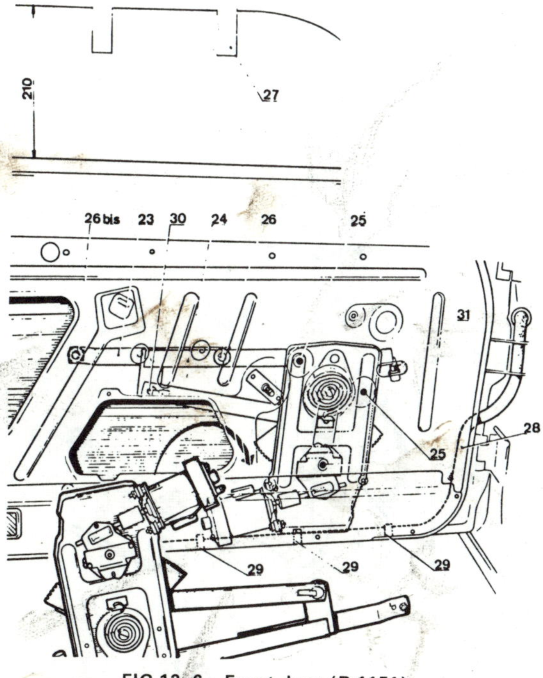

FIG 12:6 Front door (R.1151)

Key to Fig 12:6 23 Roller arm 24 Upper mechanism 25 Nuts 26 Roller 26 Bis roller 27 Tape 28 Front 29 Clips 30 Nut

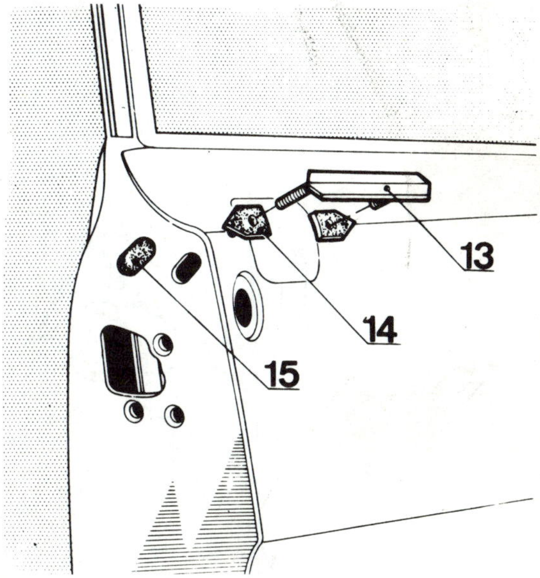

FIG 12:9 Door handle

Key to Fig 12:9 13 Handle 14 Seal 15 Rubber plug

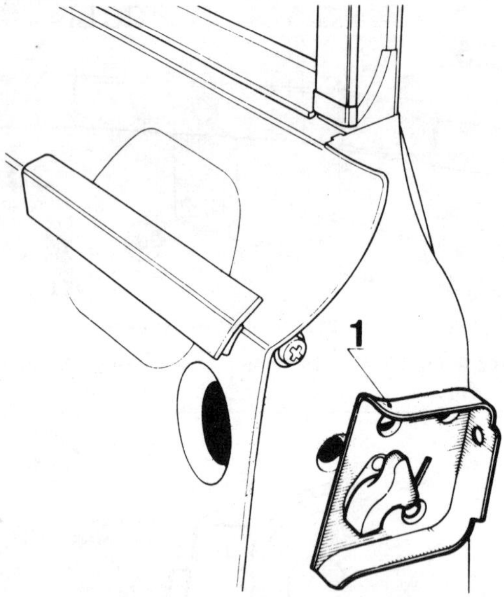

FIG 12:10 Door lock (first position)

Key to Fig 12:10 1 Plate

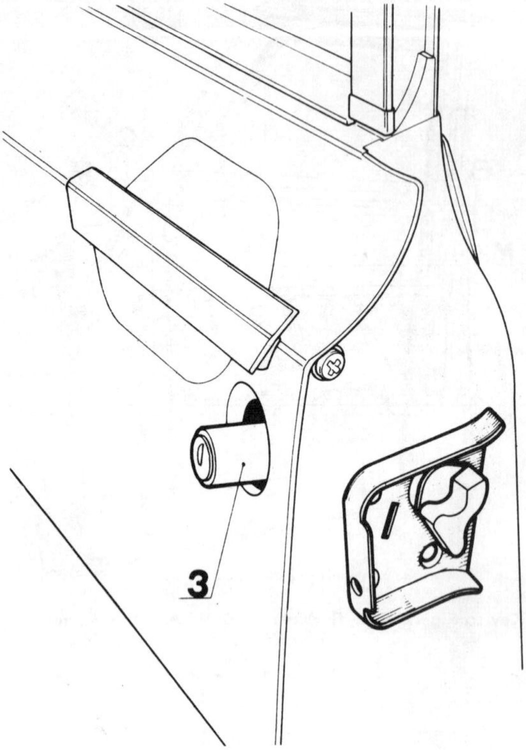

FIG 12:12 Door lock (third position)

Key to Fig 12:12 3 Plunger

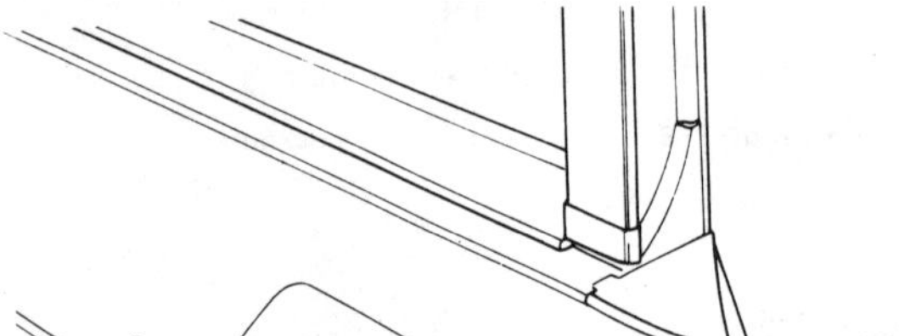

FIG 12:11 Door lock (second position)

Key to Fig 12:11 2 Plate

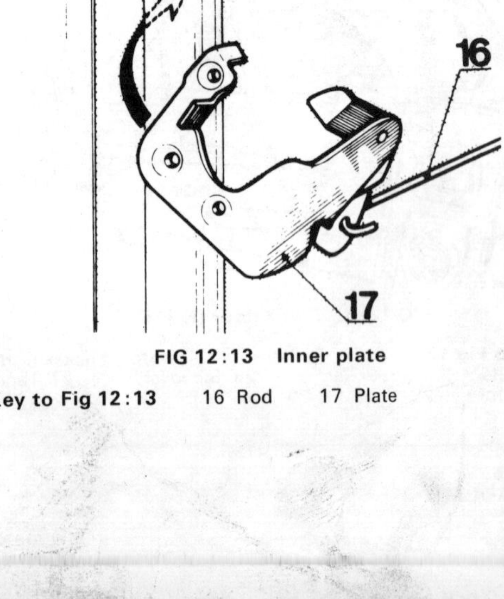

FIG 12:13 Inner plate

Key to Fig 12:13 16 Rod 17 Plate

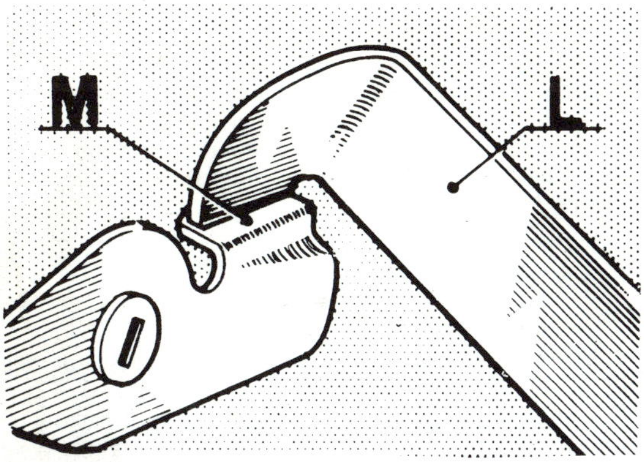

FIG 12:14 Lever assembly

Key to Fig 12:14 **L** Lever **M** Lug

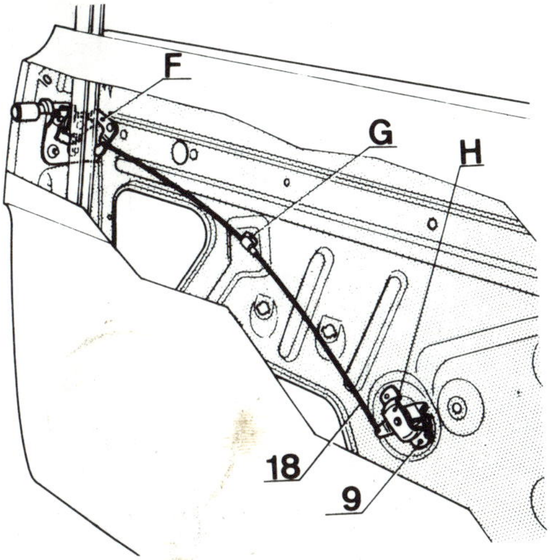

FIG 12:15 Remote control mechanism

Key to Fig 12:15 9 Screws **F** Upper lever **G** Clip **H** Lower lever 18 Hinge

Dismantling:

Unscrew the two screws securing the arm rest and remove the inside door handle which is secured by either a screw or roll-pin. Lift off the detachable portion of the ashtray and remove the screws securing the inner part. Remove the window winder handle in the manner described in **Section 12:1,** the sealing panel, the lower door trim, the lock and remote control rod and the interior door handle which is secured by two screws. With the window in the upper position free the window winder return spring and with the winder mechanism in the lower position free the window winder. Remove the clips and mechanism from the window bottom. Undo the three window winder fastenings and take the window winder out through the hole in the bottom of the door body. Unscrew the screws on the rear pillar and rear body and free the sixth and seventh clips. Free the glass channel and the rear pillar in an upwards direction together with the polished aluminium frame 7 in **FIG 12:17** and remove the glass from the top by swinging the front corner of the window downwards.

Refit by reversing the dismantling procedure.

12:5 Rear door lock

With regard to **FIG 12:9** fit the outer door handle 13 together with its seals 14 and rubber plug 15. Fit the door lock as detailed in **Section 12:3** and the rubber sealing ring on the plunger button. Fit the remote control 30 in **FIG 12:18** to the inner plate and fit the inner plate by passing it behind the window slide, shown by the arrow in **FIG 12:18.** Secure the lock and the plate to each other. Fit the remote control to the inside door handle hinge 31 in **FIG 12:19** the plate is secured by two

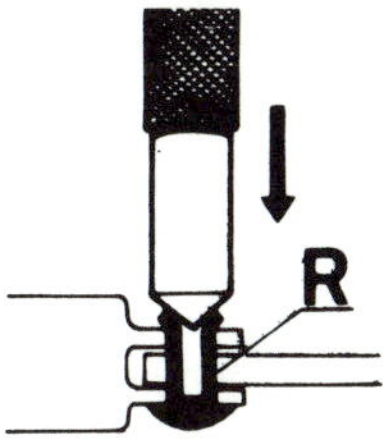

FIG 12:16 Hollow rivet

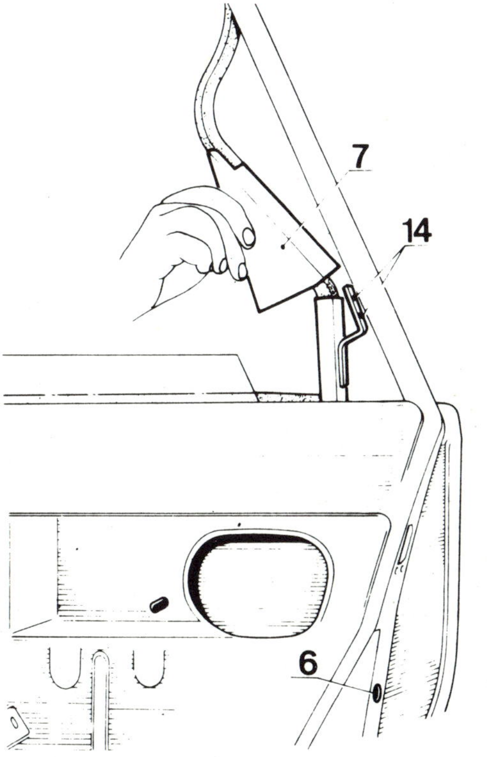

FIG 12:17 Aluminium frame

Key to Fig 12:17 7 Frame 14 Channel

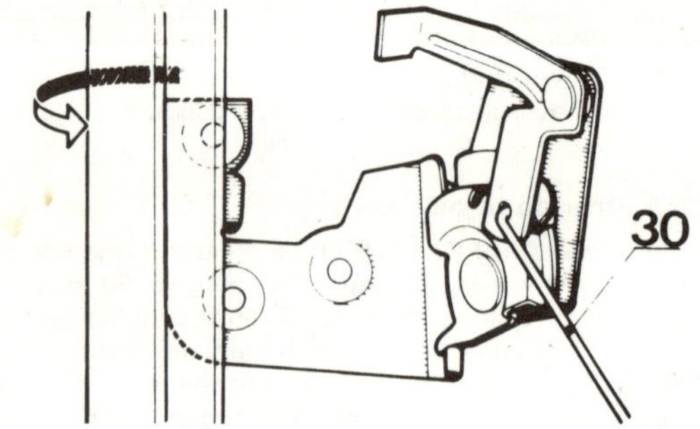

FIG 12:18 Remote control rod

Key to Fig 12:18 30 Rod

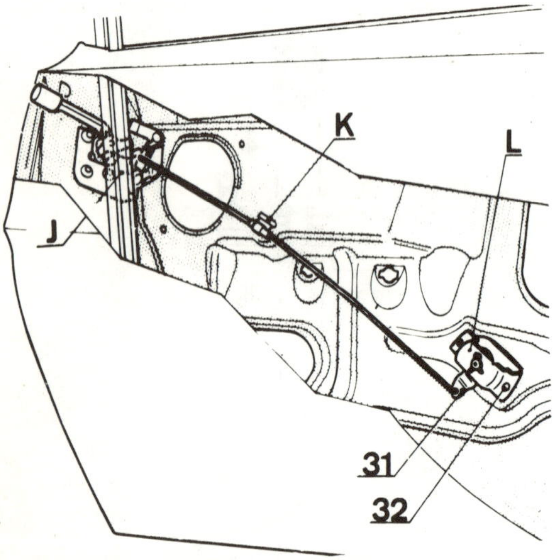

FIG 12:19 Remote control mechanism (rear door)

Key to Fig 12:19 31 Hinge 32 Screw **J** Upper swivel **K** Clip **L** Lower swivel

screws 32. Fit clip K to the door body, ensure that the lock operates correctly and then tighten the screws 32 in **FIG 12:19.** Fit the plastic clip cover.

12:6 Bonnet

The bonnet can be removed either by taking out the four side securing bolts 1 in **FIG 12:20,** which means adjusting the bonnet on refitting or by removing the retaining circlips on the hinge pins 2. This last operation will involve removing the scuttle grille (see **Section 12:7**).

Modification:

In order to improve the position of the bonnet the rubber guide stop has been moved and as a result a new bonnet has been manufactured. As only the new type bonnet can be obtained vehicles manufactured before the modification took place will have to be modified.

With regard to **FIG 12:21** drill the two holes 2 and 4 which are $\frac{5}{16}$ inch (8 mm) in diameter the holes 1 and 3 being those formerly used.

Bonnet lock:

To remove the lock with reference to **FIG 12:22** remove the fastenings on the radiator grill panel 1, push out the roll-pin 2 and take out the tumbler.

Refit the lock by carrying out the removing operations in reverse. The locating lug is adjusted through aperture 3 in **FIG 12:22.**

12:7 Scuttle grille

Removal:

Remove the two wiper arms, the two windscreen bearing nuts and the five screws 1 in **FIG 12:23** together with the 'rapid' nuts behind them. Unscrew the locating dowel 2 and the two side sheet metal screws 3.

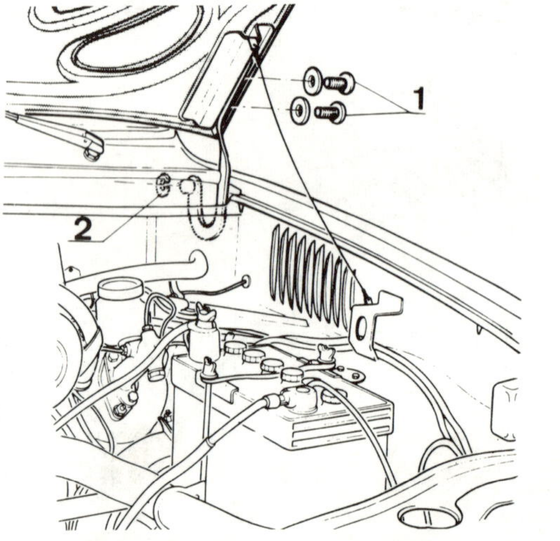

FIG 12:20 Removing the bonnet

Key to Fig 12:20 1 Bolts 2 Circlip

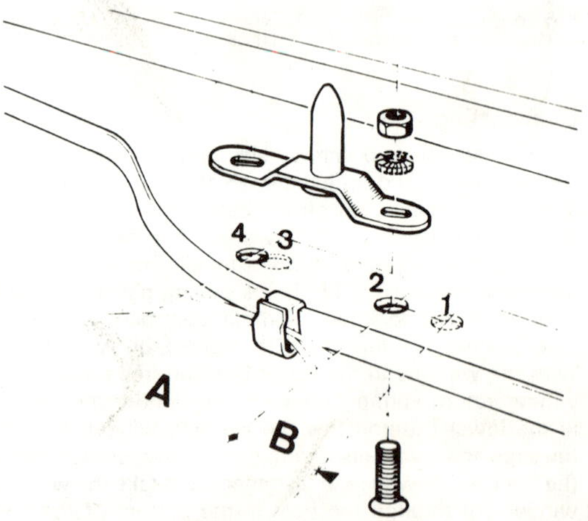

FIG 12:21 Guide stop

Key to Fig 12:21 A=2$\frac{1}{2}$ inch (63 mm) B=$\frac{43}{64}$ inch (16 mm)

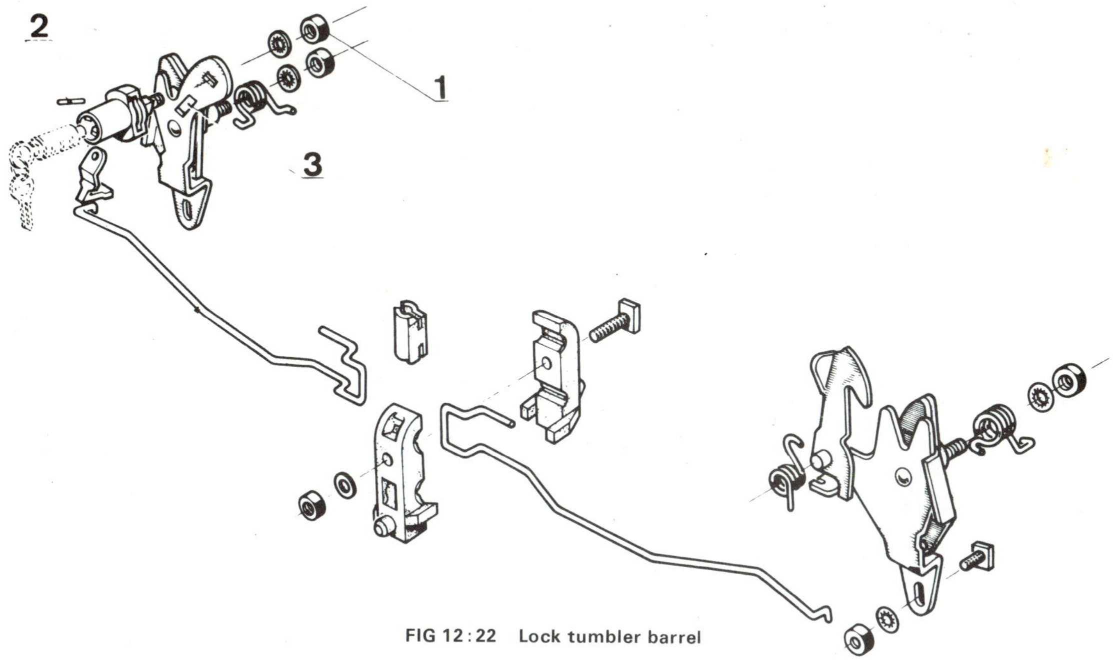

FIG 12:22 Lock tumbler barrel

Key to Fig 12:22 1 Nut 2 Roll-pin 3 Aperture

Modification:

The addition of a ventilation flap (see **FIG 12:24**), operated from the dashboard by means of a knob and cable passing through the heater casing and under the upper part of the glove compartment tray panel and a new bonnet locating dowel, the fitting of which has involved the removing of one of the retaining screws on the scuttle crossmember.

Refitting:

Before refitting the scuttle grille, seal it by means of strips of 503 compound 4 in **FIG 12:23,** cut to the correct length. To make positioning the scuttle grille with the bonnet in position easier, an assistant should lower the bonnet to the partially closed position, to permit it to pass, so as to prevent any risk of scratching the paint work.

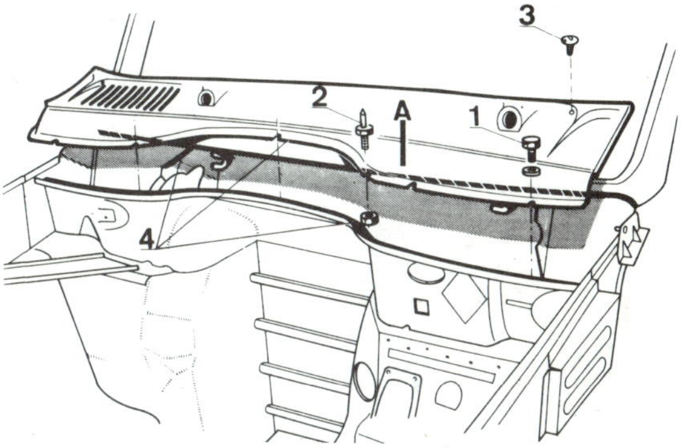

FIG 12:23 Scuttle grille

Key to Fig 12:23 1 Bolt 2 Dowel 3 Screw 4 Compound

12:8 Ventilator flap cable

To remove the cable slightly lift the scuttle crossmember at the flap end to gain access to the cable fastening 3 in **FIG 12:24.** Free the clip by pushing on its end at 4 and take off eye-end 5 with a screwdriver.

The cable can be refitted by carrying out the removing operations in reverse, it is however, advisable to release the cable at the control panel or the dashboard in order to have further clearance at the flap end. Take care to prevent the cable slipping under the glove compartment tray panel by attaching it to a piece of wire.

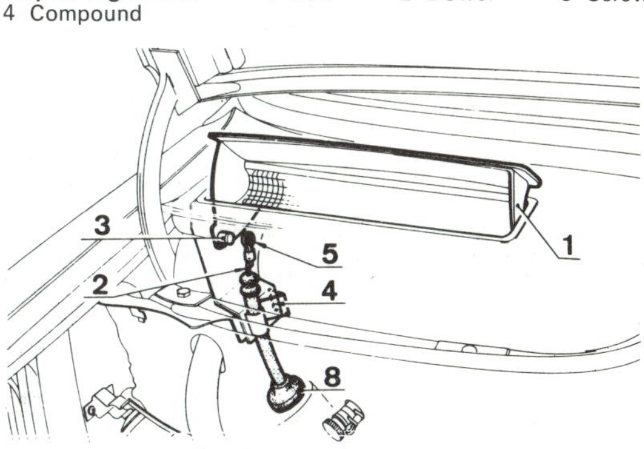

FIG 12:24 Ventilator flap cable

Key to Fig 12:24 1 Flap 2 Cable 3 Dowel 4 Clip 5 Eye-end 8 Knob

12:9 Tail gate

To remove a tail gate remove the counterbalances which are secured to the tail gate body by means of

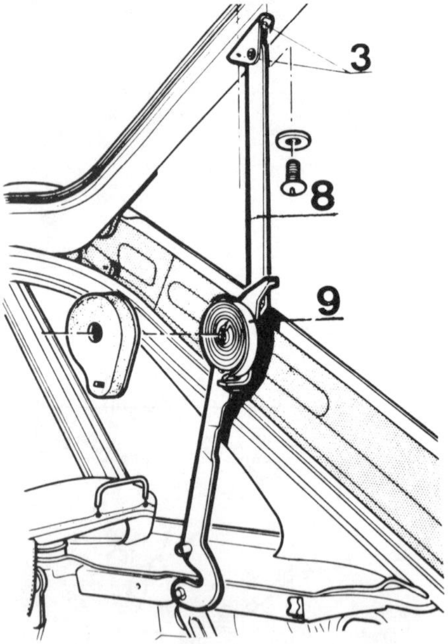

FIG 12 : 25 Tail gate counter balance

Key to Fig 12 : 25 3 Screws 8 Arm 9 Spring

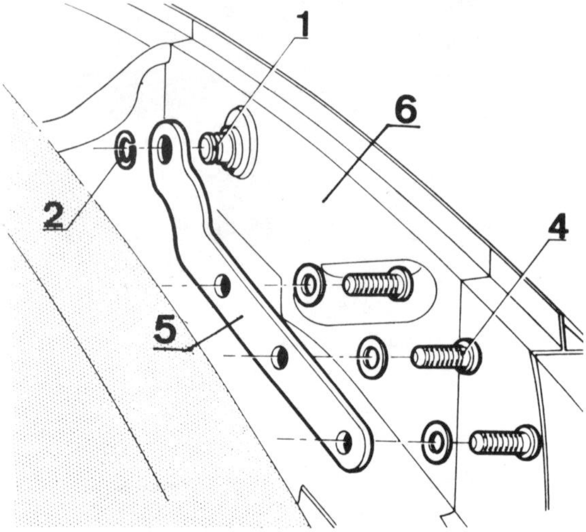

FIG 12 : 26 Tail gate hinge arms

Key to Fig 12 : 26 1 Dowel 2 Clip 4 Screw 5 Arm 6 Moulding

screws 3 in **FIG 12 : 25** and unscrew the hinge arm securing screws 4 in **FIG 12 : 26** on the tail gate body.

To refit the tail gate fit the hinge arms 5 and clips 2 in **FIG 12 : 26** to the hinge pins before positioning the tail gate and secure the tail gate in place by means of bolts 4. Refit screws 3 in **FIG 12 : 25**.

Tail gate tumbler:

To replace a tumbler remove the two nuts 1 in **FIG 12 : 27** on the inner tail gate body and take out the assembly. Remove the tumbler after having pushed out the roll-pin 2. Refit by reversing the removal procedure, adjusting by means of elongated holes 3.

12 : 10 Dashboard (R.1150)

With reference to **FIG 12 : 28** remove the hold bar which is secured by three screws 1 on the righthand side and one screw 2 on the lefthand side. Take out the ash-tray support which is secured by three sheet metal screws 3 behind the ashtray and one screw 4 on the side and the lefthand hold bar support which is held by two screws 5. Remove the instrument panel capping which has two force fit covers 6 and is secured by four screws 7. Disconnect the battery and the three switches which are a force fit in the instrument panel capping 8 and remove the instrument panel lighting rheostat 9. Disconnect the speedometer drive cable and remove the instrument panel which is retained by three screws 10, the righthand embellisher which is secured by four screws 11 and the lefthand embellisher which is secured by one screw 12. With regard to **FIG 12 : 29** remove the demister flaps by inserting a screwdriver T between the flap D and the dashboard, taking great care as studs P are easily broken. Finally unscrew screws 13 and 14 in **FIG 12 : 28** which secure the trim.

Refit by reversing the removal procedure.

12 : 11 Dashboard (1967 model)

With regard to **FIG 12 : 30** unscrew screw 1 to loosen the righthand trim and loosen the lefthand trim undoing screw 2 and screw 3. Remove both trims by unscrewing studs 4. Remove the five screws 5 and the trapped nuts securing the demisting grille but note that to prevent the screws falling into the grille they are retained by a rubber clip consequently they have to be unscrewed partially and then the grille has to be slightly lifted at one end in order to see the point at which each screw comes out

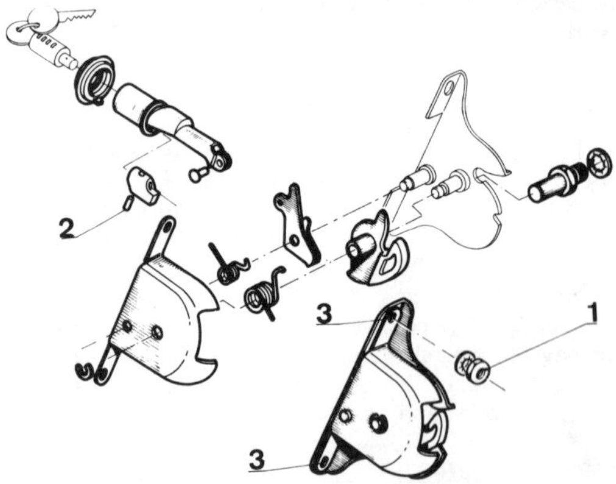

FIG 12 : 27 Tail gate tumbler

Key to Fig 12 : 27 1 Nut 2 Pin 3 Holes

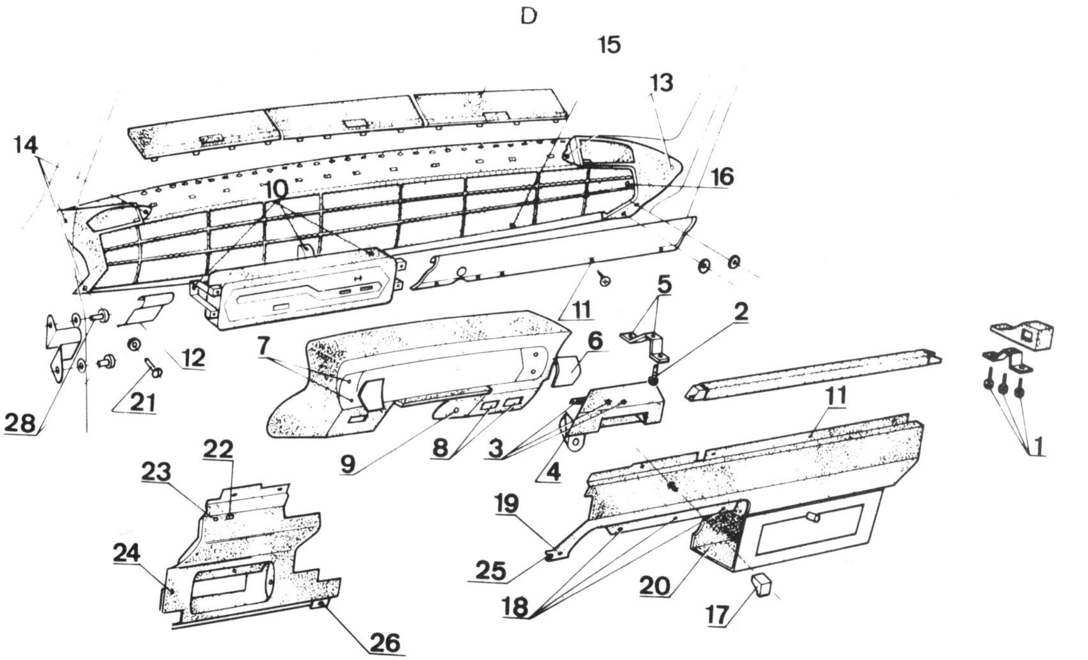

FIG 12:28 **Dashboard (R.1150)**

Key to Fig 12:28 1 Screw 2 Screw 3 Ash tray 4 Screw 5 Screw 6 Cover 7 Screw 8 Capping 9 Rheostat 10 Screw 11 Screw 12 Screw 13 Screw 14 Screw 15 Bottom 16 Ends 17 Knob 18 Screw 19 Screw 20 Screw 21 Fastening 22 Flasher unit 23 Knob 24 Bracket 25 Bracket 26 Centre scuttle section

from its nut. Remove the hold bar which is secured by screw 6 and two screws 7 and remove the cigar lighter 8. Remove the two blind nuts 10 in **FIG 12:30** and a screw 11 under the instrument panel capping retaining the protective casing. Remove the heater control panel which is secured by three nuts 12 in **FIG 12:31**, the flap control cable which is retained by a cable cover end stop 13 and a retaining pin 14. Unscrew the two screws 15 securing the ashtray unit, access being made easier by holding the ashtray cover in the half-open position. Take out the righthand glove compartment tray by removing the hold handle, the upper screw 11, the ashtray, the capping, the heater flap knob 17, the three screws 18, the choke support screw 19 and the four screws 20 inside the casing. Take out the lefthand tray by removing the capping, the switches, the lower trim fastening 21, the flasher unit 22, the battery, the heater control knob 23, the handbrake bracket 24, the choke bracket 25, the lower bracket on the centre scuttle section 26, the lower lighting switch housing and the two handbrake securing bolts.

Refit the dashboard by reversing the dismantling procedure. Before positioning the heater control panel place a small washer at point 16 (see **FIG 12:31**) and place the eye-end of the flap cable 14 onto its shaft, and tighten the cable cover end clamp 13 and nuts 12. Ensure that the flap operates correctly by moving handle 19 and fit the coverplate which is secured at points 10 and 11 and the hold handle.

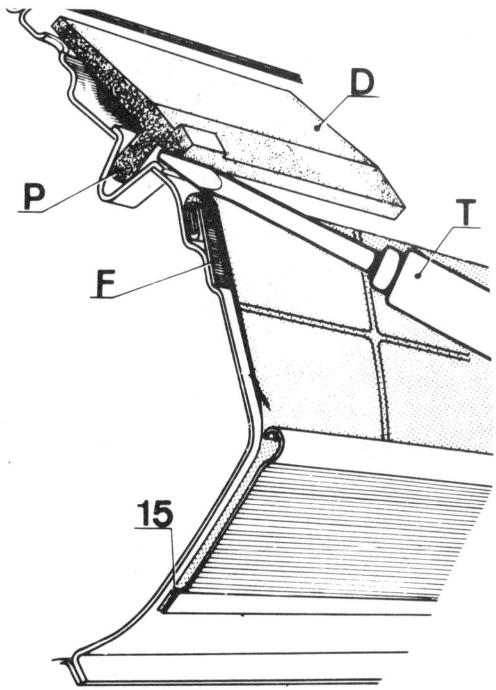

FIG 12:29 **Removing the demisting flaps**

Key to Fig 12:29 **D** Flap **F** Strip **P** Stud **T** Screwdriver 15 Bottom

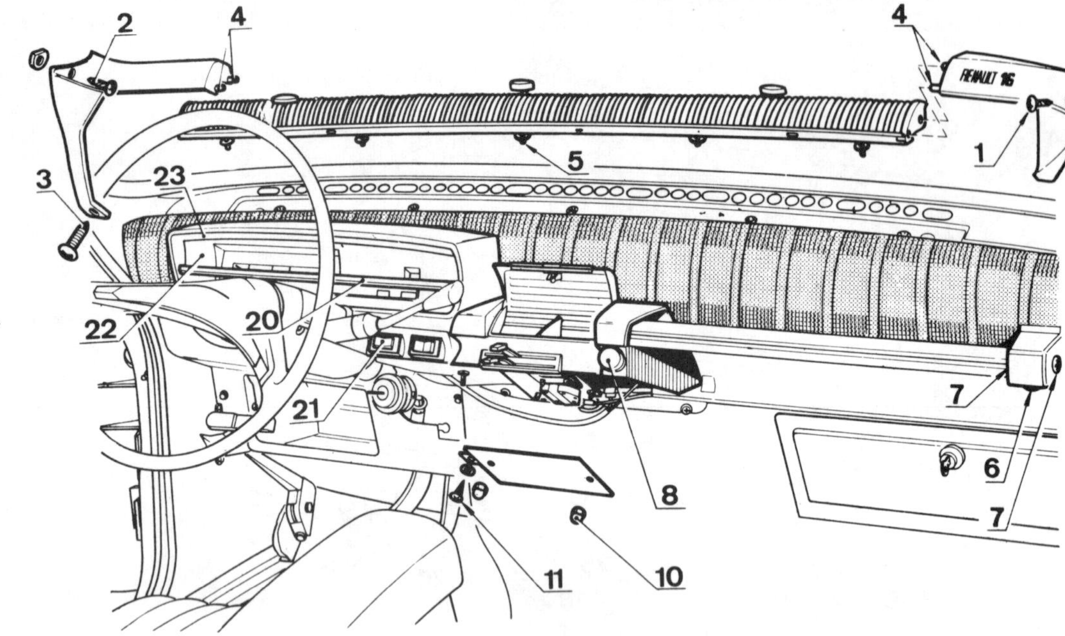

FIG 12:30 Dashboard (1967 model)

Key to Fig 12:30 1 Screw 2 Screw 3 Screw 4 Stud 5 Screw 6 Screw 7 Screw 8 Cigar lighter 10 Nuts 11 Screw 20 Bead 21 Switches 22 Panel 23 Capping

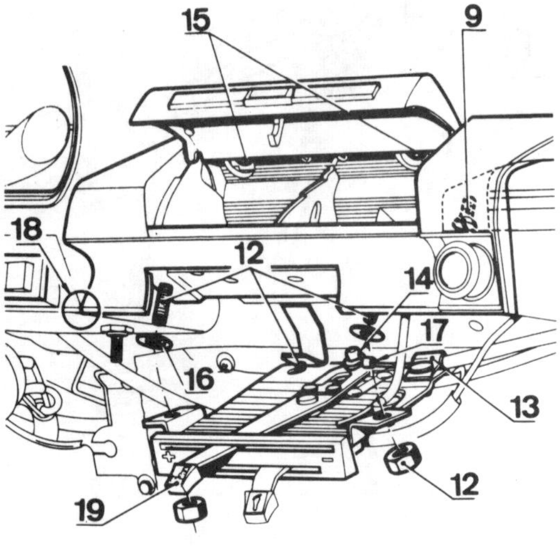

FIG 12:31 Heater controls

Key to Fig 12:31 9 Screw 12 Nuts 13 End stop 14 Pin 15 Screw 16 Point 17 Eye 18 Alignment 19 Knob

12:12 Sun roof (R.1151)

Removal:

With the roof in the forward position remove the cover casing 12 in **FIG 12-32** which is secured by six screws, unscrew the screws 13 and bring bearing 14 towards the inside by moving lugs A. Lift the front of the sun roof from inside the vehicle and remove it. Remove the spacers 15 in **FIG 12:33** in order to avoid the rear rubber seal tearing away.

Refitting:

Insert a piece of cardboard on the current feed track 16 in **FIG 12:33,** clear the lead ramps 18 and grease them lightly. Position the sun roof, tilting it slightly to the rear and engage the retaining springs 19 under the roof and pads 17 on the centre track.

Spacers 15 in **FIG 12:33** are supplied in four different thicknesses, denoted by different colours, and they are used to ensure that the roof is flush with the actual roof panelling. It is possible for two spacers of different thicknesses to be fitted to any one given vehicle.

Adjusting:

Bring the roof to approximately $5\frac{7}{8}$ inch (15 cm) from the front edge and after fitting the pinions on the racks apply the guide bearings 14 in **FIG 12:34** against the side pieces. Pull them back to leave a $\frac{1}{16}$ inch (1.5 mm) clearance between them and tighten securing nuts 13. Refit the cover casing 12 in **FIG 12:32.**

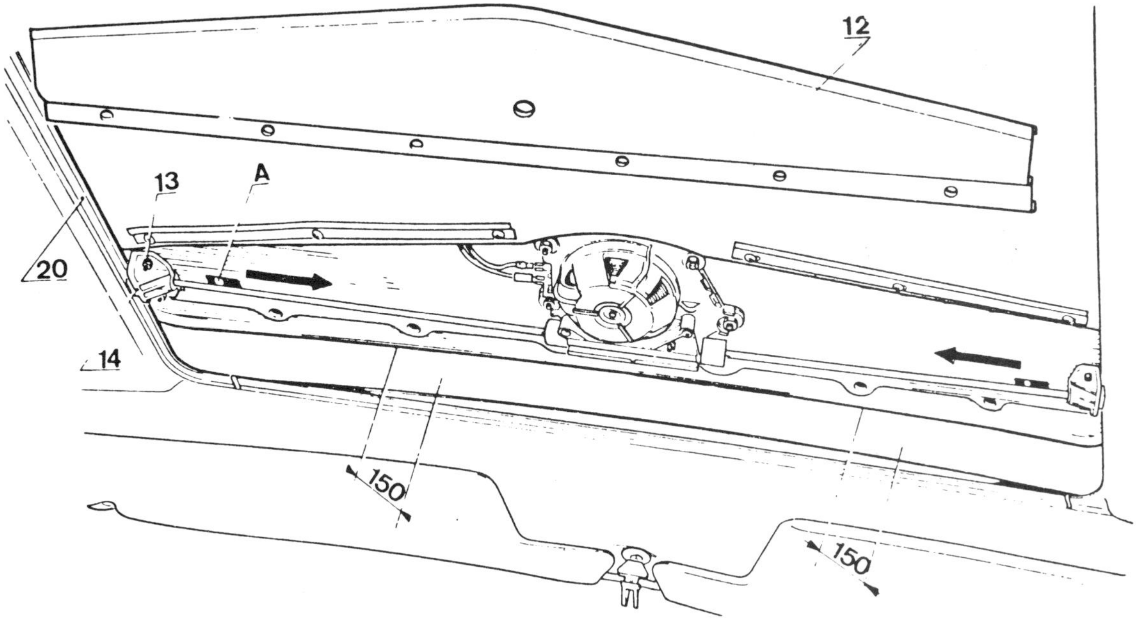

FIG 12:32 Removing the sun roof

Key to Fig 12:32 12 Casing 13 Screws 14 Bearing 20 Side pieces

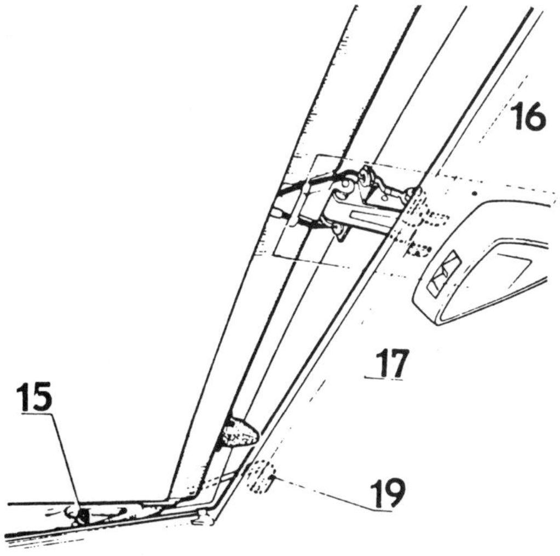

FIG 12:33 Refitting the sun roof

Key to Fig 12:33 15 Spacer 16 Track 17 Pad 19 Spring

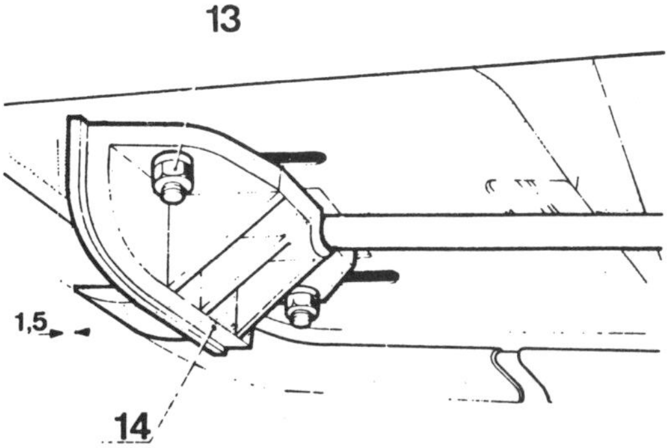

FIG 12:34 Adjusting the sun roof

Key to Fig 12:34 13 Nuts 14 Bearing

APPENDIX

TECHNICAL DATA

ENGINE

R.1150 specifications

Construction	Four-cylinder in-line vertical, working on the four stroke cycle fitted with a five bearing crankshaft
Type 697.01	8.6 compression ratio
Type 697.02	7.6 compression ratio
Type 697.03	7.25 compression ratio
Brake horsepower (8.6 CR)	63 at 5000 rev/min
Brake horsepower (7.6 CR)	60 at 5000 rev/min
Maximum torque (8.6 CR)	76 lb ft (10.8 m.da.N) at 2800 rev/min
Maximum torque (7.6 CR)	72 lb ft (10.2 m.da.N) at 2800 rev/min
Bore	2.992 inch (76 mm)
Stroke	3.189 inch (81 mm)
Cubic capacity	90 cu in (1470 cc)
Combustion chamber shape	Bathtube
Initial timing at the pulley	0 ± 2 deg.
Operating temperature (normal)	84°C (183°F)
Operating temperature (Hot countries) ...	73°C (163°F)

R.1151 specifications

Construction	Four-cylinder in-line vertical, working on the four stroke cycle fitted with a five bearing crankshaft
Compression ratio	8.6:1
Brake hoursepower	87.5 at 5750 rev/min
Maximum torque	90 lb/ft (12 m.da.N) at 3500 rev/min
Bore	3.032 inch (77 mm)
Stroke	3.307 inch (84 mm)
Cubic capacity	95.5 cu in (1565 cc)
Combustion chamber shape	Hemispherical
Normal timing at the pulley	0 ± 2 deg.
Operating temperature (normal)	84°C (183°F)
Operating temperature (Hot countries) ...	73°C (163°F)

Crankshaft

Type	Roll hardened five main bearing
Main journal diameter	2.158 inch (54.8 mm)
Main bearings	Thinwall, steel-backed
Undersizes	—.010 inch (.25 mm) and —.020 inch (.5 mm)
Grinding tolerance	+.0007 inch (.014 mm) —.0001 inch (.002 mm)

Pistons

Type	Aluminium, solid skirt
Top ring	A 'firing' square section chrome plated ring
Second ring	A non-phosphated taper compression ring
Oil control ring	A U-flex pre-run-in oil control ring
Ring gaps	Preset by manufacturer
Piston pin type	Semi-floating (press fit in the piston)

Camshaft

End play at flange	.002 to .0045 inch (.05 to .12 mm)

Cylinder head

Standard depth (R.1150)	3.175 inch (80.65 mm)
(R.1151)	3.681 inch (93.5 mm)

Minimum depth (R.1150)	3.163 inch (80.35 mm)
(R.1151)	3.670 inch (93.2 mm)
Maximum permissible bow	.002 inch (.05 mm)
Combustion chamber volume (R.1150) ...	2.483 cu in (40.7 cc)
(R.1151) ...	2.652 cu in (43.45 cc)
Valves	
Seat angle (inlet and exhaust)	45 deg.
Inlet maximum seat width	.063 inch (1.33 mm)
Exhaust maximum seat width	.079 inch (1.73 mm)
Inlet valve head diameter (R.1150)	1.575 inch (40 mm)
Exhaust valve head diameter (R.1150) ...	1.378 inch (35 mm)
Valve guides	
Original size (R.1150)	.512 inch (13 mm)
Oversize (R.1150)	.522 inch (13.25 mm)
Valve springs	
Inlet and exhaust (R.1150) free length ...	1 $\frac{23}{64}$ inch (48.4 mm)
Inlet and exhaust (R.1151) free length (outer)	2 $\frac{5}{32}$ inch (54.3 mm)
(inner)	1$\frac{3}{4}$ inch (44.7 mm)
Wire diameter (R.1150)	.150 inch (3.8 mm)
(R.1151 outer)	.166 inch (4.2 mm)
(R.1151 inner)	.118 inch (3 mm)
Colour (R.1150)	Green
(R.1151) inner and outer	Light green
Number of effective coils (R.1151 inner) ...	6
(R.1151 outer) ...	5
Valve timing and clearance	
Timing marks	Indent point on crankshaft and camshaft sprockets
Rocker clearance inlet	.008 inch (.20 mm)
exhaust	.010 inch (.25 mm)
Oil pump	
Type	Eccentric rotor
Clearance between teeth (minimum) ...	.001 inch (.02 mm)
(maximum) ...	.006 inch (.14 mm)

COOLING SYSTEM

Thermostat setting	84°C (183°F)
Water pump belt tension	$\frac{5}{32}$ inch (4 mm)
Capacity	10$\frac{1}{2}$ pints (5.8 litres)
Radiator	Fin type
Water pump type	Centrifugal
Cooling	Electric fan operated by a temperature switch

FUEL SYSTEM

Solex carburetter (319)	
Choke tube	27
Main jet	140
Air compensator jet	135
Idling jet	50
Needle valve	1.5 mm
Float	7.3 gr
Pump injector	50
Pump stroke	5 mm
Solex carburetter (365)	
Choke tube	27
Main jet	142.5

Air compensator jet	160
Idling jet	42.5
Needle valve	1.5 mm
Float	7.3 gr
Pump injector	40
Pump stroke	3 mm

Solex carburetter (370)

Choke tube	27
Main jet	142.5
Air compensator jet	160
Idling jet	42.5
Needle valve (first setting)	1.5 mm
(second setting)	2 mm
Float	7.3 gr
Pump injector	40
Pump stroke	3 mm

Solex carburetter (376)

Choke tube	26.5
Main jet	142.5
Air compensator jet	155
Idling jet	50
Needle valve	1.7 mm
Float	7.3 gr
Pump injector	50
Pump stroke	3 mm

Solex carburetter (366 H.A)

Choke tube	26.5
Main jet	142.5
Air compensator jet	145
Idling jet	50
Needle valve	1.7 mm
Float	7.3 gr
Pump injector	50
Pump stroke	3 mm

Weber carburetter

Choke tube (first barrel)	24
(second barrel)	26
Main jet (first barrel)	140
(second barrel)	150
Air compensator jet (first barrel)	190
(second barrel) ...	140
Idling jet (first barrel)	50
(second barrel)	80
Needle valve	1.75 mm
Float	11 gr

Zenith carburetter

Choke tube	27
Main jet	135
Air compensator jet	100
Idling jet	40
Needle valve	1.5 mm
Pump injector	40
Pump stroke	3 mm
Throttle initial setting	.95 mm

IGNITION SYSTEM

Coil	Ducellier

Distributor type	Ducellier
Rotation of rotor arm	Anticlockwise
Cam form	Four-cylinder high-lift
Cam closed period	60 deg. $\pm$ 4 deg.
Cam open period	30 deg. $\pm$ 4 deg.
Automatic advance commences	1800 rev/min (crankshaft speed)
Maximum advance	18 deg. at 5400 rev/min (crankshaft speed)
Firing order	1–3–4–2
Sparking plugs	14 mm long reach

CLUTCH

Type	Renault 200.D
Thickness of disc	.304 inch (7.7 mm)
Facing material	Ferodo
Spring	Diaphragm plate
Clearance measured at withdrawl fork ...	$\frac{1}{8}$ inch (3 mm)

TRANSMISSION

Type	336
Construction	Pressure die-cast aluminium housing separated into two parts
Number of forward gears	Four
Synchromesh	All forward gears
Ratio—top	1.03:1
third	1.48:1
second	2.25:1
first	3.61:1
reverse	3.07:1
Speedometer drive (9 tooth pinion) ...	6 start worm and 12 tooth pinion
Speedometer drive (8 tooth pinion) ...	6 start worm and 14 tooth pinion
Crownwheel	34 teeth
Pinion	8 or 9 teeth
Capacity	3 pts (1.64 litres)
Oil grade	EP.80

STEERING

Type	Rack and pinion
Steering wheel turns	4
Reduction ratio	23:1
Overall length of the rack	$21\frac{1}{2}$ inch (546 mm)
Steering wheel diameter	$16\frac{1}{8}$ inch (410 mm)
Turning circle diameter (between kerbs) ...	32 ft 10 inches (10 m)
Turning circle diameter (between walls) ...	34 ft 9 inches (10.6 m)

SUSPENSION

Front

Type	Torsion bar
Length of bar	$40\frac{3}{4}$ inch (1.035 m)
Diameter of bar (good road version) ...	.685 inch (17.4 mm)
Diameter of bar (bad road version)	.716 inch (18.2 mm)

Rear

Type	Torsion bar
Length of bar	$40\frac{9}{32}$ inch (1.023 m)
Diameter of bar	.850 inch (21.6 mm)
Diameter of bar (1968 models)	.886 inch (22.5 mm)

Number of splines (suspension arm end) ...	30
Number of splines (anchor casing end) ...	28
Dampers	Double acting with override pads

BRAKES

Master cylinder diameter	.812 inch (20.6 mm)
Master cylinder travel	$\frac{17}{32}$ inch (31 mm)
Brake pressure limiting valve setting: Bendix brakes first model	515 lb sq in (36 bars)
Brake pressure limiting valve setting: Bendix brakes second setting	470 lb/sq in (33 bars)
Brake pressure limiting valve setting: Girling brakes	470 lb/sq in (33 bars)
Front disc brakes	
Caliper diameter	1.889 inch (48 mm)
Disc diameter	$9\frac{7}{8}$ inch (250 mm)
Disc thickness	.354 inch (9 mm)
Thickness of pad (piston side old type) ...	$\frac{15}{32}$ inch (12 mm)
Thickness of pad (opposite side old type) ...	$\frac{15}{32}$ inch (12 mm)
Thickness of pad (piston side new type) ...	$\frac{35}{64}$ inch (14 mm)
Thickness of pad (opposite side new type)	$\frac{33}{64}$ inch (13 mm)
Rear drum brakes	
Wheel cylinder diameter (Bendix first model)	$\frac{3}{4}$ inch (19 mm)
Wheel cylinder diameter (Bendix second model)	$\frac{7}{8}$ inch (22 mm)
Wheel cylinder diameter (Girling)	$\frac{7}{8}$ inch (22 mm)
Drum diameter (normal)	9 inch (228.5 mm)
Drum diameter (maximum)	$9\frac{3}{64}$ inch (229.5 mm)
Width of linings	$1\frac{19}{32}$ inch (40 mm)
Thickness of linings	$\frac{13}{64}$ inch (5 mm)

ELECTRICAL EQUIPMENT

Battery	
Type	Fulmen AS.810 or Tudor 6.RF4
Specifications	Nine cell, twelve volt
Capacity	40 amp/hr (will supply a steady current of 4 amps for ten hours)
Ignition coil	
Type	12-volt Ducellier 2765A
Spark plugs	
Types	AC 45, Champion N5
Spark gap	.025 inch (.6 mm)
Flasher unit	
Type	12-volt, 40 to 45 watt
Motor fan unit	
Fan unit	12-volt
Relay	Cartier Ref 90
Temperature switch setting	82°C to 92°C (179°F to 197°F)
Windscreen wiper motor	
Type	Bosch WS1500 RIF
Fuse box	
Fuses	Two 25 amp
Connections	Eight tabs for clip terminals
Lighting rheostat	
Type	Continuously variable
Resistance	24 ohms
Alternator	
Make	SEV Motorola

Type	A.12/30
Nominal voltage	12
Capacity at 3000 rev/min	30 amps
Field coil resistance	5.2 ohms at 25°C
Engine to alternator pulley speed ratio	2.12:1
Weight	Approximately 4 kilograms
Belt size	13 x 8

Voltage regulator

Make	SEV Motorola
Type	E.144
Setting	14.4 volts at 25°C

Starter

Make	Paris-Rhone
Operation	Solenoid
Voltage	12
Diameter	$3\frac{11}{32}$ inch (85 mm)
Type	D.8.E.49
Locked pinion torque	8 lb ft (1.1 m.da.N)
Locked pinion current flow	Approximately 355 amps

CAPACITIES

Fuel tank (R.1150)	11 gallons
Fuel tank (R.1151)	11 gallons
Engine maximum (R.1150)	7 pints
Engine maximum (R.1151)	7 pints
Engine minimum (R.1150)	$3\frac{1}{2}$ pints
Engine minimum (R.1151)	$3\frac{1}{2}$ pints
Transmission	3 pints
Cooling system	10 pints
Cooling system (intense cold version)	$10\frac{1}{2}$ pints
Weight in running order (R.1150)	2161 lbs
Weight in running order (R.1151)	2271 lbs
Weight on front (R.1150)	1213 lbs
Weight on front (R.1151)	1279 lbs
Weight on rear (R.1150)	948 lbs
Weight on rear (R.1151)	992 lbs
Total authorized weight (R.1150)	3042 lbs
Total authorized weight (R.1151)	3219 lbs
Luggage boot (R.1150)	$12\frac{1}{4}$ cu ft
Luggage boot (R.1151)	$12\frac{1}{4}$ cu ft

DIMENSIONS

Overall length (R.1150)	13ft $10\frac{1}{2}$ inches
Overall length (R.1151)	13 ft $10\frac{1}{2}$ inches
Overall width (R.1150)	5 ft $4\frac{5}{8}$ inches
Overall width (R.1151)	5 ft $4\frac{5}{8}$ inches
Overall height (R.1150)	4 ft $5\frac{1}{2}$ inches
Overall height (R.1151)	4 ft $5\frac{1}{2}$ inches
Wheelbase (R.1150)	8 ft $8\frac{1}{4}$ inches
Wheelbase (R.1151)	8 ft $8\frac{1}{4}$ inches
Front track (R.1150)	4 ft $4\frac{3}{4}$ inches
Front track (R.1151)	4 ft $4\frac{3}{4}$ inches
Rear track (R.1150)	4 ft $2\frac{3}{4}$ inches
Rear track (R.1151)	4 ft $2\frac{3}{4}$ inches
Ground clearance (R.1150)	$5\frac{7}{8}$ inches
Ground clearance (R.1151)	$5\frac{7}{8}$ inches

TORQUE WRENCH SETTINGS

Engine	
Oil pump securing bolts ($\frac{63}{64}$ inch long) ...	20 lb ft (2.75 m.da.N)
Oil pump securing bolts ($\frac{51}{64}$ inch long) ...	15 lb ft (1.75 m.da.N)
Main bearing cap bolts	45 lb ft (6.5 m.da.N)
Flywheel securing bolts	40 lb ft (5 m.da.N)
Big-end cap bolts	30 lb ft (4.5 m.da.N)
Crankshaft sprocket bolt	45 lb ft (6 m.da.N)
Cylinder head bolts	60 lb ft (8.75 m.da.N)
Rocker arm securing nuts (R.1150) ...	20 lb ft (2.75 m.da.N)
Manifold securing nuts	20 lb ft (2.75 m.da.N)
Transmission	
Speedometer drive worm	85 lb ft (12 m.da.N)
Crownwheel securing bolts (10 mm) ...	45 lb ft (6 m.da.N)
Crownwheel securing bolts (11 mm) ...	80 lb ft (11 m.da.N)
Side coverplate securing bolts	15 lb ft (2 m.da.N)
Half housing securing bolt (7 mm)	15 lb ft (2 m.da.N)
Half housing securing bolts (8 mm) ...	20 lb ft (2.75 m.da.N)
Reverse swivel lever pivot	20 lb ft (2.75 m.da.N)
Shift control bolt	10 lb ft (1.5 m.da.N)
Shift control pivot pin	20 lb ft (2.75 m.da.N)
Steering	
Flange to coupling bolts	10 lb ft (1.5 m.da.N)
Steering box securing bolts	20 lb ft (2.75 m.da.N)
Steering link pin	30 lb ft (4 m.da.N)
Steering wheel retaining nut	35 lb ft (5 m.da.N)
Front suspension	
Hub nut	35 lb ft (5 m.da.N)
Damper pin nut	30 lb ft (4 m.da.N)
Lower ball joint nut	35 lb ft (5 m.da.N)
Upper ball joint nut	25 lb ft (3.5 m.da.N)
Steering link pivot pin	25 lb ft (3.5 m.da.N)
Lower suspension arm hinge bolt	30 lb ft (4 m.da.N)
Upper suspension arm hinge bolt	30 lb ft (4 m.da.N)
Steering ball joint nut	25 lb ft (3.5 m.da.N)
Rear suspension	
Outer bearing securing bolts	32 lb ft (4.5 m.da.N)
Rear bearing securing nut	25 lb ft (3.5 m.da.N)
Brakes	
Rigid pipe unions	10 lb ft (1.5 m.da.N)
Hose on the caliper	15 lb ft (2 m.da.N)
Bleed screw	7 lb ft (1 m.da.N)

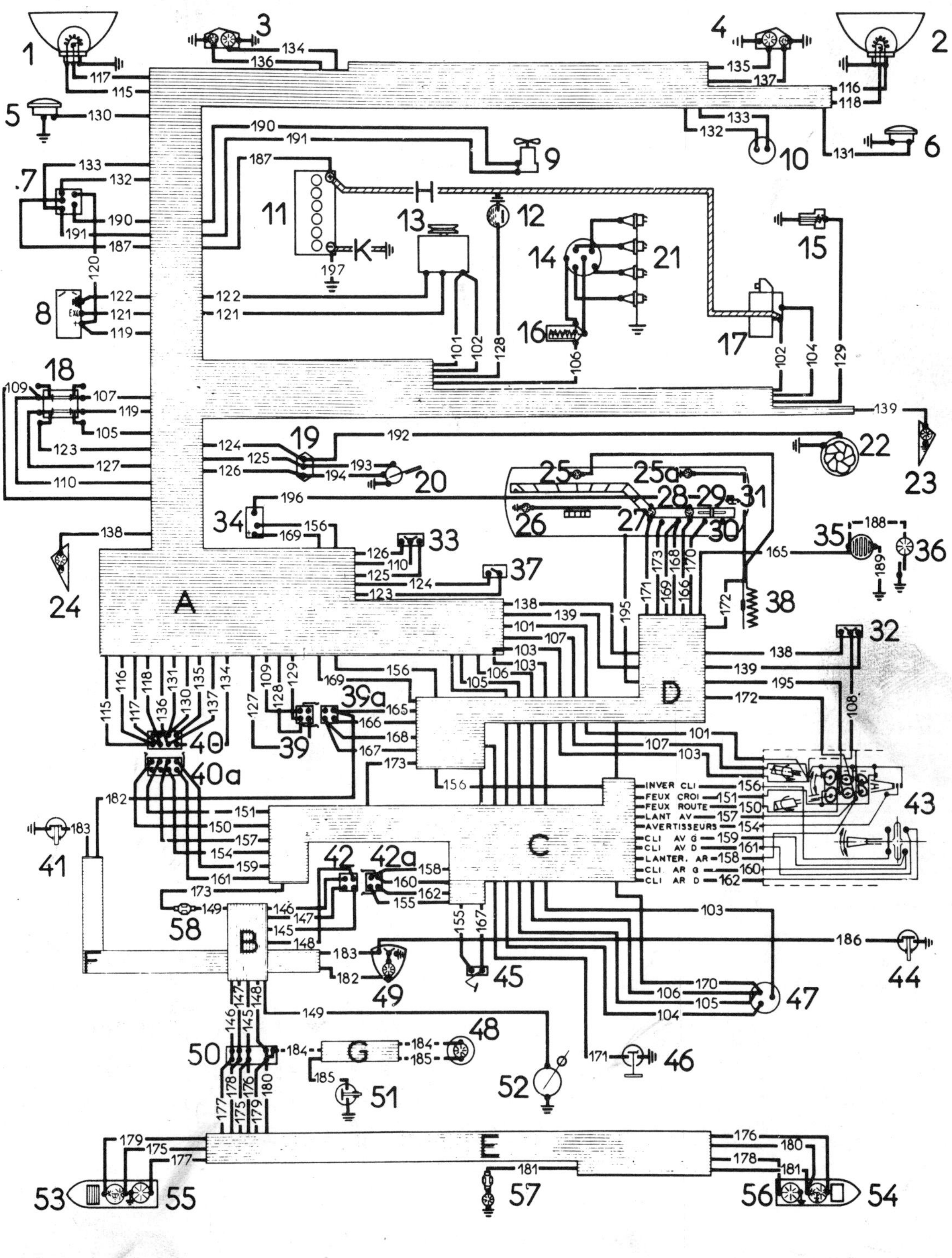

FIG 13:1 Wiring diagram R.1150 1966 model

Key to Fig 13:1 1 Lefthand headlight 2 Righthand headlight 3 Front lefthand side direction indicator light 4 Front righthand side direction indicator light 5 Horn 6 Horn 7 Motor fan unit relay 8 Voltage regulator 9 Motor fan unit 10 Motor fan temperature switch 11 Battery 12 Oil pressure switch 13 Alternator 14 Distributor 15 Temperature switch 16 Coil 17 Starter 18 Fuses 19 Connection block on scuttle panel 20 Windscreen wiper motor 21 Spark plugs 22 Heater motor 23 Righthand parking light 24 Lefthand parking light 25 25a Instrument panel light 26 Headlight telltale 27 Choke telltale 28 Fuel contents indicator 29 Oil pressure and water temperature warning light 30 Ammeter 31 Direction indicator telltale 32 Parking light switch 33 Windscreen wiper switch 34 Flasher unit 35 Cigar lighter 36 Glove compartment light 37 Heater switch 38 Instrument panel lighting rheostat 39 39a Connection block 40 40a Connection block 41 Lefthand door switch 42 42a Connection block 43 Direction indicator switch 44 Righthand door switch 45 Stop switch 46 Choke knob 47 Ignition and starting switch 48 Luggage compartment light 49 Interior light 50 Rear connection plate 51 Tailgate switch 52 Fuel contents rheostat 53 Rear lefthand stop and tail light 54 Rear righthand stop and tail light 55 Rear lefthand direction indicator 56 Rear righthand direction indicator 57 Number plate light 58 Connection between leads 149 and 173

List of harnesses **A** Engine harness **B** Chassis harness **C** Horn and lighting switch harness **D** Instrument panel harness **E** Rear harness **F** Interior light harness **G** Luggage compartment light harness **H** Positive starter lead **K** Negative starter lead

List of wires

Harness	*Wire No.*	*Colour of sleeve and wire*	*Wire connected from*	*Wire connected to*	*Wire diameter in*	*AWG No.*
A	101	Blue, yellow wire	13	43	30/10	9
	102	Covered, yellow wire	17	13	30/10	9
	103	White (light switch) blue (direction indicator switch) Buff wire	43	47	20/10	12
	104	Aluminium grey wire	47 (R)	17	20/10	12
	105	Red, red wire	47 (B)	18	16/10	14
	106	Red, salmon wire	47 (B)	16	12/10	16
	107	Blue, blue wire	43	18	16/10	14
	108	Blue, blue wire	43	32	9/10	19
	109	Blue, blue wire	18	39	16/10	14
	110	Blue, grey wire	18	33	12/10	16
	115	Green wire	40	1 head	12/10	16
	116	Green wire	40	2 head	12/10	16
	117	Salmon pink wire	40	1 C	12/10	16
	118	Salmon pink wire	40	2 C	12/10	16
	119	Red, red wire	18	8 (+ Regulator)	16/10	16
	120	Red, grey wire	8 (+ Regulator)	7 (Coil)	12/10	16
	121	Green, blue wire	8 (Fld)	13 (Fld)	16/10	14
	122	Black, white wire	8 (—)	13 (—)	16/10	14
	123	Red, grey wire	18	37	12/10	16
	124	Brown, grey wire	37 (+)	19	12/10	16
	125	Green, green wire	33 (Motor)	19	12/10	16
	126	Blue, green wire	33 (Parked)	19	12/10	16
	127	Red, grey wire	18	39	12/10	16
	128	Covered green wire	39	12	12/10	16
	129	Covered green wire	39	15	12/10	16
	130	Covered green wire	40	5	12/10	16
	131	Covered grey wire	40	6	12/10	16
	132	Black, grey wire	7	10	12/10	16
	133	Black, grey wire	10	7	12/10	16
	134	Blue wire	40	3 (Front lefthand indicator)	9/10	19
	135	Red wire	40	4 (Front righthand indicator)	9/10	19
	136	White wire	40	3 Front lefthand side light	9/10	19
	137	White wire	40	4 Front righthand side light	9/10	19
	138	Violet, black wire	32	24 Lefthand parking light	9/10	19
	139	Brown, black wire	32	23 Righthand parking light	9/10	19
B	145	Pink, salmon wire	42	50	12/10	16
	146	Violet, blue wire	42	50	9/10	19
	147	Brown, red wire	42	50	9/10	19
	148	Yellow, white wire	42	50	9/10	19
	149	White wire	58	52	9/10	19
C	150	Blue wire	43 (Headlight)	40a	16/10	14
	151	Red wire	43 dipped	40a	16/10	14
	154	White wire	43 Horn	40a	16/10	14

	155	Pink, salmon wire	45 (Stop)	42a	12/10	16
	156	Blue, salmon wire	35 Switch	43	12/10	16
	157	White wire	43 Side lights	40a	9/10	19
	158	White wire	43 Tail lights	42a	9/10	19
	159	Blue wire	43 Front lefthand direction indicator	40a	9/10	19
	160	Blue wire	43 Rear lefthand direction indicator	42a	9/10	19
	161	Red wire	43 Front righthand direction indicator	40a	9/10	19
	162	Red wire	43 Rear righthand direction indicator	42a	9/10	19
D	165	Blue, blue wire	39a	35	16/10	14
	166	Brown, green wire	39a	29	12/10	16
	167	Red, grey wire	39a	45 (+ stop)	12/10	16
	168	Red, grey wire	39a	+ Instrument panel	12/10	16
	169	Red, grey wire	+ Instrument panel	34 (+)	12/10	16
	170	White red (Instrument panel) Red (Ignition) grey wire	47 (B)	30	12/10	16
	171	Black, black wire	27	46	9/10	19
	172	Yellow, black wire	43	38	9/10	19
	173	Violet, white wire	28	58	9/10	19
E	175	Pink, blue wire	50	53 Lefthand stop lamp	9/10	19
	176	Pink, blue wire	50	54 Righthand stop lamp	9/10	19
	177	Violet, red wire	50	55 Rear lefthand direction indicator	9/10	19
	178	Brown, red wire	50	56 Rear righthand direction indicator	9/10	19
	179	Yellow, white wire	50	53 Rear lefthand direction indicator	9/10	19
	180	Yellow, white wire	50	54 Rear righthand direction indicator	9/10	19
	181	White wire	54	57	9/10	19
F	182	Blue white wire	39a	49	9/10	19
	183	White wire	49	41	9/10	19
G	184	Yellow, white wire	50	48	9/10	19
	185	Black wire	48	51	9/10	19
Single wires	186	White wire covered with orange cotton	49	44	9/10	19
	187	White, grey wire	11	7	20/10	12
	188	Blue, black wire	35	36	9/10	19
	189	Black, grey wire	35	Earth (ground)	12/10	16
	190	Red, black wire	7 (Motor)	9	16/10	14
	191	Black, black wire	9	7 (—)	16/10	14
	192	Brown, grey wire	19 (+ Motor)	22	12/10	16
	193	Green, green wire	19	20	12/10	16
	194	Blue, green wire	19 (Park)	20	12/10	16
	195	Blue wire	43	26	9/10	19
	196	Direction indicator telltale	34 (REP.)	31	9/10	19
	197	Yellow wire	11	Earth (ground) bodywork	30/10	9

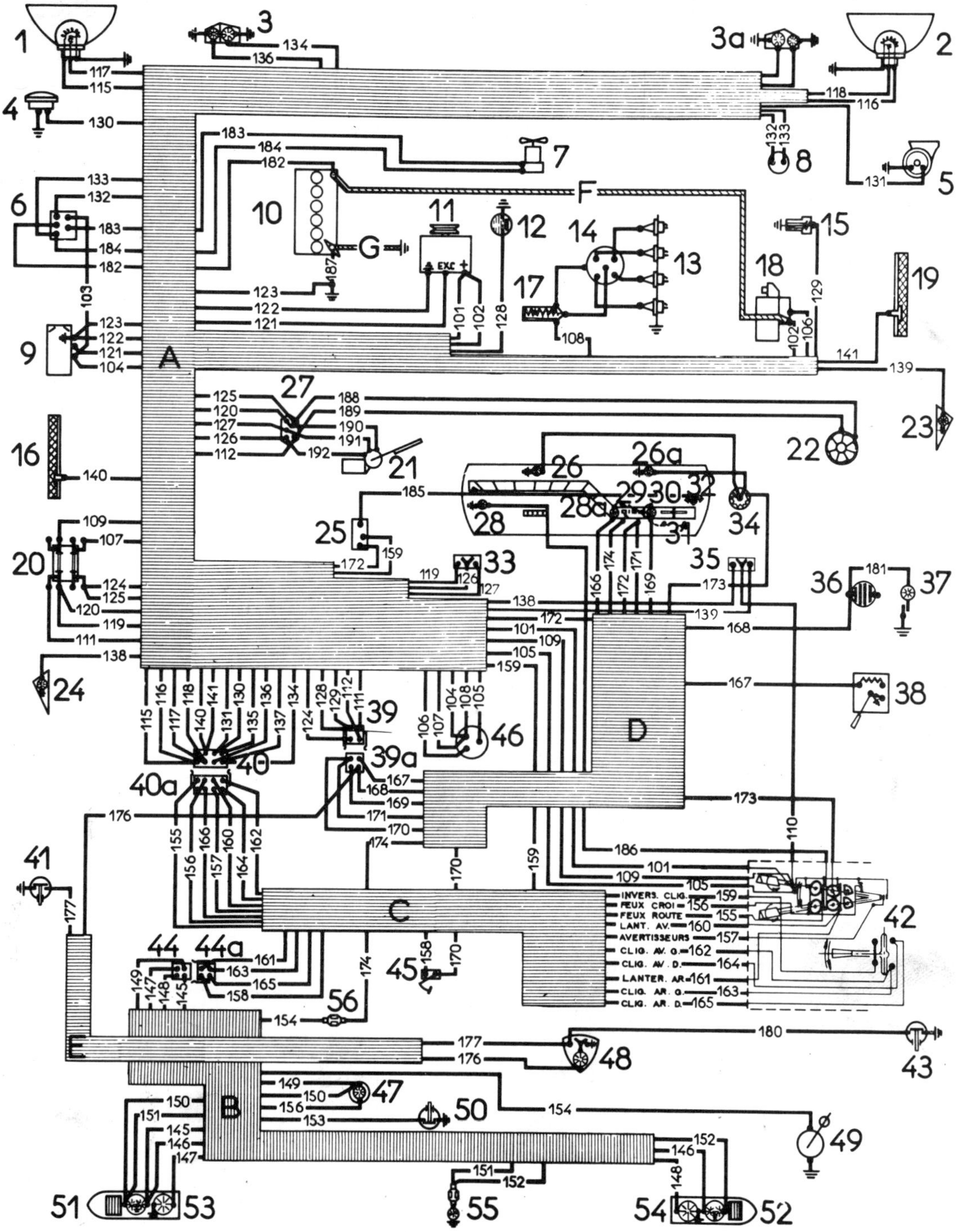

FIG 13:2 Wiring diagram R.1150 1967 model

Key to Fig 13:2 1 Lefthand headlight 2 Righthand headlight 3 Front lefthand side direction indicator light 3a Front righthand side direction indicator light 4 Lefthand side horn 5 Righthand side horn 6 Motor fan unit relay 7 Motor fan cooling unit 8 Motor fan temperature switch 9 Voltage regulator 10 Battery 11 Alternator 12 Oil pressure switch 13 Spark plugs 14 Distributor 15 Temperature switch 16 Front lefthand brake pad 17 Coil 18 Starter 19 Front righthand brake pad 20 Fuses 21 Windscreen wiper motor 22 Heater 23 Righthand parking light 24 Lefthand parking light 25 Flasher unit 26 26a Instrument panel light 27 Connection block on scuttle panel 28 Headlight telltale 28a Front brake pad wear warning light 29 Fuel contents indicator 30 Oil pressure and water temperature warning light 31 Ammeter 32 Direction indicator telltale 33 Windscren wiper switch 34 Instrument panel lighting rheostat 35 Parking light switch 36 Cigar lighter 37 Glove compartment light 38 Heater rheostat 39 39a Connection block 40 40a Connection block 41 Lefthand door switch 42 Direction indicator switch 43 Righthand door switch 44 44a Connection block 45 Stop switch 46 Ignition and starting switch 47 Luggage compartment light 48 Interior light 49 Fuel contents rheostat 50 Tailgate switch 51 Rear lefthand stop and tail light 52 Rear righthand stop and tail light 53 Rear lefthand direction indicator 54 Rear righthand direction indicator 55 Number plate light 56 Connection between leads 154 and 174

List of harnesses **A** Engine harness **B** Chassis harness **C** Horn and lighting switch harness **D** Instrument panel harness **E** Interior light harness **F** Positive starter lead **G** Negative starter lead

List of wires

Harness	*Wire No.*	*Colour of sleeve and wire*	*Wire connected from*	*Wire connected to*	*Wire diameter mm*	*AWG No.*
A	101	Blue, yellow wire	11 (+Alt)	42	30/10	9
	102	Covered yellow wire	18	11 (+Alt)	30/10	9
	103	Red, grey wire	9+Reg.	6 Coil	12/10	16
	104	Red, red wire	46 (B)	9+Reg.	16/10	14
	105	White (Neiman) Blue (Direction indicator switch)	42	46 (+)	20/10	12
		Buff wire				
	106	Aluminium grey wire	46 (R)	18	20/10	12
	107	Red, red wire	46 (B)	20	16/10	14
	108	Red, salmon pink wire	46 (B)	17	12/10	16
	109	Blue, blue wire	42	20	16/10	14
	110	Blue, blue wire	42	35	9/10	19
	111	Blue wire	20	39	16/10	14
	112	Yellow wire	27	39	12/10	16
	115	Green wire	40	1 Lefthand headlight	12/10	16
	116	Green wire	40	2 Righthand headlight	12/10	16
	117	Salmon pink wire	40	1 Lefthand direction indicator	12/10	16
	118	Salmon pink wire	40	2 Righthand direction indicator	12/10	16
	119	Blue, salmon pink wire	20	33 (+)	12/10	16
	120	Blue, salmon pink wire	20	27	12/10	16
	121	Green, blue wire	9 Exc.	11 Exc.	16/10	14
	122	Black, white wire	9 (—)	11 (—)	16/10	14
	123	Black, white wire	9 (—)	10 (—)	16/10	14
	124	Red, grey wire	20	39	12/10	16
	125	Red, grey wire	20	27	12/10	16
	126	Green wire	33	27	12/10	16
	127	Grey wire	33 (Park)	27	12/10	16
	128	Green covered wire	12	39	12/10	16
	129	Green covered wire	15	39	12/10	16
	130	Green covered wire	40	4 Lefthand horn	12/10	16
	131	Grey covered wire	40	5 Righthand horn	12/10	16
	132	Black, grey wire	6 'RAD'	8	12/10	16
	133	Black, grey wire	8	6 (—)	12/10	16
	134	Blue wire	40	3 Front lefthand direction indicator	9/10	19
	135	Red wire	40	3 Front righthand direction indicator	9/10	19
	136	White wire	40	3 Front lefthand switch	9/10	19
	137	White wire	40	3 Front righthand switch	9/10	19
	138	Black wire	35	24	9/10	19
	139	Brown, black wire	35	23	9/10	19
	140	Black covered wire	40	16	12/10	16
	141	Black covered wire	40	19	12/10	16
B	145	Salmon pink wire	44	51 Rear lefthand stop light	12/10	16
	146	Black wire	51	52 Rear righthand stop light	12/10	16
	147	Blue wire	44	53 Rear lefthand direction indicator	9/10	19
	148	Red wire	44	54 Rear righthand direction indicator	9/10	19

	149	Clear, white wire	44	47	9/10	19
	150	Clear, white wire	47	51 Rear lefthand	9/10	19
	151	White wire	51	55	9/10	19
	152	White wire	55	52 Rear righthand	9/10	19
	153	Black wire	47	50	9/10	19
	154	White wire	56	49	9/10	19
C	155	Blue wire	42 (Headlight)	40a	16/10	14
	156	Red wire	42 'Dip'	40a	16/10	14
	157	White wire	42 'Horn'	40a	16/10	14
	158	Pink, salmon pink wire	45 Stop	44a	12/10	16
	159	Blue, salmon pink wire	25 'Com'	42	12/10	16
	160	White wire	42 side	40a	9/10	19
	161	White wire	42 Rear stop light	44a	9/10	19
	162	Blue wire	42 Front lefthand direction indicator	40a	9/10	19
	163	Blue wire	42 Rear lefthand direction indicator	44a	9/10	19
	164	Red wire	42 Front righthand direction indicator	40a	9/10	19
	165	Red wire	42 Rear righthand direction indicator	44a	9/10	19
	166	Black, black wire	28a	40a	9/10	19
D	167	Yellow wire	39a	38	12/10	16
	168	Clear, blue wire	39a	36	16/10	14
	169	Brown, green wire	39a	30	12/10	16
	170	Red, grey wire	39a	45 'Stop'	12/10	16
	171	Red, grey wire	39a	+panel	12/10	16
	172	Red, grey wire	+panel	25 '+'	12/10	16
	173	Yellow, black wire	42	34	9/10	19
	174	White wire	29	56	9/10	19
E	176	Blue, white wire	39a	48	9/10	19
	177	White wire	48	41	9/10	19
Single wires	180	White wire covered with orange cotton	48	43	9/10	19
	181	Clear, blue wire	36	37	9/10	19
	182	White, grey covered wire	10	6 (+)	20/10	12
	183	Red, black wire	6 'Motor'	7	16/10	14
	184	Black, black wire	7	6 (—)	16/10	14
	185	Direction indicator telltale	25 'REP'	32	9/10	19
	186	Blue wire	42	28	9/10	19
	187	Yellow wire	10	Earth Body. (ground)	30/10	9
	188	Red, grey wire	27	22	12/10	16
	189	Yellow wire	27	22	12/10	16
	190	Blue, salmon pink wire	27	21	12/10	16
	191	Grey wire	27	21 Park	12/10	16
	192	Green wire	27	21	12/10	16

HINTS ON MAINTENANCE AND OVERHAUL

There are few things more rewarding than the restoration of a vehicle's original peak of efficiency and smooth performance.

The following notes are intended to help the owner to reach that state of perfection. Providing that he possesses the basic manual skills he should have no difficulty in performing most of the operations detailed in this manual. It must be stressed, however, that where recommended in the manual, highly-skilled operations ought to be entrusted to experts, who have the necessary equipment, to carry out the work satisfactorily.

Quality of workmanship:

The hazardous driving conditions on the roads to-day demand that vehicles should be as nearly perfect, mechanically, as possible. It is therefore most important that amateur work be carried out with extra care, bearing in mind the often inadequate working conditions, and also the inferior tools which may have to be used. It is easy to counsel perfection in all things, and we recognize that it may be setting an impossibly high standard. We do, however, suggest that every care should be taken to ensure that a vehicle is as safe to take on the road as it is humanly possible to make it.

Safe working conditions:

Even though a vehicle may be stationary, it is still potentially dangerous if certain sensible precautions are not taken when working on it while it is supported on jacks or blocks. It is indeed preferable not to use jacks alone, but to supplement them with carefully placed blocks, so that there will be plenty of support if the car rolls off the jacks during a strenuous manoeuvre. Axle stands are an excellent way of providing a rigid base which is not readily disturbed. Piles of bricks are a dangerous substitute. Be careful not to get under heavy loads on lifting tackle, the load could fall. It is preferable not to work alone when lifting an engine, or when working underneath a vehicle which is supported well off the ground. To be trapped, particularly under the vehicle, may have unpleasant results if help is not quickly forthcoming. Make some provision, however humble, to deal with fires. Always disconnect a battery if there is a likelihood of electrical shorts. These may start a fire if there is leaking fuel about. This applies particularly to leads which can carry a heavy current, like those in the starter circuit. While on the subject of electricity, we must also stress the danger of using equipment which is run off the mains and which has no earth or has faulty wiring or connections. So many workshops have damp floors, and electrical shocks are of such a nature that it is sometimes impossible to let go of a live lead or piece of equipment due to the muscular spasms which take place.

Work demanding special care:

This involves the servicing of braking, steering and suspension systems. On the road, failure of the braking system may be disastrous. Make quite sure that there can be no possibility of failure through the bursting of rusty brake pipes or rotten hoses, nor to a sudden loss of pressure due to defective seals or valves.

Problems:

The chief problems which may face an operator are:

1 External dirt.
2 Difficulty in undoing tight fixings.
3 Dismantling unfamiliar mechanisms.
4 Deciding in what respect parts are defective.
5 Confusion about the correct order for reassembly.
6 Adjusting running clearance.
7 Road testing.
8 Final tuning.

Practical suggestions to solve the problems:

1 Preliminary cleaning of large parts—engines, transmissions, steering, suspensions, etc.,—should be carried out before removal from the car. Where road dirt and mud alone are present, wash clean with a high-pressure water jet, brushing to remove stubborn adhesions, and allow to drain and dry. Where oil or grease is also present, wash down with a proprietary compound (Gunk, Teepol, etc.), applying with a stiff brush—an old paint brush is suitable—into all crevices. Cover the distributor and ignition coils with a polythene bag and then apply a strong water jet to clear the loosened deposits. Allow to drain and dry. The assemblies will then be sufficiently clean to remove and transfer to the bench for the next stage.

On the bench, further cleaning can be carried out, first wiping the parts as free as possible from grease with old newspaper. Avoid using rag or cotton waste which can leave clogging fibres behind. Any remaining grease can be removed with a brush dipped in paraffin. If necessary, traces of paraffin can be removed by carbon tetrachloride. Avoid using paraffin or petrol in large quantities for cleaning in enclosed areas, such as garages, on account of the high fire risk.

When all exteriors have been cleaned, and not before, dismantling can be commenced. This ensures that dirt will not enter into interiors and orifices revealed by dismantling. In the next phases, where components have to be cleaned, use carbon tetrachloride in preference to petrol and keep the containers covered except when in use. After the components have been cleaned, plug small holes with tapered hard wood plugs cut to size and blank off larger orifices with grease-proof paper and masking tape. Do not use soft wood plugs or matchsticks as they may break.

2 It is not advisable to hammer on the end of a screw thread, but if it must be done, first screw on a nut to protect the thread, and use a lead hammer. This applies particularly to the removal of tapered cotters. Nuts and bolts seem to 'grow' together, especially in exhaust systems. Generous use of a penetrating oil usually helps to overcome this problem.

Tight bushes or pieces of tail-pipe rusted into a silencer can be removed by splitting them with an open-ended hacksaw. Tight screws can sometimes be started by a tap from a hammer on the end of a suitable screwdriver. Many tight fittings will yield to the judicious use of a hammer, but it must be a soft-faced hammer if damage is to be avoided, use a heavy block on the opposite side to absorb shock. Any parts of the steering system which have been damaged should be renewed, as attempts to repair them may lead to cracking and subsequent failure, and steering ball joints should be disconnected using a recommended tool to prevent damage.

3 It often happens that an owner is baffled when trying to dismantle an unfamiliar piece of equipment. So many modern devices are pressed together or assembled by spinning-over flanges, that they must be sawn apart. The intention is that the whole assembly must be renewed. However, parts which appear to be in one piece to the naked eye, may reveal close-fitting joint lines when inspected with a magnifying glass, and, this may provide the necessary clue to dismantling. Left-handed screw threads are used where rotational forces would tend to unscrew a right-handed screw thread.

Be very careful when dismantling mechanisms which may come apart suddenly. Work in an enclosed space where the parts will be contained, and drape a piece of cloth over the device if springs are likely to fly in all directions. Mark everything which might be reassembled in the wrong position, scratched symbols may be used on unstressed parts, or a sequence of tiny dots from a centre punch can be useful. Stressed parts should never be scratched or centre-popped as this may lead to cracking under working conditions. Store parts which look alike in the correct order for reassembly. Never rely upon memory to assist in the assembly of complicated mechanisms, especially when they will be dismantled for a long time, but make notes, and drawings to supplement the diagrams in the manual, and put labels on detached wires. Rust stains may indicate unlubricated wear. This can sometimes be seen round the outside edge of a bearing cup in a universal joint. Look for bright rubbing marks on parts which normally should not make heavy contact. These might prove that something is bent or running out of true. For example, there might be bright marks on one side of a piston, at the top near the ring grooves, and others at the bottom of the skirt on the other side. This could well be the clue to a bent connecting rod. Suspected cracks can be proved by heating the component in a light oil to approximately 100°C, removing, drying off, and dusting with french chalk, if a crack is present the oil retained in the crack will stain the french chalk.

4 In determining wear, and the degree, against the permissible limits set in the manual, accurate measurement can only be achieved by the use of a micrometer. or vernier gauge. In many micrometers the wear is given to the fourth place of decimals; that is in ten-thousandths of an inch. This can be read by the vernier scale on the barrel of a good micrometer. Bore diameters are easily determined using a vernier gauge. In other cases, the shank of a twist drill of known diameter is a handy check.

Many methods have been devised for determining the clearance between bearing surfaces. To-day the best and simplest is by the use of Plastigage, obtainable from most garages. A thin plastic thread is laid between the two surfaces and the bearing is tightened, flattening the thread. On removal, the width of the thread is compared with a scale supplied with the thread and the clearance is read off directly. Sometimes joint faces leak persistently, even after gasket renewal. The fault will then be traceable to distortion, dirt or burrs. Studs which are screwed into soft metal frequently raise burrs at the point of entry. A quick cure for this is to chamfer the edge of the hole in the part which fits over the stud.

5 **Always check a replacement part with the original one before it is fitted.**

If parts are not marked, and the order for reassembly is not known, a little detective work will help. Look for marks which are due to wear to see if they can be mated. Joint faces may not be identical due to manufacturing errors, and parts which overlap may be stained, giving a clue to the correct position. Most fixings leave identifying marks especially if they were painted over on assembly. It is then easier to decide whether a nut, for instance, has a plain, a spring, or a shakeproof washer under it. All running surfaces become 'bedded' together after long spells of work and tiny imperfections on one part will be found to have left corresponding marks on the other. This is particularly true of shafts and bearings and even a score on a cylinder wall will show on the piston.

6 Checking end float or rocker clearances by feeler gauge may not always give accurate results because of wear. For instance, the rocker tip which bears on a valve stem may be deeply pitted, in which case the feeler will simply be bridging a depression. Thrust washers may also wear depressions in opposing faces to make accurate measurement difficult. End float is then easier to check by using a dial gauge. It is common practice to adjust end play in bearing assemblies, like front hubs with taper rollers, by doing up the axle nut until the hub becomes stiff to turn and then backing it off a little. Do not use this method with ballbearing hubs as the assembly is often preloaded by tightening the axle nut to its fullest extent. If the splitpin hole will not line up, file the base of the nut a little.

Steering assemblies often wear in the straight-ahead position. If any part is adjusted, make sure that it remains free when moved from lock to lock. Do not be surprised if an assembly like a steering gearbox, which is known to be carefully adjusted outside the car, becomes stiff when it is bolted in place. This will be due to distortion of the case by the pull of the mounting bolts, particularly if the mounting points are not all touching together. This problem may be met in other equipment and is cured by careful attention to the alignment of mounting points.

When a spanner is stamped with a size and A/F it means that the dimension is the width between the jaws and has no connection with ANF, which is the designation for the American National Fine thread. Coarse threads like Whitworth are rarely used on cars to-day except for studs which screw into soft aluminium or cast iron. For this reason it might be found that the top end of a cylinder head stud has a fine thread and the lower end a coarse thread to screw into the cylinder block. If the car has mainly UNF threads then it is likely that any coarse threads will be UNC, which are not the same as Whitworth. Small sizes have the same number of threads in Whitworth and UNC, but in the $\frac{1}{2}$ inch size for example, there are twelve threads to the inch in the former and thirteen in the latter.

7 After a major overhaul, particularly if a great deal of work has been done on the braking, steering and suspension systems, it is advisable to approach the problem of testing with care. If the braking system has been overhauled, apply heavy pressure to the brake pedal and get a second operator to check every possible source of leakage. The brakes may work extremely well, but a leak could cause complete failure after a few miles.

Do not fit the hub caps until every wheel nut has been checked for tightness, and make sure the tyre pressures are correct. Check the levels of coolant, lubricants and hydraulic fluids. Being satisfied that all is well, take the car on the road and test the brakes at once. Check the steering and the action of the handbrake. Do all this at moderate speeds on quiet roads, and make sure there is no other vehicle behind you when you try a rapid stop.

Finally, remember that many parts settle down after a time, so check for tightness of all fixings after the car has been on the road for a hundred miles or so.

8 It is useless to tune an engine which has not reached its normal running temperature. In the same way, the tune of an engine which is stiff after a rebore will be different when the engine is again running free. Remember too, that rocker clearances on pushrod operated valve gear will change when the cylinder head nuts are tightened after an initial period of running with a new head gasket.

Trouble may not always be due to what seems the obvious cause. Ignition, carburation and mechanical condition are interdependent and spitting back through the carburetter, which might be attributed to a weak mixture, can be caused by a sticking inlet valve.

For one final hint on tuning, never adjust more than one thing at a time or it will be impossible to tell which adjustment produced the desired result.

GLOSSARY OF TERMS

AF Across Flats. Width across the flats of nut or bolt heads, or between jaws of associated spanners.

Alternator Electrical generator producing alternating current. Rectified to direct current for battery charging.

Ambient temperature Surrounding atmospheric temperature.

Annulus Used in engineering to indicate the outer ring gear of an epicyclic gear train.

Armature The shaft carrying the windings, which rotates in the magnetic field of a generator or starter motor. That part of a solenoid which is activated by the magnetic field.

Asymmetrical Not symmetrical.

Axial In line with, or pertaining to, an axis.

Backlash Play in meshing gears.

Balance lever A bar where force applied at the centre is equally divided between connections at the ends.

Bendix pinion A self-engaging and self-disengaging drive on a starter motor shaft.

Bevel pinion A conical shaped gearwheel, designed to mesh with a similar gear with an axis usually at 90 deg. to its own.

bhp Brake horse power, measured on a dynamometer.

bmep Brake mean effective pressure. Average pressure on a piston during the working stroke.

Brake cylinder Cylinder with hydraulically operated piston(s) acting on brake shoes or pad(s).

Brake regulator Control valve fitted in hydraulic braking system which limits brake pressure to rear brakes during heavy braking to prevent rear wheel locking.

Camber Angle at which a wheel is tilted from the vertical.

Capacitor Modern term for an electrical condenser. Part of distributor assembly, connected across contact breaker points, acts as an interference suppressor.

Castellated Top face of a nut, slotted across the flats, to take a locking splitpin.

Castor Angle at which the kingpin or swivel pin is tilted when viewed from the side.

cc Cubic centimetres. Engine capacity is arrived at by multiplying the area of the bore in sq cm by the stroke in cm by the number of cylinders.

Clevis U-shaped forked connector used with a clevis pin, usually at handbrake connections.

Clockwise In the direction of rotation of the hands of a clock, movement in the opposite direction is normally referred to as anti-clockwise.

Collet A type of collar, usually split and located in a groove in a shaft, and held in place by a retainer. The arrangement used to retain the spring(s) on a valve stem in most cases.

Commutator Rotating segmented current distributor between armature windings and brushes in generator or motor.

Compression ratio The ratio, or quantitative relation, of the total volume (piston at bottom of stroke) to the unswept volume (piston at top of stroke) in an engine cylinder.

Condensor See capacitor.

Core plug Plug for blanking off a manufacturing hole in a casting.

Crownwheel Large bevel gear in rear axle, driven by a bevel pinion attached to the propeller shaft. Sometimes called a 'ring wheel'.

'C' Spanner Like a 'C' with a handle. For use on screwed collars without flats, but with slots or holes.

Damper Modern term for shock-absorber used in vehicle suspension systems to damp out spring oscillations.

Depression The lowering of atmospheric pressure as in the inlet manifold and carburetter.

Dowel Close tolerance pin, peg, tube, or bolt, which accurately locates mating parts.

Drag link Rod connecting steering box drop arm (pitman arm) to nearest front wheel steering arm in certain types of steering systems.

Dry liner Thinwall tube pressed into cylinder bore.

Electrode Terminal part of an electrical component, such as the points or 'electrodes' of a sparking plug.

Electrolyte In lead-acid car batteries a solution of sulphuric acid and distilled water.

End float Or end play. The endwise movement between associated parts.

EP Extreme pressure. In lubricants, special grades for heavily loaded bearing surfaces, such as gear teeth in a gearbox, or crownwheel and pinion in a rear axle.

Fade Of brakes. Reduced efficiency due to overheating.

Field coils Windings on the polepieces of motors and generators.

Fillets Narrow finishing strips usually applied to interior bodywork.

First motion shaft Input shaft from clutch to gearbox.

Fullflow Oil filters. Filters all the oil pumped to the engine. If the element becomes clogged, a bypass valve operates to pass unfiltered oil to the engine.

FWD Front wheel drive.

Grommet A ring of protective or sealing material. Can be used to protect pipes or leads passing through bulkheads.

Gudgeon pin Shaft which connects a piston to its connecting rod. Sometimes called 'wrist pin', or 'piston pin'.

Halfshaft One of a pair transmitting drive from the differential gearing to the wheel hubs.

HC High-compression. See Compression ratio.

Helical In spiral form. The teeth of helical gears are cut at a spiral angle to the side faces of the gear wheel.

Hot spot Hot area that assists vapourisation of fuel on its way to cylinders. Often provided by close contact between inlet and exhaust manifolds.

HT High Tension. Applied to electrical current produced by the ignition coil for the sparking plugs.

Hydrometer A device for checking specific gravity of liquids. Used to check specific gravity of electrolyte.

Hypoid bevel gears A form of bevel gear used in the rear axle drive gears. The bevel pinion meshes below the centre line of the crownwheel, giving a lower propeller shaft line.

Idler A device for passing on movement. A free running gear between driving and driven gears. A lever transmitting track rod movement to a side rod in steering gear

IFS Independent Front Suspension.

Impeller A centrifugal pumping element. Used in water pumps to stimulate flow.

Journals Those parts of a shaft that are in contact with the bearings.

Kerosene Paraffin.

Kingpin The main vertical pin which carries the front wheel spindle, and permits steering movement. May be called 'steering pin' or 'swivel pin'.

Layshaft The shaft which carries the laygear in the gearbox. The laygear is driven by the first motion shaft and drives the third motion shaft according to the gear selected. Sometimes called the 'Countershaft' or 'Second motion shaft'.

lb ft A measure of twist or torque. A pull of 10 lb at a radius of 1 ft is a torque of 10 lb ft.

lb/sq in Pounds per square inch.

LC Low Compression. See 'Compression ratio'.

Little end The small, or piston end of a connecting rod. Sometimes called the 'Small end'.

ls Leading shoe in brake drum. Tends to wedge into drum, when applied, so increasing the braking effect.

LT Low Tension. The current output from battery.

Mandrel Accurately manufactured bar or rod used for test or centring purposes.

Manifold A pipe duct, or chamber, with several branches.

Needle rollers Bearing rollers with a length many times their diameter.

Oil bath Reservoir which lubricates parts by immersion. In air filters, a separate oil supply for wetting a wiremesh element and holding the dust.

Oil wetted In air filters, a wiremesh element lightly oiled to trap and hold airborne dust.

Overlap Period during which inlet and exhaust valves are open together.

Panhard rod Bar connected between fixed point on chassis and another on axle to control sideways movement.

Pawl Pivoted catch which engages in the teeth of a ratchet to permit movement in one direction only.

Peg spanner Tool with pegs, or pins, to engage in holes in the part to be turned.

Pendant pedals Pedals with levers that are pivoted at the top end.

Phillips screwdriver A cross-point screwdriver for use with the cross-slotted heads of Phillips screws.

Pinion A small gear, usually in relation to another gear.

Piston-type damper Shock absorber in which damping is controlled by a piston working in a closed oil filled cylinder.

Preloading Preset static pressure on ball or roller bearings not due to working loads.

Radial Radiating from a centre, like the spokes of a wheel.

Radius rod Pivoted arm confining movement of a part to an arc of fixed radius.

Ratchet Toothed wheel or rack which can move in one direction only, movement in the other being prevented by a pawl.

Ring gear	A gear toothed ring attached to outer periphery of flywheel. Starter pinion engages with it during starting.
Runout	Amount by which a rotating part is out of true.
SAE	Society of Automotive Engineers.
Semi-floating axle	Outer end of rear axle halfshaft is carried on bearing inside axle casing. Wheel hub is secured to end of shaft.
Servo	A hydraulic or pneumatic system for assisting, or augmenting a physical effort. See 'Vacuum Servo'.
Setscrew	One which is threaded for the full length of the shank.
Shackle	A coupling link, used in the form of two parallel pins connected by side plates to secure the end of the master suspension spring, and absorb the effects of deflection.
Shell bearing	Thin walled, steel shell lined with anti-friction metal. Usually semi-circular and used in pairs for main and big-end bearings.
Shock absorber	See 'damper'.
Silentbloc	Rubber bush bonded to inner and outer metal sleeves.
Socket-head screw	Screw with hexagonal socket for an Allen key.
Solenoid	A coil of wire creating a magnetic field when electric current passes through it. Used with a soft iron core to operate contacts or a mechanical device.
Spur gear	A gear with teeth cut axially across the periphery.
Stator tube	A stationary tube inside the steering column, carrying wiring to steering wheel controls.
Stub axle	Short axle fitted at one end only.
Tachometer	An instrument for accurate measurement of rotating speed. Usually indicates in revolutions per minute.
TDC	Top Dead Centre. The highest point reached by a piston in a cylinder, with the crank and connecting rod in line.
Thermostat	Automatic device for regulating temperature. Used in vehicle coolant systems to open a valve which restricts circulation at low temperatures.
Third motion shaft	Output shaft of gearbox.
Thrust bearing or washer	Used to reduce friction in rotating parts subject to axial loads.
Torque	Turning or twisting effort. See lb ft.
Track rod	The bar(s) across the vehicle which connect the steering arms and maintain the front wheels in their correct alignment.
ts	Trailing shoe, in a drum brake assembly. Tends to be pushed away from drum.
UJ	Universal joint. A coupling between shafts which permits angular movement.
Vacuum Servo	Device used in brake system, using difference between atmospheric pressure and inlet manifold depression to operate a piston which acts to augment brake pressure as required. See 'Servo'.
Venturi	A restriction or 'choke' in a tube, as in a carburetter, used to increase velocity to obtain a reduction in pressure.
Vernier	A sliding scale for obtaining fractional readings of the graduations of an adjacent scale.
Welch plug	A domed thin metal disc which is partially flattened to lock in a recess. Used to plug core holes in castings.
Wet liner	Removable cylinder barrel, sealed against coolant leakage, where the coolant is in direct contact with the outer surface.
Wet sump	A reservoir attached to the crankcase to hold the lubricating oil.

INDEX

THE AUTOBOOK SERIES OF WORKSHOP MANUALS

Make	*Author*	*Title*
AUSTIN		
A30 1951–1956	Ball	Austin A30, A35, A40 Autobook
A35 1956–1962	Ball	Austin A30, A35, A40 Autobook
A40 Farina 1957–1967	Ball	Austin A30, A35, A40 Autobook
A40 Cambridge 1954–1957	Ball	BMC Autobook Three
A50 Cambridge 1954–1957	Ball	BMC Autobook Three
A55 Cambridge Mk 1 1957–1958	Ball	BMC Autobook Three
A55 Cambridge Mk 2 1958–1961	Smith	BMC Autobook One
A60 Cambridge 1961–1969	Smith	BMC Autobook One
A99 1959–1961	Ball	BMC Autobook Four
A110 1961–1968	Ball	BMC Autobook Four
Mini 1959–1970	Ball	Mini 1959–70 Autobook
Mini Cooper 1961–1970	Ball	Mini Cooper 1961–70 Autobook
Mini Cooper S 1963–1970	Ball	Mini Cooper 1961–70 Autobook
1100 Mk 1 1963–1967	Ball	1100 Mk 1 1962–67 Autobook
1100 Mk 2 1968–1969	Ball	1100 Mk 2, 1300, America 1968–69 Autobook
1300 1968–1969	Ball	1100 Mk 2, 1300, America 1968–69 Autobook
America 1968–1969	Ball	1100 Mk 2, 1300, America 1968–69 Autobook
1800 Mk 1 1964–1968	Ball	1800 Autobook
1800 Mk 2 1968–1969	Ball	1800 Autobook
Maxi 1969	Ball	Austin Maxi 1969 Autobook
AUSTIN HEALEY		
100/6 1956–1959	Ball	Austin Healey 100/6, 3000 1956–68 Autobook
Sprite 1958–1969	Ball	Sprite, Midget 1958–69 Autobook
3000 Mk 1 1959–1961	Ball	Austin Healey 100/6, 3000 1956–68 Autobook
3000 Mk 2 1961–1964	Ball	Austin Healey 100/6, 3000 1956–68 Autobook
3000 Mk 3 1964–1968	Ball	Austin Healey 100/6, 3000 1956–68 Autobook
BEDFORD		
CA Mk 1 and 2 1961–1969	Ball	Vauxhall Victor 1, 2, FB 1957–64 Autobook
Beagle HA 1964–1966	Ball	Vauxhall Viva HA 1964–66 Autobook
BMW		
1600 1966–1969	Ball	BMW 1600 1966–69 Autobook
1600–2 1966–1969	Ball	BMW 1600 1966–69 Autobook
1600TI 1966–1969	Ball	BMW 1600 1966–69 Autobook
1800 1964–1968	Ball	BMW 1800 1964–68 Autobook
1800TI 1964–1968	Ball	BMW 1800 1964–68 Autobook
2000 1966–1969	Ball	BMW 2000, 2002 1966–69 Autobook
2000A 1966–1969	Ball	BMW 2000, 2002 1966–69 Autobook
2000TI 1966–1969	Ball	BMW 2000, 2002 1966–69 Autobook
2000CS 1967–1969	Ball	BMW 2000, 2002 1966–69 Autobook
2000CA 1967–1969	Ball	BMW 2000, 2002 1966–69 Autobook
2002 1968–1969	Ball	BMW 2000, 2002 1966–69 Autobook
COMMER		
Cob Series 1 1960	Ball	Hillman Minx 1 to 5 1956–65 Autobook
Cob Series 2 1960–1963	Ball	Hillman Minx 1 to 5 1956–65 Autobook
Cob Series 3 1963–1965	Ball	Hillman Minx 1 to 5 1956–65 Autobook
Imp Vans 1963–1969	Smith	Hillman Imp 1963–69 Autobook
DE DION BOUTON		
One-cylinder 1899–1907	Mercredy	De Dion Autobook One
Two-cylinder 1903–1907	Mercredy	De Dion Autobook One
Four-cylinder 1905–1907	Mercredy	De Dion Autobook One

Make	Author	Title
FIAT		
500 1957–1961	Ball	Fiat 500 1957–69 Autobook
500D 1960–1965	Ball	Fiat 500 1957–69 Autobook
500F 1965–1969	Ball	Fiat 500 1957–69 Autobook
600 633 cc 1955–1961	Ball	Fiat 600, 600D 1955–69 Autobook
600D 766 cc 1960–1969	Ball	Fiat 600, 600D 1955–69 Autobook
850 Sedan 1964–1969	Ball	Fiat 850 1964–69 Autobook
850 Coupé 1965–1969	Ball	Fiat 850 1964–69 Autobook
850 Roadster 1965–1969	Ball	Fiat 850 1964–69 Autobook
850 Family 1965–1969	Ball	Fiat 850 1964–69 Autobook
124 Saloon 1966–1969	Ball	Fiat 124 1966–69 Autobook
FORD		
Anglia 100E 1953–1959	Ball	Ford Anglia Prefect 100E Autobook
Anglia 105E 1959–1967	Smith	Ford Anglia 105E, Prefect 107E 1954–67 Autobook
Anglia Super 123E 1962–1967	Smith	Ford Anglia 105E, Prefect 107E 1954–67 Autobook
Capri 109E 1962	Smith	Ford Classic, Capri Autobook One
Capri 116E 1962–1964	Smith	Ford Classic, Capri Autobook One
Classic 109E 1961–1962	Smith	Ford Classic, Capri Autobook One
Classic 116E 1962–1963	Smith	Ford Classic, Capri Autobook One
Consul Mk 1 1950–1956	Ball	Ford Consul, Zephyr, Zodiac 1, 2 1950–62 Autobook
Consul Mk 2 1956–1962	Ball	Ford Consul, Zephyr, Zodiac 1, 2 1950–62 Autobook
Corsair V4 3004E 1965–1969	Smith	Ford Corsair V4 1965–69 Autobook
Corsair V4 GT 1965–1966	Smith	Ford Corsair V4 1965–69 Autobook
Corsair 2000, 2000E 1966–1969	Smith	Ford Corsair V4 1965–69 Autobook
Cortina 113E 1962–1966	Smith	Ford Cortina 1962–66 Autobook
Cortina Super 118E 1963–1966	Smith	Ford Cortina 1962–66 Autobook
Cortina Lotus 125E 1963–1966	Smith	Ford Cortina 1962–66 Autobook
Cortina GT 118E 1963–1966	Smith	Ford Cortina 1962–66 Autobook
Cortina 1300 1967–1969	Smith	Ford Cortina 1967–69 Autobook
Cortina 1500 1967–1969	Smith	Ford Cortina 1967–69 Autobook
Cortina 1600 (including Lotus) 1967–1969	Smith	Ford Cortina 1967–69 Autobook
Escort 100E 1955–1959	Ball	Ford Anglia Prefect 100E Autobook
Escort 1100 1967–1970	Ball	Ford Escort 1967–70 Autobook
Escort 1300 1967–1970	Ball	Ford Escort 1967–70 Autobook
Prefect 100E 1954–1959	Ball	Ford Anglia Prefect 100E Autobook
Prefect 107E 1959–61	Smith	Ford Anglia 105E, Prefect 107E 1954–67 Autobook
Popular 100E 1959–1962	Ball	Ford Anglia Prefect 100E Autobook
Squire 100E 1955–1959	Ball	Ford Anglia Prefect 100E Autobook
Zephyr Mk 1 1950–1956	Ball	Ford Consul, Zephyr, Zodiac 1, 2 1950–62 Autobook
Zephyr Mk 2 1956–1962	Ball	Ford Consul, Zephyr, Zodiac 1, 2 1950–62 Autobook
Zephyr 4 Mk 3 1962–1966	Ball	Ford Zephyr, Zodiac Mk 3 1962–66 Autobook
Zephyr 6 Mk 3 1962–1966	Ball	Ford Zephyr, Zodiac Mk 3 1962–66 Autobook
Zodiac Mk 3 1962–1966	Ball	Ford Zephyr, Zodiac Mk 3 1962–66 Autobook
Zodiac Mk 1 1953–1956	Ball	Ford Consul, Zephyr, Zodiac 1, 2 1950–62 Autobook
Zodiac Mk 2 1956–1962	Ball	Ford Consul, Zephyr, Zodiac 1, 2 1950–62 Autobook
Zephyr V4 2 litre 1966–1969	Ball	Ford Zephyr V4, V6, Zodiac 1966–69 Autobook
Zephyr V6 2.5 litre 1966–1969	Ball	Ford Zephyr V4, V6, Zodiac 1966–69 Autobook
Zodiac V6 3 litre 1966–1969	Ball	Ford Zephyr V4, V6, Zodiac 1966–69 Autobook
Capri 1300, 1300 GT 1968–1969	Ball	Ford Capri 1968–69 Autobook
Capri 1600, 1600 GT 1968–1969	Ball	Ford Capri 1968–69 Autobook
HILLMAN		
Hunter GT 1966–1970	Ball	Hillman Hunter 1966–70 Autobook
Minx Series 1 1956–57	Ball	Hillman Minx 1 to 5 1956–65 Autobook
Minx Series 2 1957–1958	Ball	Hillman Minx 1 to 5 1956–65 Autobook
Minx Series 3 1958–1959	Ball	Hillman Minx 1 to 5 1956–65 Autobook
Minx Series 3A 1959–1960	Ball	Hillman Minx 1 to 5 1956–65 Autobook
Minx Series 3B 1960–1961	Ball	Hillman Minx 1 to 5 1956–65 Autobook

Make	*Author*	*Title*
Minx Series 3C 1961–1963	Ball	Hillman Minx 1 to 5 1956–65 Autobook
Minx Series 5 1963–1965	Ball	Hillman Minx 1 to 5 1956–65 Autobook
Minx Series 6 1955–1967	Ball	Hillman Minx 1965–67 Autobook
New Minx 1500, 1725 1966–1969	Ball	Hillman Minx 1966–69 Autobook
Imp 1963–1969	Smith	Hillman Imp 1963–69 Autobook
Husky Series 1 1958–1959	Ball	Hillman Minx 1 to 5 1956–65 Autobook
Husky Series 2 1960–1963	Ball	Hillman Minx 1 to 5 1956–65 Autobook
Husky Series 3 1963–1965	Ball	Hillman Minx 1 to 5 1956–65 Autobook
Super Minx Mk 1 1961–1962	Ball	Hillman Super Minx 1, 2, 3 1961–65 Autobook
Super Minx Mk 2 1962–1964	Ball	Hillman Super Minx 1, 2, 3 1961–65 Autobook
Super Minx Mk 3 1964–1965	Ball	Hillman Super Minx 1, 2, 3 1961–65 Autobook
Super Minx Mk 4 1965–1967	Ball	Hillman Minx 1965–67 Autobook

HUMBER

Sceptre Mk 2 1965–1967	Ball	Hillman Minx 1965–67 Autobook
Sceptre 1967–70	Ball	Hillman Hunter 1966–70 Autobook

JAGUAR

XK 120 1948–1954	Ball	Jaguar XK 120, 140, 150 Mk 7, 8, 9 1948–61 Autobook
XK 140 1954–1957	Ball	Jaguar XK 120, 140, 150 Mk 7, 8, 9 1948–61 Autobook
XK 150 1957–1961	Ball	Jaguar XK 120, 140, 150 Mk 7, 8, 9 1948–61 Autobook
XK 150S 1959–1961	Ball	Jaguar XK 120, 140, 150 Mk 7, 8, 9 1948–61 Autobook
Mk 7 1950–1954	Ball	Jaguar XK 120, 140, 150 Mk 7, 8, 9 1948–61 Autobook
Mk 7M 1954–1957	Ball	Jaguar XK 120, 140, 150 Mk 7, 8, 9 1948–61 Autobook
Mk 8 1956–1961	Ball	Jaguar XK 120, 140, 150 Mk 7, 8, 9 1948–61 Autobook
Mk 9 1958–1961	Ball	Jaguar XK 120, 140, 150 Mk 7, 8, 9 1948–61 Autobook
2.4 Mk 1 1955–1959	Ball	Jaguar 2.4, 3.4, 3.8 Mk 1, 2 1955–67 Autobook
2.4 Mk 2 1959–1967	Ball	Jaguar 2.4, 3.4, 3.8 Mk 1, 2 1955–67 Autobook
3.4 Mk 1 1957–1960	Ball	Jaguar 2.4, 3.4, 3.8 Mk 1, 2 1955–67 Autobook
3.4 Mk 2 1960–1967	Ball	Jaguar 2.4, 3.4, 3.8 Mk 1, 2 1955–67 Autobook
3.8 Mk 2 1959–1967	Ball	Jaguar 2.4, 3.4, 3.8 Mk 1, 2 1955–67 Autobook
240 1967–1969	Ball	Jaguar 2.4, 3.4, 3.8 Mk 1, 2 1955–67 Autobook
340 1967–1969	Ball	Jaguar 2.4, 3.4, 3.8 Mk 1, 2 1955–67 Autobook
E Type 3.8 1961–1965	Ball	Jaguar E Type 1961–69 Autobook
E Type 4.2 1964–1969	Ball	Jaguar E Type 1961–69 Autobook
E Type 4.2 2+2 1966–1969	Ball	Jaguar E Type 1961–69 Autobook
E Type 4.2 Series 2 1969	Ball	Jaguar E Type 1961–69 Autobook
S Type 3.4 1963–1968	Ball	Jaguar S Type and 420 1963–68 Autobook
S Type 3.8 1963–1968	Ball	Jaguar S Type and 420 1963–68 Autobook
420 1963–1968	Ball	Jaguar S Type and 420 1963–68 Autobook

JOWETT

Javelin PA 1947–1949	Mitchell	Jowett Javelin Jupiter 1947–53 Autobook
Javelin PB 1949–1950	Mitchell	Jowett Javelin Jupiter 1947–53 Autobook
Javelin PC 1950–1951	Mitchell	Jowett Javelin Jupiter 1947–53 Autobook
Javelin PD 1951–1952	Mitchell	Jowett Javelin Jupiter 1947–53 Autobook
Javelin PE 1952–1953	Mitchell	Jowett Javelin Jupiter 1947–53 Autobook
Jupiter Mk 1 SA 1949–1952	Mitchell	Jowett Javelin Jupiter 1947–53 Autobook
Jupiter Mk 1A SC 1952–1953	Mitchell	Jowett Javelin Jupiter 1947–53 Autobook

MG

TA 1936–1939	Ball	MG TA to TF 1936–55 Autobook
TB 1939	Ball	MG TA to TF 1936–55 Autobook
TC 1945–1949	Ball	MG TA to TF 1936–55 Autobook

Make	Author	Title
TD 1950–1953	Ball	MG TA to TF 1936–55 Autobook
TF 1953–1954	Ball	MG TA to TF 1936–55 Autobook
TF 1500 1954–1955	Ball	MG TA to TF 1936–55 Autobook
Midget 1961–1969	Ball	Sprite, Midget 1958–69 Autobook
Magnette ZA, ZB 1955–1959	Ball	BMC Autobook Three
Magnette 3, 4 1959–1968	Smith	BMC Autobook One
MGA 1500, 1600 1955–1962	Ball	MGA, MGB 1955–69 Autobook
MGA Twin Cam 1958–1960	Ball	MGA, MGB 1955–69 Autobook
MGB 1962–1969	Ball	MGA, MGB 1955–69 Autobook
1100 Mk 1 1962–1967	Ball	1100 Mk 1, 1962–67 Autobook
1100 Mk 2 1968	Ball	1100 Mk 2, 1300, America 1968–69 Autobook
1300 1968–1969	Ball	1100 Mk 2, 1300, America 1968–69 Autobook
MORGAN		
Four-wheelers 1936–1969	Clarke	Morgan 1936–69 Autobook
MORRIS		
Oxford 2, 3 1956–1959	Ball	BMC Autobook Three
Oxford 5, 6 1959–1969	Smith	BMC Autobook One
Minor Series 2 1952–1956	Ball	Morris Minor 1952–69 Autobook
Minor 1000 1957–1969	Ball	Morris Minor 1952–69 Autobook
Mini 1959–1970	Ball	Mini 1959–70 Autobook
Mini Cooper 1961–1970	Ball	Mini Cooper 1961–70 Autobook
Mini Cooper S 1963–1970	Ball	Mini Cooper 1961–70 Autobook
1100 Mk 1 1962–1967	Ball	1100 Mk 1 1962–67 Autobook
1100 Mk 2 1968–1969	Ball	1100 Mk 2, 1300, America 1968–69 Autobook
1300 1968–1969	Ball	1100 Mk 2, 1300, America 1968–69 Autobook
1800 Mk 1 1966–1968	Ball	1800 Autobook
1800 Mk 2 1968–1969	Ball	1800 Autobook
PEUGEOT		
404 1960–1969	Ball	Peugeot 404 1960–69 Autobook
RENAULT		
R8 956 cc 1962–1967	Ball	Renault R8, R10, 1100 1962–69 Autobook
R8 1108 cc 1966–1969	Ball	Renault R8, R10, 1100 1962–69 Autobook
1100 1108 cc 1964–1969	Ball	Renault R8, R10, 1100 1962–69 Autobook
R10 1108 cc 1967–1969	Ball	Renault R8, R10, 1100 1962–69 Autobook
RILEY		
1.5 1957–1965	Ball	BMC Autobook Three
4/68 1959–1961	Smith	BMC Autobook One
4/72 1961–1969	Smith	BMC Autobook One
Elf 1961–1970	Ball	Mini 1959–70 Autobook
1100 Mk 1 1965–1967	Ball	1100 Mk 1, 1962–67 Autobook
1100 Mk 2 1968	Ball	1100 Mk 2 1300, America 1968–69 Autobook
1300 1968–1969	Ball	1100 Mk 2, 1300, America 1968–69 Autobook
ROVER		
60 1953–1959	Ball	Rover 60–110 1953–64 Autobook
75 1954–1959	Ball	Rover 60–110 1953–64 Autobook
80 1959–1962	Ball	Rover 60–110 1953–64 Autobook
90 1954–1959	Ball	Rover 60–110 1953–64 Autobook
95 1962–1964	Ball	Rover 60–110 1953–64 Autobook
100 1959–1962	Ball	Rover 60–110 1953–64 Autobook
105R 1957–1958	Ball	Rover 60–110 1953–64 Autobook
105S 1957–1959	Ball	Rover 60–110 1953–64 Autobook
110 1962–1964	Ball	Rover 60–110 1953–64 Autobook
2000 SC 1963–1969	Ball	Rover 2000 1963–69 Autobook
2000 TC 1963–1969	Ball	Rover 2000 1963–69 Autobook

Make	*Author*	*Title*
3 litre Saloon Mk 1, 1A 1958–1962	Ball	Rover 3 litre 1958–67 Autobook
3 litre Saloon Mk 2, 3 1962–1967	Ball	Rover 3 litre 1958–67 Autobook
3 litre Coupé 1965–1967	Ball	Rover 3 litre 1958–67 Autobook
3500 1968–1970	Ball	Rover 3500, 3500S 1968–70 Autobook
3500S 1968–1970	Ball	Rover 3500, 3500S 1968–70 Autobook
SINGER		
Chamois 1964–1969	Smith	Hillman Imp 1963–69 Autobook
Chamois Sport 1964–1969	Smith	Hillman Imp 1963–69 Autobook
Gazelle Series 2A to 5 1958–1965	Ball	Hillman Minx 1 to 5 1956–65 Autobook
Gazelle Series 6 1965–1967	Ball	Hillman Minx 1965–67 Autobook
New Gazelle 1500, 1725 1966–1969	Ball	Hillman Minx 1966–69 Autobook
Vogue Series 4 1965–1967	Ball	Hillman Minx 1965–67 Autobook
New Vogue 1966–1970	Ball	Hillman Hunter 1966–70 Autobook
SKODA		
440, 445, 450 1957–1969	Skoda	Skoda Autobook One
SUNBEAM		
Alpine Series 1 1959–1960	Ball	Sunbeam Rapier Alpine 1959–65 Autobook
Alpine Series 2 1960–1963	Ball	Sunbeam Rapier Alpine 1959–65 Autobook
Alpine Series 3 1963–1964	Ball	Sunbeam Rapier Alpine 1959–65 Autobook
Alpine Series 4 1964–1965	Ball	Sunbeam Rapier Alpine 1959–65 Autobook
Alpine Series 5 1965–1967	Ball	Hillman Minx 1965–67 Autobook
Alpine 1969–1970	Ball	Hillman Hunter 1966–70 Autobook
Rapier Series 3 1959–1961	Ball	Sunbeam Rapier Alpine 1959–65 Autobook
Rapier Series 3A 1961–1964	Ball	Sunbeam Rapier Alpine 1959–65 Autobook
Rapier Series 4 1963–1965	Ball	Sunbeam Rapier Alpine 1959–65 Autobook
Rapier Series 5 1965–1967	Ball	Hillman Minx 1965–67 Autobook
Rapier H.120 1967–1970	Ball	Hillman Hunter 1966–70 Autobook
Imp Sport 1963–1969	Smith	Hillman Imp 1963–69 Autobook
Stilletto 1967–1969	Smith	Hillman Imp 1963–69 Autobook
TRIUMPH		
TR2 1952–1955	Ball	Triumph TR2, TR3, TR3A 1952–62 Autobook
TR3 1955–1962	Ball	Triumph TR2, TR3, TR3A 1952–62 Autobook
TR3A 1958–1962	Ball	Triumph TR2, TR3, TR3A 1952–62 Autobook
TR4 1961–1965	Ball	Triumph TR4, TR4A 1961–67 Autobook
TR4A 1965–1967	Ball	Triumph TR4, TR4A 1961–67 Autobook
TR5 1967–1969	Ball	Triumph TR5, TR250, TR6 1967–70 Autobook
TR6 1969–1970	Ball	Triumph TR5, TR250, TR6 1967–70 Autobook
TR250 1967–1969	Ball	Triumph TR5, TR250, TR6 1967–70 Autobook
1300 1965–1969	Ball	Triumph 1300 1965–69 Autobook
1300TC 1967–1969	Ball	Triumph 1300 1965–69 Autobook
2000 1963–1969	Ball	Triumph 2000 1963–69 Autobook
Herald 948 1959–1964	Smith	Triumph Herald 1959–69 Autobook
Herald 1200 1961–1969	Smith	Triumph Herald 1959–69 Autobook
Herald 12/50 1963–1967	Smith	Triumph Herald 1959–69 Autobook
Herald 13/60 1967–1969	Smith	Triumph Herald 1959–69 Autobook
Spitfire 1962–1969	Smith	Triumph Spitfire Vitesse 1962–69 Autobook
Vitesse 1600 and 2 litre 1962–1969	Smith	Triumph Spitfire Vitesse 1962–69 Autobook
GT6 2 litre 1966–1969	Smith	Triumph Spitfire Vitesse 1962–69 Autobook
VANDEN PLAS		
3 litre 1959–1964	Ball	BMC Autobook Four
1100 Mk 1 1963–1967	Ball	1100 Mk 1 1962–67 Autobook
1100 Mk 2 1968	Ball	1100 Mk 2, 1300, America 1968–69 Autobook
1300 1968–1969	Ball	1100 Mk 2, 1300, America 1968–69 Autobook

Make	*Author*	*Title*
VAUXHALL		
Victor 1 1957–1959	Ball	Vauxhall Victor 1, 2, FB 1957–64 Autobook
Victor 2 1959–1961	Ball	Vauxhall Victor 1, 2, FB 1957–64 Autobook
Victor FB 1961–1964	Ball	Vauxhall Victor 1, 2, FB 1957–64 Autobook
VX 4/90 FBH 1961–1964	Ball	Vauxhall Victor 1, 2, FB 1957–64 Autobook
Victor FC 101 1964–1967	Ball	Vauxhall Victor 101 1964–67 Autobook
VX 4/90 FCH 1964–1967	Ball	Vauxhall Victor 101 1964–67 Autobook
Velox, Cresta PA 1957–1962	Ball	Vauxhall Velox Cresta 1957–69 Autobook
Velox, Cresta PB 1962–1965	Ball	Vauxhall Velox Cresta 1957–69 Autobook
Cresta PC 1965–1968	Ball	Vauxhall Velox Cresta 1957–69 Autobook
Viscount 1966–1969	Ball	Vauxhall Velox Cresta 1957–69 Autobook
Viva HA (including 90) 1964–1966	Ball	Vauxhall Viva HA 1964–66 Autobook
Viva HB (including 90 and SL90) 1966–1969	Ball	Vauxhall Viva HB 1966–69 Autobook
Victor FD 1599cc 1967–1969	Ball	Vauxhall Victor FD 1600, 2000 1967–69 Autobook
Victor FD 1975cc 1967–1969	Ball	Vauxhall Victor FD 1600, 2000 1967–69 Autobook
VOLKSWAGEN		
1200 Beetle 1954–1966	Ball	Volkswagen Beetle 1954–67 Autobook
1200 Karmann Ghia 1955–1965	Ball	Volkswagen Beetle 1954–67 Autobook
1200 Transporter 1954–1964	Ball	Volkswagen Transporter 1954–67 Autobook
1300 Beetle 1965–1967	Ball	Volkswagen Beetle 1954–67 Autobook
1300 Karmann Ghia 1965–1966	Ball	Volkswagen Beetle 1954–67 Autobook
1500 Beetle 1966–1967	Ball	Volkswagen Beetle 1954–67 Autobook
1500 Karmann Ghia 1966–1967	Ball	Volkswagen Beetle 1954–67 Autobook
1500 Transporter 1963–1967	Ball	Volkswagen Transporter 1954–67 Autobook
WOLSELEY		
1500 1959–1965	Ball	BMC Autobook Three
15/50 1956–1958	Ball	BMC Autobook Three
15/60 1958–1961	Smith	BMC Autobook One
16/60 1961–1969	Smith	BMC Autobook One
6/99 1959–1961	Ball	BMC Autobook Four
6/110 1961–1968	Ball	BMC Autobook Four
Hornet 1961–1970	Ball	Mini 1959–70 Autobook
1100 Mk 1 1965–1967	Ball	1100 Mk 1 1962–67 Autobook
1100 Mk 2 1968	Ball	1100 Mk 2, 1300, America 1968–69 Autobook
1300 1968–1969	Ball	1100 Mk 2, 1300, America 1968–69 Autobook